James DeForest Murch   1892-1973

ADVENTURING
FOR CHRIST
In Changing Times

An Autobiography of
JAMES DEFOREST MURCH

Restoration Press
1973

The manuscript for this book was completed January 1, 1972, and no major changes have been made in it since that date.

RESTORATION PRESS

Box 391

Louisville, Kentucky 40201

Printed by The Standard Printing Co., Inc., Louisville, Kentucky, U.S.A.

CONTENTS

Foreword

Introduction

Works of James DeForest Murch

Index

FOREWORD

This volume is far more than a book about a man. It is a record of an era.

There is no living man within the religious fellowship known as the American Restoration Movement who is held in higher esteem than is Dr. James DeForest Murch. He is viewed with affection by those who hold Jesus Christ to be Lord, who believe His Gospel to be the Church's essential message, and who receive the Scriptures as the authentic record of God's self-revelation to men.

Dr. Murch has diligently kept open the lines of communication with key people in all nuances of the movement, and has done as much as any living Christian to preserve relationships where there is any ground for relationship.

Reaching beyond his most intimate fraternal group, Dr. Murch has given his life sharing his burning desire for Christian unity on the basis of "the ancient order" as revealed in Scripture with communions, groups and individuals who are open to these precepts.

That DeForest Murch must be assigned a significant role among Christian leaders can scarcely be gainsaid. He has gained this stature legitimately through several avenues of service and a plurality of disciplines. He is a great preacher, a distinguished author, an effective teacher and lecturer, and an esteemed editor. To each of these separate professions he has brought the knowledge of several disciplines: Christian Education, History, Ecclesiology and Theology, to name a few.

He brings to his writings the seasoning and perspective that only the years can supply. Perhaps as much as any other single quality, it is this breadth of perspective which makes Dr. Murch's counsel so highly regarded. This present volume becomes the pinnacle in the entire array of the countless contributions from his pen, for it draws together all the ingredients that make James DeForest Murch God's statesman for this hour.

W. F. LOWN

President Manhattan Christian College

President (1973) North American Christian Convention

INTRODUCTION

These memoirs are written in response to requests from many teachers of church history in schools and colleges of the Christian Churches and Churches of Christ. Dean E. Walker, professor of Church History in the School of Religion, Butler University, and later president of Milligan College, was the first to suggest it. It was the belief of these men that the story of my life, covering as it did a period of more than a half century of crucial historical developments in the life of the Restoration Movement in America, would be of considerable corollary value to them in the teaching process. It so happened that I was involved in one way or another, either as a participant or a first-hand observer, in those events, and also in contemporary Christian action in the evangelical world at large. I doubt that I would have written such a book except for the insistence of these brethren.

My reminiscences are not history, biography, nor a diary, although they comprise something of each. Because I was often involved in many different situations and events at one and the same time, I faced the problem of relating them in a way that would not be confusing to the reader. I finally decided to write the book on the basis of episodes, as the Table of Contents will reveal. These episodes often overlap chronologically, but I have tried to maintain a logical continuity and relatedness conducive to a total life story that may be of value. The greatest difficulty confronting me was that of recounting my share in the many events involved without giving my acts an unwarranted prominence.

The book is not written in the hope that it may have literary merit. The motive that induces me to write is not that of authorship. The historic import of some of its portions is my only claim to attention. It is my hope, however, that something in the telling may inspire in others an ambition to serve Christ and His Cause with their whole heart, as God may call them and give them to see the Way. No other cause in the world can match it in rewards in the NOW and in the Hereafter.

JAMES DeFOREST MURCH

James DeForest Murch

Episode I

Childhood and Youth

Shakespeare never wrote a truer word than, "A son's form is by his father imprinted." It is especially true in my case. Everett Delonzo Murch was undoubtedly the greatest single human influence on my life.

My father was born in the "Western Reserve" of Ohio at North Amherst, October 25, 1861 — the year the Civil War (or the "War Between the States") began. His forebears were Scotch-English. I shall never forget the thrill I got on my first trip to England seeing the name "D. J. Murch" on a plaque on the wall in the Stoke Poges Church, made immortal in Gray's "Elegy in a Country Churchyard." Dad used to say that the Murches in the old country were mostly "independent" religiously. In America they boasted a long line of "fishermen and Baptist preachers," though some became Presbyterian missionaries of note. One of the latter discovered the first Tell-el Amarna tablets while serving in Egypt. This find has been appropriately recognized by scholars to be as significant, in some respects, as that of the Moabite Stone. It made possible the scientific confirmation of the Scripture accounts of Egyptian-Israeli life around 1500-1350 B.C.

There is an unconfirmed family tradition that the Scotch-English Murches had their origin in the Spanish province of Murcia. As the story goes, the princes of Murcia outfitted and staffed one of the great frigates of the famous Spanish Armada which King Philip of Spain sent against England in his effort to return the hated Anglican Protestants to the suzerainty of the Pope of Rome. When the Armada was wrecked by the "winds of God" the Murcian craft came to rest on the coast of Scotland. Its crew and its soldiers who survived were eventually converted and became ardent Protestants. The name Murch is supposedly an eversion of Murcia. Believe it or not!

But back to Father. At age eleven he was left an orphan. His father, Stephen, a veteran of the Civil War, died of wounds received as a Union soldier in the Battle of Gettysburg. His mother died of childbirth. There were no near relatives to whom the young lad could turn, so he was apprenticed to a farmer by the name of Sessions near Gallatin, Missouri. In a checkered series of events he found his way back to Lorain County, Ohio, where he determined to become a public-school teacher. At Elyria, in the providence of God, he visited a tent meeting being held by the Garvin Brothers and learned for the first time of the movement to restore the New Testament church in "doctrine, ordinances, and life." He was thrilled by the idea, bought a Bible, investigated the teaching concerning the Gospel plan of Salvation, and gave his life to

1

Christ. A wealthy farmer from North Eaton by the name of James Robinson, who was backing the meetings financially, took a liking to the earnest and intelligent young man and made a mental note to watch his development in the faith. That fall Father enrolled in what later became Ohio Northern University at Ada, to train for the teaching profession. Dr. H. S. Lehr, president of the school, was an ardent Disciple, as were other members of the faculty. Professor J. G. Park, teacher of English, had the habit of asking his pupils to diagram Bible sentences like Acts 2:38 and certain Restoration shibboleths like "Where the Bible speaks, we speak; and where the Bible is silent we are silent." He never missed an opportunity to teach his pupils "the way of the Lord more perfectly" and frequently baptized converts made in his classes. Father, like P. H. Welshimer and others, credited Professor Park with his decision to enter the ministry. The word of that decision got to "Uncle Jim" Robinson, who wrote Dad a letter addressed to Alpena, Michigan, where he was spending his vacation trying to earn funds by fruit-picking and packing. The letter was like manna from heaven. It offered to underwrite the cost of his preparation for the Christian ministry at the College of the Bible in Lexington, Kentucky, in the hope that Dad would devote his life to establishing and shepherding rural and small-town churches in southern Ohio. The proposition was accepted. Under the tutelage of men like J. W. McGarvey, I. B. Grubbs, Robert Milligan, and Robert Graham, he learned how to "handle aright the word of truth." During his college days he preached for the old Stony Creek Church, near Nicholasville, and I treasure the record book he meticulously kept of his sermon outlines and the names of his converts. For many years I kept his class notes based on McGarvey's outlines of the Book of Acts. This, next to his New Testament, was his doctrinal guide throughout his ministry.

When he returned to Lorain County "Uncle Jim" and the elders at North Eaton Church asked him to become its minister until he was able to make contacts with churches in southern Ohio. While here he met, converted, and married a wonderful Methodist girl by the name of Ella Savage, a resident of Elyria. Soon a call came to the churches at New Vienna and New Antioch, in Clinton County. They had been having their troubles and were glad to have the help of the young Timothy. New Antioch was one of the noted churches of the early Restoration movement. It was founded by Samuel Rogers, who converted a whole congregation of Baptists and remained as their minister for many years. He was a close friend and co-worker of Barton W. Stone, as was his better-known brother, John. History buffs still journey to New Antioch to visit the grave of this "hero of the faith." Father preached "half time" at both churches.

New Vienna was the home of W. D. Moore, then retired. Moore was one of a number of brilliant self-made preachers who excelled in debate during this period of Restoration history. He especially distinguished himself in the Carleton-Moore debates on Universalism at Union City,

Indiana, and Pricetown, Ohio. The Union City debate was published and widely distributed. It is said that when Moore had concluded his week-long argument under an arbor at Pricetown, the noted Boston cleric was so soundly defeated that Universalism in southwestern Ohio received its death blow. Practically the whole Universalist Church at Pricetown presented themselves for baptism on the closing day. Moore and his ailing wife died at New Vienna during Father's ministries. It was during this pastorate that a youngster by the name of James DeForest Murch was born, October 23, 1892, in New Vienna.

Discouraged by results of his first ministry there, Father received a call to the churches at Rutland and Zion, Meigs County, and the Murches soon after packed their belongings and headed east. Meigs County was a strong center for the Restoration cause, its churches dating back to a great revival that swept the area under the leadership of Barton Stone. Here the young minister struck his stride. His leadership was accepted by the whole community and his influence went far beyond to Middleport, the largest town in the county, and Pomeroy, the county seat. He became easily the most popular preacher in the county. When the Zion church house was destroyed by fire, he led in its rebuilding. At Rutland he converted and baptized many young people who became business and professional leaders in the area. Among them was an Englishman by the name of Thomas L. Lowe, who later became one of the leading ministers in Ohio with distinguished pastorates at Athens and Columbus. A handful of brethren at Athens, county seat of Athens County, and the home of Ohio University, called him to hold a tent meeting on the college campus. It later resulted in establishing the church in this strategic city.

The news of Father's accomplishments filtered back to New Vienna and a turn of events there resulted in a call to return to this former field of labor. Many times during his ministerial career he was to have second pastorates. Most ministers say such pastorates are usually unsuccessful, but in every such case Father's "return engagement" was more fruitful than the first. It was not long until the church building could not hold the growing audiences. Some of the leading business and professional men of New Vienna joined the church. The building was enlarged and remodeled. The new bell tower was topped by a gold-leaf pinnacle that was the marvel of the town. I can yet remember Dad's artistic lettering across the interior wall above the pulpit, which greeted the congregation at every service: "In faith, unity; in opinions, liberty; and in all things, charity." Here be began to preach "chart sermons" that were basic to a "teaching ministry" and people came from miles around to hear the young minister expound visually the Word of God. Here was where my "theological" training began. Looking over Dad's shoulder as he painted his charts, I first learned the letters of the alphabet, then to read, and to discover the fundamentals of the Christian faith.

Alanson Wilcox, then secretary of the Ohio Christian Missionary

3

Society, came to visit us one day. After dinner he looked at me and said, "DeForest, what are you going to be when you grow up?" Unhesitatingly I replied, "A preacher." "Well, what will you preach?" queried the great man. Again unhesitatingly, I said, "The Gospel of Jesus Christ, God's side and man's side." Wilcox said, "That's the best answer I ever heard to such a question." What had happened was that Dad was just completing a chart sermon entitled, "God's Plan of Salvation: God's Side and Man's Side," and I had committed much of it to memory.

Alanson Wilcox was just one of the great "worthies" of the "brotherhood" who came to our home in New Vienna. Others were F. D. Power, of the Garfield Memorial Church in Washington, Mary Alice Lyons, Robert Moffett, J. V. Updike, Charles Freer, J. A. Lord, and J. H. Fillmore. Many of them stayed over night and ate at our table. Who can measure the influence of their conversations and their personalities on a growing boy? And our prayer times together!

The fame of Dad's chart sermons spread throughout Highland, Clinton, Adams, and Brown Counties and he was on constant demand for "protracted meetings." He preached with the Bible in one hand and a pointer in the other. He quoted Scripture after Scripture from memory. I often watched him turn pages to give the impression that he was reading from the Book, but he was really quoting from memory. This was an ability he acquired at the College of the Bible in Lexington, where the teachers insisted on their students' memorizing large sections of the New Testament. People often said, "If you don't have a Bible around when you want to take a legal oath, just call in Murch and put your hands on his head. It's all there."

In some of the rural areas he did his work under rather primitive conditions. I remember hearing him tell about a meeting at May Hill when the church was packed to capacity and he was about to give the invitation; the house was so quiet under the spell of his appeal to accept Christ that you could have heard a pin drop. Then suddenly a little tot who had crawled down under the seats, jumped up in front of him and yelled "BOO!" at the top of his voice. The service was over. Dad had hundreds of confessions and baptisms in these meetings, most of the baptisms in running streams. He had some eighty charts which were a match for if not exceeding in quality those in Z. T. Sweeney's brochure of chart sermons published by Standard. In later years, I wanted to publish them but was never able to get approval of a publisher.

Grandmother (Mother's mother) came to live with us at New Vienna and stayed in the home the rest of her life (she died aged one hundred years). She was a Presbyterian and loyal to her faith. We were always talking about our beliefs and one day she said, "Everett, I like you and I like to go to church and hear you preach. I agree with most that you say, but get this straight, I am a Presbyterian and I expect to remain one as long as I live. Above all, let up on that baptism business!" Dad did

4

(he was always considerate of "Grandma Savage") but one Lord's Day morning there were several confessions and there were baptisms at the conclusion of the service. The congregation retired to a nearby creek for the baptisms. At the conclusion, Grandma got up and moved toward the pool saying, "Everett, I want to be baptized." Dad was shocked. She had made no preparations, so he baptized her in her Sunday finery. When she came up out of the water she shouted, "Hallelujah!" in a very un-Presbyterian-like manner. Afterward she said, "I studied the Scriptures on baptism and found out what I ought to do, but I was too proud and stubborn to do it. Now I am the happiest woman in the world." I owe much to Grandma. She was baby-sitter and maid around the house for many years with never a note of complaint. Her service made it possible for Mother to be a veritable assistant pastor to Dad. Quiet and retiring and of a sweet disposition, she was a living example of Christian womanhood at its best.

Father's popularity as a preacher soon made him, because of his personality and active abilities, a leader in every phase of community life. He hated the liquor traffic and he mounted a campaign that voted New Vienna "dry." He discovered that the head of the public schools denied the deity of Christ, the authenticity of the Bible, and often spoke in favor of "free love." He was opposed to essential discipline, advocating "rule by love," with the result that there was little order in the classes. The job of educating New Vienna's children and youth was not getting done. Dad initiated a vote of the citizens for the recall of the superintendent and won his case by an overwhelming vote. Then leaders of the community came to Dad and said, "You won, now it is up to you to get us a good superintendent of schools." Fortunately, he was able to persuade E. P. Tice of the Buford congregation, a graduate of Ohio State, to take over the schools. Tice was most successful. Later he went to Columbus to organize and head what is now a multi-million-dollar insurance company.

Socially inclined, Dad became a great "Odd Fellow." The Independent Order of Odd Fellows had a strong lodge in New Vienna with a luxurious lodge hall. All the leading men in town were members. He was made chaplain and lecturer. So well did he acquit himself that he was persuaded to "do the chairs" and eventually head the order. He became known state-wide and was for many years the state chaplain of I.O.O.F. Mother was a member of Rebekah, the woman's auxiliary, and very popular among the ladies.

Every time the community promoted a big event Father made his contribution. I remember when President William McKinley was assassinated and the town was in mourning, Dad was asked to direct the memorial services in the City Hall auditorium. He planned the program, organized a community chorus composed of members of all the church choirs in town, and at the insistence of the committee preached the memorial sermon. I can still recall this impressive event.

While standing foursquare for his Restoration position, he was friendly with all the religious leaders of the community. He gladly participated in "union meetings." When it came his turn to preach, it was a sermon in some form or other on "The Plea." He didn't label it but he presented it in all its Scriptural and undenominational beauty and power. He made many a "convert" as a result. When there was a revival in the Baptist, the Methodist, or the Friends church, he would attend at least one night with the whole family and often participate in the prayer periods. The Church of Christ was the most rapidly growing church in town, and at times there was considerable jealousy exhibited on the part of the other groups, but Dad was always irenic and courteous in his attitude toward all. During this ministry the church doubled and trebled in membership. What was the smallest and most insignificant congregation in New Vienna at the time of his first ministry was, when Dad finally left the community, the largest and most influential.

While in New Vienna Dad received an inheritance. It was small and totally unexpected, but it was a great windfall for the "poor-as-church-mice" Murches. Dad had an uncle in Cincinnati by the name of Chauncey M. Murch. He was a successful inventor and businessman. I could write a page or two about this great soul. When he died, he was childless and left his considerable fortune to his wife; but, on attorney's advice, he recognized the possible claims of his multitudinous nephews and nieces. In his will he satisfied these claims by giving them each $2,000 (big money in those days). I took my first trip on a railroad train when I accompanied Dad to the "Queen City of the West" where he received his share of the inheritance. With part of his "fortune" he bought a horse and modern "rubber-tired buggy," a "roll-top desk," a letter file, and a Williams (later a Blickensderfer) typewriter. This evidence of affluence was greatly deplored by "the brethren." They never knew that most of this money was given to the church over the next few years.

That typewriter was my pride and joy. I mastered it immediately and, among other things, produced a small newspaper for distribution in the neighborhood. Though no one suspected it, even myself, here was born my predilection to writing and publishing.

There are a score of memories of my childhood at New Vienna that come crowding. Some of them are undoubtedly influenced by family tradition and not distinctly my own. Many of them are of a personal sort and have no place in a book of this kind. But I remember being entranced by the "tunes" played by dear Brother W. D. Moore's gold cuff buttons on his celluloid cuffs when he presided at the Lord's Table (he suffered from "shaking paralysis"). A preacher as great as Brother Moore had to be recognized even though he was past the days of his usefulness. One of Dad's other problems in keeping the peace among the brethren was a moronic creature who attended midweek prayer meeting regularly and always prayed. He inevitably started out by

6

saying, "Lord, I thank Thee that it is as well with me as what it is." There were many and varied comments on this repetitious introduction, as the reader may well imagine, but I realized later in life that I had received a great blessing from it. Many is the time, when I was at the end of my tether, that I paused in my self-pity and prayed from the heart, "Lord, I thank Thee that it is as well with me as what it is." It is a good line to remember and to use when all seems to be going wrong.

I was only nine years old when we departed New Vienna, in the fourth grade in school, but it was quite a sad occasion for me to leave the little village. It has to this day a warm place in my heart. Through the years I have frequently been called to preach there on special occasions (once in a meeting with twenty-three additions) and these memories always overwhelm me. I can still name scores of people — long passed to their reward — whom I loved and cherished and who made their contribution to my life.

In 1900 Dad was called to the church at Hillsboro, county seat of Highland County. It was a city of above 5,000, much larger than New Vienna. The church there was of comparatively recent origin. Though there were a dozen or so good rural churches of Christ in the county, the county seat awaited the coming of the great evangelist J. V. Updike in 1888 for the planting of a New Testament congregation. Under a tent for a month, more than two hundred responded to the Gospel invitation. A rather impressive frame edifice was erected, but in 1900 it was about to be sold under the hammer for debt. The membership was of the lower middle class (with a few exceptions) with very little money. The community was unaware of the accomplishments of the new parson and classed him with his underprivileged parishioners. The church itself was elated with the prospect of his leadership and at first gave him their enthusiastic support. He was able to lead them in paying off the debt and receiving many new additions to the membership.

In 1902 my beloved sister Frances was born in Hillsboro. She was ten years my junior. More later about her.

The liquor issue arose. Hillsboro was where the great national Christian Women's Temperance Crusade was born during a union revival led by Lorenzo Dow. Here, in the home of the daughter of former Governor Trimble, what later became the Women's Christian Temperance Union was organized. It was destined to grow into an immense power for good and a mighty factor in bringing about the passage of the Eighteenth Amendment. (Roy Haynes, editor of the *Hillsboro Dispatch*, was to become the first National Prohibition enforcement officer in Washington.) But at the beginning of the new century Hillsboro was infested with law-breaking saloons and beset by crime. Dad's reputation as a leader in voting New Vienna "dry" became known and he was plunged into a fight to rid Hillsboro of the "demon rum." The little church was filled to overflowing every Sunday night to hear the valiant David as he challenged Goliath. All the ministers and the moral leadership of the community cooperated in the campaign. Outstanding temperance orators were brought in, including John Gough. There were repercussions for the "preacher's kid." One day after school a gang of roughs, led by a kid by the name of Dillon, whose father owned the largest saloon in town, kidnapped me, took me into a back alley and beat me unmercifully. To make a long story short, the city rose up and voted liquor out. I can still remember hearing the church bells ringing and the mill whistles blowing when the results of the vote were announced. But there were some in the church who were unhappy about having a preacher who was "too active in politics." Dad was of a disposition that even though the great majority was with him, a small minority could trouble him. He felt that they could be the nucleus of constant irritation and opposition to his plans and programs. So with a heavy heart he resigned after only a little more than a year in Hillsboro.

Like old Elijah, who retreated to a cave, Dad decided to give up the full-time ministry and go to farming. He bought twenty-five acres in southwestern Highland County and became, as he often said, "just an old hayseed," or as others put it (because he owned only one horse) "a one-horse preacher." I went to a one-room country school. Dad, however, was not cut out to be a farmer. He was first, last, and always a preacher. The church people of the area would not let him alone. He was called to preach in several rural ministries — Pricetown, Union, South Liberty, and Buford. He held "protracted meetings" everywhere.

Maybe I should describe our rural setting. The land was gently rolling and situated just at the edge of a small settlement called by three names: East Danville, the name of the railroad station; Winkle, the name of the post office; and Straightout, the original native nickname. There were about a hundred inhabitants in this rural "metropolis," a one-room school, three stores, a flour and feed mill, a lumber "saw" mill, a tile mill, a feed center, and a stockyard, where cattle, sheep, and hogs were brought for shipment. In the upper stories of the stores, three lodges met — the Odd Fellows, the Modern Woodmen, and the Knights of Pythias. There was no church building, as most of the residents attended services at either Union or Danville Church of Christ. After we moved away, the rural Sonner's Chapel U. B. Church moved its building to East Danville to complete the picture of a typical southern Ohio village.

Caley's Store was the popular gathering place. It was run by Andy Caley, the town's nabob. Jovial Andy knew everybody for miles around. He was not only the proprietor of the store, but postmaster and railroad station agent. His establishment had everything country folk needed. There were rolls of "dry goods" and sewing supplies for the women; there were barrels of salt mackerel, salt pork, pickles, salt, sugar, coffee, and what-have-you. For a nickel you could get a bag of cheese and crackers, or bologna and crackers — very satisfying to a hungry boy. The tobacco counter had cigars (five for a dime), Star Plug and

Granger's Twist chewing tobacco, and Durham's or Duke's Mixture for roll-your-own cigarettes, and Prince Albert for pipe smokers. To the rear were cheap hats and bonnets; shoes and boots; brooms and brushes; tinware and tubs strung on wires and suspended from the walls; rows of shot, gunpowder, nail kegs, and kegs of New Orleans molasses and native corn whiskey. Just name it, Andy had it. Much of the trade was in the form of barter. The women brought dozens of eggs for which Andy allowed ten cents a dozen. They brought butter and other products of their kitchens. There was a good market for spring chickens that Andy shipped to Hillsboro in crates. The "trade" was usually unsatisfactory; angry customers often threatened "murder," but Andy was usually adamant and told them to "take it or leave it." All the latest gossip was purveyed around the potbellied stove. The solons of the community discussed politics and religion so seriously that there were occasional brawls that Andy had to settle with a broomstick. I always welcomed being "sent to the store" because that was where the action was in Straightout.

The farm was a small one, but Dad tried to produce everything that Mother Nature would grow. Our garden was a sight to behold. Dad was a master gardener and I thought he drove me to work it like Simon Legree. We had lettuce, radishes, onions, spinach, beets, parsnips, celery, salsify (vegetable oysters), tomatoes, turnips, cucumbers, corn, rutabagas, cabbage, cauliflower, brussels sprouts, potatoes (Irish and sweet), popcorn, watermelons, cantaloupes (muskmelons), horse radish, rhubarb, asparagus and everything else — you name it. Then there were grapes, strawberries, blackberries, raspberries, dewberries, blueberries, gooseberries, currants. There were apple and peach orchards, plums, pears, cherries — all of which had to be picked. Mother, grandma, and sister Frances kept busy in season canning all kinds of food for winter use. There were hickory nuts, hazel nuts, chestnuts, walnuts, persimmons, paw-paws, and other goodies growing wild.

Then there were the chickens. Dad prided himself on the pure strains of white Plymouth Rocks, white Wyandottes, and white Leghorns — all kept in separate runways connected with a chicken house he built according to the latest ideas of the best poultry men. People came from miles around to see that building and get eggs for setting hens. All those white chickens made a beautiful picture when they were feeding in the chickenyard. Then there were hogs that had to be fed, fattened, and butchered.

We raised wheat, corn, oats, and hay. Dad claimed he produced (with the help of fertilizer that the neighbors swore would kill his crops) the most bushels to the acre of all three of the grains. Events of great importance were the visits of the threshers and haybailers. Neighbors always "helped out" and then we reciprocated when they needed help. There was a fine community spirit. I can even remember a "barn-raising" in which the farmers did their own work under the direction of an old retired carpenter.

Food! Food! It makes my mouth water to think of the meals we enjoyed at home, at "threshings," "family reunions," "church home-comings," and the like. There were fried chicken, roast pig, turkey, duck, goose, squirrel, rabbit, pheasant, hot biscuits, salt-rising bread, fresh boiled corn-on-the-cob, succotash, butter beans, string beans, tomatoes, peas, Irish potatoes, sweet potatoes, buttermilk, sweetmilk, clabber, melons — and everything else in season; apple butter, stuffed peppers, pickles (cucumber, green tomato, beet, cauliflower, bean sprout, string bean, etc.); apple pie, peach pie, pumpkin pie, cherry pie, whip-cream pie, apple dumplings, peach cobbler, angel food cake, devil's food cake, chocolate cake. Highland County was the land flowing with milk and honey, corn and wine. Beulah Land had been reached as far as I was gastronomically concerned. They had a custom of inviting the preacher to dinner — each family taking its "turn" — on "preaching Sundays," along with all the families of the elders and "close relations." I have seen as many as sixty people at one of these dinners served at three or four tables in succession. As the preacher's son I was always given special attention, sometimes at more than one table. I still maintain, after nearly eighty years of experience, that Highland County, Ohio, cooks, in those days, were the best in the world.

One day the Highland County Republican Party bosses came to offer Dad a spot as senator in the State Legislature. With the tide for Pro-hibition running high, they said, we will elect you with the greatest majority in the history of the party. This was not idle talk. They would have done it. They even held out prospects of his moving up the political ladder and becoming District Representative in Washington. He asked for time to consider, then this "too political" preacher gave them an unalterable "No!" He said, "I had a clear call to preach the Gospel, I committed my life and my all to that ministry, and I am not going to turn back." Among his accomplishments during this period was the establishment of the new church at Mowrystown.

At first my life on the farm was unhappy. I got a taste of all kinds of farm work. I learned to plow, to plant and replant, cultivate, cut, shock and shuck corn, milk the cows, slop the hogs, mow, rake and stack hay, build fences, trim hedges, saw and split firewood, paint buildings, pick and store apples, etc. I was less than enthusiastic about farm work. Dad was often asked whether I liked the farm and his stock answer was, "Yes, I think DeForest likes everything about the farm, *except the work.*"

Then came one great decision — my acceptance of Christ as Saviour during a meeting at Union under the preaching of Edgar Hayes. I was baptized the same "hour of the night," in below-zero February weather with ice floating on the water, in old Smokey Row Creek. Then I rode home in an old buggy, two and a half miles, wrapped in a horse blanket, with a rejoicing father and mother, to start my Christian life. I remember, a few weeks later, walking down a dusty road at twilight when a strange, warm feeling came over me and I cried out, "I am going to give everything that I am or hope to be to Christ to serve Him to the end." This experience had an increasingly vital meaning to me as the years passed. I was constantly in prayer about it.

Parenthetically, a word about the church at Danville, two and a half miles up the "pike." A gang of us boys used to make pilgrimages there at protracted-meeting time and on Sunday nights when there were no services at Union. Danville in those days was rather primitive. It had once indulged in "footwashing" but had returned to orthodox religious practices. The elders sat in an "Amen Corner" at all services, headed by patriarchal Elder Joshua Hawk, the wealthiest and most prominent citizen of the community. Emmanuel Roush led the music, ostentatiously handing out the limited number of songbooks at the beginning of each service. Sometimes he would pitch them out from the platform to good singers (and catchers) in the middle of the house. The seating arrangements included a reverse center-pew on each side of the aisle so the brethren could gather closer to the potbellied stoves on cold days and also to accommodate the tobacco-chewing men — a sawdust-filled Star Tobacco box provided nearby. Even the most proficient marksmen missed the box occasionally, so the deacons felt it necessary to have two gold-lettered signs framed and hung on each wall. One read, "Those Who Expect-to-Rate as Gentlemen, Will Not Expectorate on the Floor"; the other, "Do Not Spit on the Floor — Remember the Johnstown Flood." In the wintertime the officiating fireman often made himself obnoxious by pokering up the fires and pouring in more coal right in the midst of the services. Once, I remember, Frank Foust, who was preaching on the occasion, stopped his sermon because the stove-stoking was so loud the audience could not hear what he was saying. I wish I could recall Frank's remarks, which were appropriately hot and to the point. He did not resume his sermon until the fires were roaring again. But despite old Danville's shortcomings it developed into one of the finest and largest rural churches in the county and through the years made many worthwhile contributions to the Restoration cause.

A few years later a note of encouragement came to me when the Boxwell Law passed the State Legislature, making it possible for rural children with only a one-room schooling to take a county examination and qualify for high school. I took the exam, passed with flying colors, spoke at the Boxwell Commencement (reciting Tennyson's "Charge of the Light Brigade"), and was soon enrolled in the Hillsboro High School. During the school year I got up every school day at 4:00 a.m., milked the cows, ate my breakfast, and caught the 6:00 a.m. C.P.&V. (later the N.&W.) Hillsboro train at East Danville, returning after school for more farm work.

One thing that helped introduce the country boy to his high school compatriots was the fact that the editor of the weekly *Hillsboro Dispatch* asked me (or did I ask him?) to write a column of high school news for each issue. Background: I had been for some time the weekly news correspondent for East Danville, our farm community, and had written a "History of East Danville" which appeared in several issues, causing wide and favorable comment. To do this latter job I spent weeks interviewing the oldest residents of the neighborhood and quoted extensively from their recollections and the accepted folk tales of their ancestors. The editor had a "scoop" and was my friend from that time on. I was immediately asked to become a member of the staff of *Trident,* the high school monthly, and at the conclusion of my Junior year was elected editor.

A combination of events, among which was my parents' concern for my education, led Dad to accept one of several repeated calls from the Hillsboro church for him to return to the pastorate there. His second ministry was amazingly successful.

We were on the verge of what later became the "Golden Age" of the Sunday school and Dad reorganized the Bible school on a graded plan with strong emphasis on organized Bible classes. We soon had the largest school in the city, entertained a countywide Church of Christ Sunday School Convention that jam-packed the church edifice and gave new stimulus to all our congregations. One of the chief factors in the successful gathering was the leadership of the Farises of Lynchburg (L. L. and Lillie) both of whom later became state and national experts of note. The supreme attraction at the convention was the noted Herbert Moninger, author of *Training for Service,* editor of *The Lookout,* and founder of the World-Wide Loyal Movement. Moninger was easily the most popular Sunday-school man in America at this time. His teacher training textbooks were used by all the churches. He, himself, had conducted a training class in Cincinnati's Music Hall, said to be the largest such class in the world, with thousands receiving diplomas. His text was used by millions for more than a generation, then was revised by C. J. Sharp and others for use even to this day. His Loyal Movement infused new life into the organized Bible classes of America. At Hillsboro we had thriving Loyal Women, Loyal Men, Loyal Berean, Loyal Boys, and Loyal Girls classes which were following with much profit Moninger's directions for work and growth. The prestige of the Hillsboro Church was greatly enhanced because of our ability to secure the services of this great man. I remember having quite a conversation with him. He put my name in his notebook and I had a letter from him on his return to Cincinnati. He was especially interested in what I had done to promote the convention through the columns of the Highland County press and invited me to report news of Sunday-school progress for *The Lookout.*

At that time, wearing my high school Cadet uniform, I taught Bible every Sunday to a class of forty Junior boys. As a special attraction I conducted a military drill for the lads every Saturday on "the commons,"

12

each kid carrying a sawed-off broom handle for a gun. The other churches in town had a hard time keeping their Junior-age boys in the "home paddock."

My own Bible class was the Berean Boys composed almost entirely of high school kids. We majored on Bible study but had many activities. One of these was a quartet of which I was a member. As I recall, I sang bass; Halford Conwell, alto; Glenn Faris, soprano; and Jimmy Day, tenor. Our fame spread beyond our own congregation and we had frequent invitations to sing on special occasions both religious and secular. Our peak performance was at the annual Highland County Farmers' Institute in Bell's Opera House. We were to sing "Old MacDonald Had a Farm." When we came out on the stage we succumbed to a bad case of stage fright. Jimmy Day gave us the pitch but we couldn't manage the harmony. He tried a second time with the same result. When the third trial failed, Jimmy fainted and the other three of us carried him out through the wings. We would not give up, however. We asked to try again later in the program and "made it good with a vengeance" amid wild applause that called for an encore. The Berean Boys had taught the great lesson that "perseverance wins"!

Christian Endeavor was the accepted medium for the expressional training of our youth. I plunged zealously into the work of our society. One day I wrote to the State secretary, a young man by the name of Daniel A. Poling, about the possibility of organizing a county union. Dan responded pronto and proposed that we set up a temporary committee and tour the county, lining up the youth groups of all the churches. A neighbor of ours, a young German Reformed Church minister by the name of Emerson Tobias (serving the Mt. Zion and Danville charges), joined me in the plan and was named chairman of the committee. This was my first introduction to inter-church work. My father approved enthusiastically. He said, "Wherever we can work with other Christian people *without sacrificing our convictions* and for the common good of the cause of Christ, we should do it." That has been my belief and practice from that day to this. To make a long story short, Dan Poling came down to Highland County and with "Toby" and me, using Toby's horse and buggy, we toured the county and set up the organization. I recall speaking in Presbyterian, Reformed, and Quaker churches and forming friendships that lasted through the years. For, from that time I was "in" with Dan Poling and moved up into state work. More about Dan later.

While we lived in Hillsboro, the thrill of a lifetime came. In 1909 the "Centennial Convention" of the Disciples of Christ was held at Pittsburgh — the greatest gathering of Restoration brethren in the history of the Movement. I never knew for sure where poor Dad got the money, but he scraped together enough shekels to take Mother and me with him to that tremendous event. My description of the Centennial, to be found in *Christians Only,* my definitive history of the Restoration

13

Movement, will have to suffice, except for a few personal impressions. The "great men" of the churches were there. The most publicized was the Honorable Champ Clark, then Speaker of the House of Representatives and the leading candidate for the Democratic nomination as President of the United States. When he came on the program the crowd was immense. He came to the podium, paused, and said "Brethren!" at which the place went wild. Then he continued, "I am a Democrat and a 'Campbellite' and if that won't take a man to heaven, I don't know what will." The multi-millionaire Robert A. Long, of Kansas City, president of the Long-Bell Lumber Company, then the largest lumber company in the world, chartered a special train to bring in the Kansas City delegation and leased the entire facilities of the Schenley Hotel for their entertainment. Here I met, thanks to Dad, the outstanding men of the Brotherhood. I shall never forget meeting John W. McGarvey of Lexington, Dad's old teacher. He was a little wizened old man (he died soon after Pittsburgh) so hard of hearing that he carried an ear trumpet into which I had to speak. He complimented Dad for his loyalty to the faith, and then putting his hand on my shoulder said, "My boy, you can't do better than follow the example of your father; be loyal to the Book and preach the everlasting Gospel." I witnessed the dedication and launching of the *Oregon,* the first missionary steamboat used on the Congo River in Africa. Everybody was proud of the great work our missionaries were doing in the Congo country. Thousands had been won and baptized into Christ. I shall never forget Royal J. Dye and his tearful and consecrated appeal to our people to evangelize Africa and the world. After the convention the boat was dismantled and packed for the long ocean journey. It was the means of reaching thousands who never would otherwise have heard the Gospel. The culminating thrill of the convention was the observance of the Lord's Supper in Forbes Field, then the newly-constructed home of the Pittsburgh Pirates. Earlier the Pirates had won the National League pennant there, but the crowd that gathered to remember the "death and suffering of Christ" on that closing Lord's Day of the week-long meeting exceeded that of America's baseball fans — thousands of our people jamming the stands and standing in the field. It was estimated that more than 30,000 partook of the emblems. The gathering was without benefit of "P.A." and loud speakers, but out of habit we followed the signs, sang the old hymns under the direction of W. E. M. Hackleman, guessed at what Wallace Tharp the "M.C." was saying, and "ate the bread and drank of the cup" together in solemn, prayerful, and impressive stillness. Here was a testimony for the Lord and the Movement unlike anything in our history. The high school boy from Hillsboro came back home talking for weeks about "nothing else" but Pittsburgh, the Centennial, and the Restoration Movement.

It was evident to everybody in the Hillsboro church, except a few stingy and stubborn church officers, that the time had come to enlarge the church building to house the large audiences and provide proper accommodations for the growing Bible school. Dad, with the help of local builders, drew a plan for the structure. He was backed by such forward-looking businessmen as Elder Chauncey Gross, of the Gross-Feibel Safe and Lock Company, who promised to handle the necessary financing — but to no avail. By close votes the project failed. Father resigned and Gross left the congregation for the Baptists (for many years, along with Lumberman Charles Whistler, he was their leading layman and most liberal giver). How many of our churches have been hindered in growth and influence by short-visioned, narrow-minded lay leaders? Hillsboro in later years repented of its shortcomings and became one of the greatest churches of our people in Ohio, particularly under the outstanding ministry of the brilliant and popular Paul Jones.

When the news of Dad's decision got out, he received a number of calls to other fields. One especially appealed to the family — Mount Healthy Church, Cincinnati. This was the prestigious old "A. McLean church" where he lived and worked through his early years with the Foreign Christian Missionary Society. But Dad thought this was too much of a leap forward for a rural and smalltown man, so he turned it down to accept the call of the church at Rantoul, Champaign County, Illinois. Today Rantoul is the home of mammoth Chanute Field (built by the U. S. Government during the Second World War), but then it was a village of 900 with mud streets and many wealthy retired farmers.

I was pretty blue about the change of events. It meant that I would have to forego editing *Trident,* the high-school paper. It meant rifts in close friendships. When the Archer brothers, owners of the *Hillsboro Dispatch,* heard the news they approached me with what I thought was a wonderful proposition. They were buying up a chain of weekly county-seat papers. They had purchased one at Caldwell, Noble County, and they proposed to set me up as its quasi-editor under the guidance of one of the brothers. They offered the, to me, fabulous salary of $800 a year. Dad soon dampened my ardor for acceptance by telling me that I was not yet twenty-one, scarcely "dry behind the ears," and that I had little or no education to speak of. "Accept the Caldwell job," he said, "and you will be a second-rate reporter on a small-town newspaper the rest of your life." I went west with little enthusiasm and certainly not as a brave frontiersman eager to "grow up with the country," as Horace Greeley once advised the youth of America. Even yet I weep a little when I think of the cost of "leaving Hillsboro forever."

Going to Rantoul was for me like going to a foreign land. In place of the beautiful hills and dales of southern Ohio were vast stretches of black prairie-flat farmland. I could stand at the rail crossing of the Illinois Central and see the next towns on a clear day — Thomasboro to the south, Gifford to the east, Fisher to the west, and Ludlow to the north. The farmers were wealthy. Their forebears had bought up I.C. mile-wide, right-of-way government land grants for as low as forty cents an acre (in many cases) and now their holdings were worth from $600 to $1,000 an acre. They raised the finest corn in America and fed it to the finest hogs in America, sold both at top prices and piled up their profits in completely reactionary self-satisfaction. The streets of Rantoul were mud most of the year as were all the rural roads. Nobody wanted to spend the money to build "hard" streets or roads. In fact, some of the old-timers contended that there was no bottom to Illinois mud and that to put macadam, concrete, or blacktop on it would result only in their sinking out of sight during the next spring thaw. The only way Dad could call on his rural parishioners in the winter was to take advantage of a "road-drag" just before a big freeze which would result in a hard, level surface until the next thaw.

The church was "rich" — with the wealthiest per capita membership in town. There were only about 150 members, many of them bankers, merchants, and village officials, with the rest well-to-do active and retired farmers. Some of Illinois' best preachers had served the church — men like H. H. Peters, who had recently become State secretary. Dad measured up in the pulpit, but he expected the church to "do great things for God," to reach others for Christ, and to set an example in church growth. The "brethren" liked the preaching but not the "pushing."

About the only break-through Dad got was with the young people. We organized a splendid Christian Endeavor Society with a strong appeal to all the young people in the town. A "Red-and-Blue" contest built up the membership to over a hundred. Kids who had never shown an interest in the church suddenly pitched in and became hard workers. I remember the case of "Little Doc," as we called him (the unpredictable son of the leading physician of Rantoul). We had a point system in the contest which included ten points each for participation in the meetings. A prayer counted fifteen points. On the last night the race was close and "Little Doc" prayed, to everybody's amazement. His petition was simple and sincere, "O Lord, bless our side. I hope we beat. Amen." His side did beat and this was a turning point in his life. He became chairman of the missionary committee, raised the money for the support of an orphan in India; then moved up to become president of the society, and much later a leader in the church.

Father took advantage of this youth situation and announced a series of Sunday night sermons for young people on "Love, Courtship, and Marriage." All our high school friends turned out and packed the auditorium with the largest audiences seen in years.

Christian Endeavor success at Rantoul somehow got to the ears of E. P. ("Pearly") Gates, the State secretary in Chicago. He contacted me and we worked out a plan to organize the "Eastern Illinois C. E. Union" covering four or five counties in our area. I soon had to leave, but the plan worked out with a very successful first convention held in Danville. "Pearly" was, from then on, one of my closest friends and helped to introduce me in later years to possible fields of service at the national level of Christian Endeavor.

An outstanding experience of the Rantoul days was the opportunity to meet Charles Reign Scoville and see him in action. He was the greatest evangelist our people produced during the so-called "Billy Sunday Era" in American evangelism. He was holding a meeting for Stephen E. Fisher and the great University Church in Champaign located across the street from the University of Illinois campus. He packed the building twice or three times a day. At this time he preached the old Gospel without compromise, broad, but in the spirit of the Restoration Movement and not in a sectarian manner. He gave the Acts 2:38 answer to the question, "What must I do to be saved?" and made a great deal of the baptismal services. As I recall, there were nearly 1,000 additions, making the University Church one of the largest churches of the Brotherhood. Dad and I were present every night we could make it. Scoville was an earnest and fluent speaker, somewhat flamboyant in his manner. He would come down the aisles when he offered the invitation, and get audience response in many ways. All Christians were urged to speak to others in the pews about decisions for Christ. When the "call of the Gospel" came there was no doubt about whether there would be confessions; many moved down the aisles to confess, "I believe with all my heart that Jesus is the Christ the Son of the Living God and my personal Saviour." Through the years a number of Illinois' largest churches availed themselves of his services. His good friend State Secretary H. H. Peters (former minister at Rantoul) wrote his biography.

My high-school experience was quite rewarding, despite the disappointment at leaving Hillsboro in my senior year. I was elected editor of the school annual. I reported school events for the weekly *Rantoul Press*. My teachers were capable men and women who took a personal interest in my education. Realizing my bent toward journalism, my English teacher promised to get me a scholarship in the School of Journalism at the University of Illinois in Champaign-Urbana. I deeply treasured my diploma. The following summer Editor Riker took me on as "printer's devil" and reporter for the *Press*. I was inducted into the fraternity the first day by learning what "printer's lice" were. I became a "jack of all trades" for "Rike." When he said "Jump," I jumped. When he said "Stop," I stopped. At various times I operated the linotype, fed the old flat-bed press, tinkered with the old gasoline engine, canvassed the stores and offices for news, ran the mailing machine, read proof, pasted up dummies, and learned the job-printing business. There developed a camaraderie in the office and shop that was so deep that when I left for Ohio there was a suspicion of tears on several faces including "Rike's" and mine. It was a great experience, a "liberal" education.

The "handwriting" was "on the wall" before the first year of Dad's ministry expired. He would not stay in a field where meaningful church growth was impossible. One day, in what he considered "the Lord's leading," he received a letter from C. E. Starr, a businessman-elder in the church at Athens, Ohio — a man whom he had baptized when he preached at Rutland — offering him the pastorate of this growing congregation. Starr said several of Dad's former parishioners at Rutland were then leaders at Athens. A Rutland convert, T. L. Lowe, had recently concluded a successful ministry there to take the West Fourth Avenue Church in Columbus. This had a strong emotional appeal but other factors predominated. The congregation serves as the "university church" to Ohio University (the oldest state university west of the Allegheny mountains), it had a burgeoning Sunday school, and in its relations to the churches in southeastern Ohio offered Dad the opportunity to serve them in harmony with his promise to his mentor "Uncle Jim" Robinson to minister to rural and small-town areas of southern Ohio. Dad recalled, too, that while at Rutland he had helped to organize the Athens church in a tent meeting held on the campus of the university. Athens it was! His two pastorates in this strategic location were to constitute one of the greatest achievements of Dad's life for Christ.

We arrived in Athens in the midwinter of 1912 just in time for me to take entrance examinations and matriculate at Ohio University in the Winter Quarter. The church was housed in an unpretentious frame building at the corner of Washington and Congress Streets. The Bible school overflowed into a residence and the nearby lodge halls of the Red Men and the Odd Fellows. You had to come early to get a seat at worship services in the sanctuary. I was immediately catapulted into leadership in the school as teacher of the Garfield Class (university men) and later as general superintendent. The Christian Endeavor society made me president.

Early in Dad's ministry he persuaded the brethren to call the Fife Brothers for a revival. Clyde (the preacher), Bob (the businessman), and Earl (the music director) had made a great reputation for evangelism a la Scoville and Billy Sunday. I was charged with the task of supplying publicity for the local papers. When the opening service was held, more than 300 people were turned away from the little church. We went to the Methodist church, the largest church auditorium in the city, and turned hundreds away the next night. Then to the University Auditorium with the same experience. Immediately plans were laid to build a tabernacle seating 2,000. In a sensational move, believe-it-or-not, *we built it in a day* on a prominent lot at the head of Court Street. "Everybody in Athens" swarmed around to see the impossible actually achieved. It was filled the first night and every night thereafter for more than three weeks, despite the worst flood in the history of the Hocking River, which came toward the end of the series. The flood seemed to help. It cut off all roads into Athens, but the Athens people filled the building, eagerly seeking salvation. I never saw anything like it. People from all the churches and from no church came. The old Gospel was

18

preached in all its fullness. My dad baptized scores of people every night in the temporary baptistery high over the great chorus. All the lights in the tabernacle were turned out except those in the baptistery. This feature of the meeting made a great impression in the predominantly pedo-baptist community. Many, dissatisfied with their sprinkling, came for Scriptural baptism. The closing day, with the flood waters subsided, was a veritable Pentecost. People came from miles around. We had 1,011 in Bible school at an early hour. Four services were held during the day to accommodate the thousands in attendance. On Sunday night it was announced that more than 600 had been added to the Athens church. Beyond this fact, the whole community was cleansed and blessed. As recently as September 21, 1969, the *Athens Daily Messenger* gave a full page to a story recalling this remarkable event in the religious life of the city. The Fifes went on to nearby Jackson where they repeated their Athens record. It was apparent to everybody in our congregation that something would have to be done to enlarge our borders if we were to conserve the fruits of victory. Almost immediately the church voted to buy a new strategic location at State and Congress Streets (where it was believed the new Elks temple would be constructed) and proceed to lay plans for a new building. The First Christian Church morale had come up from nonentity to the status of a major religious influence in the life of the community. Dad was everywhere recognized as a leading figure — a man to be consulted about every forward movement in the area.

The chief significance of Athens to my life was, of course, the university. It early appeared that my chief interest was in English, Language, Philosophy, and History studies. I took everything I could get in these areas. My professors were capable and took a real interest in me. I recall particularly Drs. Edwin Watts Chubb and Hiram Roy Wilson in English. I was soon chosen a member of the English Club and the Booklovers Club. In History I had Dr. H. W. Elson (former Lutheran minister, author of a noted history textbook and later president of Theil College) and Dr. Thomas Hoover (a Harvard Ph.D.). In Languages, Dr. Mary T. Noss (Romance Languages) and Dr. David W. Evans (Latin). I was elected to membership in the Cercle Francaise; took four years of college Latin. In Philosophy, I was fortunate to have the tutelage of Dr. Frederick Treudley and Dr. Geoffrey Morgan. Parenthetically, I should note that Dr. Treudley was an elder in our church. He came from Hiram, Ohio, where he taught at one time in Hiram College, and from the distinguished Atwater family, which had made such a fine contribution to the Restoration cause in the early days. Treudley was said to have one of the four or five "greatest minds in America." It was a real privilege to sit in his classes. One of the buildings on the modern Ohio campus was named in his honor.

Because of my commitment to Biblical Christianity, I could not accept many of the philosophical ideas advanced in Dr. Treudley's classes and

I brashly challenged them. We often wasted (?) a whole hour of class time arguing, with the good professor tolerant and kind in his attitude. I really loved him and I think he loved me because our friendship lasted until his death, though he was to be on the liberal side and I on the conservative in the controversies that were to wrack the Brotherhood.*

Another scene of controversy was the biology classes under Dr. W. F. ("Bugs") Mercer. Evolution was the issue. I, of course, was thoroughly committed to creationism and abhorrently opposed the idea that man was descended from the apes. I would come home from the class discussions outlining evolutionary views and Dad would fill me with ammunition for the next session. He gave me copies of Alfred Fairhurst's *Organic Evolution Considered* and his *Theistic Evolution,* which I devoured. We settled nothing in the class discussions but I became an even more confirmed creationist from that time on. Mercer was a loyal churchman and told the class that he was a believer in a type of "theistic evolution" which was not out of harmony with the Genesis account of origins.

It might be well to say a word about Dr. Fairhurst. A professor in Transylvania University, he was probably the most effective opponent of evolution in the educational field of his day. He was often challenged to debates by leading scientists and professors of the major universities. With his keen, incisive questions he could slay the Goliaths with ease. He never came off second best. His books (published by Standard) had a wide sale for many years. I once met him. He was a rather slender, unimpressive mustached man with a high piping voice, but he knew his science and his Bible, as his books amply testify.

Other professors whose names come to me were Dr. Pierce (Speech) and Dr. MacKinnon (Journalism). I was in the first Journalism class offered in the history of the university which later developed into a department and then into the School of Journalism headed for many years by the distinguished Dr. David Starr Lasher. This connection later resulted in my election as an honorary member of Sigma Delta Chi.

One of my first extra-curricular activities was as a member of the staff of *Green and White,* the student publication. In my Junior year I became editor, changed the format to that of an eight-column newspaper and won recognition for the school at state and national college journalistic levels. In my Senior year I was editor of *Athena,* the university annual.

Wherever there was action, I was there. If I had given as much attention to my studies as I did to student activities I might have been a scholar. Here is a part of my record:

As a member of the College Y I moved up to become President and

*Dr. Treudley's daughter Esther (Esther Treudley Johnson) was at one time editor of World Call. Later she married wealthy E. M. Bowman of the Bowman Milk Company of Chicago and avidly supported the work of the UCMS. Another daughter, Mary, a brilliant Ph.D., taught for many years in Gingling College (for women) in Nanking, China.

then General Secretary (a salaried job). I remember we put on a campaign for new members with a goal of enrolling every man in the university and we did it. Our Y program at Ohio U. was distinctly evangelical in character. We had nationally-known Y lecturers visit the university, speaking on life career choices, Christian commitment, moral issues (with a "men-only" meeting dealing frankly with sex), and undisguised evangelism. We had "gospel teams" that visited the mining camps and villages around about and teams of teachers who served in mission Sunday schools. I particularly remember being a member of a gospel team that held a weekend of meetings at Beverly, Ohio, in the Christian, Methodist, and Presbyterian churches with crowded houses and many decisions for Christ. I had the privilege of attending state Y leadership conferences in Otterbein College and Ohio Wesleyan University and one summer in an outdoor camp in the Adironacks at Eaglesmere. Several leaders urged me to make YMCA a life work, but I saw trends that compromised the biblical faith and I never could become enthusiastic about such a career.

In the literary society field I became a Philomathean and in due time president. I went out for inter-collegiate debate and made the team, also membership in Tau Kappa Alpha.

In the fraternity field, despite bids to Beta Theta Pi and Phi Delta Theta, I chose Phrenecon and became a "Barbarian." The issue was drinking and dancing. The Phrenecons were a bunch of puritans and this was "my dish." In my Senior year I was appointed a delegate to a fraternity conference at Miami University where chapters from four schools (Miami, Ohio U., Ohio State, and Center) united in the formation of Phi Kappa Tau, now one of the major social fraternities of the nation, with Ohio U. as Beta chapter).

My general college leadership qualities were recognized by my election to Omicron Delta Kappa, national honorary fraternity.

Athletics had little or no appeal to me, although I was always an enthusiastic rooter for our teams and attended practically every game of football, basketball, and baseball, as well as most track events. I had many warm friends among the letter men because of the headlines I gave them in the college paper.

My interest in student politics led to contracts with Athens city politicians. As I approached twenty-one and the casting of my first vote for president of the United States, I became a passionate "Bull Mooser," welcoming every opportunity to make stump speeches for "T.R." (Theodore Roosevelt). Athens was a hotbed of Progressive Party strength. "T.R." came to Athens during the campaign and spoke from the courthouse steps to a tumultuous throng of thousands. I was promptly made a "clerk of elections" and was urged by the political "powers that be" to choose politics as a life vocation. I was tempted then and was tempted later, but the Lord threw up enough roadblocks to save me from such a fate.

I must relate an interesting incident from the previous year. Dan Poling became the Prohibition Party candidate for Governor of Ohio. He needed a field man to make arrangement for his appearances in the southern counties of the state. He asked me to take the job. He had no money. I was to contact the members of the Prohibition Party (a pretty sad collection of oldsters) in each county-seat town, solicit campaign funds, and get permits for meetings. All summer I canvassed the counties and had some interesting experiences. When I came to Cincinnati, the county-seat of Hamilton County, I was to contact first a lawyer by the name of Hawk. I arrived in the city around six o'clock with only a quarter and two nickels in my pocket. With one nickel I called Hawk's downtown office, but he had left for his home in Terrace Park. With the other nickel I phoned him there. He said he was sorry but he couldn't possibly see me before ten o'clock the next morning. I knew nobody in the city. I had no dinner. I had no place to sleep. So I determined to go to the waiting room of the old Union Terminal at Third and Central and try to act like somebody going some place. Around one in the morning I made the mistake of sitting down on a bench and nodding off to dreamland. A policeman asked me where I was going and I told him the truth. I also told him I had only a quarter in my pocket. He was little impressed and told me he might have to arrest me for vagrancy and let me sleep in jail. Then he had a happy thought and said, "I know the proprietor of a flop house on Central Avenue. I might persuade him to take you in for the night." He did. Despite the filthy bed and an assortment of bedbugs, I got some rest, cleaned myself up the next morning and presented myself at the lawyer's office. He welcomed me, gave me a ten-dollar bill, and sent me on my way. Dan Poling had a hearty laugh when he heard my story and said, "Cheer up, I will make you my secretary of state when I get to Columbus." Dan made a thrilling campaign and got the largest vote the Prohibition Party ever polled in Ohio. (Of course, a Republican won.)

An incident in my Senior year was to have a great effect on my life. In one of Dr. Geoffrey Morgan's classes, The History of Education, we were studying about Ciceronianism in the Roman culture and its effect on the thinking of early Christian leaders. I saw a striking comparison to the conflict of "modernism" and "fundamentalism" just beginning to develop in American Protestantism and decided to write an article for Christian Standard entitled "Christ or Cicero — Which?" I had little hope it would be published, but — lo! and behold! — in a few days there came a telegram from S. S. Lappin, the editor, asking me to send my photo and some biographical notes; they were planning on making it the lead article in the next issue. The eventualities related to that incident were to result in my long and profitable relationship with the Standard Publishing Company. Letters from Lappin and Russell Errett opened the gates for the publication of further contributions.

My religious activities were many and varied during my college career. Beyond those already mentioned were Christian Endeavor concerns. I was early involved as president of the local church organization. With the cooperation of a fine group of young people we set many new records in attendance, social and spiritual development. As in Father's previous pastorates, I soon found myself elected president of the Athens County C. E. Union. In annual conventions held in New Marshfield, Nelsonville, and Athens we broke all records in attendance and new societies organized. Dan Poling came to the little village of New Marshfield, where the largest auditorium in town — the Methodist Protestant Church — could not begin to hold the crowds which overflowed into outdoor meetings. Our success led to involvement in state work. We had large delegations at the state conventions and the summer conferences at Summerland Beach and I was appointed to the state publicity committee and to workshop leadership. All this was to have a determinative effect on my future life work. At the Columbus state convention in Memorial Hall I responded to Dan Poling's appeal for life work decisions. I vowed there to give my life in service for Christ and the Church along with scores of others in a moving experience that I never forgot. Whether I understood all the implications of that decision is doubtful, for I had many wrestlings of spirit in later years as to my life work. But I owe to Christian Endeavor a great debt for its aid and direction. I still believe that its youth program is the finest ever conceived and that the churches made a grave mistake when they abandoned it as the medium of expressional activity for their youth. I shall have more to say about Christian Endeavor as I continue to tell my story.

While I was at Athens the Ohio Christian Missionary Society greatly honored me by inviting me to give the youth address at its Crooksville state convention. I think the address was rather effective but an amusing incident took place which ought to be recorded. The time was rather limited and I was given a minute stop-warning just as I got to the poem that was to conclude the talk. The poem had three or four verses and read something like this:

> I want to let go,
> But I will not let go;
> I am, it is true,
> Discouraged and blue,
> Worn out, through and through;
> But I will not let go!

As my time ran out the timekeeper rose and pulled my coat tail once, twice, thrice as I persisted in repeating with the refrain, "I will not let go!" The big audience veritably split its sides with laughter as I retired from the platform with a very red face. My youthful enthusiasm was generously forgiven, but I was taught a valuable lesson — the necessity of proper "terminal facilities" in public address.

After the New Marshfield Christian Endeavor convention, the brethren in the Church of Christ there got the idea that I might make them a good half-time preacher. I was invited to preach a "trial sermon." I knew that I was very, very young and that I did not have the preparation to render such a service to even a small village congregation. I consulted with Father and he said, "Go ahead and preach for them. It will be an interesting experience for all concerned." So I preached my first sermon at age nineteen. I leaned heavily on some of W. H. Book's dissertations from his *Columbus Tabernacle Sermons* at both morning and evening services. No one suspected that many of my ideas were Brother W. H. Book's because they lacked the personality, the conviction, the quality, and the spirit of the author. When the elders failed to give me a call to the pulpit, I suspected that I had been a great disappointment to the New Marshfield brethren. Thereafter I decided to be Murch and not somebody else in the pulpit, and to lean for my support upon the Bible and the Spirit of God.

Despite my failure at New Marshfield, within a couple of weeks I had two calls to serve as student minister to the Athens county churches at Trimble and Millfield. I accepted and continued for nearly three years in that capacity. When I was to leave them they urged me to stay as their full-time pastor.

Trimble was a rather substantial congregation (founded in 1845) and responded in a wonderful way to my youthful leadership. The elders were considerate and helpful in every way. It was at Trimble that I was ordained by them to the Christian ministry at a simple "laying on of hands" ceremony during a regular morning service. To those who might object to the validity of such a procedure, I would remind them that many of our ministers in those days were never formally ordained. The State Society had not yet come to exercise its self-appointed hierarchal powers, and the local churches persisted in the traditional belief that their elders had sufficient authority to "set apart" those who were "Scripturally qualified for the ministry." Audiences grew. The Bible school more than doubled in attendance. Ours became known in the community as "the young people's church." Out of our strong Christian Endeavor society came two young Timothies who were to serve the Brotherhood as ministers in later years. I recall holding an evangelistic meeting in which many young people accepted Christ and were baptized. My sermon on baptism caused quite a sensation among the Methodist young people who frequented our services. Although they desired to do so, their parents would not permit them to "join the Christian Church." However, the youngsters were so touched by the meetings that at their own preacher's next appointment they responded to the invitation and requested "baptism by immersion." The preacher and their parents did their best to dissuade them from such "foolishness" but they stood their ground. The Methodist preacher had never immersed anyone and he was greatly embarrassed. Nevertheless, he found a pool in the river near Redtown and immersed them one Sunday afternoon as many of our young people watched from the riverside. It was a victory for the plain teaching of the New Testament that was not soon forgotten in that community.

Millfield was a weak and untaught congregation. There were very few male members and women often officiated at the Lord's Table. They virtually kept the doors open. Millfield was a divided town consisting of the old community of Protestant Anglo-Saxons and the new community (built around Poston's Coal Mine) of Roman Catholic "hunkies" (as they were commonly known) of Polish ancestry. Like the Jews and the Samaritans they had little or no dealings with one another. Our church house was in a dilapidated condition. One of the first things I did was to recruit a gang of young men who joined with me in painting the building and making necessary repairs on the roof. I was soon able to win several of these to Christ and gradually a number of men "returned to the fold." Among the latter was John Wade, the finest specimen of the *genus homo* in Millfield, in charge of the blacksmith shop in the mine, and respected by everybody, even the gang of toughs who often invaded old Millfield. At our evening services I often dealt with community issues. Once, I recall, I took a strong stand against Sunday baseball and preached a hot sermon on "Lord's Day Observance." The toughs swore vengeance on me. That night two-hundred-pound Wade put his big arm around me as I was leaving the building and said, "Preacher, you are going to need some help tonight and I think you and I both will be a match for any trouble." I usually took the K & M train for Athens after the service and had to wait about an hour or so at the railroad station. The gang was there ready to attack me, but Wade made a little speech, backed up by some effective gestures of his right arm, and I "departed in peace."

One Lord's Day, thanks largely to the influence of the Fife Brothers meeting in Athens, I was thrilled at the conclusion of my morning sermon to see four couples come down the aisle to confess Christ and be baptized. These people were among the leading citizens of the community and their coming strengthened the church immeasurably. They had voluntarily held a prayer meeting in one of the homes and mutually decided upon their course of action.

I made several efforts to penetrate the barrier between the two communities, but with little success. I got almost no encouragement from our church members. But one Lord's Day I was surprised during the Gospel invitation by the response of a woman and her young daughter who came from "hunky-town." They had been attending our Bible school but were often treated as "untouchables." A few weeks later I had an invitation to visit their home for dinner. I did not accept immediately because I knew I would be greatly criticized if I fraternized too much with the "great unwashed." Then one Sunday in a blinding blizzard I ploughed through the snow up a railroad spur to the little slab-sided cabin where these people lived. I learned that the woman had a bad reputation although she was then "going straight." She earned a bare living by taking in washing and doing cleaning. Her mother was confined to her bed with terminal cancer. The home was so poverty-stricken that we sat on boxes at a rickety table with only hard bread and boiled potatoes to eat. They gave me the only table knife, fork, and spoon they owned, while they shamefacedly ate with kitchen spoons and their fingers. After the meal I stayed an hour or so, read from the Scriptures, dealt with their problems, and offered prayer. Later I was able to get them a little financial help. They were the most appreciative people I ever knew. Some years later I was speaking one night in the Church at Glouster — many miles "up the track" from Millfield. After the service I was shaking hands with people at the door when this woman and her daughter came out weeping and shook my hands warmly. I expressed surprise at seeing them and said, "How did you get here?" "We walked," they said, "and now we are going to walk back." I expressed my appreciation and the mother said, "Brother Murch, you are the only preacher who ever treated me like I was a human being and a Christian, and you will never know how much it has meant to all of us in our little family." I have often wished that I could have spent more time among the people of "hunky-town" ministering to them in the name of Christ.

I should add that for three years on "fifth Sundays" I also preached for the good people at Airline Church, near Albany. They claimed to be the oldest Church of Christ in Athens County. They worshiped in an old frame building with two entrances — one for men and the other for women. The pulpit was located between the two entrances with the congregation seated facing those who came into the meetings. To all who "passed the examination" I preached on Saturday night, Sunday morning, and Sunday night, and we had some good times together. The elders carried on between "preaching Sundays," teaching the Word and observing the weekly Communion services. The last I knew, the congregation, with never more than fifty members, is still carrying on for the Lord in their rural setting — a living example of what can be done by a group of consecrated and indoctrinated farmers and their families.

Episode II

Columbus and Pittsburgh

Meanwhile, matters in First Church, Athens, had taken a turn for the worse. A reactionary element had thrown roadblocks in the way of immediate erection of the new church building and growth was considerably slowed. Dad became discouraged, resigned, and, as he did in Hillsboro, decided to "leave the ministry." He was offered a job as regional representative of the LeFebure Ledger Company, and Elijah-like withdrew to the "wilderness" of first, Lima, Ohio, and then, Parkersburg, West Virginia. Thus, I was left to finish my college days alone. From then on in life, I was "on my own" like the proverbial bird pushed from the nest.

In June, 1915, I received my "sheep-skin" as a Bachelor of Arts (inscribed in Latin) and faced the three possible choices for the year ahead. Dr. Chubb offered me a scholarship in English literature at Ohio State University where I might secure my Master's. Dr. Elson offered a similar scholarship in History. Both professors felt that I could have a bright future as a teacher in some university. At the same time my friend Dan Poling offered me the job of Field Secretary of the Ohio Christian Endeavor Union and the editorship of *The Ohio Endeavorer* with offices in Columbus. The latter open door was chosen after much thought and prayer. Here was an opportunity to carry out my life-work decision. It should also be said that I had the help of a certain young lady in making up my mind.

Olive Cameron was an outstanding member of our youth group in First Church. She was the daughter of Henry and Ella Cameron. Henry was a leading business man of Athens, a trustee of the church, and a warm friend of father's. Olive had a secretarial job in her father's office and was taking work in the University. She was socially inclined, was a founder of the Ohio chapter of Alpha Delta Pi, and recognized as a leader among the girls on campus. She was active in Sunday school and Christian Endeavor Society work. I think it was while she was chairman of the Social Committee of the society and staged a number of successful parties that I first began to realize that she was the girl for me. Quite naturally I began squiring her to and from school and church events and kept blithely on until it became a habit I didn't want to break. She was always sympathetic with my ideas and my plans, often offering her very efficient help to realize them. A short time before graduation she consented to be my wife. She liked the idea of my having a paying job and of living in Columbus. It meant marriage immediately. Her "vote" was a deciding factor in my saying "yes" to Dan Poling. The wedding was a simple afternoon affair in the Cameron home with George Owen, the new minister at First Church, performing the ceremony, August 25, 1915. I had rented a furnished house on West Fourth Avenue in Columbus, near our West Fourth Avenue Church. After a delightful reception we took the Hocking Valley train to Ohio's capital city. A crowd of fraternity and sorority members and young people from the church cheered and showered us with rice as we took refuge in the parlor car amid the knowing smiles of all the passengers. It was a step I have never regretted.

We were given a warm reception in Columbus both by associates in the office and friends in the church. T. L. Lowe was pastor of the West Fourth Avenue Church, then our largest in the city. Its Bible school averaged around a thousand in attendance and it had a large youth group, many of its members students in Ohio State University. Lowe was father's Timothy dating back to Rutland days. He immediately took a fatherly interest in us, often dropping in for calls and even meals and encouraging me to assist in youth and Bible class work as time would permit.

I was associated with Stanley B. Vandersall, who was executive secretary of the Ohio C. E. Union (a brother-in-law of Dan Poling). My chief task was the production of the state paper which at that time was a twenty-four page monthly. The cost was considerable and it was financed by soliciting advertising for special county editions. No sooner had I landed in Columbus than I was assigned to Newark and Licking County where I sold advertising by day and spoke to youth groups at night. I made many friends with leaders of the county organization who willingly helped me to achieve a fine record. I covered large sections of the state, thoroughly enjoying my work.

I recall especially my trip to Cleveland and Cuyahoga County. At that time "The Sunrise Union" was the largest in the state and one of the largest city unions in America. Fred L. Ball, young executive of the Park Drop Forge Company, was the outstanding leader. The union gave me a dinner reception my first night in the city. When I was introduced, I said, "All those who like cherry pie put up your hands." Everybody did and I said, "That's my favorite pie. With this in common we are on the way to having a fine week together." To my surprise the next morning I was served cherry pie for breakfast, and the entertainment committee saw to it that I had cherry pie at every meal for "the duration." I was never in my life so sick of cherry pie. There were fun, and work, and deep spiritual experiences which I shall never forget. I spoke in many churches of all denominations and reached hundreds of young people "for Christ and the Church" (the Christian Endeavor motto). Largely through the influence of Fred Ball we went "over the top" in our advertising drive.

As I got around as a guest over the state I personally made a special effort to contact our Christian Churches and Churches of Christ. I was often invited to supply the pulpits of these congregations. *The Christian Standard,* during those months, carried a weekly news letter over my name under the acrostic heading "*Over-H*eard *In O*hio" which was appreciated by all those who were mentioned. As one result of this service, there came the opportunity to prepare the two-column weekly comments on the C. E. lessons for *The Lookout* — an arrangement which was to last for many years.

Many of our preaching brethren kept urging me to devote my talents more exclusively to the Restoration Movement. After about six months in Columbus these pressures finally crystallized in a call from the Western Pennsylvania Christian Missionary Society to come to Pittsburgh and undertake a mission ministry with the Observatory Hill Christian Church. When I shared my problem with Stan Vandersall, he immediately got in touch with Dan Poling and suggested a promotion which would keep me in C. E. ranks. Poling proposed that I become executive secretary of the Oregon Society with headquarters in Portland. When I turned down this opening, Dan was greatly disappointed and for a long time was quite cool toward me. I felt the strong call of a life of service with "our own people" and never regretted the move to Pittsburgh. Christian Endeavor continued to be a major interest, as my story will confirm.

We arrived in the then "Smoky City" (and I mean *smoky*) in the dead of winter. The church we were to serve was about ready to close its doors. Observatory Hill was all that remained of a tragic split from First Church, Allegheny, in which a brilliant showman and pulpiteer, whose name escapes me now, had been fired for misconduct. With his very considerable popular following he had led in the erection of the frame building at the corner of Wilson and Drumm Streets (near Perrysville Avenue) and for several years enjoyed a prosperous pastorate. When his questionable proclivities again manifested themselves he left for "parts unknown" and only a mere handful of committed brethren remained. Our first Lord's Day was very discouraging. The ground was covered with deep drifting snow and only about twenty-five or thirty people greeted the preacher in what had once been a men's class room, poorly heated by a small gas stove. We turned the occasion into a prayer meeting and pledged ourselves to build anew "the walls of Zion." The sanctuary had been closed for some months. The fellowship hall was filled with trash. "Death" stared at us from every angle of what had once been a rather attractive building.

As spring dawned I urged our people to clean up the church house inside and out. We painted the sanctuary, varnished the pews, installed new lighting fixtures, put new runners down the aisles, and announced services for Easter. Then came the cleanup of the fellowship hall and the rehabilitation of the kitchen and furnace room. Outside we laid sod on the barren lot, planted boxwood hedges, painted the entrance ways, and set up a bulletin board. All this was done because our own people gave their spare time night and day until the job was done. I rolled up my sleeves and worked right with the men. The whole community was electrified at what was going on, and our audiences began to grow. I visited every person and family on the church roster, inspired the faithful to participate in a calling program, and some of the prodigals began to drift back to our services.

Christian Endeavor was a medium of enlistment of new members for Observatory Hill Church. A number of young people from First Church joined in the rehabilitation program. We entertained city union meetings. I was called for speaking engagements in youth rallies and street meetings. We got the name of being a young people's church.

An interesting event occurred that summer when a Seventh-Day Adventist evangelist pitched his tent in our community and began teaching his strange doctrines. Several of our best older members who were not well indoctrinated were greatly interested and about to be led away from us. I had a number of Bible studies in their homes. Then I challenged the evangelist for a debate. We set a tentative date with the meetings to be held in our building, but finally, he was too busy "rebuilding the walls of Jerusalem to come down into the plains of Ono" and argue with a preacher who was "hardly dry behind the ears." I then advertised a Sunday evening study of Seventh-Day Adventism (thanks to the New Testament and D. M. Canright's book "Seventh-Day Adventism Renounced") which filled our sanctuary and put an early end to the proselyting program around the corner.

Probably one of the most valuable contributions my Memoirs can make to Restoration history is my impressions of great figures in the Movement of my time. Wallace Tharp was pastor of First Church, Allegheny, the largest church of our people in the area. He filled its spacious sanctuary every Lord's Day. Undoubtedly he was a great preacher and orator — one of our most magnificent when he was at his best. He often went into the pulpit chewing tobacco and would spit out his cud just before the sermon. Often after the sermon he would greet his parishioners at the door with some such word as "How did I do this morning? Didn't you think it was great?" And it probably was. He thrived on the encomiums of an admiring people. They often said he was the greatest preacher in Pittsburgh. Sometimes, however, they failed to get his wave-length. Old Dr. Cook, father of Walter Scott Cook, once told me the story of his experience at the Toronto International Convention, where Tharp was to have the main address at an important evening session. He was a flat failure. As Cook told the story: "I ate too much watermelon that night and was sitting on the curb of the street in front of the hall, 'heaving up Jonah.' Friends came along and said, 'Doc, what's the matter?' to which I replied, 'O, but I'm sick. I don't know what caused it unless it was that speech of Wallace Tharp's."

Tharp looked with little enthusiasm upon my efforts at Observatory Hill. One day I called on him in his office. He was smoking a cigar. He greeted me with the alibi, "Just burning a little incense. I usually start the day that way." He asked how I was getting along, then said, "Why don't you close the thing up. It never should have been started in the first place."

Tharp knew "the Plea" and could defend it with vigor and effectiveness. Several years after I had left Pittsburgh, he invited me to return and speak at a youth rally in First Church. He was the very soul of Virginia hospitality. I think he really had a warm place in his heart for me.

It was a real privilege to have fellowship with the churches and church leaders in Greater Pittsburgh. This was once the home of Walter Scott, Thomas Campbell, Isaac Errett, J. F. King, and other great heroes of the faith. Among those who were carrying on in that faith were the Latimer Brothers (consecrated laymen), C. B. Thurgood, F. A. Bright, Wallace Tharp, W. H. Hanna, A. C. Young, Walter Scott Cook and many others I might mention. We had a well-attended monthly fellowship meeting in the various churches where reports of evangelistic and educational achievement and inspirational messages were given. A luncheon was usually served. These meetings were a great encouragement to me.

However, it was in Pittsburgh that I was first confronted by the subversive influences of "modernism" and departures from the "faith once for all delivered." The nucleus of this movement existed in the wealthy and influential East End Christian Church where the brilliant John Ray Ewers ministered. I can remember a visit with Ewers in which he tried to sell me on "open membership" and his ideas on biblical inspiration. I was deeply impressed with his superior learning and culture and felt greatly honored that he would take the time out of his busy life to contact a poor young preacher like me. Fortunately I shared this incident with my father who gave me the answers to "liberalism" and taught me to beware of "wolves in sheep's clothing." From then on I was alert to the trends and gave much time to reading and study on the issues involved. (Not long after I left Pittsburgh, Ewers' policy split the East End Church. The "loyal" brethren withdrew, bought the old Conservatory of Music in the Schenley Park area and organized the "Central Church.")

Among the interesting people in my congregation on the Lord's Day was a little old shriveled-up lady of evident culture and intelligence. I got her name — I think it was McGee — and called on her. She was a member of First Church but the preacher there had no time to visit her. She lived in a magnificent but decaying old Victorian hilltop mansion overlooking the river and downtown Allegheny. I learned that she was the daughter of J. F. King, the great preacher who had built First Church into a power for the Restoration cause. Her husband had once been a wealthy oil man but she said he was ruined by the ruthless, lawless competitive onslaught of John D. Rockefeller in his effort to build the Standard Oil Company into a monopoly of the oil industry. (Ida M. Tarbell has told the true story in her so-called "muck-raking" book, *The*

31

History of the Standard Oil Company.) Poor little Mrs. McGee lived in the past and was bitter when she talked of the old days; yet she had a strong faith in Christ and looked to the day when all her troubles would vanish and she would live triumphantly with Him. When she talked about the future her eyes would light up with hope and courage. Her son-in-law, a successful business man, was John Ray Ewers' right hand man at East End Church. When she talked of him she would shake her head and say, "He's a nice fellow but he doesn't know what the Church is all about. They are running little more than a social club at East End." Her niece and lovely family lived nearby and were members and dependable workers at Observatory Hill. They were always an inspiration to me — the "cream of the crop."

Then, like a "bolt from the blue," one day I got a phone call. The voice said, "This is E. W. Thornton of the Standard Publishing Company in Cincinnati. I am at the Fort Pitt Hotel. Can you run down for a chat?" Thornton was at that time managing editor. He had made a special trip to Pittsburgh at the behest of Russell Errett to offer me a position on the editorial staff of the Company. I could scarcely believe my ears! This was my fondest dream come true. I had been in Pittsburgh only a little more than six months and the Observatory Hill work was just beginning to show signs of real growth. I knew I would be severely criticized if I resigned and walked out on those faithful souls who had made sacrifices to follow my leadership. What was I to do? Maybe such an offer would never come again. When A. C. Young, the State secretary, and Walter Scott Cook heard what had happened, they brought every pressure to bear to keep me from accepting. Both of these men were strongly "Establishment" and "anti-Standard" but they had been wonderful to me in their encouragement of my efforts. They said, If you accept this proposition and associate yourself with that Cincinnati cabal your prospects for advancement in the Brotherhood will be ruined. Your life will be poisoned with the "reactionism" and "bitter spirit" of the Erretts and their associates. Besides, you are under contract with the Western Pennsylvania Christian Missionary Society and are obligated to remain in Pittsburgh. (Of course, there was a sixty-day clause which either party could exercise for a separation).

After much prayer and wrestling of mind and spirit, I accepted the Standard offer. I felt that the Lord had clearly endowed me with abilities for a career of religious journalism and that it was He who was opening the door of opportunity. I could not refuse even though many would not understand. D. Park Chapman succeeded me at Observatory Hill and the work went on to new highs in growth and spiritual achievement. Years later I was called back to dedicate their remodeled church building amid joyous reunions with old friends.

So in September, 1916, I began what proved to be a nearly thirty-year association with Standard.

Episode III

Christian Standard

The Standard Publishing Company was the largest and most influential publishing house of the Christian Churches and Churches of Christ in the world. It was owned by the Errett family, descendants of Isaac Errett, founder of the *Christian Standard*. (See my estimate of the man in Chapter 11 of my book, *Christians Only*.)

For many years all publishing houses serving the churches were privately owned. Standard's most serious competitor was the very much smaller Christian Publishing Company of St. Louis, Missouri, owned by the Garrison family. It was a generally-accepted principle in those days that a church publishing house owned by "the church" (or a representative self-perpetuating board) would tend to become "official" and assume dangerous prerogatives in directing the thought and life of the Brotherhood. If privately owned, the brethren would accept it for what it was and nothing more. The views expressed in its publications would be considered merely as the private opinions of the writers. Its journals would be purchased and used in the churches on the basis of superior merit and not because of exclusive control of the market. It was also believed that competion would assure increasingly high quality of the materials being made available.

In 1909 R. A. Long purchased the St. Louis house and "gave it to the Brotherhood." It was chartered as a corporation not for profit under the laws of Missouri in 1911. Some years later it became an agency of the International Convention. This changed the picture somewhat in the publishing field, but Standard continued to maintain its supremacy.

Standard's dominance of the market was largely due to the business genius of Russell Errett (son of Isaac) with whom my lot was cast. He was probably the most misunderstood and maligned person in the Brotherhood (see *Fifty Years of Attack and Controversy* by Stephen J. Corey). Russell Errett had a brilliant mind, was a facile writer, and he understood, perhaps better than any of his contemporaries, the history and principles of the Restoration Movement. He had complete commitment to Christ and the Bible and had purposed in his heart to carry forward the great work his father had begun at whatever cost to his person, his family, his friends, his interests, or his property.

When I arrived at the Standard headquarters at Eighth, Ninth, and Cutter Streets, I was immediately taken to his office. He was sitting at a cluttered desk in an out-of-the-way part of the building. As he stood to greet me he appeared to be a tall, ungainly, Lincolnesque figure, with tousled hair, a full, trimmed beard and eyes which looked piercingly at me from under shaggy eyebrows. He said, "We have been watching you ever since 1915 when you sent us that piece for the *Standard*. ("Christ or Cicero — Which?"). We are glad to have you with us. You will serve temporarily as office editor of the *Standard*. What you do thereafter will depend largely on you and the service you are able to render. You will have a great deal of freedom to develop your talents. When men are given plenty of rope they can either climb it or they can hang themselves. I wish you the best of success." I found out later that he was thinking of me especially in terms of the editorship of *The Lookout*, then the magazine of largest circulation in the Brotherhood.

I was to learn that Standard was a benevolent patriarchate ruled by one man. When he said "yes" things moved; when he said "no" things stopped. If he embarked on a course of action he would put all the resources of the company behind it and spare no effort to make it a success. This accounted for the tremendous service Standard provided for the Sunday schools of America. It was he who launched the *Young People's Standard* (later *The Lookout*), *Buds of Hope* for the Primary child, *Boy Life* and *Girlhood Days* for the Juniors until, when I arrived in Cincinnati, Standard had some fifty Bible school publications entered as second-class matter in the Cincinnati post office. A wide variety of supplies was also available.

The Standard's presses were the finest made. I remember when one of America's leading secular publishers, S. S. McClure, of New York, faced a strike situation, he appealed to Mr. Errett to print all his publications for the duration, including the big-circulation, slick-paper *McClure's Magazine* and *Saint Nicholas*. Mr. Errett agreed and put on two additional shifts of printers, ran the presses twenty-four hours around the clock, and did a superb job. During the long strike Mr. McClure came to Cincinnati to express his appreciation and offered either to buy the Standard plant or take Mr. Errett and his printshop foreman to New York City to run his establishment. He is reported to have said, "Come to New York; work with me and I will make you a wealthy man." Of course, Mr. Errett turned him down. He was in business only for the Lord.

Russell Errett was the first businessman in Cincinnati to erect a concrete and steel building — the eight-story structure at the corner of Eighth and Cutter. He was the first religious publisher in America to recognize the importance of offset printing. He installed a battery of color presses occupying the entire eighth floor and was soon turning out the finest art reproductions for use in church and Bible school work available anywhere. To back up his supply of source materials he assembled (with the help of artist Otto Stemler) the largest collection of famous religious paintings (copies) owned by any religious publishing house in America. It was not long until Standard was printing Sunday school picture rolls and cards for most of the leading religious publishers of the nation. Then came art calendars and a wide variety of church supplies for an ever-increasing market. Mr. Errett was always in the forefront of every new development of the graphic arts in the religious field. Nothing was too good for our churches. Sometimes he would pour so much of his profits into a new idea that his line of credit would be temporarily impaired, but nothing could stop him if he felt it was the Lord's will to move ahead.

Mr. Errett's jealous enemies started rumors that he was in business only for the money and that he was not even a member of the church. He was, of course, a member and elder for many years in Central Christian Church; later in the Madisonville Church (nearer the ancestral home in Terrace Park). Until advanced age made it impossible, he was at the Lord's Table every Lord's Day and was the most liberal supporter financially at Madisonville. He saw the church grow from a small mission to over one thousand members. Mr. Errett experienced many disappointments in his family life which I will not recount here. It could well be said that he was married to Standard to which he gave "his last full measure of devotion." His gifts to worthy undertakings of the brotherhood agencies ran into many thousands of dollars every year — the Ohio Christian Missionary Society, the American Christian Missionary Society, the Foreign Christian Missionary Society, the Board of Church Extension, etc., etc. This continued until he was finally convinced that liberalism had so completely infiltrated these organizations that he could no longer in good conscience support them. Bethany College, Transylvania, Butler, and many other schools were continuously beneficiaries of his generosity. Besides these good works he spent thousands of dollars in the support of independent evangelists who majored in the establishment of new churches, financed conferences on Evangelism, Doctrinal Congresses, and Sunday School conventions galore. Only at the Last Day when "the books are opened" will it be known how much of the profits of Standard in his day found their way into enterprises committed to the development of the Plea at home and abroad.

Russell Errett was among the first Brotherhood leaders to discover liberal trends in agency leadership and educational circles. He early allied himself with John W. McGarvey and men of that type in a war against these subversive forces. McGarvey's department of "Biblical Criticism" in the *Christian Standard* was swift to detect heresy and deal with it effectively. (The survey of this era in my book *Christians Only* in Chapters 15, "The Great Apostasy" and 16, "The Great Controversy," will give background essential to understanding Standard's policies and programs in the early decades of the 1900's.) Had it not been for Russell Errett and the *Christian Standard* the "progressive" Christian Churches and Churches of Christ might well have been swallowed up in the abyss of liberalism that destroyed Bible-believing elements in many communions of American Protestanism.

As "office editor" or "assistant editor" of the *Christian Standard,* I was assigned to a little "cubbyhole" adjacent to the office of the new editor, George P. Rutledge.

S. S. Lappin was just closing a long and prosperous editorship during which time the paper reached its largest circulation and was noted as the "newspaper of the brotherhood." Whether people liked its policies and programs or not, they took the *Standard* because it had the most complete coverage of men and events available anywhere. Lappin was a born editor and writer coming to Cincinnati from a country town by the name of Geff in Illinois. He had a genius for a style of speaking and writing that appealed to middle America and he had no peer in that appeal. I was disappointed that I was not to serve as his helper. He moved out to become minister of First Church, Bedford, Indiana, then one of our largest in the Central States.

Rutledge was a more highly educated and polished man, short in stature and very "cocky." He was a chain smoker of big black cigars while Lappin was an ardent anti-tobacco crusader. Rutledge was one of the famous "four-horsemen" from Virginia, the others being W. H. Book, Robert E. Elmore, and B. A. Abbott (later editor of the *Christian Evangelist*). Rutledge was the author of several books, such as *Center Shots at Rome* and *Miracle of the Ages,* and came to Cincinnati from Columbus, Ohio, where he had a very successful ministry with the Broad Street Church. Rutledge had no more than arrived until he was deeply embroiled in the attack on liberalism in Transylvania and the College of the Bible at Lexington, Kentucky. He told me that he would look after the editorials and essays and the rest of the paper was mine. So that was the way it was for the two years or more of my residence in the "cubbyhole."

I succeeded Edwin R. Errett as office editor. His secretary Clara Luskey (later to become his first wife) became my very efficient helper. Edwin, educated in Bethany and Yale, became Bible school lesson commentator and editor. I shall have much more to say of him later on in my story. We became warm friends and in the future we were to work together in many tasks for the Lord.

I sought to continue *Standard's* reputation for news coverage in "From the Field," "Among the Brethren," and city, state and regional news letters. I introduced first-page features of the largest churches in the Brotherhood which made a hit and resulted in a long waiting list eager to get such recognition. Then I departmentalized certain phases of the news such as "Sounds of Hammer and Chisel" which featured, with accompanying illustrations, the scores of new church buildings being erected across the nation in those days. It was always a pleasure to "scoop" the *Christian Evangelist,* which we did with great frequency.

But almost like a "pall" the Lexington controversy hung over the office next door. There was little else talked about but ways and means of purging the temples of learning and their classrooms of liberalism. Evidence of heresy piled high and all sorts of strategies were devised for

36

the removal of recalcitrant professors. I was not directly involved, but who could stay in the *Standard* offices and not be affected by what was going on? At that time I did not realize that the Lexington aftermath would deeply influence my career in later years. (For my historical report of the controversy see pages 241-244 of Chapter 16 in my book *Christians Only*.)

As was to be true during my entire life, I had "other irons in the fire." Besides the *Christian Standard*, I continued to serve in the field of Christian Endeavor. I was elected president of the Ohio C. E. Union, then rivaling California as the largest state union in the nation. Russell Errett approved my taking time for weekend trips all over the state, speaking in city rallies and county conventions. The state convention came to Cincinnati that year and it was the largest in history — young people of thirty denominations filled Music Hall for the main sessions, Emery Auditorium for the Intermediate sessions and Odeon Hall for the Junior sessions. When I made my "Presidential Address" the first night Mr. Errett was in the balcony cheering me on with the rest of the "kids."

Afterward he asked me how I would like to edit a journal on the order of *The Lookout* exclusively for Endeavorers. I jumped at the chance. He gave me carte blanche and soon *Something Doing* was launched together with a training book, *Pocket Manual of Endeavor*. I never knew for certain whether he had in mind a test to see what I might be able to do at the helm of *The Lookout* or whether he expected me to build a big new Christian Endeavor journal. Suffice to say, the new magazine was soon merged with *The Lookout* and I became its editor in 1918. I also became editor of a new *Christian Endeavor Quarterly* which rendered long and effective service to societies all over the nation.

During this period I received a personal call one day from the famous Robert M. Hopkins asking me to accept the executive secretaryship of the National Board of Christian Endeavor of the Disciples of Christ, which I turned down. I had contacts with members of the Board which caused me to believe that the Disciples were soon to abandon Christian Endeavor, following the example of the Presbyterians and the Methodists. Christian Endeavor was too biblical and evangelical and had too much to say about Christian unity to please the "powers that be" in the denominational world. I announced these fears in *Something Doing* and called a rally of youth to meet in Kansas City in connection with the International Convention that year at which we proposed to draft a resolution to be presented to the Convention calling for the perpetuation of Christian Endeavor in our churches. At that time Claude E. Hill, pastor of the large First Church, Tulsa, Oklahoma, was chairman of the National Board. He was a great soul. He insisted that there was no move for the elimination of Christian Endeavor by what I now call the "Establishment." I am sure he knew nothing of the plan. He had tears in his eyes when he asked me to call off the meeting scheduled for the parlor of the Muelebach Hotel. We held the meeting but it failed to accomplish its purpose, and in a few short years Christian Endeavor was dead so far as the Disciples hierarchy was concerned. A new liberal "Youth Program" was soon inaugurated. Christian Endeavor continued, however, in the free churches and was to have yet many prosperous years among us.

While I am telling the Christian Endeavor phase of my story I might as well add, though a bit out of order chronologically, the fact that I was invited by the International Society to succeed the late Dr. Amos R. Wells as editor of the *Christian Endeavor World*. In those days the *World* was one of the major journals in the religious field. Wells was a versatile and vigorous writer and had "made" the magazine a power for righteousness. He was also for many years author and editor of *Peloubet's Notes* on the International Uniform Sunday School lessons and the author of many religious books. He had frequently asked me to contribute to the columns of the *World*. It was indeed a great honor to be asked to go to Boston and take over the editor's chair, but I had seen the "handwriting on the wall" for Christian Endeavor and felt that the magazine would eventually cease to have the influence it once commanded. My decision to decline the honor was a wise one. During my active years in the organization I contributed several books besides the *Pocket Manual*, such as *Successful C. E. Prayer Meetings, Christian Endeavor Publicity,* and *Christian Endeavor Essentials,* to say nothing of the thousands of weekly lesson commentaries I had written for *The Lookout, Standard C. E. Quarterly,* and the *Christian Endeavor World.* Only the Lord knows how many young lives were touched "for Christ and the Church" through these writings. I spoke in C. E. conventions — state, regional, and national — from coast to coast and had rich fellowship with a whole generation of secretaries and superintendents. I treasure in my library autographed copies of the autobiographies of Christian Endeavor's founder, Dr. Francis E. Clark *(Memories of Many Men in Many Lands);* Dr. William Shaw *(The Evolution of an Endeavorer),* and Dan Poling *(Mine Eyes Have Seen).*

In 1917 there was a "blow up" in affairs at the Christian Board of Publication which resulted in Standard's acquiring the services of four of its leading employees. I never knew exactly what caused the trouble except that there had been a revolt against the high-handed policies of A. C. Smither, the new manager. Smither had been pastor of First Church, Los Angeles, and was an Establishment "wheeler dealer" of the "first water." Willard Mohorter, son of J. H. Mohorter the executive secretary of the National Benevolent Association, is credited with engineering the coup-d'etat that brought us this "windfall." The new men were: Mohorter, who became assistant editor of the *Christian Standard;* Charles C. Buss, who became assistant manager of the Company; T. B. Booth, who took over the management of the Merchandise Department; and the noted Frederick D. Kershner, who became "Book Editor" or "Literary Editor." This event was the Brotherhood "sensation of the year." Buss and Kershner did not remain long in Cincinnati. Buss, who had once been a popular trumpet-playing song evangelist, soon proved himself inadequate in the discharge of his new duties. Kershner, after producing the very valuable *Restoration Handbook,* went to Butler University to become the dean of the new School of Religion — a position he held the remainder of his life. He was one of the greatest scholars in the ranks of the modern Restoration Movement. He had served with great distinction as president of Texas Christian University and as editor of the *Christian Evangelist.* It was a distinct privilege to be associated with him briefly at Standard. Booth became one of the most valued employees of the Company and built its book and supply business into one of the major services of its kind in American Protestant publishing houses. I was later to be very closely associated with him. Mohorter was to become a tremendous behind-the-scenes factor in determining Company policy, especially in its relationship to Brotherhood affairs. More of that anon.

Episode IV

The Lookout

In 1918 I became editor of *The Lookout*. I could scarcely believe that such a high honor had come to me and I began what proved to be the happiest and most rewarding period of service in my nearly thirty years with Standard.

I succeeded E. J. Meacham and Hallie Errett (Slifer) who had been joint editors for several years. Meacham, a Tennesseean, had been a very successful "Bible-school pastor" and came to Cincinnati from First Church, Portsmouth, Ohio, where he had a school of over a thousand in attendance. Like many successful pastors, he was not equipped to be a successful editor. Hallie Errett was a daughter of Russell Errett, a woman of culture and deep concern for the Kingdom, who spent most of her *Lookout* years traveling and studying abroad.

The Lookout had an interesting history. It was first called the *Young People's Standard* and was supposed to be a youthful version of *Christian Standard*. Then came the Christian Endeavor Movement and the periodical became a medium for its promotion. The name "Lookout" came from the "Lookout Committee" which was considered to be the major committee in Christian Endeavor's committee system. Among its editors in this early day were Jessie Brown (Pounds), author of many storybooks and such hymns as "The Way of the Cross Leads Home," and Mattie Boteler, also an author of note. *The Lookout* of that time was pretty much of a story paper distributed free by the churches to their youth on Sunday morning. Then came the Sunday school revival which brought Herbert Moninger to Standard and the editorship of *The Lookout*. Meacham succeeded Moninger.

Moninger deserves a special place in my memoirs because he was a real inspiration to me, and the service he rendered *The Lookout* made it possible for me to achieve the measure of success I enjoyed as its editor. I met him first at Hillsboro, Ohio (as I have already noted), and ever after eagerly watched the papers for news of his activities. I have previously spoken of his career with Standard, but I am now interested in recording what he did for *The Lookout*. He took page after page to tell of successful teacher training classes, organized Bible classes and would list attendances of outstanding schools. He promoted, promoted, and promoted for bigger and better schools. He organized the Worldwide Loyal Movement with *The Lookout* as its organ. The Movement was little more than a series of manuals which told Bible classes from the Junior Department up how to carry on an efficient program of study and growth. These booklets were simple and brought results. Classes using them were asked to change their names and include the word "Loyal." There were pins, pennants, and other gadgets provided to enlist interest. Standard sold, sold, and sold Sunday school supplies as it had never sold before. *The Lookout* was the source of enthusiasm and know-how in this field for the whole Brotherhood, and it broke all circulation records. Others tried to duplicate Moninger's system but they failed. He was the unique man for the time. When God made him He must have broken the pattern. His death at an early age was mourned by the whole Brotherhood.

I assumed the editorship in what is often called the "Golden Age" of the Sunday school (or "Bible school" — Standard's preferred nomen). The most striking single development of the period was the increase in adult Bible study. An age of business efficiency began to reflect itself in the work of "teen-age" and adult groups in the schools. Business organization and method, social effort, Bible lectures and addresses, contests and prayer circles — all inspired by carefully prepared propaganda — made a tremendous impact upon the church and society. Adult class enthusiasts often went to extremes in their desire for numbers, even breaking connection with the churches and forming community classes meeting in motion-picture theaters and public halls, where religion was popularized and diluted and education was a misnomer. In many places politicians took control of men's classes and used them to promote their political party's candidates for office. However, a fair evaluation of the total values of this development would reveal a tremendous weight of good. Simultaneously a deep educational consciousness gripped the Sunday school movement of the period. Christian educators of prominence in the secular field began to devote their careers to church schools with a resulting emphasis upon graded instruction according to the needs and capacities of age groups. It was an ideal time for me to come into leadership in this field.

As the seven big bound volumes of *The Lookout* produced during my years in the editor's chair will testify, many changes were made in its format and its areas of service were greatly expanded. The new by-line "Magazine of Christian Education" hinted at these changes. The organized Bible classes usually had front-page billing with photos of great classes which proved an inspiration to others. Each front-page feature was accompanied by the story of how the class was built, promoted, and was achieving its purpose. The leading essays dealt with educational principles or feature stories of church school success. The editorials were short, spicy, and designed to inspire schools and classes to greater accomplishment. There were a short story and a continued story in each issue. The news section reported progress everywhere. There was a statistical report of attendances of all schools with records of 300 or more present. The ten top schools were given special recognition. (On special days as many as twenty churches would report a thousand or more in attendance.) All Bible classes reporting an attendance of twenty-five or more were listed. Many a class was inspired to build its membership by the promise of listing in *The Lookout* when it reached or passed the twenty-five mark.

When I get enthusiastic about the "Golden Years" of the Sunday School before an audience of the "now generation" there are lifted eyebrows and other evidences of doubt. But the facts are that in the years that I was editor of *The Lookout* the Sunday School movement reached its peak. I have taken the trouble to verify the fantastic figures of attendance reported by our Christian Churches and Churches of Christ in *The Lookout* in 1925. The highwater mark was reached on Easter Sunday April 12 when we received reports from 320 schools totaling an attendance of 192,991. On the basis of this showing I estimated that 2,500,000 attended the 9,000 Christian Bible Schools in America that day. There has been nothing like it before or since.

Here is the Easter record (pp. 17, 18, issue of April 26) of attendance in the major schools subscribing for *The Lookout:*

Tulsa, Okla. (First) 4,274
Long Beach, Calif. (First)..3,798
Indianapolis, Ind. (Third) ..3,616
Canton, Ohio (First) 3,605
Indianapolis, Ind.(Central) 3,080
Oklahoma City, Okla.
   (First) 3,016
Enid, Okla. (Central) 2,922
Dallas, Texas (First) 2,455
Kansas City, Mo.
   (Independence Blvd.) 2,005
Coffeyville, Kans. (First) ..1,990
Washington, D. C.
   (Ninth St.) 1,869
Colorado Springs, Colo.
   (First) 1,655
Independence, Kans. 1,496
Indianapolis, Ind.
   (Seventh) 1,401
Youngstown, Ohio
   (Central) 1,400
Indianapolis, Ind.
   (Englewood) 1,355
Huntington, Ind. (Central)..1,335
Akron, Ohio
   (East Market St.) 1,297
Johnson City, Tenn.
   (First) 1,276

Shreveport, La. (Central) ..1,231
Marshall, Mo. 1,231
Hutchinson, Kans. 1,219
Portsmouth, Ohio (First) ..1,206
Council Bluffs, Ia. (First)..1,188
Ft. Worth, Tex. (First) 1,175
Pittsburg, Kans. 1,170
Bedford, Ind. (First) 1,168
Kansas City, Mo. (Central).1,164
Newcastle, Ind. (First) 1,162
Lima, Ohio (South Side) 1,134
Toledo, Ohio (Central) 1,098
Sapulpa, Okla. 1,093
Ashland, Ky. (First) 1,085
Anderson, Ind. (Central)....1,073
Centerville, Ia. 1,072
Lincoln, Ill. 1,068
Ponca City, Okla. (First) ..1,064
Akron, Ohio (South) 1,050
Franklin, Ind. 1,034
Indianapolis, Ind.
   (Olive Branch) 1,021
Miami, Fla. (First) 1,017
Indianapolis, Ind.
   (North Park) 1,014
Terre Haute, Ind.
   (Central) 1,007

There were ten other schools which just missed the 1,000 mark by a hair's breadth: East Liverpool, O. (First); Arkansas City, Ark. (Central); Zanesville, O. (First); Neodesha, Kan.; Muncie, Ind. (Jackson St.); Norwood, O.; Leavenworth, Kan.; Boone, Ia.; Huntington, W. Va. (Central); and Washington, Ind. (First). There were undoubtedly many others in that class that were not reported to us. If the reader wants an exercise in pessimism let him compare these figures with the attendance of these same schools last Easter.

The treatment of the International Uniform Sunday School lessons was one of our big features. In this we enlisted the pens of outstanding Brotherhood leaders and scholars (example: Edwin R. Errett's "Untying Some Knots"). P. H. Welshimer, teacher of the largest adult class in the Brotherhood (with over a thousand in attendance each Sunday), was given a big spread with his photo and headed "Welshimer's Bible Class." This feature alone sold thousands of copies. George Taubman, teacher of a great men's class in the Municipal Auditorium at Long Beach, California, did a column on men's work. Henrietta Heron, popular Standard staff editor and later national president of the Baraca-Philathea Movement, did one on women's work. The Loyal Movement under the leadership of its current head, Traverce Harrison, was given large space to promote its work. "Ways of Working" was a page devoted to methods of building church schools. Christian Endeavor and the Mid-week Prayer Meeting had weekly lesson treatments. "Clipped Cream" carried short, spicy comments of great men and short inspirational poems. "Fun Foundry" was filled with jokes and "bright remarks" which often found their way into other church papers all over the nation. When Standard added J. H. Shonkwiler, noted cartoonist of the day, to its staff we induced him to create a character by the name of "Simon Sledge" and draw a panel each week for *The Lookout*. Simon, as a rural-type Sunday school zealot, said many pointed things no one else dared say about the way some churches were "run," and the way the people that "ran" them conducted themselves. He was both critical and complimentary and conducted himself in such a way that Simon Sledge was for our purposes as popular a cartoon character as Dick Tracy or Charlie Brown. Special campaigns with high goals were staged at frequent intervals, such as "Anti-Summer Slump," "Pre-Easter," "Teacher Training," "Rally Day," "Youth Week," etc., etc. There was "something doing" in our columns all the time. We had special issues such as "Book Number," "Evangelism Number," "Anti-Cigarette Number," etc.

Thereby hangs a tale. HEW (Health, Education, and Welfare) was not then on the scene to back up a popular crusade against the cigarette. We "went out on a limb" to combat a very popular but dangerous habit. I had Shonkwiler draw a full front-page picture of a death skull formed by smoke from a cigarette on an ashtray for the Anti-Cigarette Number. Inside we had articles from scientists and moralists which urged abstinence. A member of the Errett family in the company was a chain smoker and a favorite of Aunt Jane Errett who had her office down the hall from mine. Aunt Jane stormed into my office right after the edition came from the press and read the riot act to me for daring to print such a thing. From that day on for many months she would not speak to me or have any dealings with me whatsoever. Eventually we became friends again but the incident was never again mentioned. Aunt Jane was a daughter of Isaac Errett, who never married and was a devout worshiper at the shrine of her sainted father. She and her brother Russell were frequently at sword's points on the way the company was run. Russell always prevailed and she drew her dividends and her bonuses without a murmur. No more opinionated or bigoted person ever lived. If she liked you, she would do anything in the world to help you. If she hated you, she would sit up nights devising ways to destroy you. I got both kinds of treatment as her mood varied from time to time. The man involved took the issue as a huge joke and kidded me about it every time we met. One day, however, I said, "If the cigarette habit is as harmless as you say it is, and you could stop it any time you take a notion, why don't you stop it and prove your case?" "Okay," he said, "here goes." He took the cigarette out of his mouth; crushed out the coals on his ashtray; took his pack of cigarettes out of his pocket and threw it into the wastebasket. Some days or weeks went by; then his usual cheery greeting became a grumpy "Hi!" He was still off the habit but the experience was beginning to hurt. He developed a case of nerves and his secretary told me he had seen a doctor for medicine to stop the craving that had become almost unbearable. Then one day he met me in the hall puffing away as usual. He hailed me with old-time cordiality and said, "Well, Jim, you win! It's a bad habit but I get a kick out of it that is worth the price."

The Lookout during those years became the most popular religious journal in the Brotherhood. Its St. Louis rival, *The Front Rank,* almost went out of business. One day Russell Errett dropped into my office with a broad smile on his face and said, "Well, you've done it! *The Lookout* has passed its old circulation record under Moninger and the print order is still climbing by leaps and bounds." This was an unusual departure from Mr. Errett's habitual silence even when he was pleased with what one of his employees was doing. Silence from the front office was supposed to denote approval or indicate that "all was well." I always treasured that visit.

Quite naturally I was invited to speak at special Bible school and class functions across the land. These visits gave me a great opportunity to get acquainted personally with many lay leaders and ministers. I could fill another book with memories of those contacts. The P. H. Welshimer contact is a good illustration of the blessings of these occasions. My first trip to First Church, Canton, was on a Rally Day in "the largest Bible School in the world." Thousands were present and the great auditorium was filled to overflowing for the address to the adults. I felt like a pigmy in a giant's castle. I have no idea what I said, and I am sure it

44

was inadequate for the occasion. P. H., however, was very, very gracious and generous and said it was "fine." At least "the editor of *The Lookout*" had appeared and that was sufficient for our thousands of readers in the Canton area. I was entertained at the Welshimer manse and had the privilege of meeting Mrs. Welshimer, Helen, Mildred, and Ralph, all of whom I came to know well in the years that were ahead. We talked "Bible school" continually and I got some insight into what made First Church tick. Welshimer was a people's preacher and teacher; he (as he often said) "put the hay down where the horses could reach it." He made the Bible a living book, essential and relevant to daily living. He had organizational and promotional ability that would have made him a successful head of a firm like Procter and Gamble or General Motors. I recall overhearing a conversation in the kitchen that day. P. H. was looking over the record of attendance of his teachers. He asked Mrs. Welshimer about certain absentees among teachers in the children's division. The eavesdropper then heard the word, "She has been absent two Sundays in a row without excuse. Out she goes Monday morning. Whom have we got to take her place?" It was remarkable how he could see the school in the large and in minutest detail at the same time. He made short shrift of drones. In every word he spoke and every move he made he seemed to be perfectly relaxed and certain of his course of action. Evangelism was the watchword in his whole program. Everything was "in order to win souls to Christ." There were additions and baptisms every Sunday. P. H. always said, "The way to build a great church is to have a great Bible school. Reach them, teach them, and baptize them is the divine order. How he found time, with his busy schedule (including scores and scores of sick calls, funerals, marriages, and out-of-town engagements) to write his weekly lesson for *The Lookout* and many "best-seller" books on Bible school methods and theological issues was always a marvel to me.

This living dynamo for God was easily the most influential local church leader in the life of the Brotherhood in his day. Later references to him will validate this estimate.

Another rich experience was a trip to the West Coast to be with George P. Taubman and First Church, Long Beach, California. Taubman was a "man's man" and one of the first things he did after he had arrived from a very successful pastorate in First Church, Portsmouth, Ohio, was to organize a great men's Bible class. It outgrew its church facilities and moved to the Long Beach Municipal Auditorium on the famous pier overlooking the Pacific Ocean. To everyone's amazement that building was filled with men every Sunday to hear "George" teach the Bible school lesson. Long Beach in those days was his town and he could get almost anything he wanted. He was erecting what was to be the finest church building in Long Beach when a devastating earthquake hit and its big dome collapsed and wrecked the whole edifice. There was no such thing as insurance against earthquakes. Taubman wasn't fazed in the least. With great faith in the Lord he announced that the debris would be cleared and construction would be resumed. The whole city of Long Beach came to his aid and the splendid structure still houses First Church there. It was to this great congregation that I came for Rally Day. I spoke first to over a thousand men in the Taubman class. I was introduced by E. B. Buffum of Buffum's Department Store and later mayor of Long Beach. The lesson was broadcast over the local radio station. (Years later this was the site of the international broadcasts of Dr. Charles E. Fuller's "Old-fashioned Revival Hour.") Then I preached to a wonderful audience at the churchhouse with the balcony and gallery packed to the limit. It was a truly great experience. I was entertained in the Taubman manse. Never have I enjoyed more gracious hospitality. The Taubmans were FFV's of the old school and ties were established that weekend which endured for many years to come. When liberalism took over historic Disciple institutions in Southern California, George Taubman and First Church became a rallying point for our "loyal brethren" and stemmed the tide which threatened to engulf them.

One more example of my field experiences while editor of *The Lookout:* my visits to the old Tabernacle Church in Columbus, Indiana, where W. H. Book was minister. Here was another of the great Bible schools which averaged over a thousand a Sunday. Book wrote the Midweek Prayer Meeting topics for *The Lookout.* He had a unique style which appealed to the common people. His books of sermons had wide distribution. He was a strong believer in the importance of the Bible school in the local church's program. It was in the Columbus parsonage that I first met his son Abbott Book, who later became one of the major leaders in Christian education at the local church level.

Parenthetically, I would like to pay tribute to Abbott. He was personally thoroughly committed to the evangelical biblical faith, but he spent most of his professional career in the camp of the liberals. His first venture was as a Director of Christian Education in the Walnut Hills Church, Cincinnati, where Robert E. Elmore was then minister. (Elmore was a half-brother of W. H. Book.) When the FCMS (Foreign Christian Missionary Society) open membership controversy broke, Walnut Hills was embroiled to such an extent that a church split seemed inevitable. Abbott's program of Christian education was completely stymied. He never got over the frustrations he experienced there. He vowed that he would thereafter "stick to his knitting" and never again become involved in a church fight of any kind. He went from Walnut Hills to First Church, Oklahoma City; then, to Union Avenue Church, St. Louis. Finally, he became executive secretary of the Council of Churches in San Francisco and continued in that position until his death. During all those years in which we were on opposite sides of the inevitable institutional confrontation, we remained close personal friends and spent many happy hours together.

46

But, back to Columbus. On this Rally Day occasion I was entertained in the palatial Irwin mansion, set in a beautiful formal Italian garden, which occupied a whole city block. The Irwins were nabobs of the city and pillars of the Tabernacle Church. Joseph I. Irwin, the founder of Irwin's Bank, was the patriarch of the family. He was succeeded by his bachelor son, William Irwin, who expanded the family fortune to include the Indiana National Bank in Indianapolis, a controlling interest in Campbell Soups, and other large business corporations. When his chauffeur invented the first American diesel automotive engine, Irwin backed him in obtaining patents of immense value and formed the Cummings Engine Company. This multi-million-dollar enterprise now forms the bulk of the huge Irwin-Miller estate. Will Irwin became a power politically in Indiana and the nation. He was a member of the National Republican Committee (once its chairman) and frequently entertained the entire committee at his own expense at nearby plush French Lick Springs. It was the Irwins who underwrote the expansion of Butler University and made possible the launching of its well-endowed College of Religion. One of Will Irwin's sisters married the internationally noted Z. T. Sweeney (once pastor of Tabernacle Church); another married Hugh T. H. Miller, then Lieutenant-Governor of Indiana, and a staunchly conservative elder in Tabernacle. It was quite an experience to be entertained in such surroundings and to meet such noted people. Again, I felt like a pigmy among giants, but formed acquaintances there which meant much more to me and to the cause of Christ in years to come.

One particularly wild journey was to a Rally Day affair in First Church, Dodge City, Kansas. This was the southwestern Kansas metropolis noted for its cowboy raids and the law and order campaign of Wyatt Erp. It had developed far beyond that stage when I visited the place, although it had a long way to go to attain its present prestige and prosperity. The roads of the area were atrocious. I went out on a Santa Fe railroad pass to Bucklin and expected to make connections there with a "puddle-jumper" train that ran up to Dodge City on a spur. Unfortunately, I arrived too late on Saturday night and missed the train. I telephoned the minister, Leon L. Myers, and he made arrangements for me to "put up" at a railroad hotel in Bucklin and promised to have a man to drive me over to Dodge City Sunday morning before Bible-school time. It had been raining and the roads were in terrible condition. At about five o'clock the next morning an old Ford appeared and I got in the back seat. The driver said, "That will never do. Now follow my directions. Get on the box there and hold tight to the back of the front seat. The only way we can make it is to follow the deep ruts in the road, and it will be a pretty rough ride." I never experienced anything like it in my life. I was shaken and tossed about like a frail reed in a storm. Two or three times the car got stuck and we almost had to give up the trip. Finally, however, around noon we arrived in Dodge City and got to the church just as the morning service was being dismissed. The rally had drawn about 1,500 people and had been a success, but the main speaker of the day failed to show. That night I preached to a full house despite a downpour of rain and had wonderful fellowship with a great people. After a visit to Cimarron the next day I took the Santa Fe back East and added an interesting experience to my docket.

I would not want to leave the impression that I only visited the largest churches in the course of my field activities. I went wherever I could be of help, be it a small country or mission congregation or one that was strategically located and doing great things for God. I often was responsible for "the Standard booth" at state and national conventions where I met hundreds of preachers and local church leaders.

One of the problems that beset me as editor of *The Lookout* was the need for a capable secretary and office editor. After many efforts to contact such a person, in desperation I advertised for one. There were many responses, but one stood out above the rest — a letter from one Mildred Covington who was secretary to the president of the State Normal College at Ada, Oklahoma. When we gave her a call, Mildred's mother came to Cincinnati to size up the editor and see whether he was the kind of man she would approve. The first question she asked me was, "What was your father's name?" I said "Everett." "Did he ever live on a farm near Gallatin, Missouri?" she continued. "Yes," I said, "he was apprenticed to William Sessions at that time." To which she responded enthusiastically, "Then your father was my first beau. We liked each other and if he hadn't moved back to Ohio, his native state, we might have married." I got the maternal okay that resulted in Mildred's many years of efficient editorial service with Standard. The Covingtons had fine family connections. The town of Covington, Oklahoma, was named after Mildred's forebears. She measured up in every way to the best tradition of the family. She taught an adult Bible class in the Walnut Hills Church for many years and was active in community affairs. At one time she was president of the Business and Professional Women's Club of Cincinnati.

During my editorship I was deeply concerned with every movement which sought to improve and escalate Christian Education in the local church. When the "Daily Vacation Bible School" idea was launched, Standard was among the first publishing houses in the United States to provide programs and supplies. The tendency was to provide sets of books already published (lesson topics, songbooks, workbooks, handwork and art portfolios, etc., with an accompanying manual or guide for use of the teachers). DVBS workers had to buy whole libraries in order to operate their schools. E. W. Thornton and I conceived the idea of providing everything essential in three large, artistic, comprehensive volumes: Primary, Junior, and Intermediate. The idea caught the market like wildfire and for many years Standard's product outsold that of any other publishing house in the land. I worked with T. B. Booth, head of the Merchandise Department, in helping to provide Sunday school helps of all sorts.

I encouraged all efforts to set up Bible school workers' conferences in connection with rallies and conventions to improve the quality of work being done in our schools. I was conscious of the fact that many of them were not worthy of the name "school" and that very few Bible school superintendents and departmental workers had the background or broad understanding of the educational task essential to effective leadership. In the last year of my editorship, when Cincinnati Bible Institute was launched, I was asked to take over responsibility for its Department of Christian Education. I became conscious of the fact that most of the textbooks available for use in my classes were tinctured with a liberal philosophy of education. I assembled a library of some two hundred volumes none of which I could approve for use. So I began to lecture on the subjects offered. Mildred Covington accompanied me to the class sessions and took down my lectures in shorthand. From these notes I began the development of a textbook of my own which eventuated in *Christian Education and the Local Church.* First published by Standard in 1943, this 400-page book has had and continues to have (revised in 1958) a tremendous sale and use in Christian colleges and seminaries all over the world. It is particularly popular in our own schools, but has had wide acceptance in evangelical educational institutions of all denominations. It has been used of the Lord to raise the standards and encourage more effective work in thousands of Bible schools. I have been pleased to discover that even in some liberal institutions this book has been made available for seminar use as "the best of such texts based on a 'fundamentalist' philosophy of education." Of course, the word should be "biblical" and not "fundamentalist"!

In 1925 I resigned as editor of *The Lookout* for reasons which I will elaborate later. When I went to Russell Errett's office to tell him of my decision, he was really shocked. After I told him why, he said, "I think you are making a great mistake. You have made a place for yourself here that will not easily be filled. I will let you go on one condition. Get me a man who can carry on the work you have begun. Can you do that?" I immediately replied, "I think I can. His name is Guy P. Leavitt, of Council Bluffs, Iowa. He superintends one of the biggest and best Bible schools in Iowa. For a time he was a reporter on the *Omaha Bee.* He now edits the house organ, *Northwest Bell,* for the Northwest Bell Telephone Company." Then I told Mr. Errett of the articles Guy had written for *The Lookout* and our relationships through the years in Christian Endeavor (a former state president in Iowa) and Bible school work. Immediately Mr. Errett responded, "Wire him at once and invite him here for a conference." Guy told me later that the receipt of that telegram was like a dream come true. When he arrived in Cincinnati his visit was only for arranging the details of his employment. He was to continue until September 30, 1956 (when he retired and moved to Florida) after achieving new highs for *The Lookout* in every phase of its service to the Bible schools of the Brotherhood.

At Guy's invitation, I wrote "On the Outlook" and "Deacon Jones Says" for years, sharing his editorial page. During the "Christian Action Crusade" I wrote hundreds of pages in its promotion for *The Lookout*. Occasionally I would write a scholarly treatise on Christian Education. Even today when its editor (Jay Sheffield) asks me to "do a piece" for him, I get nostalgic thrills. *The Lookout* will always have a warm place in my heart.

Episode V

Richmond Street Church

Our local church relationship in Cincinnati began in the historic Richmond Street Christian Church. The first Sunday we were in the city we went to the Central Christian Church. We enjoyed the service but no one spoke to us and we got the impression that no one cared. The same week, however, a cordial Britisher by the name of Joseph Keevil, pastor at Richmond Street, dropped in my office to welcome us to Cincinnati and offer his services to help us find a suitable place to live. His approach was just right to convince us that we should make Richmond Street our church home.

Richmond Street was located in the West End of Cincinnati just a block from the Standard Publishing Company's plant. It was housed in a beautiful old brick Gothic edifice originally designed for the Episcopal Church of Saint James-the-Less and purchased by our old Sixth Street Church. Its solid walnut furniture and vaulted roof beams would have brought a fortune if sold on the lumber market. One of its stained-glass windows was dedicated to David S. Burnet of the prominent Cincinnati family of that name. (See *The Story of D. S. Burnet* by Noel Keith). Burnet was one of the church's earliest and most noted members. In the rear were two marble tablets on either side of the entrance to the sanctuary — one commemorating the fact that the Christian Women's Board of Missions was organized in the building October 24, 1874; and the other a memorial to the late E. W. McDairmid, an editor of the *Christian Standard* and a past president of Bethany College, who had been an elder in the church. A third might have been added to recall that the prayer-meeting which eventuated in the organization of the Foreign Christian Missionary Society, the following year at Louisville, was held there. Richmond Street was holy ground.

In its early days the congregation was rather aristocratic and exclusive and numbered in its membership some of the wealthiest Restoration leaders in the city. When we came its halcyon days had long gone and it was having a struggle for its very existence in an area which promised to become a part of the "ghetto" in the "inner city." Brother Keevil had come from the Greenpoint Church in Brooklyn, which had similar problems, and he was well equipped to lead in such a situation.

I was soon elected an elder and teacher of the men's Bible class. Olive became a teacher in the Primary Department and active in the women's work. The young people looked to us for leadership. We were deeply involved in every effort for the good of the church from that day on.

One of the first problems we faced was the Negroes who were rapidly infiltrating the community. Our doors were open to folk of all races, but it soon became evident that if we wanted to help the Negroes we would have to do something for and with them as a distinct and separate people. With the leadership of Brother Keevil we discovered two or three struggling store-front churches in the West End which claimed the name Christian. We called their leaders into conference with our elders and asked them to suggest a progressive course of action for the future. After several meetings it was decided to merge these little assemblies into one strong church. We discovered on nearby Kenyon Avenue, a substantial church building lately abandoned by the Methodists. It had an auditorium seating around 250, a good pipe organ, and several classrooms for use of the Bible school. We enlisted the financial aid and cooperation of our "white" churches and bought the building. When it came to transferring title to the new "Kenyon Avenue Christian Church," the Negroes insisted that we vest it in a board of whites and blacks, with "whites predominating." The chief leaders confided in us, "At this point we don't trust enough of our brethren to set up a totally black board of trustees with full powers. They might run away with such a fine property. Maybe later we can qualify for complete ownership." I served on this board for nearly ten years and had the privilege of visiting the services and preaching from the Kenyon Avenue pulpit many times. The church developed into a strong testimony for the Lord in the West End. A number of its members became prominent in the life of the city. One of them Jesse B. Locker, became U.S. Ambassador to Liberia. We rejoiced to have a part in this great work.

It was while I was teacher of the men's Bible class at Richmond Street that I had the privilege of making the first radio broadcast of the Sunday school lesson in history. Powell Crosley's Station WLW, Cincinnati, was just beginning to make a name for itself. KDKA, Pittsburgh, was its only rival as claimant for first place in the infant industry. Fred Smith, a good friend of mine, was in charge of broadcast programs at WLW. One end of Crosley's shop had been hung with heavy black velvet curtains to make a sound-proof broadcasting studio. All equipment was quite primitive. Music was the major feature. One day Fred asked me how I would like to broadcast the Sunday school lesson some Sunday morning with the idea that churches over the listening area might pick it up and feature it as an advertising stunt. I readily agreed. At Richmond Street we set up a receiving set in the Fellowship Hall and packed it with men for the event. Fred was pleased with the results. Letters came in from many Eastern and Central States cities and the press gave the event considerable space. We finally decided, however, that the Sunday morning hour was too competitive, interfering with the regular teaching programs of the churches. Then the thought came that many teachers of the International Uniform Series would appreciate a preview of the lesson if broadcast on Friday night. We switched the program and the new format had even greater acceptance. Soon WLW began to realize that such a program should be sponsored and paid for. Smith gave Standard Publishing first opportunity to become sponsor, but the management balked. They said radio broadcasting was only a fad which would soon pass and there was no possibility of getting returns adequate to justify the outlay of funds. At which Smith approached the Methodist Book Concern with headquarters in Cincinnati. They "jumped at the chance," took the time, but specified that one of their own staff of Sunday school lesson editors be the broadcaster. (They were on the air for many years.) Fred said, "Sorry, Jim," and that was the end of that. But for many years there was a plaque in the lobby of WLW's broadcasting studios listing the station's "firsts" in the history of the industry and my name appeared as the first person in America to broadcast Sunday school lessons.

As we carried on at Richmond and Cutter we put strong emphasis on evangelism. We made many canvasses of the community and organized many teams for personal evangelism. Some of the most effective evangelistic teams of the day came to lead us in special services, notably those of William John Minges, Ben Edwards, and the Owen Walkers. Many were won to Christ but there was a big turnover in our membership so that the church never became a large one.

We were inevitably embroiled in the controversies which were taking place in the Brotherhood. After the organization of the United Christian Missionary Society we withdrew support from all the agencies reporting to the International Convention and became an "independent" church. Sometime before this action there was an effort made by leaders in Central Church to interest Richmond Street in a merger proposition. The idea was plausible. Central was experiencing all the growing problems of a downtown church; we were facing the problems of survival in a deteriorating community. The church buildings were only about ten blocks apart. Charles Sebastian was pastor at Central and F. W. Burnham, then president of the American Christian Missionary Society, was chairman of the Board. Brother Keevil as minister and I, as chairman of our board, had many meetings with the joint board. Finally, the issues that proved stumbling blocks were "open membership" and support of the "recognized agencies." We could not get the satisfactory guarantees which we believed essential to the "preservation of the faith" in the unified church and the union never took place. Afterward some of us came to believe that the concern for unity on the part of Burnham and his agency associates in Central Church, was primarily in order to taking over the Sidney S. Clarke Estate, legally under the guardianship of the elders of Richmond Street.

Since there is little known about the Clarke Estate and since there is little source material available, I think it might be well to incorporate my knowledge of some facts about this historic "independent" evangelistic agency in my memoirs.

Sidney Smith Clarke (1805-1871) was intensely interested in Home Missions, and, being a shrewd businessman, he determined that every cent he gave for the preaching of the old Jerusalem gospel, and the establishment of churches of Christ in destitute fields, should be used toward that end.

In his will he provided that the residue of his estate, following the death of his wife, and the satisfaction of his heirs, should be devoted to home missionary work. The original $50,000, which was the residue of his estate, has brought an income of many thousands of dollars. Almost every cent of this has been used in actual evangelistic effort, and the principal is more than intact. Mr. Clarke stipulated in his will that the residue of his estate should be administered by not more than three trustees nominated by the board of elders of the Richmond Street Christian Church to the Probate Judge of Hamilton County and appointed by him. There have (since 1871) been seven groups of trustees:

1. H. Pearce, M. A. Clarke, and C. C. Cockerill.

2. H. Pearce and C. C. Cockerill.

3. H. Pearce and H. T. Atkins.

4. H. T. Atkins.

5. C. D. Saunders, Horace William Vaile, and James DeForest Murch.

6. James DeForest Murch.

7. John Hudson and Roger Dornette.

For the most part, the early trustees were fortunate in securing missionaries and evangelists of a very high type, which, in a large measure, has made possible the excellent results achieved. The records show the names of such men as Justin N. Green, W. N. Hull, C. A. Freer, E. D. Murch, Allen Wilson, B. W. Huntsman, S. M. Martin, T. N. Kincaid, H. A. Blake, Vernon Stauffer, J. S. Raum, Henry Pearce Atkins, Joseph A. Pine, C. M. Keene, J. L. Deming, E. Joseph Myers, W. H. Kindred, R. S. Creasman.

Through the untiring labors of these men the following and other churches of Christ were organized after the New Testament pattern:

Greenfield, Ohio
Chillicothe, Ohio
Belding, Michigan
Jett, Oklahoma
Lucien, Oklahoma
Blanchard, Oklahoma
Konawa, Oklahoma
Deer Creek, Illinois
Batesville, Arkansas
Malvern, Arkansas
Oak Grove, Arkansas
Roanoke, Virginia (Belmont)
Aurora, Illinois
Elgin, Illinois

Columbus, Ohio (East Side, now Wilson Avenue)
Cincinnati, Ohio (Columbia Avenue)
Heavener, Oklahoma
Nash, Oklahoma
Nowata, Oklahoma
Verdon, Oklahoma
Battle Creek, Michigan
Pocahontas, Indiana
Camden, Arkansas
Mount Ida, Arkansas
Tiger, Arkansas

Many weak churches were assisted to self-support; building funds were created; buildings were erected; evangelistic meetings were held; many struggling, disorganized churches were "set in order." The records show the following to be some of the places thus assisted:

Cincinnati, Ohio (Madisonville)
Martinsville, Ohio
New Castle, Virginia
Cincinnati, Ohio (Fourth)
Modest, Ohio
Adrian, Michigan
Enid, Oklahoma (University Place)
Medford, Oklahoma
Pond Creek, Oklahoma
Manchester, Oklahoma
Peckham, Oklahoma
Newkirk, Oklahoma
Watonga, Oklahoma
Haskell, Oklahoma
Boynton, Oklahoma
Altus, Oklahoma
Coldwater, Oklahoma
Lahoma, Oklahoma
Drummond, Oklahoma
Ramona, Oklahoma
Glencoe, Oklahoma
Ripley, Oklahoma
Waynoka, Oklahoma
Hinton, Oklahoma
Billings, Oklahoma
Oklahoma City, Oklahoma (Capitol Hill)
Oakland, Oklahoma
Dunkirk, Indiana
Monroe, Wisconsin
Corpus Christi, Texas
Wilsey, Kansas
Council Grove, Kansas
New Hampton, Missouri
Martinsville, Missouri
Palisades, Colorado
Golden, Colorado
Blanca, Colorado
Floris, Iowa
Storm Lake, Iowa
Brighton, Iowa

Rockwell City, Iowa
Castana, Iowa
Stillwell, Illinois
Bowen, Illinois
Decatur, Illinois
Kewanee, Illinois
Saybrook, Illinois
Chandlerville, Illinois
Gridley, Illinois
Arkadelphia, Arkansas
Okolona, Arkansas
Sherrell, Arkansas
Beebe, Arkansas
Newark, Arkansas
Des Arc, Arkansas
Lonoke, Arkansas
Parry, Arkansas
Lebanon, Ohio
Coyle, Oklahoma
Quinlan, Oklahoma
Clinton, Oklahoma
Summer, Oklahoma
Stillwater, Oklahoma
Britton, Oklahoma
Sapulpa, Oklahoma
Antioch, Illinois
Cerro Gordo, Illinois
Oreana, Illinois
Owosso, Michigan
Kalamazoo, Michigan
Adrian, Michigan
Luther, Michigan
Mt. Pleasant, Michigan
Saginaw, Michigan
Sylvan Lake, Michigan
Woodward, Michigan
St. Johns, Michigan
West Sebowa, Michigan
Saranac, Michigan
Tarryton, Michigan
Pentwater, Michigan
Hart, Michigan

Coats Grove, Michigan
Hot Springs, Arkansas
Gurdon, Arkansas
Gordyce, Arkansas
Sheridan, Arkansas
Smithton, Arkansas
Mountain Valley, Arkansas
Crystal Springs, Arkansas

Magnet, Arkansas
Hooper, Arkansas
Zion, Arkansas
Oakgrove, Arkansas
Gifford, Arkansas
Traskwood, Arkansas
Butterfield, Arkansas

It was in 1919 that I became a trustee of the Estate. The residue of the Clarke Estate at that time was invested in nontaxable, interest-bearing securities, and two very desirable Cincinnati "ground rents." The trustees had full power to make any disposal of the holdings of the estate which might be proved to the Probate Court to be for the best interests of the work. Biennially we were required to make a report to the court of our stewardship.

Missionaries, or evangelists, were employed by the estate upon recommendation of the board of elders of Richmond Street Church and were under yearly contract, directly responsible to the trustees. The trustees have always demanded that the representatives of the estate be true to the "old Book."

As time passed, the trustees more and more conformed their efforts to a literal interpretation of the will in regard to the choice of fields of operation. The term "destitute places" has, by several rulings of the estate's attorneys, been interpreted to mean communities where there is no New Testament church of Christ. There is now less disposition to assist weak churches than formerly, all efforts lately having been directed to the organization of new churches, and fostering them until they are ready for self-support. It has been rather an unwritten law in recent years that no missionary shall give more than one year to one field, but that aid should thereafter be given to a settled minister.

The will provided, in case the Richmond Street Church might be disbanded, or fail to discharge the obligations of the will, that any Christian Church in Cincinnati which stands for the New Testament plea may, upon proper legal action, become the guardian of the fund. The present trustees were nominated by the Westwood-Cheviot Church of Christ, and appointed by the Court. I was made chairman and served in that capacity until 1958, the last six years as sole trustee.

Under our trusteeship over seventy churches were planted or reopened. Among the evangelists employed were Thomas H. Adams, J. H. Pickle, C. M. McKay, Edward Clutter, J. S. Raum, F. W. Strong, J. Marion Small, C. C. Root, Russell Martin, and many others. I conducted all the correspondence with local church leaders and with the evangelists authorized and examined the field surveys entailing an immense amount of my time. Vaile and Saunders handled all fiscal matters. Among the churches we established or assisted in establishing were Yuma, Prescott, Flagstaff, and Chandler, Arizona; Anaheim (Knott Avenue),

Culver City, La Habra, Montebello, National City, Oxnard, San Fernando, and Torrance, California; Gallup and Grants, New Mexico; Bluffton and Montpelier, Indiana; Pierre, South Dakota; and Madison (First), Beloit, Kenosha, and Racine, Wisconsin. Because we were especially interested in the development of the cause in or near Greater Cincinnati, we established quite a number of churches in this area: Milford, Montgomery Road, Delhi, Lockland, Cleves, Loveland, Taylor's Mill, Marshall, and Bainbridge. I simply call these to mind as I write. The complete records of the Estate would reveal many more.

As the "official" missionary agencies came under fire because of their disloyalty to the Restoration Plea, many brethren wrote the Clarke Estate asking to have fellowship in its ministry by the contribution of funds. I conceived the idea of enlarging the fund in a grand effort to "cover North America with the Plea." Our attorneys, however, advised us that the original trust could not be changed in any way. They suggested that we adopt a similar name (The Clarke Fund), set up a Board of Trustees, and become another independent home missions agency.

At the next meeting of the trustees it was agreed that an Advisory Board of ministers of churches of Christ should be formed in the interest of wise administration of all funds which would be contributed. The board chosen was made up of five men elected for five, four, three, two, and one years, respectively, and was composed of P. H. Welshimer, minister of First Christian Church, Canton, Ohio (five years); A. B. Philputt, minister of Central Christian Church, Indianapolis, Indiana (four years); C. J. Sharp, general superintendent of Group Evangelism, Hammond, Indiana (three years); C. R. Stauffer, minister of Norwood (Ohio) Christian Church (two years); and Mark Collis, minister of Broadway Christian Church, Lexington, Kentucky (one year). The advice of these men was to be solicited by the trustees in every action of importance concerning the "Clarke Fund," such as employment of missionaries, the choice of fields of work, etc.

The trustees of the Clarke Estate became the officers and trustees of the new Clarke Fund and I was elected President. We maintained offices in free facilities provided by Richmond Street Church. Almost immediately the loyal brotherhood responded to our appeals for money and the Fund grew by leaps and bounds. John Chappell, a retired banker and elder from Barnesville, Ohio, was so enthusiastic about our venture of faith that he volunteered at his own expense to become office manager and rendered yeoman service in that capacity for many years. John and his fine family became members of the Richmond Street Church.

As the missionary situation in the Brotherhood continued to worsen, it was proposed that the new Clarke Fund should be reorganized to serve as a clearinghouse for a whole new free agency complex. Several independent agencies had indicated their desire for such a cooperative venture: (1) In 1919, after the comity agreement in Mexico, Enrique T. Westrup had organized the Mexican Christian Missionary Society and salvaged the work in Monterrey and other cities. (2) In the same year M. B. Madden, who had disagreements with the FCMS Japan Mission, set up the Osaka Christian Mission in Japan's second largest city. (3) The Christian Woman's Benevolent Association, of St. Louis, was operating an independent Mothers' and Babies' Home, Christian Hospital, and Christian Old People's Home. (4) The Christian Normal Institute (later Kentucky Christian College), of Grayson, Kentucky, and other independent schools of a distinctly evangelical character were also in this growing orbit of so-called "free agencies."

The Clarke Fund had initiated a National Evangelism Rally which was meeting annually in the Richmond Street Church. Upon the advice of leading brethren, early in 1925, the trustees decided to issue a call for the next Rally to consider the possibility of reorganizing the Fund for larger service to the Brotherhood. Accordingly, on September 1, 1925, the Christian Restoration Association was organized in the historic building where the Christian Woman's Board of Missions and the Foreign Christian Missionary Society had been born. The first Board of Trustees consisted of JDM as president; L. L. Faris, vice president; Horace Wm. Vaile, secretary-treasurer; and E. W. Thornton, Ralph L. Records, Cameron Meacham, O. A. Trinkle, Ransom Perry, and Ira M. Boswell. P. H. Welshimer headed an Advisory Board of outstanding brethren. "Thus endeth the lesson." Later in the book I shall deal with the CRA as a separate episode in my life.

During the days when Richmond Street was a "cooperative" church a number of meetings were held in our building at which speakers like A. McLean, Abe Cory, F. W. Burnham, W. A. Moore, and Stephen J. Corey spoke. On one occasion I was sitting next to A. McLean (see W. R. Warren's *Archibald McLean*) who was very cordial. He said to me, "You're with Standard. I expect you have heard about me. I just want to say for the record that I hold no ill will toward Russell Errett. He did what he thought was right in our unfortunate clash over the Rockefeller grant to the FCMS, and I did, too. As things are now beginning to shape up in the Foreign Society, I am greatly disturbed about its future. I am opposed to open membership, but there are others now in control of affairs who are not. I wish things were different."

While Arthur Talmage Abernathy was our minister at Richmond Street he was able to bring a number of nationally prominent figures to our pulpit. One of these was William Jennings Bryan. He came at about the time of the famous Scopes trial. He preached (he was at one time Moderator of the Presbyterian General Assembly) at Richmond Street in the morning, at Covenant-First Presbyterian Church in the afternoon, and at Walnut Hills First Presbyterian at night. All the churches were crowded to capacity to hear him on "Creationism vs. Evolutionism." I was on the committee that welcomed Bryan to the city. We had dinner at the old Roof Garden of the Gibson Hotel and I shall never forget the stir our party created when we came into the room. People flocked to our table to greet the famous man who twice ran for President and served under Wilson as Secretary of State. He was a great soul — the "last of the Mohicans" in his denomination who fought for the evangelical, biblical faith and lost. We were truly "in heavenly places" on that historic occasion. Abernathy came to our people from the Methodists (his father was president of Trinity College, one of the schools which merged to form Duke University). He had a successful career in secular journalism and was a writer of some literary merit. He wrote two books, published by Standard, while he was at Richmond Street and brought considerable distinction to our congregation. He went from Cincinnati to be pastor of First Church, Asheville, N. C.

We had many, many happy days of fellowship at Richmond Street and for the most part it was all for the glory of God and the extension of His Kingdom.

But the Richmond Street episode would not be complete without the story of the "Great Schism." During the ministry of Orval W. Baylor the Ku Klux Klan infiltrated the congregation to such an extent that kleagles occupied the pulpit and men chosen for leadership virtually had to be members of the lodge in good standing. The preacher was the most popular Klansman of the city and one of our elders (George P. Rutledge, then editor of the *Christian Standard*) was a national officer. The Klan in those days was anti-Negro, anti-Jew, and anti-Roman-Catholic. As a result racial tensions were greatly heightened in our community. Our auditorium was frequently used for Klan rallies and packed to "the guard rails." When some of us protested, we were told to "go peddle our fly papers" or we would be ousted. The issue finally came to a focus when the Klan element proposed to adopt a new church constitution and elect a completely new slate of officers. The daily press got wind of our predicament and soon had front-page stories about us that brought reproach on the whole cause of Christ. In a crucial congregational meeting at which the new constitution was to be adopted and "the church purged of its bosses," policemen and lawyers were present to prevent a fist fight and to assure a legal and honest vote count. The anti-Klan forces won by a very narrow margin. The next Sunday morning the preacher and his cohorts rose in the morning worship service and left the church after announcing that a new congregation would be organized in a hall on Central Avenue. I had the responsibility for continuing the service and preaching an impromptu sermon. Our depleted ranks carried on for several years, but it became evident for many reasons that the days of our usefulness in that location were nearing an end. We eventually sold our building to the Southern Baptist Church, a Negro organization, moved to Price Hill and, under the leadership of George Mark Elliott, organized the Western Hills Church of Christ, now one of our finest congregations in the city. The ill-fated Central Avenue Church died after a few years. Its members were scattered to various churches in the area or were altogether lost to the cause. After that experience I vowed that I would never participate in a church fight again — that I would leave any church so involved, and I have "kept the faith."

An urban redevelopment project finally demolished the old Richmond Street building and a busy new freeway now occupies the site. I have a "catch in my throat" every time I pass it.

Episode VI

Cincinnati Bible Seminary

As the Clarke Estate-Clarke Fund program of home evangelism grew it became evident that one of our greatest problems was to find ministers who would take over our mission churches after our evangelists had left the field and build them into self-supporting and well-indoctrinated congregations. The colleges which were producing our preachers were one by one being infiltrated by liberalism. Their product was lacking in commitment to Bible doctrine and the Restoration Plea. We had several examples where churches we had founded were lost to the cause because of liberal preachers they had called to their pulpits. Our trustees were determined that we were not going to spend time and effort bringing new congregations into existence for the strengthening of the enemy's camp. We decided that the only thing we could do was to set up a "crash program" of new schools that would begin to turn out preachers loyal to the faith. We began to pray about it and ask the Lord to provide. Almost immediately we received word that a good brother in the Phillipsburg, Pennsylvania, congregation had died and left the Clarke Fund the sum of around $15,000 to be used for educational purposes. We created an Education Department of the Clarke Fund and began to plan for the opening of a new school in the fall of 1923.

We had heard of John W. Tyndall in North Carolina who was having considerable success in training young men for the ministry in an independent school known as Southern Christian Institute. He was to hold a summer session on the campus of Milligan College and I was dispatched to Tennessee for the purpose of sizing up the man and his program with a view to giving him a call to become the "educational evangelist" of The Clarke Fund and head up our proposed institution. Tyndall appeared to be an ideal man for our purposes. He was strong on Bible instruction and evangelism. Many of his students were becoming outstanding preachers. Before I left the Milligan campus Tyndall had agreed to come to Cincinnati and join us in planning for "Cincinnati Bible Institute."

I went to Russell Errett, told him of our plans and he was deeply interested. He pledged $1,500 to the school and consented to permit several Standard staff-members to teach classes there provided it did not interfere with their editorial work. He permitted me to use many columns of free advertising in the *Standard* and *Lookout* announcing our plans. We began thinking in terms of a school similar to the old Phillips Bible Institute which had recently "folded" at Canton, Ohio. We consulted with P. H. Welshimer and gained much valuable information from him. Our curriculum was patterned after Phillips. I made a trip to Butler, Pennsylvania, to interest the Phillips Family in our project and got a check for $2,500 from B. D. Phillips. Other support was assured.

Next we had to secure quarters for the school. Providentially the rather impressive old building of a defunct Roman Catholic boys' school on West Eighth Street only two blocks from the Standard Publishing Company became available. We leased it, renovated it, and began furnishing it with dormitory and classroom equipment. Working night and day we were able to open the school on time. Teachers besides Mr. Tyndall were Robert E. Elmore, Traverce Harrison, Edwin R. Errett, James DeForest Murch, E. W. Thornton, C. J. Sharp, J. E. Sturgis, and Orval W. Baylor. Board, room, tuition, and fees were to be granted for $30 per month. I was made "Regent" of the school to act as the go-between for the Institute and the Clarke Fund. The trustees of the Fund were made trustees of the school. Well over one hundred students were enrolled for the year.

Then came simultaneous news stories in the *Christian Standard* of the opening of Cincinnati Bible Institute and "McGarvey Bible College," of Louisville, Kentucky. We had no idea that MBC was even being planned. What had happened was that a group of professors of Transylvania and the College of the Bible, at Lexington, completely disillusioned as to the future of those institutions, had decided to set up a new school continuing after the pattern of the old College of the Bible in the days of J. W. McGarvey. Leaders in the move were R. C. Foster, Henry F. Lutz, and Ralph L. Records who composed the faculty, along with such lecturers as W. H. Book and Ira M. Boswell who took time out of busy pastorates at Columbus, Indiana, and Georgetown, Kentucky, to encourage the venture. Only a small student body had been enrolled at Louisville. It was apparent to all that two schools located so close to each other and with so much in common should plan to merge at the earliest possible date. I immediately opened correspondence with President Lutz proposing a conference looking in that direction. Several meetings between the interested parties were held with eventual agreement that at the close of the school year a merger would be announced and that the combined schools would open in the fall of 1924 at Cincinnati under the name "Cincinnati Bible Seminary."

It was unanimously agreed by the faculties and trustees of both institutions that Mr. Tyndall should not be considered in plans for the reorganization. He was quite cool to the proposed merger and threatened to withdraw from CBI and start his own school. He was beginning to introduce cultist doctrines and strange practices, causing much criticism. All students were required to dress in prescribed patterns. Coffee and tea were eliminated from dining hall menus and classed with the drinking of intoxicating beverages. It fell to my lot to deal with him on these and other administrative matters, always in company with one or more of our

62

trustees as witnesses. Tyndall would promise to meet us and then feign illness to avoid a showdown. While we did everything possible to avoid public confrontations, the student body became aware of the situation. Fortunately only a few upheld Tyndall in his views and there was almost unanimous and enthusiastic approval of the merger idea. We were able to close the year on a reasonably high note and hold the allegiance of most of the one hundred students who formed over ninety percent of the new Seminary student body. Tyndall went to Texas and set up another school which had little support. He died a few short years later.

The owners of the West Eighth Street property would not renew our lease and we were faced with the almost insurmountable task of finding facilities appropriate for the new school within two months time. The MBC group were unable to give us any help whatsoever. We had all the furniture necessary for classroom and dormitory use but a pitiful balance of only about $1,600 in our education account. Fortunately Mr. Vaile and I knew a very well-to-do widow by the name of Mrs. Carrie Stewart, a former member of the Richmond Street Church. She had died within the year and left a wonderful piece of residential property on Price Hill bounded by Grand, Maryland, and Chateau Avenues. There were nearly thirty rooms involved. We immediately contacted the executor of her estate, a stepson who was an Episcopalian and lived in Chicago. We found she had provided in her will that these houses be given to the National Benevolent Association of the Christian Churches for use as an old people's home. However, Ohio law required that wills for such charitable gifts had to be made more than one year prior to death of the testator. Mr. Lovell was glad to hear of our interest in the property and came to Cincinnati for a conference. Mr. Vaile and I met him on the premises. He asked many questions, and quoted a very reasonable price. The conference lasted for a couple of hours. When he asked us how much we could advance for a first payment we told him frankly that we had some property but only $1,600 in cash. We also told him of our friendship with his mother and her concern for the work of the Christian Churches and Churches of Christ. We expressed our feeling that if she were alive she would welcome the use of her property for an educational institution such as ours. He paused for a long time before answering. You could have heard a pin drop in the silence of that room. Vaile and I were praying as we had never prayed before. Finally Mr. Lovell shoved his chair back from the table where we were sitting, and said, "Gentlemen, I don't know why I am doing this but I feel a very strong inner urge to sell you this property at the figure proposed with a down payment of $1,600." Within hours the papers were signed and we had a place to open Cincinnati Bible Seminary — a site which was occupied by the school for many years.

But this was far from being ready for opening day. An immense amount of work had to be done to clean up the rooms, make necessary repairs, move and install furniture, etc., etc. Then, providentially, I had a caller. He was a middle-aged, gray-haired, rough-looking British sailor by the name of Joe Hoskins. He told how he had been converted aboard ship and had decided to go to school and enter the ministry. I assured him that we would do everything we could for him. He forthwith took off one of his brogans, extricated $300 in cash and asked that I accept it as a down-payment for his first year's expenses. "Now," he continued, "if I can be of any help as a janitor or a carpenter I will gladly give my services free of charge. In my time I have had a great deal of experience as a sailor and as ship's carpenter. What do you say?" We immediately went out to Price Hill. I showed him what had to be done. To make a long story short, Joe Hoskins took charge and with those whose help he enlisted, did a miraculous job and had the properties ready on schedule for the opening of school. One other thing our trustees did was to lease the chapel of nearby Westminster Presbyterian Church (later purchased by the Seminary) for assembly purposes.

There were many problems involved in accomplishing the merger of the two schools. The institute idea was not too well received by the Louisville contingent, but we of the Clarke Fund insisted that students who for one reason or another did not have the generally accepted entrance credentials, or were too old to consider a long academic career, or who did not have the ability to compete with other students on a higher intellectual level, should have the opportunity to receive at least a certificate for academic work based on a thorough training in English Bible. The McGarvey idea involved basic Greek and Hebrew, Bible study, and a more comprehensive literary and scientific training. I acted as spokesman for CBI in the lengthy conferences on curriculum. It was finally decided to have two-schools-in-one — the Institute offering both certificates and diplomas in English Bible, and the College offering traditional A.B., A.M., and B.D. degrees. There were also courses in the Institute for young women seeking to qualify as secretaries and directors of Christian education in local churches.

The Clarke Fund was to remain as the holding corporation and its president was charged with over-all administrative responsibilities. General supervision of the Fund's educational arm was committed to a newly-created executive council of eleven persons: W. R. Walker (chairman), Ralph L. Records (secretary), James DeForest Murch, Edwin R. Errett, H. F. Lutz, Horace Wm. Vaile, Ira M. Boswell, Marshall T. Reeves, W. H. Book, John Chappell, and Ransom Perry.

Names of members of the first faculty were Ralph L. Records (dean), W. C. Sayrs, Henry F. Lutz, E. W. Thornton, R. C. Foster, James DeForest Murch, Edwin R. Errett, Robert E. Elmore, Traverce Harrison, Henrietta Heron, Florence M. Waterman, and L. G. Tomlinson.

There was considerable argument as to whether a president of the Seminary should be chosen. There were three candidates (all from MBC) who were contending for the position. The choice of any one of them would have caused hard feelings. The situation was further complicated by the fact that the president of the Clarke Fund had been given certain administrative authority which might impinge upon the powers of such an official. Dr. Lutz, who had been president at Louisville, acquired nominal recognition as "president" but he was soon stricken with a serious illness which caused his early death. In actual fact I was "interim president" from the beginning with an office on campus, until the choice of Ralph L. Records as president in 1928. Records served in that capacity for twenty years, resigning in 1948.

There were 150 students enrolled in the opening session and the school was launched with glowing prospects. As a faculty member I was assigned the Department of Christian Education and continued to teach the classes I had initiated at CBI. Miss Heron and Mrs. Waterman offered courses in the department. I also taught a class in Missions for several years. My "presidential" responsibilities were not so easily discharged. I was under constant fire by the Louisville contingent. Records insisted on maintaining a salary relationship with Marshall T. Reeves and The Christian Foundation and did not consider himself responsible to The Clarke Fund in any way. Foster was highly critical of everything I did, contending that I was in no way fitted to discharge my responsibilities. At one time in board meeting he called for my resignation because I had "mismanaged funds to the point of practical embezzlement." When I demanded an immediate audit by a reputable firm of certified public accountants, he backed down with apologies. Others who had a reputation for anti-ism and other reactionary ideas were constant thorns in my side. The organization of the Christian Restoration Association in 1925, to succeed the Clarke Fund, (see Episode VIII) with its broader responsibilities, complicated my position. It was not long after this it became increasingly apparent that there ought to be a separation of the two organizations so that the Seminary would be free to pursue its own course independently with all proper academic freedoms. Accordingly in 1928 the official separation took place in all good spirit with the Seminary remaining in the orbit of the "Associated Free Agencies" (about which more will be said later in my story). I remained a member of the faculty and the Seminary's Board of Trustees until 1934.

These years of "blood, sweat, and tears" resulted in certain gains for the Seminary. I was able to raise most of the funds necessary for the operation of the school. We acquired additional property to the East for expansion purposes beyond our Chateau Avenue limits. I was able to interest W. P. Foster, a wealthy member and elder of the First Church, Kirksville, Missouri, in the school. Foster had been a liberal giver to "the organized work of the Brotherhood" but had been disillusioned by their liberal policies, particularly the practice of "open membership" on the foreign field. I was surprised one morning to find in my CRA mail a letter from Foster enclosing several good-sized checks for the CRA's work in the Philippines, South Africa, and Tibet, together with one for our evangelistic work in America. He said he expected to continue his support as the Lord prospered him. Shortly thereafter I went to Kirksville as a guest of the Fosters who wanted to know more about our work. At that time I was able to present the educational appeal in such a way as to elicit a good-sized check for the support of the Seminary. Later we presented our needs in terms of the indebtedness on our buildings at CBS, as a result of which (1930) Mr. Foster was very largely responsible for its total liquidation. He remained a warm friend of the institution until his death. Too, I was able to get a great deal of free advertising from Standard periodicals and to secure the continued contribution of the free services of prominent editors as members of the faculty. Without this aid the Seminary would have been severely crippled in its educational status in the Brotherhood.

Unfortunately the reactionary elements in the Seminary grew to such proportions that the whole original spirit of the school was eventually changed. Classes were used for attacks on the UCMS, the NACC, persons (such as P. H. Welshimer) who retained relationships with "the organized work," and those who failed to agree with certain legalistic interpretations of the New Testament held by prominent professors. All other conservative schools in the Brotherhood (such as Johnson Bible College) were openly criticized and boycotted on the ground that only CBS had remained loyal to Restoration principles. The CRA came under the same critical attacks. Everybody was considered "apostate" who did not bear the brand of approval of a small coterie of men who set themselves up as "judges of the universe." A generation of graduates infected with this spirit went out to spread confusion and controversy in the churches, resulting in many church splits and the hindrance of many worthy cooperative efforts at home and abroad. The "gall of bitterness" pervaded college halls and many areas of Brotherhood life.

As vigorously and aggressively as I opposed error, I could never bring myself to *major* in anti-rationalism, anti-denominationalism, anti-ecclesiasticism, anti-jesuitism and anti-UCMS-ism. I was opposed to the creation of an "anti-UCMS denomination" which made opposition to the Society a test of fellowship. I sought to recognize as my brethren all sincere believers in Christ as Lord and Saviour and all sincere seekers for New Testament Christianity wherever they might be found. In my activities definitely outside the orbit of the Society I sought to be constructive within a strictly biblical and evangelical frame of reference, helping to "get the job done" according to the pattern that was outlined for the church of Jesus Christ in the New Testament.

Things got to the point at the Seminary where a man with my views had as little chance of survival as the proverbial "snowball in hell." It came as no surprise when I was dropped from the faculty and the Board of Trustees. For more than twenty years my name was anathema in its precincts. The lies and aspersions Seminary men cast at me dogged my path wherever I went.

I could think of scores of examples of this but I will tell only one story with a happy ending. A very capable graduate of the Seminary as a pastor had split three churches with his reactionary views. Finally he had changed his ideas and his tactics and built one of the largest churches in Florida. One day, when we were both in St. Louis at the Mark Twain Hotel for a meeting of the continuation committee of the North American Christian Convention, he asked me to come to his room. "Brother Murch," he said, "I want to apologize to you." "Apologize?" I said, "For what?" "Well," he replied, "there was a time that I could not say mean enough things about you, due to Seminary propaganda. Then after I had split three churches I came to the conclusion that it was I and my views, rather than the elders and leaders of those churches, which had caused my trouble. I went back to my New Testament, and I studied many of your writings which had been so unmercifully criticized, and the whole course of my life was changed. I went to a little mission church in Florida and instead of measuring everybody by my "iron bedstead" and training our leaders to detect apostasy, I accepted all men lovingly on their confession of faith in Jesus Christ and their obedience to His commands. My attitude toward the many denominational visitors at our services was one of friendliness, welcoming them to the Lord's Table and inviting them to be a part of our Bible class and social programs. When such persons decided to locate permanently in Largo and they asked to be received into membership of our congregation, I asked for the privilege of a visit in their homes to "teach them the way of the Lord more perfectly." I found them eager to do the Master's will and I baptized a constant stream of such dear people. Some of my most dependable workers are now folk I would have most certainly alienated if I had continued in my old strategies. Today we have the second largest church in the state and it is still growing. The spirit of the congregation is wonderful. When I would attend conventions where you were present, I once delighted snubbing you and warning people against you. For this I beg your pardon. You have been a wonderful inspiration in my personal life and in my ministry." We were both in tears when he finished.

I may as well conclude the "CBS Episode" here, although the remaining remarks are out of chronological order.

After more than twenty years of ostracism from the Seminary campus, I was in Cincinnati for a series of "Deeper Life" meetings with William Harold Hockley and the Westwood-Cheviot Church. I received an early morning telephone call at the Sheraton Gibson Hotel where I was stopping. "This is Woodrow Perry," the voice said. "We would like to have you speak at chapel at Cincinnati Bible Seminary tomorrow." I could scarcely believe I was not being spoofed by some prankster. I said, "You mean this is actually the president of Cincinnati Bible Seminary?" "Yes," he said, "we saw you were in the city and we would be delighted to have you as our guest." "Why, of course I'll come," I replied. The reception I got on the new campus was very cordial. Not an unkind word was said about the past. Later I was invited to come from Washington and bring a series of lectures at the Seminary on the modern ecumenical movement. On that occasion I was honored by the faculty at a dinner. Since that time I have had the privilege of being a rather frequent visitor on the campus and a contributor to the program of the institution. The whole atmosphere had changed in the intervening years. CBS is now one of our largest and finest educational institutions, making a tremendous contribution to the ongoing of the Kingdom in thousands of ministers, missionaries, and church leaders serving in every area of the church's life. I am proud to have had a part in founding the school and helping in many ways to build it in its earliest and most crucial years — the years of "blood, sweat and tears."

Episode VII

Christian Restoration Association

My decision to resign as editor of *The Lookout* and accept the full-time presidency of the newly-formed Christian Restoration Association came after many months of prayer and conflicting emotions. I had been chiefly concerned at Standard with its constructive services to the local churches in the field of Christian education, but I was all the time conscious of the controversies dealing with basic theological and ecclesiastical issues. I think that Russell Errett did not want me to become involved in the fight, feeling that I would make a greater contribution to the Company and to the Brotherhood at large if I were isolated from it all. But this could not be. I had a conscience about basics and wanted to be where the action was as a "defender of the faith once for all delivered."

I was in Cincinnati when Standard was leading the opposition to the merger of the American Christian Missionary Society, the Christian Women's Board of Missions, the Foreign Christian Missionary Society, the Board of Church Extension, the National Benevolent Association, and the Board of Ministerial Relief to form the United Christian Missionary Society. I was present at the sessions of the 1919 "rump convention" at the IOOF Temple in Cincinnati where the opposition voiced its dissent. Later I was in Music Hall when the vote was taken to create the new Society and voted against it. But I was on the "side lines" so to speak. As an observer I noted that our opposition was hopelessly outclassed when it came to political strategy and parliamentary procedure in the Convention. The Liberal Disciples Establishment held the key positions. They maneuvered the business sessions to limit and control debate and to provide the necessary votes for victory. It was that way in 1919 and it has been that way to a greater or lesser degree in every International Convention since that day. I came to believe firmly that if the things we stood for in education, missions, and the other functional areas of the church's life were to be preserved and advanced it would have to be done outside the framework of the older agencies.

I did not lose my faith in the Brotherhood at large, but I did lose faith in the old agencies. I saw nothing wrong with the idea of creating new agencies which could adequately serve our historic aims, while recognizing the fullest freedom for others who might wish to carry on their programs in different ways. (See my apologetic on "Freedom of Association" in my book, *The Free Church*.) I remembered what Isaac Errett had said in an editorial in the *Christian Standard* in 1867: "We have no idolatrous attachment to the General Missionary Society. If it can do the work proposed, we will encourage it. If it fails to command sufficient confidence and sympathy to enable it to do its work wisely and well, we shall go in for whatever form of associated effort the general wisdom of the brotherhood may approve." In this widely accepted doctrine I saw hope for the future.

Having been providentially entrusted with the direction of the Clarke Estate and the Clarke Fund, I had a medium through which contacts were established with a number of voluntary free agencies serving in the fields of evangelism, missions, education, and benevolence. Churches and individuals that had lost faith in the older agencies gradually transferred their support to these groups. Deeply concerned brethren began to talk about providing ways and means by which these agencies could make a united appeal for brotherhood-wide support. Correspondence and conferences resulted finally in the organization of the Christian Restoration Association, September 1, 1925 (see story in Episode V: Richmond Street Church). I was elected president of the Association and served in that capacity until 1933.

There was no tidal-wave call for this move. Indeed, there was much opposition to it. Many of our outstanding conservative leaders felt that there was still hope for changing the liberal policies of the International Convention and its associated agencies. While I had little faith in any strategy looking to such a change, I went to the conventions and co-operated with these brethren in every way I could. I was in St. Louis (1920) where open membership in the China Mission was exposed. In 1921 and 22 I was at the Winona Lake conventions, although Standard refused to provide exhibits. I skipped the Colorado Springs (1923) and Cleveland (1924) gatherings, but was present at Oklahoma City (1925) where the encouraging but ill-fated Sweeney Resolution was passed. And then came Memphis (1926) which was "the end of the road" for thousands of our loyal ministers and churches.

By this time the CRA was in business with an office and staff of workers. Our little *Facts* bulletin which was published to promote the Clarke Fund's work was enlarged and renamed, *The Restoration Herald*. It was a 24-page magazine representative of several of our free agencies. The first issue (Volume IV, Number 9, September 1925) in the new format featured the work of W. D. Cunningham and The Yotsuya Mission in Japan. *Christian Standard* began to say kind words about us and it became increasingly evident that there was need for the services we could render.

I wish I had the space to summarize the contributions *The Restoration Herald* made to the cause of so-called "independent missions." It has never received its due. Above all else the *Herald* made clear the big, broad issues involved in our new crusade. I recall one of our finest contributions we were able to make: a comprehensive, in-depth critique of the Laymen's Foreign Missions Inquiry Report. Dr. W. E. Hocking, noted humanist philosopher of Harvard, had headed the Inquiry heavily subsidized by the Rockefeller Foundation.

Its theological findings and its proposed revolutionary program originated in the minds of highly-placed liberal administrators in the major denominational missionary boards, who, daring not to make known their own unorthodox views, took advantage of lay anonymity to spread their poison. I sensed immediately that this was the blueprint for future ecumenical missionary strategy and would mark the death knell of evangelical missions unless it was exposed and opposed. The *Herald,* at considerable cost, produced a 32-page edition devoted almost entirely to the Hocking Report. It was received with a rather lukewarm response by our own constituency, but it was widely acclaimed by the evangelical Protestant community. Among those who strongly commended it was Dr. Robert E. Speer of the Presbyterian U.S.A. Board of Foreign Missions, himself the author of a trenchant brochure, "Rethinking Missions."

Through the years I, as editor, gained greater insights and tried to make it clear that the things the CRA stood for and the things the UCMS growingly stood for were totally antagonistic to each other. We stood for those motivating factors which for 2,000 years made the Christian Church a mighty evangelizing force in the world:

We believed in the Bible as the infallible Word of God.

We believed in the Gospel centered in the atonement of Christ, His bodily resurrection, and implicitly demanding that every Christian is a missionary under orders to evangelize the world.

We believed that man is lost in sin, corrupt, guilty, threatened with eternal punishment, called to repentance, obedience, and forgiveness of sin.

We believed that it is impossible to be saved through non-Christian religions.

We believed that the plan of salvation is clearly taught in the New Testament and that we have no right to offer pardon on any other terms.

We believed that the Church is a redemptive fellowship which, while separate from the world, is willing to identify itself with lost mankind for the purpose of evangelizing the world.

On the other hand, the UCMS, while protesting its innocence, actually —

Disowned an authoritative Bible.

Made evangelistic theory man-centered and God-centered rather than Christ-centered.

Rejected the idea that man was lost in sin and can be saved only by accepting and obeying the Christian Gospel.

Saw the core of all creeds and religions as a nucleus of religious truth and in the human soul an inalienable religious intuition comparable to the Christian faith.

Accepted the establishment of "God's Kingdom" (a redeemed society) as the mission of the Church, and expressed a readiness to cooperate with all agencies, whether Christian or not, for social improvement and the building of modern Utopia.

The events of the past thirty years have proved the validity of our position.

With an almost dramatic suddenness, came the opportunity to assist in salvaging the Philippine Mission. John T. Brown, who visited India, China, and the Philippines to investigate the practice of open membership in UCMS missions, discovered the practice in the Taft Avenue Church in Manila. E. K. Higdon, the head of the mission, was found to be in favor of it. Leslie Wolfe, secretary of the mission, opposed it. Instead of recalling Higdon, the UCMS voted to recall Wolfe. The news of the situation gradually filtered through to America and because of serious repercussions the UCMS sent out an investigating committee of its own headed by Cleveland Kleihauer, noted advocate of open membership, withholding final action on Wolfe until its decision. The Philippine Mission was plunged into a divisive fight over the issue. The largest church in Manila, Gastambide, voted to back Wolfe and oppose open membership, with the result that its doors were padlocked and a thousand members denied admission to the house of worship they had helped to build. Wolfe decided to come back to America, a defeated man. It was at this crucial moment that I called a meeting of our executive committee and recommended that the CRA send him $500 at once and promise him monthly support if he would carry on as a missionary of the CRA. Wolfe accepted and remained to develop the great Philippine Christian Mission.

This event became the center around which developed the crucial Memphis Convention debacle. The Kleihauer investigating committee was scheduled to report at Memphis with a complete whitewash of UCMS missions, exonerating its leaders from any responsibility in the practice of open membership. Wolfe and the nationals who supported him in the Philippines were to be smeared by attacks on their character. At this point Standard's new anti-UCMS journal, *The Touchstone,* edited by Robert E. Elmore, stepped into the picture, furnishing funds to bring Wolfe, Felino S. Orlina of the Gastambide Church, and Juan L. Baronia, president of the Manila Bible Institute, to America. Elmore demanded a hearing for the Filipinos before the Memphis convention and joined forces with a "Committee on Future Action" to stage a pre-Convention Rally in the Pantages Theatre where the open-membership issue affecting the whole Brotherhood and its agencies in particular could be aired.

There were many attempts made by UCMS leaders to forestall the *expose* of liberalism and "open membership" in its foreign mission stations. Frequent private personal approaches were made to our leaders.

I mention only the major "star chamber session" that preceded the public meetings. President F. W. Burnham of the UCMS called a meeting of *Standard* representatives whom he considered "moderates" (including Edwin Errett, S. S. Lappin, and myself) and presented to us the "documentary evidence" from enemies of Orlina and Baronia concerning their "immoral conduct." Burnham said he wanted to keep us from "making a grievous mistake" in having anything to do with men of this character. He intimated that if necessary this evidence would be introduced in the International Convention business sessions. We asked for time to consider the documents and confer with Orlina, Baronia, and Wolfe. Wolfe satisfied our minds completely as to the source of the scurrilous attacks on the native leaders. We returned the papers to Burnham with "thanks." They were not used in the Convention but were often referred to by innuendo and were circulated surreptitiously in an "underground" effort to undermine confidence in our reports of heresy in the Manila mission.

Memphis was a repetition of Cincinnati (where the UCMS was organized). Our opposition was hopelessly outclassed when it came to political strategy and parliamentary procedure in the Convention. The Liberal Disciples Establishment held the key positions. They maneuvered the business sessions to insult saintly men like W. D. Cunningham and Mark Collis; to assassinate the characters of our men from Manila; to exalt Kleihauer and the report of his commission (which by the events of later years was proved to be a "whitewash") and to endorse the Liberal administrative policies of the agency leaders. The forces of the conservative opposition were ignominiously defeated. The great majority of those who had participated in the Pantages Theatre meetings were convinced that there was no hope left in the Convention for the "faith once for all delivered" and for those who were committed to it. They vowed that this was the last International Convention they would attend and that their churches would withdraw all support from agencies which reported to it.

A post-convention meeting of the evangelical elements of the brotherhood was held November 12, 1926, and set up a "Committee on Future Action." Named to the committee were P. H. Welshimer, chairman, W. R. Walker, O. A. Trinkle, W. E. Sweeney, F. S. Dowdy, Robert S. Tuck and Mark Collis. This committee later decided to issue a call for a "North American Christian Convention" to be held in Indianapolis, October 12-16, 1927. I was closely associated (for more than forty years) with those who determined the policies and the programs of the NACC from that time forward and helped in many ways in its development into one of the largest and most influential national religious gatherings in America. It was not a "church convention." Not an "agency convention." It was not intended to be divisive in any way. We hoped and prayed that it would be a free, voluntary medium through which unity might come again to God's people — but a unity based on the New Testament Gospel and the Restoration Plea. Its strong, clear testimony was a trumpet call for action on the part of the great majority of the common people at the home base — the grassroots of the Brotherhood. I could well write a book on the NACC dealing with the personalities and the forces external and internal which sought to shape it and did shape it through the years, but for the purposes of this work I shall simply say that with the advent of the NACC I thanked God and took courage, and I still do! (See my brief history of the Convention published in the *Christian Standard* February 25, 1973.)

Our next world move, after entering the Philippines, was another that almost matched it in dramatic interest. The story of the heroic attempts of Disciples to penetrate forbidden Tibet began with the adventure of Dr. Susie Rijnhart and her husband, Petrus. Petrus and their infant son were lost soon after they arrived in the border lands in 1895. Then came the J. C. Ogdens, Dr. A. L. Shelton, and Dr. Z. S. Loftus. Dr. Loftus died of typhus fever and Shelton was killed by bandits. Shelton was spared enough years to lead in erecting a good hospital and establishing a splendid mission at Batang on the Tibetan border. The stories of his achievements are among the most inspiring annals of the entire mission enterprise in the Far East. It was rumored that Shelton had been able to penetrate Tibet itself many times and once to have ministered either to the Dalai Lama himself or to one of his inner cabinet members in Lhasa. On one of his furloughs to America Shelton contacted a young student in Phillips University by the name of Russell Morse and persuaded him to go to Tibet, which he did in 1921. After Shelton's death, the UCMS decided to close the mission, but Morse determined to carry on. He had the deep conviction that he had given God his life to be used in Tibet and that he had promised Dr. Shelton to carry on until his dreams for Tibet were fully realized. The word got to me that Morse would be interested in becoming an independent missionary. Again the CRA cabled money and offered support which eventually resulted in Morse's opening of a new mission in West China not far from the Tibetan border. There are many stories afloat about details of Morse's break with the Society and events leading up to his work with the Lisus. Whatever credence may be given them the fact of his successful missionary career remains. In 1932 he reported 118 baptisms and preaching appointments in 22 villages. He said the Lisu tribes were turning to Christ "in unprecedented numbers." Over a hundred native workers had been trained. Then came the Communist revolution and almost unbelievable persecutions. Morse early left the employ of the CRA but we continued to support and encourage him in many ways. I shall never forget hearing him tell years later in Taft Auditorium in Cincinnati the story of his imprisonment by the Reds in Yunnan Fu as "an agent of imperialist America." He was deprived of all contacts with his family and told they were all dead. For months he was brainwashed, stripped naked, starved, beaten, and caused to endure every devilish inquisitorial device known to man. I heard him tell how the Communists denied him his Bible and how he had only the sustaining words of Scripture he had committed to memory when he was a Junior in an Oklahoma Sunday School, his faith in victorious prayer, and the very real experience of the presence of Christ through the Holy Spirit to keep him from going mad. I heard him tell how he was miraculously restored to his family. Every eye of the over two thousand people who heard him was filled with tears as he stirred us to new commitment to the missionary cause. After the meeting I met him and with tears he said, "Dear Brother Murch! It is good to see you again. We shall never forget what you did for us when we were reaching our decision to return to the field. We have never regretted that decision!" There have been many criticisms of Morse in later years when weakened by his sufferings, he said many strange things and acted in questionable ways, but I am sure that there is laid up for him a crown of everlasting life which the Lord, the Righteous Judge, will give him in the last day. He was one of the great missionary heroes of the Restoration. Many of the hundreds now serving in independent missions around the world are there because of the inspiration they derived from the Morse saga.

One day when I was in Louisville meeting with the trustees of the McGarvey Bible College, W. H. Book asked me whether the CRA would be interested in taking over the work of the African Christian Missionary Society. I gave him a favorable answer and a few weeks later I met with "The African Missionary Board of the Tabernacle Church of Christ," Columbus, Indiana, to conclude arrangements.

The meeting was held in the home of the Honorable Hugh T. H. Miller, an elder, who had married into the Joseph I. Irwin family — noted Columbus banker and benefactor. Miller himself was prominent in public affairs and had served as Lieutenant Governor of the State. Hugh T. H. was the father of Irwin Miller who years later inherited control of the vast Irwin Estate. Irwin was then in Oxford University in England completing his education. None of us that day could foresee that he was to join the Disciples liberal Establishment, underwrite the publication of the *Christian Century,* make possible the liberal rape of the College of Religion and Butler University, become the first lay president of the National Council of Churches, and split the Tabernacle Church in a futile effort to control it.

The ACMS had its origin in the work of Thomas Bambesi Kalane, a native of South Africa. Kalane came to America and studied at Wilberforce University, Xenia, Ohio. Early in his university experience he went to Columbus to see and hear W. H. Book and to learn more about the Restoration Movement. To make a long story short, the Tabernacle Church underwrote Kalane's return (1921) to his native land as a missionary. Scores of native denominational churches in his home community turned to the simple faith of the New Testament and hundreds were baptized. Kimberley, the industrial and mining center of South Africa, became the headquarters of the work. When Kalane died another native minister, Simon B. Sibenya, succeeded him as mission director. Then the racist doctrine of apartheid was introduced into the government of South Africa. No enterprise of any kind could be carried on among the blacks or coloreds without an approved white sponsor. Sibenya appealed to the Columbus board for such a man and O. E. Payne, a capable retired business man and elder in the University City Church in St. Louis, was sent to Kimberley. He gave wise guidance while allowing the native workers to carry on their work in ways common to their racial traditions. Payne died in May, 1925, and was succeeded by C. B. Titus, a former missionary to China. On June 21, 1926, we announced that the CRA would henceforth be responsible for the work of the ACMS. Thousands were saved and the work became one of the most promising independent missionary endeavors of the time. There were many problems — personal, congregational, social, political, and otherwise. It seemed like we were in "hot water" with the government and the natives most of the time. What many of our brethren did not understand was that the mission program was carried on under circumstances totally different from ours in America. Social conditions were many levels below those obtaining in the worst American ghettos. Those in leadership were well indoctrinated and the ideals held before the people were strictly according to the New Testament. An institute for the training of native leaders and workers had been initiated and began to turn out capable men in increasingly larger numbers year after year. Yet there were many instances in the general community of immorality, "open membership," and polygamy comparable to those which the apostle Paul encountered in his mission work in the pagan cities of Asia Minor.

One year we sent out over my protest a young American couple to assist Brother Titus. The man had proved a "hothead" in Seminary and had neither the training nor the aptitude for missionary leadership. He had not been in South Africa long until he broke with Brother Titus, demanding a thorough "purge" of the mission and total reorganization under his direction. He was recalled but not before he had spread a distorted story of heresy in the South African mission. On his arrival in America he went to the UCMS headquarters in Indianapolis and gave them information which was used extensively to discredit not only the work of the CRA in South Africa but all the independent missionary work of the brotherhood.

Despite such problems the mission grew and prospered. Eventually it solidified its gains centering in the great Observatory Church of Christ, Polo Road, Cape Town, and a Bible Institute in Kimberley. The work now extends over an area of approximately 400,000 square miles. Some forty Negro churches have scores of outstations and preaching points which carry on the Kalane vision to the glory of God.

I will cite one more major concern of the CRA proper in its early expansion program — the work in Poland. Joseph Keevil, former pastor at Richmond Street Church, put us in touch with a young man by the

76

name of Konstantine Jaroszewicz who headed up the Union of Churches of Christ in Poland. He had come to America some years before and was preaching on the streets of Brooklyn, New York, when Brother Keevil, then the minister of the Flatbush Christian Church, heard him and was taken with the fact that the doctrines the young Pole expounded were similar to his. Keevil learned that there were a number of churches in Poland which had been established by the Russian Restoration Movement. Jaroszewicz said he had the ambition to get college training in America so that he could return and serve his brethren more effectively. Keevil immediately sent him to Johnson Bible College and got the necessary support for his room and tuition. We contacted this man who had achieved great power and influence among his people and in 1921 reached an agreement with him by which the Polish work became associated with our missionary program. A wonderful group of evangelists and teachers covered Poland with the Gospel. Great evangelistic meetings were held, with as many as a hundred converts being immersed at one time and many churches being established in small villages and towns. At one time the Union of Churches of Christ in Poland received official government recognition as the chief Protestant body in the nation.

Jaroszewicz was a dynamic speaker and in our Restoration rallies throughout America he was able to hold audiences spellbound as he recounted tales of victory for the simple New Testament Gospel in his native land. In these rallies I often teamed up with him and heard him speak repeatedly.

One of his stories I remember had to do with the scarcity of the Holy Scriptures in Poland. A great crowd was gathered in the public square of a town to hear the evangelist expound on the Word of God. He showed that it contained the only hope of their salvation. They were breathless as he read from the sacred pages and pleaded with him to sell them copies. Inquiry proved that the book he held in his hand was the only one in the town. Then in answer to their tearful pleas he began to tear pages from the Bible and hand them out one to each family upon their promise to read them and pass them on to other families in exchange for their pages, until they had read the whole Bible. After this moving address, the offering plates were passed and filled to overflowing with money for Bibles in Poland.

Another story had to do with the controls which the Polish government exercised over the churches. No foreign denomination was permitted to carry on work. Only Polish preachers and teachers in good standing could instruct the people. One Lord's Day when one of the churches was assembled for worship, the police arrived, marched to the front of the room and demanded the preacher and elders answer their questions.

Q. What is the name of your church?

A. The Church of Christ.

Q. Where are your headquarters?
A. In heaven.
Q. Who is the head of your church?
A. Jesus Christ.
Q. Where are your constitution and by-laws?
A. Here in the Bible.
Q. Where was it printed?
A. In Warsaw.
Q. In what language is it printed?
A. The Polish language.
Q. What do you preach?
A. The Gospel of Jesus Christ.
Q. What does your Gospel teach about government?
A. To obey those in authority, according to Romans 3.

Aftr an hour or so of such answers the gestapo were completely confounded. They then took their places in the audience and demanded that a sermon be preached so they could judge for themselves whether or not the church was a subversive instrument of some "foreign imperialism." So persuasive was the message that two of the police accepted Christ and were immersed at the conclusion of the service.

Some of our people felt that Jaroszewicz's stories were almost too good to be true, but brethren from America who visited Poland confirmed the validity of the work being done. Even Jesse Bader of the World Convention of Churches of Christ visited the field, endorsed the work, and invited the Union to join the World Convention. Leaders of the United Presbyterian Churches (the old psalm-singing denomination before the merger) saw what was being done and asked for the privilege of sending a Christmas offering from all their churches. When this became known among some of our people they raised "a great hue and cry" about it. I remember I wrote to President Montgomery of Muskingum College, then moderator of their General Assembly, explained our problem and asked him for a letter stating frankly the UP relationship with the Union. He very graciously replied to the effect that the UP leaders were well aware of the fact that our Polish churches were not Presbyterian but, since they were doing such a marvelous work, all Protestants should rejoice with them and support them generously. The UP Christmas offerings sent direct to the field were a source of great encouragement to the Polish brethren.

Before the Republic of Poland was overrun by Soviet Russia and religious work was severely restricted, there were more than 250,000 members in churches and meetings known to the Union. There were 134 evangelists on the field; 65 organized churches, hundreds of scattered meetings, and 206 regular preaching points in 26 counties and in 10 provinces.

With all these new developments CRA did not lose its early concern for the evangelization of the USA. The Clarke Estate continued to function, working in cooperation with the CRA. An interchange of evangelists between the two organizations made it possible to keep several good men constantly in the field. Adams, Raum, Root, Strong, (J. Marion) Small, Pickle, Clutter, Snyder, and others became expert in church-planting strategies. There was seldom a year that went by without our establishing a new church every month, sometimes more.

In this expansion program I remember a number of outstanding incidents. In Cedar Rapids, Iowa, there was a wealthy business man by the name of Fred Shaver who was greatly concerned about church closings in nearby communities. The State society had adopted a policy of retrenchment for Iowa's rural and village churches on the ground that social trends had doomed hopes for church growth and development in such areas. Fred was then teaching the large men's Bible class in First Church. He conceived the idea that evangelists could be brought in to preach the old Gospel, revive these churches, and reopen their buildings. He saw capable men from his class lending aid in reorganizing a local leadership. He invited me to come to Cedar Rapids and meet a volunteer committee in his offices. As a result we cooperated by providing evangelists in about a dozen closed churches and bringing new life to the cause in and around Cedar Rapids. Fred and I became close friends. I was several times entertained in his beautiful home. His wife was a wonderful soul. He told me that his father had indoctrinated him in the Bible and the Restoration plea as a boy, but that he had been a sort of "prodigal son" in his youth. During a Billy Sunday meeting in Cedar Rapids, he had been converted and restored to an active life for Christ and the Church. He loved to give his personal testimony about the crisis years of his Christian experience and did it so effectively that he won many men to Christ. I had the good fortune to arrange for his appearance in many of our rallies. He always paid his own expenses for entertainment and travel and often dropped a good-sized check in the offering plate to help defray general expenses. We kept up a lively correspondence dealing with brotherhood problems until his death. The church in Cedar Rapids went liberal under pressures from Drake University and the State office, a situation which broke his heart and hastened his death.

George Taubman, Bruce Brown, and C. C. Root saw the tremendous population explosion of Southern California as a challenge to establish new churches in new communities. They brought me out to survey the field and to tell the CRA story to the growing number of churches which were withdrawing support from the UCMS. I remember our first rally in Bruce Brown's church which packed the building and had in attendance the "top brass" of the State missionary society. In a two-hour question-and-answer session they grilled me about our program, with salutary results for the cause. The Pacific Coast became a veritable hot-bed of evangelical effort. Clayton Root grew to be one of the most effective evangelists and church-organizers in the Brotherhood. The

CRA entered into a contract with him for his full-time services. Eventually the area churches came to accept complete responsibility for his program and backed him in founding over twenty churches in strategic centers before his untimely death. Some of the finest congregations we have in that area were the fruit of his labors. The Harris family in Beverly Hills, which had built a fortune in the lumber business, entertained me in their beautiful mansion overlooking Los Angeles, for the purpose of laying the groundwork of a Seminary patterned after our school in Cincinnati. I returned later to advise with a committee, which included Mrs. Harris, in the formation of Pacific Bible Seminary (later Pacific Christian College) and the opening of its first sessions in the Alvarado Christian Church. This school furnished many capable leaders for the new congregations being established.

Arizona was a fruitful field for our CRA evangelists. Due to the strong leadership of Robert E. Elmore and P. Y. Pendleton in the First Church, Phoenix, practically all of the Arizona churches withdrew support from the UCMS and voted to separate the Arizona Christian Missionary Society from the International Convention. The ACMS turned its attention almost exclusively to the planting of new churches in the state. They sought our advice and the aid of our evangelists. I could recount many stories of church-plantings, but the Yuma story must suffice. We sent Tom Adams to this torrid Mexican border city, then noted for its gambling, its saloons, and its houses of prostitution. Tom, with his blunt British tongue and his penchant for rushing in where angels feared to tread, was the ideal man for the job. He pitched his tent downtown, got out his advertising posters and flyers, and then visited all the main saloons. This was a decidedly new approach quite unlike that of other evangelists. He would go to the bar, order a glass of milk, announce who he was and what his business was, shake hands all around, and then ask permission to offer prayer for the town, its people, and the meetings. No one denied him and from the first night the tent was filled to hear this he-man preacher. The meetings lasted for a month with over a hundred additions. Lots were purchased and a tabernacle erected. A church was organized which persisted, with many "ups and downs," until finally the cause developed a capable leadership, was housed in adequate buildings, and is now carrying on a program which is a credit to the Restoration plea in modern Yuma and the whole state. Through the years I visited Arizona many times and was always generously and hospitably received.

This is poor manuscript coordination, but I know of no better place to recount an interesting Arizona visit. I was invited to First Church, Phoenix, for special Lord's Day services and on Monday morning I received a call from John W. Loper, chairman of the church board and superintendent of the Phoenix Public Schools. He said, "How would you like to visit a Mormon Temple?" I expressed enthusiastic assent, while wondering where in the world that could happen. Loper then told me that, when he was superintendent of the Mesa Public Schools, he had formed many friendships with Mormon leaders in the community. The Mesa stake had been chosen by the Utah authorities as the site for the erection of one of its few secret Temples. The magnificent structure was soon to be dedicated and closed to the public. Loper felt he knew men who could get me permission to tour the building. So we drove down on a beautiful Arizona spring day through the colorful flower-strewn desert. Loper's man took us to the director of building operations who consented to the tour provided Loper and I would be willing to "take instruction in the Mormon faith."

We were briefed and then taken into the marble and gold central well of the building. Here were beautiful mural paintings of outstanding historical events in Mormon history, including the immersion of Joseph Smith in the Susquehanna River. In the middle of the well was the magnificent Rookwood baptismal basin mounted on the backs of a group of oxen. Here, we were told, was where "baptism for the dead" took place. Then we entered the lowest of a series of classrooms arranged in ascending spirals around the central well to the top of the building. Here in the first room were murals depicting the Adam and Eve story from the creation to the tragic break with God. We were told that each of the remaining ascending rooms represented a degree of instruction in God's plan for the ages which chosen Mormons took until they could pass the final examination and attain the sublime status of a Temple Mormon. At the top of the building was a luxurious ballroom where the final ceremonies of induction took place. Its walls were hung with velvet curtains and its floors carpeted with plush velour. Great crystal chandeliers furnished the lighting. My mind recalls only faintly the arched entrances into what I think they called the "seven heavens." In this area of the Temple was the chapel where "celestial marriages" were performed. A cushioned bench was provided where the couple was supposed to kneel, overarched with the words, "What God hath joined together, let not man put asunder." I gathered that only Temple Mormons were permitted to negotiate these secret polygamous marriages on the earth and qualify to claim their additional wives in heaven. At least that is the impression that remains with me after being rather vaguely instructed on the subject by our guide who impressed me as being extremely reluctant to tell two unregenerate Gentiles all the truth about this "precious doctrine."

It was quite an experience to visit this massive nearly-completed Temple at Mesa which in a few short days was to be closed to all but loyal Mormons.

Possibly here is as good a place as any to mention my visit to the first Mormon Temple at Kirtland, Ohio. This is where recently-converted Sidney Rigdon (Alexander Campbell's companion of early Restoration history) led the Prophet Joseph Smith for the establishment of his new Zion. The Temple had been erected at great sacrifice. Indeed, the mortar of its walls is filled with chips of donated china dishes, coins, and jewels as a testimony of that sacrifice. The Temple is now the property of the Reorganized Church of Jesus Christ of Latter Day Saints with headquarters at Independence, Missouri. When I entered the gate I presented my card which read: "James DeForest Murch, President, Christian Restoration Association, Cincinnati, Ohio." The guide was immediately taken with the word "Restoration," asked its meaning, and finally told us that Mormonism is the only true "Restoration Movement," being set to the task of restoring God's plan for the ages including the Aaronic and Melchizedekian priesthoods. When I told him about our Movement, he immediately responded, "Yes, we know of Alexander Campbell. He had a great idea but he did not go far enough in his work of restoration." In the second story of the Kirtland Temple we were shown the ornate benches in each end of the great hall where the Twelve Apostles and the representatives of the two priesthoods sat during the assemblies of the Church. We were shown many interesting relics of early-day Mormonism and given copies of tracts used by their missionaries. We asked the reasons for Smith's abandonment of Kirtland, but our guide expressed little interest in exploring the subject. I had many interesting contacts with Mormons through the years and admired their courage in standing for their beliefs which still retain a semblance of Christian orthodoxy. In this frame of reference, the practical demonstration of their moral and social idealism is most exemplary.

But — back to evangelism and the CRA. Wisconsin was the scene of many church-planting victories. I happen to recall Beloit. We sent J. S. Raum to this city where a little dilapidated frame chapel still remained as a reminder of the fact that we once had a church there. George Taubman had ministered there as a youthful preacher, but the cause had fallen on evil days. The house was soon to be sold. Raum discovered a few brethren who helped him put the building in shape for services. At the end of two weeks of revival the crowds outgrew the accommodations. A Lutheran church building in the center of the city was for sale. Raum was able to rent it and he filled its auditorium with eager listeners. A congregation of more than a hundred members was organized and the building was purchased. A young man by the name of Gerald L. K. Smith, a graduate of Eureka College, was called as its minister. He had a brilliant personality and was a "stem-winder" of a preacher. We agreed to underwrite his salary for a year. In that time he received and baptized some three hundred new members and became one of the most admired preachers in Beloit. I once heard him preach a sermon on the Restoration plea which rivaled anything our best sermonizers could do. We all thought we had discovered in Gerald the coming leader of our cause that we were praying for. But the Disciples' Establishment became enamored of the young "prophet" too and took him away from Beloit to be the pastor of the wealthy and influential Kingshighway Christian Church in Baton Rouge, Louisiana. There he went on the air over the

South's most powerful radio station and became one of America's most popular preachers. Then he decided he had been called to be America's new Messiah and organized a socio-political crusade that rivaled the Ku Klux Klan in its racist, fascist, and nationalist overtones. The Baton Rouge Church was split and his relations with the Christian Churches and Churches of Christ were at an end. The Beloit Church had benefited from his early ministry and went on to become one of our strong Wisconsin congregations. Church plantings followed at Kenosha, Racine, and other cities. When testing days came later in our history almost every church in the state remained loyal to "the faith once for all delivered."

So successful was our effort to "Cover North America with the Plea" that many independent area groups were organized to plant new churches. We worked out a plan by which the CRA cooperated with these groups, supplementing their funds and their leadership and doubling the effectiveness of our program. With limited funds which had been given or willed us we set up a miniature "Church Extension" system, loaning funds to new congregations ready to build. This grew with the years. Shortly before I resigned as president we had prospects for a great evangelistic forward movement.

One day I got a special delivery letter from W.H. Marler, an evangelist in Texas, which bore the news that A. D. Milroy had died leaving $250,000 for evangelistic work under the CRA. Soon afterward I took a train for Beaumont where I met Brother Marler. That night I preached in a new church he was planting in a suburban area and the next morning we took off for Brenham to meet the Milroy family and learn about the great gift. I found out that A. D. Milroy was a Britisher who had come to America as a young man and had been very successful as a cotton merchant. He was converted by B. B. Sanders and became a tower of strength to the Brenham church and our cause in Texas. He married Sarah Jackson of a prominent Brenham family. He worked hard and invested his profits in a large cotton gin operation, in Beaumont oil, the great Houston ship canal, and other successful enterprises. He became a wealthy man with a high sense of his responsibilities as a Christian steward. He liberally supported the work of the Texas Christian Missionary Society and underwrote the evangelistic ministries of a number of men like A. G. Brelos, Albert T. Fitts, John W. Tyndall, and W. H. Marler. He himself became a lay preacher, thoroughly versed in the Word of God, and gave his services to many a weak and struggling congregation. He had admired the work the CRA was doing in evangelism and wanted to have fellowship in it through his great gift. We enjoyed the visit with the family, who were most cordial, and went on to Houston to meet the trust officers of the Bank which was in control of the funds. Here we experienced the Texas "cold shoulder" and discovered Texas laws requiring the money to be administered in Texas by Texans and spent in Texas by Texans. I was treated as a "foreigner" from Ohio, but when all was said and done the CRA had access to quite a large sum of money which could be used to the glory of God and the extension of His Kingdom. We thanked God and took courage.

I journeyed to Texas several times seeking to enlist support for CRA. My contacts were with men who had been prominent in the Evangelistic Era of the state work and who were unhappy about the trends toward a centralized ecclesiasticism and theological liberalism. They were men who once had close associations with ministers and evangelists like J. H. O. Smith, S. M. Martin, E. V. Spicer, John L. Brandt, W. T. Brooks, and Charles Reign Scoville. Chief among them was multi-millionaire Luke C. Brite whose generosity made possible Brite College of the Bible at Texas Christian University. He had a mammoth cattle ranch in Western Texas and lived well at the little city of Marfa. I visited Marfa several times, especially during the pastorate of Joseph Keevil (minister of the Richmond Street Church, Cincinnati, and later field man for the CRA). It was a real thrill to ride with Brite over his ranch with its thousands of head of cattle and its own village largely populated with Mexican cowboys. Brite intended to do something for the CRA comparable to the Milroy fund, but when the Establishment saw "the way the wind was blowing" they turned loose all their propagandists to block any such gift. Mrs. Brite was the one who finally convinced Luke that he should have nothing to do with the "mavericks" from "up North." She was a dyed-in-the-wool member of the Indianapolis-controlled Christian Women's Fellowship. All her friends in the organization were "up in arms" against us and we were forced to retreat in ignominious defeat. But it was nice knowing the Brites. Luke's heart was in the right place. He knew the Plea, having been taught and baptized by old Addison Clarke, the Texas pioneer evangelist and educator. He gave thousands of dollars to TCU, to the Thomas (Africa) Mission, to Mexican evangelism, and to needy churches on the border. The story of the Brites is told fully in Noel Keith's *The Brites of Capote*.

An important phase of the work of the CRA was its "clearing house" which received and forwarded funds to all agencies who were related to "The Christian Restoration Association and Associated Free Agencies." This was a service gladly rendered to individuals, groups, and churches who did not have the addresses of works which they desired to support. Agencies which enjoyed this service also agreed to prepare a monthly news report of their accomplishments for the *Herald* and to participate in the Restoration Rallies. Once each year they were to submit reports of their accomplishments and their financial situation so that the Brotherhood could see what was being done by their "independent" agencies.

At one time there were as many as twenty such agencies holding a loose relationship with the CRA — all of them free and independent to carry on their work as the Lord led and their own wisdom determined. They were urged to take advantage of any services the CRA provided but they were under no obligation to do so.

I want to pay tribute to some of these agencies and the leaders who helped to bring some semblance of unity to the growing extra-congregational cooperative life of the Brotherhood outside the UCMS and the International Convention.

Probably the largest and most influential member of the CRA and of Associated Free Agencies was Eugene Bible University, of Eugene, Oregon, and its related institutions. Maybe the best way to state this relationship is that "E. C. Sanderson joined us." Sanderson *was* EBU in those days and had been for many years.

I shall always remember my visit to him which resulted in the relationship. He was a tall, well-proportioned man with an inscrutable bespectacled, intelligent face. He welcomed me into his home with patriarchal cordiality, indicating that he was overjoyed to know that one of a younger generation had "seen the light," realized the dangers of liberalism, and was anxious to do something about it. He welcomed me as an ally in a work which he had been engaged in for many years.

That day he quoted Luke 11:52 over and over, especially that portion which reads, "They have taken away the key of knowledge." This was his favorite passage of Scripture and he often used it as a text in his Restoration Rally addresses as he toured the country with us on many occasions. He assured me that all the resources of his "empire" would be associated with us, and those resources were mighty extensive and influential.

E. C. Sanderson went from Drake University, where he had received his education, to the Northwest. There he opened "Eugene Divinity School" in 1895 on a "shoestring." It was located near the campus of the University of Oregon. It grew scholastically, institutionally, and fiscally, until it came to serve the Brotherhood educationally as our only institution of higher education in the great Northwest. Then it became "Eugene Bible University."

The "university" idea was Sanderson's, built on the pattern of the University of London with related institutions in various places. The idea was born out of a deep concern for the educational crisis in the Brotherhood as college after college was taken over by the liberals. Sanderson determined, since no one else in the West was doing anything about it, to build up a chain of schools loyal to the faith once for all delivered.

In 1913 the beautiful, strategically-located building of Eugene Olson's "International Christian Bible College," opposite the campus of the University of Minnesota, was about to be sold at auction. Sanderson stepped in, purchased it, changed its name to Minnesota Bible College, and underwrote its program. In 1927 he purchased a site adjacent to the campus of what is now Kansas State University at Manhattan and founded "Christian Workers University," calling Dean T. H. Johnson of Johnson Bible College to be its first president. This is today Manhattan Christian College. Then followed the establishment of Colorado Bible College, using the facilities of the Central Church in Denver for its work.

Then Seattle Bible College opposite the campus of the University of Washington. And finally San Jose Bible College opposite the campus of the San Jose State College. What a complex!

As needs of various sorts arose, Sanderson moved in to supply them. There was need of a Christian Hospital in Eugene, so he set up a committee, purchased land, and erected the first building for "Pacific Christian Hospital." He established a Christian Old People's Home and a Christian Children's Home — all in Eugene. In cooperation with Leon L. Myers and First Church, Dodge City, Kansas, he built a Christian hospital there and, before the Great Depression hit with full force, had a number of other projects planned in the field of Christian benevolence.

He was adept at raising money. He had scores and scores of married couples without children, single men, single women — spinsters and widows — who deeded their properties — residences, farms, and store-buildings — to his corporations with contracts calling for the payment of lifetime annuities at high rates of interest. They all trusted him and he always "delivered."

We had splendid relations with the "Sanderson Empire" all during my administration as President of the CRA. This gave us tremendous status in the West and Middle West and had salutary results beyond measure. Eugene Bible University gave me my first honorary doctorate (D.D. in 1928).

Sorrowfully, I must record that when the Great Depression hit the Northwest in full strength the "Sanderson Empire" collapsed. E. C. gave himself poor to salvage the wreck but it was too big an undertaking for him and his loyal supporters. Bankruptcy faced all his institutions. However, in the long years which followed, much was redeemed. Today we have Northwest Christian College, Minnesota Bible College, Manhattan Christian College, and San Jose Bible College, none of which probably would be in existence today if it had not been for E. C. Sanderson. And who will ever know how many thousands of souls were saved, how many missionaries and ministers educated, and good deeds done because he lived and gave himself so sacrificially in God's service?

It was a unique privilege and experience to have been associated with this great and good man whose heart was pure and whose faith was great. If his critics can show a record half as fruitful for the Kingdom they will do well.

I want to pay tribute to Mrs. T. R. Ayars who stood by me when others failed. She was probably the most mistreated, misrepresented, and persecuted woman in the history of the Restoration Movement.

She came of the wealthy and socially-prominent Shedd family in St. Louis. Her life and her fortune were dedicated to the cause of Christian benevolence. A prominent worker in the National Benevolent Association of the Christian Church, she was honored by appointment to national offices where her natural administrative and financial abilities contributed much to the organization.

Then her heart was touched with the need for Christian services to unmarried mothers and their babies. She helped to organize the Mothers' and Babies' Home in St. Louis and gave much of the money to buy and equip property for the Home. Then pious hypocrites in the churches began to object to the church's providing an institution of this character. A debate ensued in the NBA as to the wisdom of continuing such an institution. Mrs. Ayars fought J. H. Mohorter and Mrs. J. K. Hansbrough to a finish, but lost the battle. She and her Mothers' and Babies' Home were ousted. Only her sacrificial giving and heartfelt service saved the work.

Gathering about her the remnant of her friends in the churches of St. Louis, she organized the Christian Women's Benevolent Association of the Christian Church. After the great St. Louis World's Fair she conceived the idea of buying the Fair's biggest tourist hotel in University City and turning it into a Christian home for the aged. It was a tremendous undertaking but Mrs. Ayars and her helpers succeeded in it. It continues today as a monument to her magnificent leadership.

I have a vivid recollection of the hatred toward Mrs. Ayars exhibited by the "powers that be" in the Disciples Establishment. Her noncomformity was a sin in their eyes. It was in connection with the St. Louis International Convention in 1920. The CWBA had somehow been granted the right to lease exhibit space in the Convention Hall. They had a large and very attractive booth. When the NBA discovered it, the Convention gave her legal notice to get out. When Mrs. Ayars refused to surrender her contract, the police were called and by force wrecked the exhibit and set the effects of the CWBA in an alley.

Her husband, Dr. T. R. Ayars, was a leading St. Louis surgeon. They had a dream of establishing a Christian Hospital. The NBA had lost several hospitals (such as Valparaiso and Kansas City) and benevolent leaders of the Brotherhood thought it was impossible to develop and maintain a successful venture in this field. But the CWBA, Mrs. Ayars, and a group of consecrated physicians did it. Today we have two successful Christian hospitals in St. Louis worth many millions — one downtown and the other in a northern suburb.

At Ferguson the women established a Christian Children's Home, now a youth center for juvenile court cases. Hundreds of young people have gone out from its doors to become church workers and leaders in the life of America.

When the CRA was established, Mrs. Ayars was one of the first to encourage me in the new program. She led the CWBA to become one of our Associated Free Agencies. She gladly welcomed the fellowship with others of like mind and heart. She always bore uncomplainingly her part of the financial load. She went on trips across the country, speaking in the Restoration Rallies, and inspiring other Christian women to undertake greater things for Christ and the Church.

Another major associate in our complex of agencies was Enrique T.

Westrup and the Mexican Christian Missionary Society. He was a prince in Israel. When I first met this Mexican gentleman in the States he impressed me as a well-mannered, cultured, capable businessman rather than a missionary.

Without his courageous stand for the faith in a crucial hour we might not have had a Mexican brotherhood of Churches of Christ in Monterrey, Sabinas, and Piedras Negras. He was the son of a British Baptist missionary who as a young man had been converted to the Restoration idea. His father had married a fine young lady of the Spanish-Mexican aristocracy and Enrique was educated in the best schools the country afforded. He was a master of English and tutored many business and professional Mexican leaders in the use of the language. He, too, married into the aristocracy and had a highly cultured family.

When the Indianapolis missionary hierarchy in 1919 negotiated a "comity agreement" with the denominations, they transferred all the mission property in northern Mexico to the Southern Methodists in exchange for rights to operate a mission in Aguascalientes and San Luis Potosi. They abandoned our original Mexican brethren and told them to join the Methodists.

It was then that Brother Westrup at great personal sacrifice took a strong stand against the merger, was able to salvage the property of the Central Christian Church in Monterrey and organize the Mexican Christian Missionary Society. He launched a small journal called *La Via de Paz* which circulated both in Spanish and English among the friends of the mission. The cause prospered both educationally and evangelistically under the leadership of native Mexicans whom Westrup rescued from the old mission and trained to teach and preach.

I was commissioned by our Board to go to Monterrey and persuade Westrup to join our ranks. It was a very happy experience. He met me at Laredo on the Mexican-American border and rode with me on the train to Monterrey. Our trip was an education as he acquainted me with Mexican customs, history, political and social developments. On the train many important personages (especially high up in Masonry) stopped by our compartment and visited with us. Mr. Westrup told me how the revolution, which freed Mexico from the rule of the Roman Catholic hierarchy and the "Gringo" establishment, was really staged and consummated by Mexican Masons, first in secret and then openly in a successful and almost bloodless revolution. It was an all-day journey, hot, but very enjoyable.

In Monterrey I was entertained in the modest but beautiful home of the Westrups. Next day he proudly showed me his business college and English school which occupied the entire floor of one of Monterrey's largest and most modern buildings. He took me to the government offices, introduced me to the mayor, the federal governor, the director of public education and other leaders too numerous to mention. Everywhere we went he was treated with the highest respect by everyone.

That night I preached in the Central Church which was packed to the doors. This was my first experience in the use of an interpreter in public address. I was frequently interrupted by Amens and hand-clapping, and at the close of the service was simply overwhelmed by the reception given me.

Next day we went on a tour of the nearby mission stations where I met the workers and talked with them about their plans for the future. I shall never forget a visit to a poor mission chapel in a ghetto area of Monterrey. My coming had been announced and the place was crowded with the saddest specimens of humanity I have ever seen. They were mostly women and children (a few toothless old men) shabbily dressed, ignorant, sickly, and dispirited. I talked (with Brother Westrup translating) in simple terms about the Christ who loves all men and offers salvation and better days to all who will accept and serve Him. There were two or three confessions, followed by baptism in a small stream that ran nearby. My heart has ever been deeply concerned with our Mexican work because of that experience.

The Mexican Christian Missionary Society joined our ranks and wholeheartedly cooperated in our program. In our Restoration rallies E. T. Westrup was one of our most well-received speakers. He sent his most promising young people to our independent colleges for preparation as future leaders. There is more to this story but I had left the CRA before its events transpired. I unhesitatingly say that if it had not been for the noble service of this great and good man at a crucial hour we might not have had the splendid "independent" work which is prospering so encouragingly in northern Mexico today.

I must not forget the Maddens and the Osaka Christian Mission. They were among the choicest UCMS missionaries in Japan. When confronted by the new policies of open membership and interdenominational comity, they were forced conscientiously to break with Indianapolis. They set up a modest work emphasizing evangelism and education and carried on in the second largest metropolis of the nation.

Mrs. Madden was probably the most successful author of missionary literature in the history of our people. She wrote, during her lifetime, such books as *In the Land of the Cherry Blossoms, When the East Is in the West, Where Day Dawns, Women of the Meiji Era,* and *Young Hearts in Old Japan.* Most of her books were published by Fleming H. Revell and they were widely sold through women's missionary societies of Christian Churches and Churches of Christ. Revell's broad clientele made possible even larger sales interdenominationally.

When we announced the "Associated Agencies" plan the Maddens and the Osaka Christian Mission were among the first to apply for membership. Once when they were on furlough M. B. served in the office of the CRA as office manager and did yeoman service on the field for the whole program. Providentially, after Maude's death, when M. B. was forced to retire by age and illness, he was given a home and hospitalization in the CWBA complex of institutions in St. Louis. I visited him there several times, reminiscing joyously together about the fellowship we had in the work of the CRA.

W. D. Cunningham was another tower of strength to our venture in the broad inclusive policy of the CRA. Cunningham was no new recruit in the cause of "independent missions." He and his wife volunteered to go to Japan as missionaries under the old Foreign Christian Missionary Society in 1898 and were accepted. Then W. D. suffered an attack of infantile paralysis which crippled him for life. The FCMS would not take him after that, but he and his wife felt keenly that God had called them to preach the Gospel and establish Churches of Christ in Japan, and that the mere decision of a mission board could not keep them from doing God's will.

They collected a modest sum of money from intimate friends and went to Tokyo where they began their work in a small way. Despite the opposition of the FCMS and the Disciples Establishment, they were able to get teaching positions in Japanese schools, organize Bible classes, and win their first converts. Providentially, they were able to lease for 999 years a strategic tract of ground opposite the Emperor's Palace and build the First Church of Christ, the nearest building to the royal compound. By the time the CRA came into existence the "Yotsuya Christian Mission," as the Cunninghams called their venture of faith, had twenty-four churches organized (ten self-supporting), twenty-two competent native pastors, eighty-two Bible schools. More than 6,000 Japanese had been won to Christ, among them several members of the nobility. They had developed a list of thousands of "rope-holders" in our American Churches. The mission's debt-free real estate holdings were worth more than a quarter of a million dollars in American money.

W. D. saw the CRA as an answer to his prayers — a fellowship with others of like mind, a medium which would guarantee and perpetuate the work he and his associates had accomplished. He made several trips to America, went out on our Restoration Rallies, and finally astonished us all by deeding all the property of the Yotsuya Mission to the Christian Restoration Association. He retained a life interest in the Mission as its director and made several other restrictions guaranteeing the independent future of the work and the rights and privileges of the native Christians. This arrangement existed until World War II when Japan and the USA became incolved in the great conflict that resulted in American citizens and corporations losing all their rights in the "Sunrise Empire."

The later history of the Yotsuya Mission was a tragic one in which practically all its possessions and church organizations were lost, but as long as I was president of the CRA our relationships were rich and rewarding. We pointed to Yotsuya Mission as the outstanding example of what could be done for Christ by "independent missions." The first issue of our new magazine, *The Restoration Herald,* featured the Yotsuya Mission and paid tribute to the Cunninghams and their associates. I

90

never knew a man who was more completely committed to Christ and the task of disseminating the Gospel throughout the world than W. D. Cunningham. His very presence in our Restoration Rallies electrified our people. I can still remember his impassioned plea, "The man who has never heard the Gospel has a greater right to hear it once than you have to hear it twice!" His work and his personal example will ever continue a vital contribution to the cause of Christian missions.

One of the most successful promotional plans we carried out was through the instrumentality of the area "Restoration Rallies," to which I have previously referred several times. Our conservative brethren had been deprived of the fellowship they had formerly enjoyed in district, state, and regional conventions. They were hungry for fellowship. We provided it in these rallies. In the spring and fall we drafted an itinerary covering the nation. All agencies affiliated with the CRA were invited to send a team-mate who would speak in the Rallies presenting their work. The host church was responsible for entertainment, would allow offerings to take care of promotion and travel expenses, and would cooperate with us in the choice of preachers from their area who would preach old-time Gospel sermons. We carried on high-power promotion through *The Restoration Herald* and our correspondence. The strong programs with opportunities to meet missionaries, educators, and evangelists assured good attendance in most instances. We reached thousands every year and were able to keep the fires of faith blazing constructively all over the country. I was present, supervised, and spoke in most of these meetings. Some that come to mind at the moment are: Phoenix, Denver, Clovis, Wichita, Pittsburgh, Minneapolis, Chicago (Metropolitan), Des Moines, Council Bluffs, Lexington, Indianapolis (Englewood), St. Louis, West Frankfort, Columbus, Mitchell, Bryan, New Castle, Atlanta, Louisville, Georgetown, Long Beach, Oklahoma City, Enid, Eugene, Grant's Pass, The Dalles, Spokane, and many, many more. I could tell stories about every one of them. The agency leaders who participated included W. D. Cunningham, Mrs. T. R. Ayars, Leslie Wolfe, Enrique Westrup, Dr. Zoena Rothermel, Harry Schaefer, M. B. Madden, K. J. Jaroshewicz, Russell Morse, E. C. Sanderson, J. W. Lusby. Among the preachers who thrilled us with their Gospel sermons were P. H. Welshimer, O. A. Trinkle, W. H. Book, Ira M. Boswell, Robert E. Elmore, George Taubman, E. W. Thornton, W. R. Walker, Edwin Errett, R. C. Foster, S. S. Lappin, C. J. Sharp, James Small, Mark Collis, J. H. O. Smith, J. J. Whitehouse, J. T. McKissick, F. W. O'Malley, W. E. Sweeney, T. K. Smith, L. G. Tomlinson, and George P. Rutledge.

We had no national "missionary convention" in those days. We of the CRA used our influence in every way possible to persuade the continuation committees of the North American Christian Convention to provide a day for world evangelism in their annual gatherings, but they were afraid that the missionary appeal would be so strong that it would eventually monopolize the program. Too, there was the fear that such a move would be the opening wedge for setting up a new missionary society complex comparable to the UCMS. Finally we determined that we would set up a national Restoration Rally following the general format of the regional Rallies offering a platform and exhibit booths where the missionary, evangelistic, educational, and benevolent agencies could adequately present thier appeals. We had no desire to replace the North American Convention, but we felt that this neglected field of service should be filled. (We proposed to NACC leaders that their convention, then meeting on an irregular schedule, become a semi-annual affair and that ours be held every other year. This we felt would preclude any competitive rivalry and provide a more comprehensive service to the Brotherhood. No takers!) So in May, 1932 we held the first National Restoration Assembly in the spacious old downtown Central Christian Church, Cincinnati, with most of the Free Agencies represented. Some 1,500 people were in attendance. A second and more largely attended Assembly was held in 1934. This effort is often mentioned as the forerunner of the National Missionary Convention that now is a most vital factor in the tremendous concern of our churches for winning the world to Christ.

Speaking of general assemblies, about this time Jesse M. Bader, Edwin Errett, and others conceived the idea of a World Convention of Churches of Christ which every five years would be the gathering place of all brethren of goodwill in all the sectors of brotherhood life, emphasizing the things upon which we were basically agreed, and enjoying the fellowship which would be its natural fruitage. The first meeting was held in Washington, D. C., in October 1930. I advocated the participation of the CRA and we had a booth there. While the Association refused to cooperate in later meetings, I was active in my personal support and attended every World Convention from that time on through San Juan, Puerto Rico, in 1965. Jesse Bader was a thoroughly irenic soul and was basically sound in doctrine. He was constantly handicapped in trying to be fair toward conservatives, but did everything he could to maintain balance in personnel, policy, and program. The more I knew him the more I appreciated him. He rendered a service to the Brotherhood he loved which has never been adequately recognized. After his day the World Convention became increasingly a tool of the Liberal forces of the Brotherhood and of the apostate World Ecumenical Movement.

It was during my later years with the CRA that economic depression hit the USA. I vividly remember the Hoover-Roosevelt campaign for the presidency. I was in Steubenville, Ohio, for a rally when the Roosevelt victory was announced on radio. The whole city went wild and great crowds of people surged around the downtown hotel where I was staying, shouting and making noise with every conceivable device. Shortly afterward Roosevelt closed the banks. Business of all kinds came to a halt. We, with our slim bank account, and contributions to the CRA virtually nil, were hard put to exist. For the Murches, our meals were largely cereals and milk. Fortunately we were favored by the bank which held the mortgage on our home.

All over the land jobs were lost, banks failed, mortgages were foreclosed. Hunger, rage, frustration were everywhere. The perplexity not alone of the suddenly impoverished, but also of those who were not themselves dispossessed and hungered but who were overcome by gloom, loss and shame, caused thousands of suicides and early deaths. No one but those who endured the hard times will ever know the anguish and terror of the days when suddenly there was no more money.

As I write our nation faces tragic problems but we live on the "fat of the land." In comparison we enjoy a prosperity the like of which the world has never seen. There is not an underprivileged person alive in 1970 who has suffered anything like the troubles which all America endured in the 1930's. When you talk to people about the Great Depression they are absolutely incapable of understanding what we went through. What modern Negro now can imagine the horrors of slavery? What modern Protestant can imagine the tragedy of medieval Roman Catholic inquisitions? What modern nation can understand the terror of ancient plagues that leveled whole cities with the dead lying in the streets and no one to bury them? There is no standard today by which affluent modern Americans can understand what happened in the Great Depression.

Christians found a living faith, hope, and strength they had never known before. The churches began to fill up with people who had long neglected their Lord. There were many strangers in the pews who heard the Gospel with eagerness and many souls were saved. The churches enjoyed a prosperity which they had not known for years — not a money prosperity, but a spiritual prosperity. There was a bitterness in the land toward those who had been guilty of economic larceny, but the people as a whole were drawn together in a deeper and richer fellowship than they had ever known. They shared, they helped, they were together and they came to a new appreciation of the things of life that really count.

The next generation never really knew what happened in those crucial years. They never appreciated the courage, the faith, and the perseverance of their parents in a land that had been wracked with catastrophe. Maybe they were told, but they were not interested in the past. They failed to benefit from the lessons their parents learned and went on to create for themselves a new world with mounting problems which now threaten to engulf us all.

During this period the CRA piled up a salary debt to me which they never made any move to pay. Only the Lord made it possible as doors opened providentially for me to survive financially.

In the last few years prior to my resignation as President of CRA came developments among our constituency which saddened my soul. I had given my life to Christ and the high ideals of the Restoration Movement to restore His Church in doctrine, ordinances, and life. My commitment made it necessary to stand for what I believed to be right. I hated evil and all those forces which promoted it, but I sought to love everybody who loved the Lord, regardless of their organizational commitments. I kept up many relationships with brethren who were sound in the faith but supported other agencies. I made no tests of fellowship other than those stated specifically in the New Testament. I tried to love my enemies.

Certain elements in the CRA and in the whole "independent agency" complex began to make loyalty to these agencies a test of fellowship. They hated everybody in the UCMS and the International Convention related agencies. There was nothing too mean that they could say about them, accusing them of every crime under the sun regardless of the truth. This spirit spread within the conservative camp itself with group suspicions, jealousies, hatreds, charges, and countercharges against everything and everybody that did not conform to their cunningly devised standards and interpretations which were given equal status with the Scriptures. These sectarian groups began to accuse me of compromise and saw the CRA as a new UCMS seeking to monopolize the new functional life of the Brotherhood. The North American Christian Convention was attacked as a "work of the devil." Men like P. H. Welshimer, Edwin Errett, W. R. Walker, and others of like mind and heart with whom I found happy fellowship were accused, without one scintilla of proof, of compromise and apostasy because they occasionally appeared on International and State convention programs. Local churches were being split over personal disagreements as to sectarian and cultist standards of fellowship.

It was my hope that we should seize upon every possibility of truly Scriptural fellowship remaining to us and that by cultivation we could enrich it; and that the healing rays of the love of Christ might purify us all unto that day when a reconciled community of Christians might move on to the complete accomplishment of our original purposes as a people. I saw this unity, not in something personal, nor in anything organizational (certainly not in CRA), but in the love of Christ and His kingdom as big and broad as the teaching of the Holy Scriptures.

Finally, I began to feel so frustrated in my work that I turned to Christ in prayer night and day asking for guidance out of the wilderness. It was in this period that "Christian Action" was born.

The whole story of this wonderful movement will be told as a separate Episode. It led to my early resignation as president of the CRA and eventually separation from all connections with the Association. I was succeeded by Leon L. Myers, minister of First Church, Dodge City, Kansas, and he in turn by Robert E. Elmore of First Church, Phoenix, Arizona. The negative elements of the Brotherhood in that day flocked around its standards and eventually (for a time) came into virtual control of the policies of the Standard Publishing Company.

Under a reactionary leadership the broad "associated agencies" policies and programs of the CRA were abandoned. Home evangelism shriveled to less than half its former church-planting effectiveness. *The Restoration Herald* became a medium devoted largely to diatribe, heresy hunting, character assassination and divisive propaganda. I came to rue the day that I had launched it.

As I write, however, I am thankful to say that the CRA is now staffed by a capable and progressive coterie of young men thoroughly committed to the Restoration Plea and willing to make any sacrifice to advance it both at home and abroad. The *Herald* has a fine irenic spirit, is standing for the faith once for all delivered, and is one of the chief instrumentalities in the brotherhood for encouraging and promoting aggressive Christian evangelism. God bless them all!

Episode VIII

Country Preacher

During the days leading to the Great Depression, I faced economic problems which caused me to accept weekly preaching engagements in two rural churches near Cincinnati.

As is often the case in my life story, this development proved to be of the Lord's leading. The Restoration Movement in America gained its widest acceptance in rural and small-town communities. My experience in this eleven-year ministry helped me to keep the common touch and enabled me to serve the cause more effectively in publishing and other interests at the national level.

The congregation that was nearest my heart was Union, in Highland County, Ohio, about sixty miles from Cincinnati. Here I had spent boyhood years, had made the good confession and been baptized. Here were Aunt Kit Carr, Uncle Perry Surber, and all the other "aunts" and "uncles" of that fellowship. We called each other by our first names and were truly a family in the Lord.

Union was founded in 1833 and was one of the oldest congregations in the county. Its first house of worship was built of logs and called "Union" because it was made available for whatever preachers happened to come that way. Later the appeal of the simple Gospel overcame all rival sectarian concerns. When a new frame building was erected near the present site, the name "Union" was perpetuated but with the connotation that all God's people could be made one by a return to the Bible and the Bible alone as their rule of faith and practice. In my childhood days a small but beautiful Gothic brick chapel housed the congregation. It had been dedicated by that peerless leader Z. T. Sweeney. Union's eldership was well indoctrinated, and instructed capable men of each new generation so that there had been an unbroken continuity of loyal leadership through the years.

When I began my ministry the Bible school was averaging around thirty or forty and preaching services were attended by about fifty. This was considered good for an "open country" church. With a new emphasis on the teaching function of the church the school grew to over one hundred in average attendance and our building was filled for "preaching services." We introduced modern methods of financing the church and made many improvements on the property. The old cemetery, where the bodies of many of the old heroes of the faith lay buried, had been deeded to the township and its toppling monuments were overgrown with weeds and briars. We repossessed the tract and, thanks to the donation of land by one of our neighbors, doubled the size of the burial plot. A roadway was constructed, an ornamental fence provided, a landscape expert straightened up the tombstones and planted evergreens and flowers, and ample parking space was provided. We observed Arbor Sunday and converted the barren church property into a maple grove. We built a furnace room and installed a modern heating system. Then came the need for enlarged accommodations for the Bible school and added seating for special occasions. There was considerable opposition to such a large undertaking, but finally an addition with classrooms and other facilities was built and paid for. This improvement made Union one of the best-housed rural churches in the area. I remember one Sunday evening while a group of us were talking in the front churchyard, a stranger drove up, stopped, and engaged some of us in conversation. He said, "I am a traveling salesman and I have been driving by this church for several years. I have noticed the improvements being made on your property and I think this speaks well for the kind of people who live in this community. I am a Roman Catholic. We take great pride in our church buildings. It does my heart good to see others honoring Christ in a similar way. I wish you God's speed in your work." With the new building came the opportunity of developing a community center of sorts. The Future Farmers of America and the Four-H Club were provided meeting places free of charge. Social events were held in the new rooms. We were able to hold our young people while many rural churches were losing theirs. Another project was the raising of a fund of several thousand dollars for "perpetual care" of the cemetery and other church property. In all these projects the cooperation of our fine leadership made success possible.

I think of Curtis Roler, our leading elder, and Carey Winkle, our Bible school superintendent. Other names that come to mind are Surber, Cochran, Vance, Donahoo, Ludwick, Sonner, Roush, Kibler, Robinson, Gossett, Pulliam, Fender, Ruble, Roberts and Hawk. Curt was a remarkably well informed and progressive farmer. He reminded me of Scattergood Baines, of *Saturday Evening Post* fame. When he stretched out in his favorite chair and loosened up his "think tank" he was sure to come forth with words of wisdom we all did well to follow. When crucial times came, it was Curt who knew the right moves to make and the right words to speak, that the cause might go forward to the Lord's glory.

We had a "protracted meeting" every year. I baptized over a hundred in old Whiteoak Creek during this ministry. There were marriages and funerals without number. My sermons were educational and inspirational and we enjoyed many mountaintop experiences together. The church came to have a stewardship and missionary vision and had but few financial problems. When we celebrated our Centennial we heard the history of the old church recounted and together with our friends in other congregations enjoyed a great outdoor dinner on the grounds. Our annual Homecomings were great social events of similar pattern. Union's cooks were supreme and food was plentiful and to spare.

When parting came at the end of eleven years (the longest ministry in the history of the church), there were tears and embraces I shall always treasure in loving memory.

The other church was in Blanchester, Clinton County, Ohio — a village of about 1,600 population. Here we had competition with five other churches: Methodist, American Baptist, Primitive Baptist, Universalist, and Roman Catholic. Blanchester was one of the churches established in 1900 by the Clarke Estate through the instrumentality of C. A. Freer and the Ohio Christian Missionary Society. The congregation had had its "ups and downs." At one time only a group of faithful women kept the doors open. It was in bad shape when I took over, but there had recently been some good additions of brethren who were ready for a move forward. On the first Sunday there were twenty-nine in the Bible school and a mere "handful" for preaching services. The once attractive and well-located frame building was unkempt, with a leaky roof, needing paint, its stained-glass windows partly missing. The auditorium was heated by two coal stoves that often in winter had to be "coaled up" during the services. As rapidly as we could raise the funds we renovated the building, put on a new roof, painted it inside and out, repaired the stained-glass windows, built a furnace room and installed a modern heating system, repaired the baptistery, and added to the seating facilities. We advertised our services in the local newspaper and soon we began to see acceptance in the community. Audiences grew until we had to put chairs in the aisles for the evening services. The Bible school was reorganized and new teachers and leaders were trained for more efficient service. Our first Rally Day saw over one hundred in the school and finally we were able to top the two-hundred mark in special services. Hit or miss worship services were stabilized and were dignified by the use of simple but appropriate forms. Elders and deacons were trained. Stewardship and missionary programs were adopted. Among the names of those who were faithful helpers I recall the Conners, Floreas, Wilsons, Footes, Myers, Villers, Archers, Grooms, Duvall, Garwood, and Achor.

One feature that "put us on the map" in Blanchester was a popular evening service. We had a "singspiration hour" and brought in special music from surrounding Churches of Christ. A question box dealt with all sorts of religious problems. There were frequent "Bible bowl" demonstrations by children and youth. We had special day observances. Community problems and issues were dealt with in no uncertain terms. The old-fashioned Gospel was preached without fear or favor. It was not long until these services became known not only community-wide but beyond, and there were lots of strangers in attendance — many of whom became good prospects for church growth. So successful were these meetings that in summer by popular demand they replaced Blanchester's Union Meetings. Our building would be filled while only a few

98

of "the faithful" from the other churches in town gathered for the traditional community gathering. Finally the Union Meetings were discontinued. Confessions, baptisms and transfers marked many of our evening services.

I was constantly in demand in both Clinton and Highland counties for homecomings, township and county Sunday School conventions, fifth-Sunday meetings and special days. I could not answer all the calls, but I thoroughly enjoyed many Sunday afternoon excursions. During those years I remember revival meetings at Monterey, New Vienna, South Liberty, Pricetown, Georgetown. How I was able to work all these into my schedule was miraculous, but the Lord blessed with many souls won to Christ. Both Clinton and Highland County churches had annual meetings (Clinton at the Sabina Campgrounds and Highland at the Hillsboro Fairgrounds) which drew thousands. Our congregations were always well represented, giving their testimony for the evangelical biblical faith and the Restoration plea. The ties that bound these churches in Christian love had much to do with the fact that when brotherhood problems and divisions came in later years they stood almost unanimously for the "faith once delivered."

Practically every Sunday my car would be filled with Cincinnati Bible Seminary students going out to preach in rural pulpits. I would drop them off at stated points and then pick them up in the evening as I drove home. Closed churches were opened and dying churches were restored to life as a result of these services. I think of Modest, Lerado, McKendree, and several others in this category.

It was during this decade and largely because of my Blanchester contacts, that I was tempted to enter politics. As I have indicated, our evening services drew scores of local community leaders who were not members of our congregation. Among them were the Basingers, the Snyders, the Nices, the Lashes, the Hannahs, and the Browns. The Browns were easily the "first family" of Blanchester. The Honorable Clarence J. Brown was our representative in Washington and president of the Brown Publishing Company, one of the largest commercial printers and newspaper publishers in southwestern Ohio. One time when we had a special patriotic service, we dedicated an outdoor flagpole and had a formal flagraising with Clarence Brown as the main speaker. He was running for Governor of Ohio on the Republican Ticket while I was preaching at Blanchester. I offered to write a letter to all the Christian Church and Church of Christ ministers in the state commending him and soliciting their vote for him. He was delighted with my interest and accepted my proposal. This incident was the beginning of an intimate friendship. He was defeated for the governorship, largely because of a combination of Roman Catholic and labor union opposition, but he remained our representative in Washington until his death. One day he said to me, "Why don't you go into politics? You have what it takes." Then he outlined a possible strategy. "The Hillsboro *News Herald* might be bought," he said, "and we could make you editor. The Murch name in Highland and Clinton Counties coupled with your writing and publishing abilities could put you in the state legislature in short order. From there on, with a bit of luck, you could go far. I will certainly do everything I can for you." I had a number of friends in the party. Judge George Eyrich, my neighbor on Werk Road, was the GOP "boss" of Cincinnati and Hamilton County. The Honorable Myers Y. Cooper, former governor of Ohio, an elder in the Walnut Hills Church, and his good wife were long-standing friends of the Murches. I had rewarding contacts with Senator Robert A. Taft and the Taft family while I was president of the Cincinnati Chapter of the Sons of the American Revolution. Unquestionably I could have had "plenty going for me" if I had succumbed to the appeal of power and fame, but my early commitment to a life of service for Christ and the Church prevailed. I have never regretted my decision.

Episode IX

Christian Action

This period of my life was characterized by the deepest despair and then by the highest spiritual exaltation I ever experiencd.

Conditions in the world and in the churches, to which I have previously alluded, almost caused me to lose my faith. We had come through World War I with its wholesale carnage. Millions of youth slain on the battlefields. Other millions of souls seared by hate, bitterness, resentment, and revenge. Ideals shattered. World brotherhood paralyzed. Then came the wild orgy of pseudo-prosperity in America. There was an unprecedented wild scramble by selfish business interests for post-war plunder, undeserved profits, wild speculation and extravagance. The inevitable result was the Great Depression of 1929-1936. Foreign markets were cut off by suicidal nationalism. Factories were closed. There were 10,000,000 unemployed; 20,000,000 on relief. Moral codes were abandoned. There was economic and social confusion bordering on revolution. The destruction of Western civilization was actually happening before our eyes.

The institutional churches were miserably failing to meet the situation. They were more interested in perpetuating their worn-out human dogmas, building cathedrals, strengthening their hierarchies, and raising their multimillion-dollar budgets than doing the will of Christ as revealed in the New Testament. Liberalism was rampant in their colleges and seminaries, and thousands of their ministers no longer gave credence to the Holy Scriptures and the validity of the expressed will of God revealed in them. Their church rolls were filled with hypocrites and rascals whose names were there merely to promote their selfish social and business status in the community. Paganism and worldliness impregnated most of them. Many of our own churches were just as guilty as the rest of them.

One of our largest churches in Oklahoma had a liberal minister who frequented night clubs and road houses and majored in trying to be a "good fellow" about town. When questioned by one of the elders in a meeting called to consider his conduct, he produced a little red book which showed the names of certain men of his board who were present at these resorts with women not their wives. He gave specific times and places and said, "Go ahead and call a congregational meeting to discipline me if you want to, but when you do I'll open my little red book to the public and I'll take the lid right off of things in this church." The whole matter was hushed up and the preacher was soon riding around in a fine new car purchased by the men whose names were in his little red book. Three ministers in succession had to leave the pulpit of this church for varied kinds of moral turpitude.

Our conservative churches were not particularly plagued by situations like this, but many of them were guilty of pharisaism, Sandemanianism, and other forms of legalism which had virtually destroyed the spirit of Christ and resulted in strife, division, sectarianism, and bigotry. Real prayer and Holy Spirit guidance were almost foreign to their thinking and their practice. It was this element which threatened to take over the leadership of the Christian Restoration Association, our new colleges, our mission fields, and our media of communication.

I was forced to agree with a cynical friend of mine that "America has been inoculated with a mild form of Christianity and seems to be immune to the real thing." Many a sleepless night was spent futilely in seeking a way out of my problems, my doubts and frustrations. When I was almost on the verge of losing my faith in God and man, a startling spiritual experience came to me.

One unforgettable night, after a crushing day, my heart despairingly bowed down, I awoke startled by a Voice. I looked about, but there was no one else in the room. Then there flashed into my mind like a blinding light the words of Romans 12:1,2.

I beseech you, therefore, brethren, by the mercies of God, that ye present your bodies a living sacrifice, holy, acceptable unto God, which is your reasonable service. And be not conformed to this world: but be ye transformed by the renewing of your mind, that ye may prove what is that good, and acceptable, and perfect, will of God.

I had read that passage of Scripture scores of times but now it was the special direct Word of God to me. He had spoken it by Living Presence through the Holy Spirit. IT WAS THE ANSWER TO MY PLEA! IT WAS THE WAY OUT! If the reader is interested in a more complete story of my experience, it is recorded in my book, *God Still Lives.*

As I analyzed this Scripture passage I saw in it a plan for a "Crusade for Christian Action." It had three directives: (1) *Consecration* — complete surrender and commitment to Christ. (2) *Restudy of the Scriptures* — essential to the rediscovery of the whole will of God for our lives. (3) *Experimental action* — putting rediscovered truth into action beginning in our individual lives, and then in our homes, our churches, our communities, and the world.

As I sought to carry out the plan in my own life I had another unforgettable experience which I shall relate. One Sunday as I was sitting in my library I confronted myself with the question, Are you putting Jesus Christ first in your life by complete surrender and commitment to Him? I picked up an old envelope from my desk and began to jot down the things that seemed most important in my life. The list ran something like this: My work. My family. My parents. My property. My personal comfort. My social relationships.

Then I asked myself the question, "Would I be willing to put Christ first — ahead of my social life?" Many a time I could have done some things for Christ or the church but my excuse was, "Tonight is lodge night." A long series of incidents rose into view and paraded before me. I realized that I had fallen short and I promised God that from henceforth I would always put Jesus ahead of everything in my social life.

In rapid review went other things, and I want to tell you there was some mighty surrendering going on. I had never before realized the grip the things of this world had on my life. No wonder Paul said the death of Christ was for the ultimate purpose of *delivering us from this world* (Galatians 1:3,4). Peter, in the first gospel sermon, cries, "Save yourselves from this untoward generation!" Everywhere in the Book there breathes the spirit of Christ's fiat, "He that loveth his life shall lose it, and he that HATETH HIS LIFE IN THIS WORLD shall keep it in life eternal." The great illusion which hinders mankind in its effort to discover reality is THIS WORLD. We are kept bound and gagged by our trust in temporal things. Even so-called Christians love the world more than they love Christ.

I went on until I came to my family — my wife — my dear son. God has blessed me with a wonderful family. Could I actually put Jesus first — *ahead of them?* Why should God ask any such outlandish thing? Yet I recalled that when Jesus called men to His discipleship in the old days He said: "Except a man give up father, mother, brother, sister, houses and lands for my sake he is not worthy to be my disciple."

The problem was a difficult one. If you don't believe it, try it yourself. It is the test that was put to Abraham when he was asked to take his son, Isaac, out and sacrifice him. It is the same question that Jesus put to the rich young ruler. Abraham became the Father of the Faithful, because he answered that question in God's favor. The rich young ruler "went away sorrowful" because he answered the question in what he thought to be his own favor. We who have allowed our material heritages and environments to bind, gag and deliver us to the world, the flesh and the devil, need to know the joy of release which can come alone through Jesus Christ. Well, to make a long story short, with tears that came from the depths of my soul I made the surrender. It wrenched and ground and devastated me. I know now I was being recreated — made over into a different person. I had opened my life to God in a way I had never done before and He had come in.

I was conscious of a Presence with me, and descending upon me a kind of cleansing, flushing force throughout my mind and active consciousness, much as a fireman's hose would flush out a clogged tile. Then with sterilizing effect it seemed that my entire inner being was purified as a laboratory technician cleanses his instruments or as a surgeon cauterizes a wound, and this was followed with a feeling that my whole self was being flooded with light, glorious, golden, luminous, and the Voice said, "I have forgiven thee and redeemed thee. Henceforth you are not your own; you are mine. I claim you for my witness". And a release of tension and a peace of heart came to me that was indescribably wonderful.

I have since learned the truth of what Christ said to Peter following the incident of the rich young ruler. Peter had said, "Lo, we have left all to follow Thee," (as much as to say, "What reward have we?"). Christ's reply was:

Verily, I say unto you, There is no man that hath left house, or parents, or brethren, or wife, or children, for the kingdom of God's sake who shall not receive manifold more in this present time, and in the world to come life everlasting.

From that day in my library my life has been showered with riches and blessings far greater than I had ever dared think.

Out of this experience came my song, "I'll Put Jesus First in My Life." The words and music came to me in bed one morning about three o'clock. I am no musician, so I call it "the song the Lord gave me." It starts —

The world all about me
Has now no allure:
Its pleasures bring pain
Its wisdom is vain.
I seek a foundation
That's steadfast and sure —
I'll put Jesus first in my life.

CHORUS

In all that I say,
In all that I do,
Throughout this world
Of toil and strife,
By day and by night,
Through trust in His might,
I'll put Jesus first in my life.

The Lord has used this song in a marvelous way as a factor in bringing thousands of decisions for Christ, decisions for restoration and renewal, and decisions for full time Christian service. It appears in countless hymnals and has been translated into many languages. The chorus is a favorite in revival meetings, camp meetings, and summer conferences.

Then I began an intensive restudy of the New Testament in the spirit of Thomas and Alexander Campbell to discover the pristine genius of apostolic Christianity and consider how it could be restored in my day. In it I sought guidance of the Holy Spirit that I might be able to put aside all human traditional concepts, habits, and practices and accept only the truth revealed in the Word of God. Out of this came my

Christian Action Bible Studies which might have well been titled "What It Means to Be a New Testament Christian." Multiplied thousands of these studies appeared in pamphlet and book form and had wide use around the world, being translated into many languages. Although long out of print they still keep appearing in xerox and mimeograph form issued by people who discover them and are so led to this sort of study that they organize independent groups for their use.

I was so imbued with my "magnificent obsession" that I told people about my experience everywhere I went. Some looked at me with astonishment as if thinking me a bit crazy and about to join the "holy rollers." Others were deeply impressed and urged me to set in motion a crusade in the churches to disseminate a new technique for revival and restoration based on my "discovery."

This is finally what actually happened. Our CRA executive committee approved a "change of policy" for the *Restoration Herald* in which our major emphasis would be the promotion of a "Christian Action Crusade," organizing Bible study groups and holding regional rallies for spiritual renewal.

Two documents that appeared in the *Restoration Herald* are reproduced here to keep the record straight. The first appeared on the cover page:

DUNAMIS!

TO ALL MY FRIENDS IN CHRIST:

The other day I sat down to my annual task of mapping a fall and winter program for the Christian Restoration Association.

Despite the fact that our Association will be able to report its largest results in evangelism since organization, I was forced to realize that our accomplishments are a mere *bagatelle* compared to what our brotherhood should be doing in "seeking and saving the lost." A consciousness of the futility of man-made programs gripped me.

Why is it, I said to myself, that Christians have their automobiles, their trips to the World's Fair and summer resorts, their rouge and tobacco and give little or no time or money to the extension of the kingdom?

Furthermore, I asked myself, what are all our programs availing while the civilization about us is rapidly disintegrating and the world seems headed for destruction? These things weighed upon my mind and troubled me exceedingly. A deep conviction came to me, that the reason why we are in such a desperate situation is that the power of God has ceased to be exercised through the modern churches. We are not really Christians. "The churches" are spiritually dead.

It came to me that the Roman Christians lived in a similar period — all about them the Roman civilization was in its death throes. So I turned to Romans, the 12th chapter, and as I read I saw the cure — *the only cure* — for all our ills!

First — Christians must "present themselves a living sacrifice holy and acceptable unto God." That necessitates an open and absolute break with the world.

Second — They must be "transformed by the renewing of the mind" — adventure in an honest restudy of God's word to rediscover His will.

Third — They must "prove what is that . . . perfect will of God," — DO it with all their might regardless of the consequences. "Proving" demands experimental ACTION!

Christians must *CONSECRATE! LEARN!* and *DARE TO DO!*

There it was — a universal limitless program of CHRISTIAN ACTION. Not my plan. *GOD'S PLAN!*

I pledged myself to publish that program to the church, and God helping me, to the world. THE RESTORATION HERALD for the next year will put everything else in the background and tell the story of CHRISTIAN ACTION to an impotent church.

If God's people are regenerated and if they consecrate their all to Christ, not only the problem of missionary support will be solved but every problem of the church and the world will be met and conquered.

The program is so big that I tremble at the consequences of the adventure it proposes. Its mighty implications are full of dynamite. But it is going to take the *dunamis* of God to break a highway through the chaos of a dying world.

Wherever it leads I will go! Will you join me?

In a lead article, "Our Unfinished Task," I related the new spiritual adventure to what I considered a crisis in the Restoration Movement:

> One of the modern miracles of church history is the phenomenal growth and progress of the people known as the "Disciples of Christ." In 1809 they were a mere handful, today they number over 2,000,000.
>
> These people arose in a day of intense sectarian prejudice, when bigoted and intolerant "Christians" were constantly at each others throats in bitter and ignominious warfare. The body of Christ was crucified afresh by their theological wranglings and dogmatic pronouncements.
>
> As if by an act of God (and a close student of the history of the times must believe it was indeed that), by an act of God, there arose simultaneously in widely separated sections of the English speaking world small groups who threw off the yoke of denominational bondage and took their stand on the Bible, and the Bible alone, as their only rule of faith and practice. There were the Haldanes of Scotland, Mueller of England, Dr. Abner Jones of Vermont, Thomas O'Kelly of North Carolina, Barton W. Stone of Kentucky, Thomas and Alexander Campbell, of Pennsylvania and West Virginia, Dr. Chester Bullard of Virginia, and many others who courageously led the way in this "new Reformation." Each at first unmindful of the presence of the others, upon learning of their existence, these groups gradually coalesced. By

far the large majority clustered about the distinguished leadership of Alexander Campbell and Barton W. Stone and became known to the religious world as the "Disciples of Christ."

Their ideal was "The Restoration of the New Testament Church in Doctrine, Ordinances, and Life." Under the very necessities of that early day, and in sheer self-defense from utter extinction, they became a people of argumentation and debate. Alexander Campbell was the most brainy, courageous, logical and convincing of them all. He met and vanquished the sectarian theologians of all Protestantism and then turned his brilliant powers against Archbishop Purcell of the Roman Catholic Church and Hon. Robert Owen, popular advocate of atheism. His writings and his debates stand today without a superior in the field of logical, unrefutable Bible theology. He was the peerless contender for the faith, "once for all delivered to the saints"!

Rising out of this atmosphere of theological victory came the magnificent leadership of Walter Scott in aggressive evangelism. He put the scriptural "steps into the kingdom" in such a clear, concise, and convincing manner that "fools, even though they were ignorant, could not err therein." He and his successors pleaded for the unity of Protestantism, through the Restoration of the New Testament order. The simplicity of it gripped the nation and spread like wildfire through the countryside, into the villages, the cities, and across the plains. It looked for a time that sectarianism was doomed. The passionate zeal of these evangels of a new order stands to condemn our present day indifference and halting growth.

If one were to interpret briefly the stages of our development to this present hour, it could be put thus —

First Period, Debate. Here we established the Christian System so impregnably that it stands today without a fissure or a blemish — tested by every wind of doctrine that the mind of man can conceive.

Second, Evangelism.

Third, Cooperation. The intense individualism of the early leadership, and the vigorous contention that the local church was the supreme unit of the divine order in the earth, had swung the movement to the extreme of virtual non-cooperation. Then came the persuasive voice of Isaac Errett calling to all like-minded brethren to join hands in a cooperative and aggressive program. The people, hungry for fellowship and inspiration, responded with a will and our conventions and societies began their life and growth.

Fourth, Missionary Achievement. Here A. McLean, the outwardly gruff, but inwardly ardent and consecrated man of God contributed a wonderful leadership. Forsaking home and loved ones, living on a mere pittance, working like a veritable slave, A. McLean performed the feat of imbuing a backward and visionless people with a deep missionary conviction. First hundreds, then thousands, and finally millions of dollars rolled into missionary treasuries. Young people

107

offered their lives upon the altar and went out to "the uttermost parts of the earth" to bear the glad tidings of good things to those who knew not our Lord in the pardon of their sins. What a victory!

This period marked our highest and best achievement. From then on to the present we have been losing momentum and have suffered from a dangerous defeatism.

The next period *(Fifth)* may be characterized as one of *Arrogance and Pride.* With our laurels won, and the heroic leadership of the early days laid to rest, there arose a new generation that "knew not Joseph." They dwelt with pride upon the victories of the past, the wealthy and powerful missionary organizations, the culture and distinction of our colleges, the prominence of our people in the nation and the world, our numerical strength and position among "the *other* denominations." Our society officials assumed certain ecclesiastical prerogatives and "lorded it over the flock." They "enlarged the borders of their garments" took the "chief place at feasts," and the "chief seats in the synagogue."

Sixth, Departure from the Faith. But "pride goeth before destruction!" and now entered the elements which destroyed the peace, unity, and progress of a great people. The deity of our Lord was denied, the inspiration and revelation of the Bible was flouted, open membership was practiced in the churches, modernism and secularism captured our colleges, missionary societies adopted policies of compromise. A people who once prided themselves on their Bible platform were driven by every wind of doctrine and captivated by the philosophies of men.

Seventh, Chaos. Then came a day when division and strife were fanned to white heat by our journalism, losses in receipts for missions were reported, workers were recalled from the field, mission properties were sold. Worldliness and sin gripped the churches. Disintegration and decay were evident on every hand. This is the period we live in. Our message to the religious world is today rendered *null and void* by our own shortcomings. Our leaders not only doubt the efficacy of "our plea" but openly ridicule and hold up to scorn the remnant who persist in promoting it. Chaos and confusion are everywhere!

As one contemplates this sorry condition of a movement so grand in its conceptions and so unselfish in its goals, he is moved to bitterness and tears. Were Campbell, Stone, Scott, Errett, McLean and that great host of our "princes in Israel" to come back today, they would scarcely recognize us. And we would be forced to hang our heads in shame and disgrace. But the supreme question we need to ask ourselves is, "What would we do if *Jesus Christ* were to confront us — a people who flaunt His name on their edifices but do not the things which He commanded, or live the life that He lived?" Would He not say, "This people honoreth me with their lips but their heart is far from me"?

Now to the conclusion of the whole matter: The Restoration Movement began with the aim, "The Restoration of the New Testament Church in Doctrine, Ordinances, and Life." We restored the doctrine. We have claimed to restore the ordinances. *But we have made no appreciable progress in restoring the life of that apostolic era!* We need to finish the program laid down in great wisdom by our first leaders! When we do, all our other problems will be solved.

If the "Churches of Christ" had the conception of Christian consecration which Paul had (Phil. 3:12-16 — read the whole chapter) we would be the most marvelous power for righteousness in the world today. We need to accept Jesus Christ as our all and in all. We need to give up the world, its wisdom, our conceits, our organizational prejudices, our selfishness — everything that we are and possess — lay all on the altar a living sacrifice! His thoughts need to become our thoughts, His love our love, His will our will. Then we need a restudy of "our plea" that we may *realize* it in the freshness of newly-discovered truth. It is only when we can be over-mastered with its perfect adequacy that a rebirth of passion and power will grip us. And finally we need to go out and *do* what we know and feel! Thus, and thus only, will pulsating and revitalizing LIFE be infused into the dead body of our faith.

This is the goal of the Crusade for CHRISTIAN ACTION which is being born in our midst today. There need be no flourish of trumpets, no elaborate schemes or programs, no convention endorsements, no "statesman-like" leadership — simply the opening of our hearts and lives to Christ, letting Him come in to use us to His glory! This is distinctly and wholly a *spiritual* program.

If we will practice what we have preached for 100 years, God still has a place and a use for the people called "Disciples of Christ"! If not, he will take the already-feeble torch from our hands and give it in fuller light to a people who will properly represent Him to a dying world!

"The night is far spent, and the day is at hand; let us therefore cast off the works of darkness, let us put on the armor or light, and LET US *WALK!*"

Possibly, if we do our part, "SALVATION IS NEARER TO US THAN WHEN WE FIRST BELIEVED!"

The crusade began under the auspices of the Christian Restoration Association, but those reactionary elements, to which I have already alluded, were strongly opposed to any such change. Some branded me as a heretic whose new ideas were a distinct departure from the Restoration Plea.

It was then that the Lord opened an unexpected door of opportunity, as He has often done in crucial times in my life.

One day I made a trip over to the offices of the Standard Publishing Company for a chat with my good friend Edwin Errett, editor of the

Christian Standard. During our conversation I told him about my new "obsession" and our plans for a "Christian Action Crusade." He immediately asked me to write an article about it for the *Standard.* Surprisingly he featured it as the lead article in the next issue. We were all amazed when more than six hundred letters of approval came in — an all-time record response on a purely voluntary basis.

A few weeks later I received a call from Willard Mohorter, secretary of the Company, asking me to visit his office. With little ado he offered me the position of "Book Editor" or "Literary Editor" and *carte blanche* for the promotion of Christian Action. He suggested that I might have four pages every week in the *Standard* and two pages in *The Lookout* in which the Crusade could be promoted in any way I chose. He also offered to take over the publication of the Bible Studies and any literature I deemed necessary. Furthermore, he promised that the Company would underwrite any legitimate travel expenses for rallies and conferences. It was an answer to prayer "pressed down, shaken together and running over"! Of course I accepted. Within a few weeks I had resigned as president of the CRA and was installed in my new office with two secretaries and every convenience at my disposal.

The space in the two journals was used for articles reflecting Christian Action principles, the fifty-two Bible Studies in serial form, letters and testimonies from the field, and a question-and-answer feature that became very popular. An artistic and attractive pamphlet, "What Is Christian Action?" was published and made available free for distribution by the hundreds of thousands.

It is impossible to convey to the reader the impact and the blessings of this adventure of faith. A whole set of volumes could be written about it. I shall attempt to give in brief outline form some of the results as I remember them.

Thousands of groups adopted the weekly Bible Studies, including Bible classes, community cells, home study gatherings, mid-week prayer meetings. Each participant took the following pledge: "I believe with all my heart that Jesus is the Christ the Son of the living God and I accept Him as the Master of my life. Trusting in my Lord for strength I present myself to Him a living sacrifice, and I promise Him that I will strive to do whatsoever He would have me do, as the Holy Spirit reveals His will to me, in the Word of God." Everyone had to carry his own Bible and be prepared to read the passages of Scripture assigned. The whole scheme of study was catechetical and the questions and answers were designed to give a comprehensive harmony of all the Bible taught on a given theme. At the conclusion of each study the group was asked what implications the teaching had for their everyday lives and each individual was required to put them into practice regardless of the cost. The following week personal experiences and testimonies were shared with the group. Although the course was designed to be completed in one year, many groups took two years or more for the studies. Two years later another study book, *Studies in Christian Living,* was provided with an even more popular acceptance. The news of the studies spread from church to church and beyond into the denominational world without any high-pressure promotion, with results far beyond our expectations. Years later as I covered the nation in various ministries hundreds of people came to me thanking me for these studies and told me their whole life had been changed through revitalized contacts with the living Christ.

Thousands of lives were changed. I recall a noted socialite — an alcoholic — who gave up all for Christ and was cured; a college professor who was born again; a clandestine love affair that was ended; a military cadet who renounced war; a bell-hop in a hotel who resigned because he could no longer be a party to evil deeds; an embezzler who made restitution of his defalcations; a housewife who gave up evil speaking and gossip; a discouraged preacher who had left the ministry but met Christ anew and started all over again; a timid soul who became an outstanding church leader; a vagrant saved from suicide; a broken home restored and made happy; a social worker who took Christ as a Partner in her ministries; a church leader who died to self and exalted Christ; a woman saved from insanity. This was the work that the church should have been doing all along, but thousands of congregations had lost their touch with the living Christ and were failing to be media for changing and transforming lives. Christian Action was the means God used to restore them to their apostolic task.

Speaking of the impact of Christian Action on the churches, we frequently quoted Revelation 3:14-22 in our work. I felt that we were definitely in the Laodicean age and that the churches were rich in this world's goods but paupers in the true riches — wretched, miserable, poor, blind, and naked. The call to return to their "first love" was made over and over and with encouraging results. I'll tell the story of just one Kentucky church touched by Christian Action. It served a fine residential community in a large city. It had grown to a membership of nearly a thousand, then it split over the erection of a rather elaborate new meeting house. The "bullheaded" minister and an elder clashed. Their friends took sides and many terrible exchanges occurred with the result that the elder and his friends quit attending services, the Bible school dwindled to half its former size, the church budget plummeted into the red. The building project had to be abandoned with only a basement for the church home. Finally the misfit minister resigned and was replaced by a capable, sweet-spirited man who — try as he might — was unable to restore the congregation's former peace and prosperity. He had studied Christian Action and he invited me to hold a "Christian Action" revival. He felt this might be the answer. The remarkable Payne Sisters had charge of the music. The first thing we did was to visit the elder. He was a physician — one of the city's most prominent surgeons. He had a fine knowledge of the Bible and the Restoration Plea and had been the Bible school superintendent for many years. We called him and he agreed to see us. When we arrived his office waiting room was filled with patients, but the nurse recognized us and said: "The doctor is waiting for you. Go right in." I cannot describe his warm and friendly reception. He had been reading our Christian Action literature and said, "I guess what we need in this situation is a dose of old-fashioned prayer," so the three of us got down on our knees in his office and each of us prayed earnestly for forgiveness, for the leadership of the Holy Spirit, for the meeting, and for a new day for the old church. When we got up from our knees the doctor said, "I know what I need to do and I am going to do it." That evening he was in the building for the first time in five years. Everyone was amazed. The news spread. The auditorium filled up and was crowded the rest of the week. Then I called for a great service on the Lord's Day for renewal, repentance, forgiveness, and the restoration of true Christian fellowship. The Lord gave me amazing power in the morning message and then we sang, "I'll Put Jesus First in My Life." I never have witnessed anything like the response. More than two hundred moved forward and clasped hands for the first time in years and begged forgiveness. Tears flowed freely. Everyone in the auditorium took the Christian Action pledge. We had prayer. Then came a heart-stirring Communion service followed by the immersion of eleven who accepted Christ for the first time as Saviour and Lord. After that came the singing of "Blest Be the Tie" and the benediction. Hundreds lingered, loath to go home. Shortly after this event came plans for the completion of the new building. A great ingathering of souls came from week to week. Today this is the leading church for our people in this great city.

Many ministers throughout the nation experienced spiritual renewal and came to know the living Christ. Out in Illinois a preacher of my acquaintance had an unfortunate experience in his early ministry. He had thought all elders were saints but he was so disillusioned about this that he gave up the ministry. Blaming others, he was unable to see that he himself was lacking in faith in God and untrue to his vows as a minister. He retired to a little farm and became a rural mail carrier. Then he came in contact with Christian Action. He saw himself as he really was. He had not even been attending Bible school and church services in the community, but the next Sunday he dressed in his best and went. People who knew him were amazed. He asked for the privilege of saying a word to the congregation and was granted permission. "Friends," he said, "I have been untrue to my Lord." Then he told the story of his life. When he finished there were few dry eyes in the audience. "Friends, I now realize that my supreme allegiance is to the living Christ who is all sufficient. He has promised to go with us even to the end of the world. From now on, regardless of the failures of my early associates and my own shortcomings, I will not fail Him. I am going back into the ministry a new man, and, I trust, a better servant of Christ!" He was soon in a good church, preaching with power, and turning hundreds to righteousness. I could fill scores of pages with similar testimonies. One I especially treasure is recounted in this letter from a well-known pastor:

"The act of dedication according to Romans 12:1,2, which you advised, was as definite to me as conversion. With fear and trembling I handed over my will to God in order that He might bring it into conformity with His own. This He began to do, not by a supernatural upheaval, but by a series of experiences in actual life. Circumstances became the instrument by which He shaped the life according to Philippians 1:6. Ah, it was not all a primrose path. He had to work destructively before He could work constructively. There were days when life itself was despaired of! In the dark I knew that One was wrestling with me — wrestling to get control of my stubborn will. I learned what Jacob's experience meant. And though like him I walked limpingly, I leaned upon the arm of One who was strong to uphold. Since then I have never doubted His constant presence which is of all thoughts the sweetest to me.

"Christ is my daily Companion, and at night He watches round about. He has delivered from physical and spiritual dangers which nothing but His providence can explain. Through all the years He has answered prayer. Many of the answers have been instantaneous; others were a longer time in coming. Answered prayer is a daily experience, and the answers are the tokens of His favor, the dew on the fleece.

"Jesus is my daily Guide. I follow Him all too falteringly, but I know He guides. He has chosen my fields of service. In only one or two instances have I known when concluding work in one field just where the next would be. When I closed one of my first pastorates, a veteran preacher put his hand on my shoulder and said very tenderly and sympathetically: 'Don't you worry about your next field; the Lord will guide you if you trust him.' And He always has guided.

"To cite one instance out of many: We were within a few weeks of leaving a field when the prayer for guidance was answered by a telegram. Our home had to be disposed of, and the real estate men could not sell it on a declining market. I took it out of their hands. My wife and son and I — the three of us — made it a matter of prayer. The display ad in the paper was answered by a ready purchaser at a sum above what had been the first purchase price. Along with the house, the purchaser asked to buy just the pieces of furniture we wished to sell, *without knowing we wished to sell them!* The commission was saved and the money made on the deal used for moving expenses! We had just time enough, but not a minute to spare, to wind up affairs and get away on schedule time to a distant field.

"Jesus is my Lord. It would require a book to record all His manifestations — how He has used a frail earthen vessel, making it stronger through the years; how He has brought victory out of defeat in personal life and in service on the field. But the most amazing of all has been

His grace — His patience with an erring, often-disobedient disciple, but one who, nevertheless, has ever held before him the vision splendid, *'the measure of the stature of the fullness of Christ.'*

"Jesus is my Hope. Not only in Him do I rest for complete redemption and perfection of character, but I wait for the promised *manifestation* when the sin-scarred, blood-drenched earth shall be delivered from the bondage of corruption into the glorious liberty of the sons of God. It is a glorious anticipation. For with this faith, I know that the travails of the present hour are but the birth pangs of a new age when He shall be King of kings and His principles shall become the passion and realization of mankind."

Laymen by the thousands experienced renewal and change. A social leader in a Pacific Coast city and a prominent church worker lost her faith when her only son was drowned — a college lad of great promise. Then she was touched by Christian Action, caught the meaning of Romans 12:1,2 and was restored. I want to share a portion of a letter she wrote me:

"It has been a whole year since I wrote you a letter full of selfishness and bitterness about the death of my son. It fills me with shame now to remember it because I know at that time I thought only of myself, my loss and my horrible grief. I had very little knowledge of God, so could only think of Him as being unjust and cruel to me. I hope He has forgiven me, for I cannot forgive myself.

"My grief is still just as fresh, just as hard to bear as it was when our blessed boy was taken from us, but my attitude has changed. Now I'm trying desperately to *use* my grief in helping others — others who are so terribly in need of comfort, and I am now sure that God most certainly answered my prayer when I used to pray, 'O God, keep my boy safe from all harm, never let him be hurt, let him always be sweet and fine.' Yes, I'm sure God heard and answered my prayer. He just didn't answer it the way I wanted or expected Him to.

"I wish I might talk to you and tell you all that has changed in me this last year. I was so worldly, I was a church member in name only. Sins and temptations found me an easy prey because I had never really been converted. I had never really suffered, and as E. Stanley Jones says in his beautiful book, *Christ and Human Suffering,* 'One must have a background of black' to really have character. I now have my background of black and I know it has saved my soul. But what a price to pay! It makes me heartsick now to remember with what indifference I used to take God. But now that God has opened my eyes I'm trying to make amends. I work in and for the Sunday school and church, I never miss a prayer meeting, and, oh, what a comfort, what peace it brings to me. And I've really learned to pray — pray to a loving, kind Father who forgives us. And what a joy and comfort my church friends have been to me.

"Doesn't it seem a cruel pity that some people can't see what it means

114

to be a real Christian before some heartbreaking experience comes? I hate to look back and see myself as others must have seen me."

A leading industrialist in the South was touched by Christian Action and determined to put the Christian principles he discovered in his study of the Bible into action in his woolen mills. He decided to hire only good Christians to man his mills. Then he said, "If religion is a good thing on Sunday, it's a good thing on Monday and every other day in the week, and there's no good reason prayer won't mix with business." And he started a daily prayer meeting. The whole atmosphere of the mills was changed. There were more cordiality and friendliness. Production began to mount. The people were happier. When nearby mills were tied up by strikes, prayer settled things for the Christian mills.

When days were split into two shifts some time ago, the workers had a meeting to decide whether the prayer meeting would be continued. They voted unanimously to have two meetings daily. The present system calls for meetings at 6:00 a.m. and 2:00 p.m., just before each set of employees goes to the machines.

A newspaper reporter tackled this employer one day and asked him what he thought ought to be done to settle the strikes that were perplexing the nation. "Convert the whole bunch to Christ!" he said. "I believe strongly that the principles of the Christian religion will cure any labor trouble or any other kind of trouble. But you've not only got to believe in them — you've got to practice them." Asked whether Christian principles would settle strikes so long as atheists and non-Christian religionists were involved, he said: "No, you can't get non-Christians to practice Christianity any more than you can get a confirmed Hottentot to be a good American."

He sees through the Christian program as it applies to social problems. He wrote me:

"Our daily chapel services have certainly demonstrated, as I have never seen before, the practicality of the Christian religion as a solvent of industrial problems. We have never had the slightest conflict of any sort with our employees and we never expect to have. About eighty percent of them are themselves active church members, and we are constantly urging that all become active.

"If they have their grievances, they bring them to me. If I feel they should do better I talk to their committee and we try to settle everything on Christian principles.

"I believe with you that the Christian religion is the only power known to man which is sufficient for all of the problems of life — industrial, social, or otherwise. It generates love in the hearts of men, and love is the thing that does the work. I should say in this connection, however, that these services were not organized primarily for the purpose of solving a labor problem, because that would have been a selfish motive. We did it simply because we believe it to be our duty and would be a good example to others. No one can distinguish between the management and the operatives in our meetings. We are all equal before God. Our employees have cooperated one hundred percent in these services, and if they belong to anyone in particular they are theirs."

This man is known everywhere throughout the South — has been elected to the highest offices Southern manufacturers can give him. Everywhere he goes, North and South, he preaches this thing. God is using him in a marvelous way to bring about a truly better day in industry.

It was amazing how the movement spread. Each person was inspired to do his or her "thing" to assure its widest possible outreach. One of the most unusual developments was in the life of a convict in a Western state penitentiary. A visitor had given him Christian Action literature. The "cell" idea appealed to him and with the consent of the prison authorities he opened a Bible study in the prison schoolroom meeting every Saturday. He wrote me that the men who joined him in the studies made a real sacrifice to do so. They had only Saturday afternoons, and one and one-half hours on Sunday for freedom in the yard, visiting, and sports. Yet fifteen men undertook the studies. Several found Christ as Saviour. The leader himself (No. 13187) made his full surrender and decided to study for full-time Christian service upon his release. As in so many other cases, only eternity will reveal what results came from these trysts of sincere souls with the Lord.

The most amazing expansion came when Christian Action leaped the Atlantic and entered Europe, through no planning of ours but rather the clear providence of God. A well-educated Bulgarian who had emigrated to the United States came in contact with Christian Action in a Los Angeles church. He was changed and transformed and began to write his friends and relatives in Bulgaria, translating the Christian Action Bible studies and other literature, including the song, "I'll Put Jesus First," and mailing copies with his personal correspondence. They responded enthusiastically and began setting up study groups in their homes. In one town the pastor of a Protestant church learned about the movement and set up a class in his congregation. After a year or so of study this amazing thing happened, according to my correspondent:

"Our pastor, as well as the officers of our church, studied your lessons and your personal testimony, compared them with the New Testament, and decided that we should lay aside all man-made creeds and practices and become simply an apostolic congregation. Hence on Lord's Day, March 4, with our sanctuary crowded to the doors, our pastor read from your writings in which you appealed to all Christians to leave their man-made rules, and take up the cross and follow Jesus only, that we may be living members of the true church of Christ. There was not one person in the whole congregation your request did not affect, even those who had never before bothered with any religion. All of us shed tears and I cried like a child. The action of our leaders was unanimously approved amid the singing of your song, "I'll Put Jesus First." Then came countless testimonies from the people and the service was prolonged until two o'clock in the afternoon. Not one soul stirred or even thought of eating. Finally we all fell to our knees and praised God and prayed for all who are in the Christian Action movement around the world. Since this meeting great things are happening in the various villages round about. Who knows where this revival will end?"

The last I knew, before the holocaust of World War II, the movement had spread even to Sofia, the capital of Bulgaria, where numerous cells were meeting for Bible study.

Word came from many foreign lands about victories for Christ through Christian Action. I recall letters from Australia, New Zealand, India, Japan, China, Africa, England, Scotland, Mexico and other Latin American and Caribbean countries. In the very nature of the movement there was no organization set up to promote or control these developments. Everything was personal- or group-initiated and carried on. There were no denominational or sectarian ties or barriers and all religious communions were affected.

Christian unity was advanced in many ways. Growing out of a Christian Action rally that I directed in the Keele Street Church, Toronto, Canada, came a development that was of such magnitude that I will treat it later as a separate Episode.

It was not long before there was an almost unanimous request for a national gathering of Christian Action crusaders in which they might enjoy the fellowship of others of like mind and heart and be inspired to greater service for Christ and the Church. Standard Publishing was glad to underwrite the cost of such a project. Lake James summer conference grounds, near Angola, Indiana, were chosen as the site for the first event. It proved a veritable Pentecost. We had no way of knowing how many would be present, but some five hundred came. For three years we met there annually with crowds growing until the capacity of the hotels and auditorium became hopelessly inadequate. The last year at Lake James, all the facilities of the hotels and motels within twenty miles were taken and many camped on the grounds in tents or slept under their cars or bushes. We then moved to the spacious Chautauqua Grounds near Franklin, Ohio, but they proved inadequate. Finally, we transferred these national meetings to Winona Lake, Indiana, the famous "Billy Sunday Camp Grounds," where they became one of the major gatherings held annually at that great evangelical Christian center.

The general pattern of this national gathering was: People came into the grounds in a quiet and prayerful spirit and prepared for the first session which was in the nature of a hillside vesper service overlooking the lake. Vespers came each night before the evening session in the tabernacle. Emphasis in the address was on spiritual renewal, full-surrender to Christ of body, mind, and spirit, and absolute and unwithholding commitment to the responsibilities of the Christian life. A call for open and public decision came at the close of each service and there were always large responses. The morning sessions began with prayer and expository lessons in the Scriptures. Then followed short addresses or sermons and, finally, the great sessions with S. D. Gordon, author of the world-famous "Quiet Talks," speaking in his inimitable way. The afternoons were free for group Bible study, prayer groups, serious confrontations with individuals about their moral and spiritual problems, recreation, and wonderful Christian fellowship. A veritable heavenly atmosphere pervaded the grounds. I have never known such happy and helpful fraternal experiences as we had in these unplanned, Spirit-moved hours together. At night, following vespers, we had our headline speakers in a setting of genuine prayer and praise services with singing that reached up to the walls of Zion. Meals were served in the dining halls as far as they were able to accommodate the crowds. Many brought their own cooking and eating facilities and ate in their cottages or in the out-of-doors. We would not be on the grounds long before "converts" would be giving their testimonies to groups that would listen. There were frequent "sharings" by those who told each other what the Lord had done for them through their years of service for Him. Church leaders, both ministers and elders, gathered voluntarily to share stories of new life in local congregations, in their Bible school work, their women's work, their youth work, their missionary and benevolent activities, their financial successes, and in spiritual renewal. When the week was over people were loath to leave, but they carried worthwhile blessings home with them that would last a lifetime.

Among the nationally-known brethren who were most closely associated with me in the national and regional meetings were George W. Knepper, C. G. Kindred, J. B. Hunley, Harry Poll, Aldis Webb, Ernest Hunter Wray, Homer E. Sala, and J. M. Appelgate.

George Knepper was pastor of the great High Street Church, Akron, Ohio. This church led all the churches of the nation for many years in giving to our organized agencies. When I went to Akron to confer with him about my plans he welcomed me like a "long-lost brother." He had frequented the annual deeper life conferences at Keswick, England, and was convinced that the greatest need of the Disciples of Christ was a spiritual rebirth. He placed the facilities of the church at my disposal. Once when there was doubt that we should be able to continue our program, he and friends in High Street underwrote the opening of an office in Akron. Knepper was greatly criticized by the Indianapolis Establishment for his association with me but he never wavered in his loyalty and willingness to work. His addresses were always replete with heart-warming references to the Holy Spirit. Three of his Christian Action messages on that theme were printed in tract form and widely distributed.

C. G. Kindred, then minister of the Englewood Church, Chicago, (then our largest in the city), was "closer than a brother" during the whole crusade. He brought large numbers of his people to the gatherings

118

and was ready with generous financial aid whenever needed. "Cal," as we called him, was a truly lovable character. He was strictly Biblical and evangelical in his position, yet big and broad in his sympathies for all men. He was a favorite speaker and paid his own expenses on trips that took us to all parts of the country. When it was finally necessary to conclude our nation-wide program, he protested vigorously and opened a summer conference of his own at Cedar Lake perpetuating the Christian Action spirit for many years in the Chicago-Calumet region.

J. B. Hunley had served as pastor of several leading churches of the Brotherhood — Hanover Avenue, Richmond, Virginia; First Church, Walla Walla, Washington, and was preaching in the aristocratic Tidewater district of Virginia when he and his good wife became enamored with Christian Action. He was a deeply spiritual man and the author of several books including *Pentecost and the Holy Spirit* and *Altar Fires of Faith.* As a result of our friendship he was later persuaded to conduct a daily-devotions feature of the *Christian Standard* which was a great blessing to its readers for many years. Although his contacts through the years had been largely with the Indianapolis Establishment brethren, he said he had never known such wonderful fellowship as he experienced in our Christian Action gatherings. He too, was called across the nation for conferences and special meetings.

Harry Poll was my minister at Westwood-Cheviot Church, Cincinnati, during much of the Crusade. We had a rich and rewarding fellowship. He was most helpful with the management of the huge national gatherings, along with Aldis Webb and J. M. Appelgate. I do not know what I would have done without their aid in handling the thousand-and-one details involved. All this service was rendered without financial remuneration, but these men (and others like them) considered it to be a real privilege to thus serve the Lord and make it possible for thousands to enjoy the blessings of Lake James, Chautauqua, and Winona Lake. I shall make further references to these men later in my story.

Homer E. Sala was nationally known as pastor of First Church, Miami, Florida; First Church, Decatur, Illinois, and as a successful evangelist. He saw the need of special orientation of the Christian Action idea for the youth of our churches. So I asked him and his talented wife to assume responsibility for that feature of the program the first year at Winona Lake. Bethany Camp there was owned by R. G. LeTourneau, the road-building-machinery tycoon of Peoria. I knew him and told him what we had in mind. He very graciously and enthusiastically gave us without charge the use of the modern facilities of the Camp for the week. He and his wife whose summer home was nearby were frequent visitors in the sessions. The Salas brought hundreds of young people to Winona and were able to lead them to a closer walk with Christ. Many went out to become ministers, missionaries, and leaders in their local churches.

Ernest Hunter Wray, of Buffalo, New York, brought a very special contribution to all our gatherings. He had charge of the "hillside vespers." Wray had been pastor of the wealthy and prestigious Richmond Avenue Church in Buffalo but had become distressed over the worldliness of some of its leaders. After years of effort to "restore the New Testament life" there, he resigned amid the protests of hundreds of members. Some two hundred persuaded him to remain in Buffalo. They bought a beautiful Congregational Church building and organized the Pilgrim Church which prospered for many years under the leadership of the Wrays. Mrs. Wray was a Linthicum from one of the prominent families of Birmingham, Alabama, pillars of First Church there. I never knew a more consecrated and Christ-spirited couple in my life. Just to be in their presence was a benediction. Wray's messages were all heart-warming appeals for "complete and unwithholding commitment" to Christ. He could move his audiences deeply, often to tears — tears of repentance and recommitment! He gave an invitation at the close of each message. Scores would come forward to reconsecrate their lives to Christ, to repent and make restitution for any sins or shortcomings of which they were guilty, to be "crucified with Christ" that they might live more acceptably with Him. These vespers were unforgettable experiences and had tremendous repercussions for good in the lives of all who heard the inimitable Brother Wray.

Platform courtesies were extended to outstanding religious leaders beyond the usual "Standard" constituency. Among these were —

R. H. Boll, of Louisville, Kentucky, minister of the Fairview Church of Christ and principal of the Fairview Christian School, always led the morning devotions. He was undoubtedly the greatest expository preacher of the day in the Restoration Movement. The fact that he was of the "non-instrument" persuasion in no way hindered the loving acceptance he received from everyone. His series of studies in Romans was especially rich and inspiring and was published in book form. Boll was also a devout believer in prophecy and the Second Coming of Christ. One year, by strong demand on the part of many, he gave under his own auspices a series of afternoon lectures on these themes in the Winona Lake Presbyterian Church. The building was always crowded with eager listeners. Acquaintances formed in Christian Action gatherings led many of our ministers to invite Brother Boll to their churches for Bible studies and deeper life conferences.

Raphael Harwood Miller, minister of Independence Boulevard Christian Church, Kansas City, Missouri (later minister of National City Church, Washington, D. C., and editor of the *Christian-Evangelist*), the most popular pulpiteer of the Disciples in his day, was heartily welcomed to the platform. He boldly championed the work we were doing and hailed it as a means by which brotherhood unity might be recaptured.

Frederick D. Kershner, then dean of the College of Religion, Butler

University, was a frequent speaker. He saw Christian Action as the means of bringing a new spiritual note to the Restoration message.

G. Edwin Osborn, pastor of Hanover Avenue Church, Richmond, Virginia, and later of University Church, Enid, Oklahoma (father of Ronald E. Osborn) a longtime personal friend, was especially able in his expositions of the deeper life.

"Bill" Alexander was then a young but phenomenal preacher who drew thousands to hear him in the little Oklahoma town of Stroud. His radio audience numbered hundreds of thousands. Bill was the son of a St. Louis preacher, but had become a prodigal and had wandered into "far countries." Then he had been converted while a popular MC in a metropolitan night club and was giving his life to full-time Christian service. As he gave his moving testimony in Christian Action gatherings he proved the most dynamic of all our speakers. (This is the man who later became the popular pastor of the modern First Christian Church, Oklahoma City, and America's most sought-after luncheon club speaker.) Pardon me if I tell a little story of our personal relationships. Since I had given him his first national recognition, he sought my advice repeatedly concerning the course of his life. The Indianapolis Establishment recognized his unusual leadership abilities, advised him to go to the University of Chicago for further study, and provided the means of support. I warned him against such a step as I was certain his contacts there would rob him of his evangelical faith. He assured me that nothing could do that. He went and, at first, it seemed that his faith had weathered the withering attacks of liberalism. Then came offers from Hollywood where his flair for the dramatic had been recognized. Big sums promised by national lecture bureaus tempted him to enter that field. He turned them all down. Then came the tempting call to the wealthy and influential First Church, Oklahoma City. All the while he was writing me for guidance. I frankly told him what I knew of First Church — good and bad — and how I felt he could be used of God to make it a great spiritual power house with influences reaching far beyond the state and the Southwest. He accepted. His ability to draw audiences was again phenomenal. No available building could accommodate the crowds. Then men of wealth in his congregation bought a city park and poured millions of dollars into the creation of a "campus" complex of buildings, including a mammoth auditorium. I had my last letter from him when he introduced public dancing into the church's program. I knew then that the devil had taken control of his life. From then on there was no limit to the worldly appeals made for worldly acclaim. His sermons became demagogic and humanistic with the design to entertain. In his own theater he trained young people for the stage. In his great outdoor bowl the beauteous "Miss Oklahoma" was chosen each year. In a sensational and unprecedented action he and one of his elders traded wives, all parties concerned remaining in good standing in First Church. When the Republication nomination for U. S. Senator from Oklahoma was offered him, he accepted. Although defeated he became more widely known. As a speaker in commercial conventions and luncheon clubs across the country he commanded fabulous fees. It was while flying in his private plane to an engagement at York, Pennsylvania, that he was killed in a storm, thus ending a life that might have been given to the Lord in as rich and widespread a ministry as that of Billy Graham, but it was not to be.

Two noted evangelists of the time brought stirring messages in our Christian Action conferences — Charles Reign Scoville and William Edward Biederwolf. Scoville was in his declining years but he still had the power to bring commitment, this time to unwithholding and complete surrender of Christians to their Lord. Arlene Dux Scoville, his wife, and "sweet singer of Israel," always accompanied him and she herself contributed much to our gatherings. Biederwolf was a Presbyterian but well and favorably known to our people as the author of *The Growing Christian* and other books on the deeper life. He was one of our most effective platform speakers.

I must speak more fully of S. D. ("Quiet Talks") Gordon, who was with us each year and passed to his reward shortly after our last gathering. This great man, who did more to make prayer a living, vital force in American Protestantism in his day than any other man, had written a score of volumes of "Quiet Talks" on the whole gamut of life's problems beginning with *Quiet Talks on Prayer* and was Fleming H. Revell's most popular author. He stumbled into his speaking career by leading a series of talks on prayer in a YMCA summer camp in North Carolina in his early years. The whole camp was plunged into a prayer meeting the like of which had never been known. From then on the news of this experience traveled and he was in demand as a speaker in church conferences and conventions of all denominations. Gordon had an inimitable style. He was a small, slender, dark-bearded, unattractive creature, but when he "took charge" he commanded the undivided attention of everyone in his audience and thrilled them with one electric shock after another. He could use unusual words and phrases to state in unforgettable ways the wonderful truths about prayer as "the greatest power in the world." He would quote from the Bible and then illustrate its truths with stories from life. When he came to the conclusion of his messages he would pull out and open an old hunting-case watch, attached to a heavy gold chain, and assure his audience that he would close on time. Nobody wanted him to close on time. They would have stayed with him as long as he wanted to talk. But this strategy always brought deathly silence to the auditorium and a breathless hanging on each and every word. His contribution to these gatherings could have made us "a praying people" if enough of us had followed his guidance. Gordon felt that Christian Action was his last great ministry. He frequently wrote me afterward about the rewarding experiences he had in our meetings. Then came word from his wife and daughter that he had passed to the Great Beyond where prayer became eternal reality to a great soul.

The music was largely the great hymns of the church, in which everybody participated. There was little time for "special numbers" and absolutely no time for parading the egos of people who thought they could sing. We benefited immensely, however, from the leadership of consecrated musicians like the Payne Sisters (Mesdames Edwin G. and James E. Crouch), J. E. Sturgis, the Brocks, the Walkers, and many others. I have never heard greater and more heartfelt singing than in those Christian Action gatherings.

Scores of gatherings of a local or regional nature were held from coast to coast. Memories of a few of these might be of some interest:

Dean Kershner invited me to present the Christian Action idea to the students of the College of Religion at Butler University. Word of the event got about in Indianapolis and many of our ministers and church leaders helped fill Sweeney Chapel to capacity. After the presentation I was to conduct an open forum. I fielded query after query in a tremendously enlightening period, but it was abruptly halted by a dramatic and tragic happening. Old Brother B. L. Allen, who had established many churches in the Indianapolis area and was a "Campbellite" of the old school, arose and demanded time to "reply" to my "heretical ideas." He fulminated and gestured until he grew red in the face, accusing me of reverting to a "mourners' bench" religion and laying the foundation for the practice of "open membership." So violent did he become that he suffered a stroke, fell to the floor, and died within minutes. This, of course, ended the meeting. Dean Kershner was most friendly to the movement and at one time wrote an unusually commendatory article in his page ("As I Think on These Things") in the *Christian-Evangelist*. Many Butler men took an active interest in the work.

Once I was invited to speak in the historic Factory Methodist Church in Washington, D. C. Harry Earl Woolever, a leading member of the congregation, had been very much intrigued by the Christian Action idea and had distributed hundreds of our little folders, "What Is Christian Action?" in the District of Columbia area. He was a successful advertising and public relations man who had been moved of God to start a Prayer Crusade in the Methodist Church which was assuming nationwide proportions. He saw the value of adding a deeper Christian Life phase to his program and had called this meeting to consider necessary changes. I was met at the Union Station by a committee of interested professional men, taken to the National Press Club for lunch, and given a most hospitable reception. In my presentation at the church I encountered enthusiastic approval of the Christian Action idea with the result that many of its features were adopted in the Methodist program. To my surprise one of the members of the audience was the Hon. Wilbur Carr, Third Assistant U. S. Secretary of State. He was the originator and the director of the professional diplomatic corps of the United States government which came to form the hard core of our American foreign relations system. He served brilliantly under six presidents. At various times his work took him to the foreign field, notably as U. S. Ambassador to Czechoslovakia. Carr had been born and raised in Highland County, Ohio, and still kept his membership in the Union Church of Christ which I had served for eleven years as pastor. When he visited his relatives annually he was in my audience at the little chapel and we had many chats together at the old Carr homestead. He was deeply interested in Christian Action and on this occasion invited me to stay over and be his guest in his beautiful Washington mansion where so many state dignitaries had been entertained through the years. Altogether this Washington trip was a never-to-be-forgotten experience.

Speaking of the Methodists and Christian Action: I was surprised and pleased when the Wesleyan Methodist Young People's Board requested the use of *Studies in Christian Living,* one of our Christian Action texts, for their weekly Sunday evening youth meetings for an entire year. Their national journals carried lesson treatments and wide publicity was given the series. We had many favorable comments from these good people.

Just when the Crusade had reached its highest attainments in general acceptance and transformed lives, I was called into the office of the Standard management and told that I could expect no further support from them. My pages in the *Christian Standard* and *The Lookout* were closed to me. Further printing of Christian Action literature was cut off. I was told that they had been glad to encourage the crusade but that it would have to "go it on its own" from then on. My own time devoted to its promotion was severely cut. The real source of the trouble was the insistent demand on the part of reactionary forces in the Brotherhood (the same element that had infiltrated the Christian Restoration Association) that Murch be "fired" and Christian Action be disowned. They threatened to discontinue buying Standard literature in their churches and Bible schools if their demands were not heeded. They falsely and unjustly accused me of introducing "mourners' bench religion" and "open membership" in the churches, "compromising with the denominations," and neglecting the "fundamentals of the faith."

This development plunged me into one of the greatest crises of my life. Should I accept the consequences of the management's decision or should I resign and devote full time to the Crusade that God had so marvelously blessed? I had not been barred from further interest in the Crusade. I was offered an increase in salary and a promotion if I would undertake wider editorial responsibilities with the Company. There was no indication that there was any loss of confidence in my commitment to the Restoration Plea. When the news of the ultimatum got about I was besieged with urgent requests that I devote full time to the crusade. Well-to-do crusaders like the Lawsons of Akron, the Vinsons of Huntington, and the Higleys of Butler offered to underwrite such an undertaking. I devoted days of ardent prayer seeking the guidance of the Holy Spirit in my decision. I knew I had the devoted confidence and commitment of thousands in my leadership. This was an amazing situation. All I had to do was ask their support and I would have been flooded with responses. But I also realized that such a move would let loose a controversy in the Brotherhood that might well cause another division. All the reactionary forces would move in public attack against me and against Christian Action. In such an eventuality Murch would be the issue and not Christ. I could become another Eddy or a Buchman and the wealthy leader of another sect. I shuddered at the thought of it and came increasingly to the conviction that the great biblical truths and practices that I had espoused needed no copyright and would remain and prosper whether or not I promoted them in a "Christian Action Crusade." So I decided to remain at Standard, giving whatever time I could to the crusade as the Lord might open the way.

Immediately new leaders arose ready to take responsibilities. Robert D. Higley of the Higley Printing Company took over the printing and promotion of our literature. Our little monthly magazine, *Christian Action,* was enlarged and given a color cover; I wrote and Higley published *God Still Lives,* the story of how God had used my life in the crusade; and new *Christian Action Bible Studies* were published in quarterly form. Friends in Akron, Ohio, opened promotional offices there and underwrote expenses. Plans advanced for a great assembly at Winona Lake as though nothing had happened. On all fronts the crusade moved forward with renewed vigor. Our greatest national gathering was held that year.

Then an unforeseen cataclysm brought a sudden end to all organizational promotion. The United States was plunged into World War II. All public meetings were forbidden. Travel was severely restricted. Paper supplies and circulation lists were reduced by government order. All means of promotion except word of mouth were shut off. For three years these conditions obtained and our distinctive work was ended.

As I move about the nation I still meet many who tell me they are in the ministry, on the mission field or in active leadership in local churches because of the influence of the Christian Action crusade. Only God knows the extent of the Spiritual influences He released and the Kingdom accomplishments He achieved as a result of those precious years of renewal and revival.

Episode X

Christian Unity

One of the most thrilling by-products of the Christian Action Crusade was an effort to bring about a meaningful unity between the Christian Churches and Churches of Christ (a cappella). When I was in Toronto, Canada, for a Christian Action rally I met the elders of the Fern Street Church of Christ. The rally was held in the Keele Street Christian Church, but a fine delegation of twenty or more was present at every service from Fern Street. In my closing address I expressed the hope for breaking down the "middle wall of partition" which separated the two communions. After the service the Fern Street elders came to me expressing a similar hope. One of them suggested that I get in touch with Claud F. Witty, minister of the West Side-Central Church of Christ in Detroit, Michigan, who held similar hopes. I promised to write him as soon as I got home, and suggested that one of the elders also write him relating the circumstances under which we had come together. Brother Witty responded to my letter immediately and proposed an early meeting which might eventuate in a serious effort toward unity. I was elated and we were soon in conference.

But a little background: At this time it had been seventy years since the opening wedges of division began to do their deadly work in the Restoration Movement. We all sought to restore the New Testament Church in doctrine, ordinances, and life through an appeal to the Holy Scriptures. In our effort to "speak where the Bible speaks and be silent where the Bible is silent" we had clashed over the scripturality of "conventions," "missionary societies," "the Louisville plan," "editorial jealousies," "Sunday schools," "baptisteries," "lesson leaves," "choirs," "individual communion cups," "young people's societies," "ladies aid societies," "musical instruments," "shaped notes," "church colleges," "belfries and cupolas," "orphans' homes," etc., etc.

Feverish debates were conducted, hard feelings were fanned to white heat, and many local congregations were rent asunder. Editors of our religious journals, having the only effective means of brotherhood-wide approach, soon became the leaders of the various factions. Eventually two rather clearly defined camps emerged from the foggy thinking and chaotic conditions of the time — "conservative" and "progressive." The former group insisted upon no "innovations" — no practice of any kind for which there could not be given a "thus saith the Lord." The latter group held that where the Bible did not speak on a given issue it was a matter of opinion to be settled amicably by each local congregation.

Locally these groups were variously known as "organ" and "anti-organ," "missionary" and "anti-missionary," "college" and "anti-college," but in the beginning this divisive spirit was not able to shake off a common faith in the great fundamental principles which brought them into being and a mutual recognition of the ties that bound them together in a great common task.

For instance: My sainted father was a student in the College of the Bible at Lexington, Kentucky, in the days of McGarvey, Grubbs, Graham, and Loos. The faculty members were divided on the issues above mentioned. These differences were even discussed in the classroom. On the Lord's Day morning some would worship in "organ" churches and some in "anti-organ" churches. On Thursday night the ministerial students would often go in a body to the Chestnut Street Church (where there was no instrument) for instruction in music under Professor Klingman. For years this situation obtained in utmost good spirit, "each esteeming the other better than himself." Graduates went out from those classic halls — some to "progressive" and some to "conservative" churches. My father preached for both. I can well remember, as a lad, going with him to his "half-time" appointment at "Old South Liberty" and sitting through the worship service where a dozen big, stalwart farmers, sitting on the "front seat," led us in singing the old songs of Zion. Then the next Lord's Day we would go down to "Old Union" where they had the instrument. No one ever questioned my father's orthodoxy and he was equally acceptable in both pulpits.

As a child I never knew that there was any difference between the "Old South Liberty" and "Old Union" — they were both "our people" and both GOD'S PEOPLE!

But a later generation arose which "wist not that the Spirit of the Lord had departed" from them, and it was not long until the molehills became mountains and the valleys of opinion grew into chasms of division.

It is passing strange that any division should ever have been recorded in Government statistics in view of the Scriptural principle of congregational autonomy which has been so generally accepted by both groups. We have always held that no authority could be set up to speak officially for groups of congregations. While divisions might conceivably occur in local churches, there was no man or group of men who had the right to give "official" sanction to any "set-up" of "Christian Churches" or "Disciples of Christ" as opposed to "Churches of Christ."

Brother Witty and I talked and prayed and corresponded for about a year before we made bolder moves. He invited me to be his guest in Detroit and to preach one Lord's Day morning in West Side Central in its commodious structure purchased from the Lutherans. It was something unheard of for a "Disciple" minister to preach in a non-instrument "Church of Christ." The Detroit papers advertised the meeting; the 1500-seat auditorium was packed, and hundreds were turned away. I preached a simple Gospel sermon and was warmly received by all the people. Many came to me afterward expressing surprise — "Why," they said, "you preach just like Brother Witty, and tell it just like it is in the Bible." This experience persuaded us both that the climate was about ready for bolder moves.

On the following February 23, 1937, the first of a series of "conversations" between interested brethren was held in the Central Y.M.C.A. in Cincinnati. About an equal number of "progressive" and "conservative" leaders were present. The *Christian Leader* of April 13, in commenting on the meeting, said: "A general friendly spirit pervaded the meeting. Prayer was made. Each one present was privileged to speak his sentiments on the occasion. Many helpful thoughts were presented — fine suggestions made — the necessity and beauty of unity stressed — many of the mutual problems discussed and not a few of the differences referred to, to be handled in future meetings. In all, it was a great and good day when men from opposing sides could sit face to face and talk, plan, and hope that eternal good might spring from this first, perhaps a series, of meetings, each filled with 'Thus saith the Lord,' to the end that perhaps thousands may be knit together in the bonds of peace and unity that today are separated by a chasm which needs eradicating."

Brother Witty and I then agreed on a simple plan to be publicized and presented to all the brethren everywhere. We called it —

AN APPROACH TO UNITY

1. PRAYER. Definite private and congregational prayer for unity, seeking to determine how much we have in common in faith and practice.

2. SURVEY. Seeking to determine how much we have in common in faith and practice.

3. FRIENDLINESS. Establishing individual friendly relations by exchange of fraternal courtesies and through fellowship meetings.

4. COOPERATION. In enterprises which will not do violence to our personal or group convictions.

5. STUDY AND DISCUSSION. Openminded study and humble discussion of the things which at present divide us, in order to discover the way to complete a permanent unity.

Indianapolis, Indiana, was the scene of our second meeting; Akron, Ohio, the third; Columbus, Indiana, the fourth. Meetings in Southern California were also held at Ontario and Los Angeles. In the very nature of the case there was no official character to such meetings. The brethren attending came without let or hindrance and represented nobody but themselves. There were no motions made, no resolutions passed. One or two thoughtful papers were presented dealing with the problems and issues involved. In each meeting several new men were contacted and the circle grew wider and wider.

Then we envisioned a platform meeting of more general character in which ministers of each group in equal number might preach on the

128

great fundamentals of the faith and stress the aims which we hold in common in the Restoration Movement. The minister, the eldership, and the membership of the Westside-Central Church of Christ in Detroit, Michigan, joined in placing their facilities at our disposal for this meeting. We called it the first "National Unity Meeting" and it was held May 3, 4, 1938, drawing large audiences. More than a thousand persons heard messages delivered by George Benson, H. H. Adamson, and J. N. Armstrong of the Churches of Christ and W. R. Walker, P. H. Welshimer, and O. A. Trinkle of the Christian Churches. So encouraging was the meeting that Trinkle invited us to the Englewood Christian Church in Indianapolis for 1939. Then followed national meetings in the Church of Christ at Lexington, Kentucky, the Indianola Christian Church in Columbus, Ohio, and other important centers of Brotherhood life.

Such meetings continued with encouraging interest for several years. Some fifty key men from each communion braved the criticism of many of their brethren to make valuable contributions to the venture. The chief accomplishments were: (1) a growing personal acquaintance among the brethren of both groups; (2) a growing knowledge of the current status of the churches — their teaching, their programs, their problems, their aims and accomplishments; (3) a frank study and discussion of the obstacles to unity, the impelling motives toward it, and possible methods of achieving it; (4) dramatizing and publicizing the five-point approach; and (5) the creation of a spirit of prayer and surrender to God's will as supremely important requisites to any such endeavor.

A *Christian Unity Quarterly,* edited jointly by Witty and Murch, was launched as a medium of free discussion and promotion. The *Christian Standard* gave generous space to addresses delivered in the gatherings and heartily supported the effort. A tract, *Christian Unity: Churches of Christ and Christian Churches,* was distributed by hundreds of thousands of copies. The *Christian-Evangelist* was friendly. Among the more conservative periodicals of the churches of Christ, only the *Christian Leader* and the *Word and Work* were openly friendly. The *Gospel Advocate* was at first violent in its opposition, but later joined with the *Firm Foundation* in studiously ignoring the movement. The latter two were the most widely circulated and influential of these papers.

During the years of rapprochement there were many incidents which deserve a record in history. In Indianapolis a lively and enlightening exchange developed between H. Leo Boles, editor of the *Gospel Advocate,* and Edwin R. Errett, editor of the *Christian Standard,* establishing the fact that both groups were equally zealous in their acceptance of the Bible alone as their rule of faith and practice.

W. R. Walker delivered a history-making address interpreting the "silences" of Campbell's dictum, "Where the Scriptures speak, we speak; where the Scriptures are silent, we are silent." I delivered a paper at

Columbus, Ohio, on "What I Believe About Instrumental Music," giving a new approach to the problem.

The Board of Church Extension, the Pension Fund, and the National Benevolent Association of the Disciples of Christ offered their services, without distinction or limitation, to the Churches of Christ. E. L. Jorgenson of the Churches of Christ edited a hymnbook, *Great Songs of the Church,* which was published by the Standard Publishing Company for use in Christian churches. (I prepared the Responsive Readings for the book.)

Witty was invited to read a paper before the International Convention's Commission on Restudy and to speak at Butler School of Religion, Minnesota Bible College, the Michigan State Ministers' Meeting of the Christian Churches, and the North American Christian Convention. I was invited to preach in Churches of Christ in Louisville, Nashville, Detroit, and other places.

An encouraging independence of friendly thought and action developed among young ministers of both communions. Lines were crossed in occasional exchanges of pulpits, and lecturers from one group were invited to speak in colleges and seminaries of the other.

Prayer meetings for unity were held at the graves of Campbell, Stone, and McGarvey, great leaders of the past whom both groups highly regard.

Some of these activities continue, with varying success and interest, in various parts of the country. One of the most significant later developments was led by Ernest Beam, a minister of the Churches of Christ in California, who in 1950 launched a new journal, *The Christian Forum,* dedicated to the promotion of unity. Until his death in the late 1950's he served as minister of congregations including members and practices of both groups.

A number of personal experiences stand out in memory of our "Unity Effort" —

Louisville, Kentucky, brethren arranged a demonstration of unity in which I preached one Lord's Day morning in the Highland Avenue Church of Christ, E. L. Jorgensen, minister, and in the evening at the Crescent Hill Christian Church, Joseph H. Garshaw, minister. My audiences were most responsive and included brethren of both persuasions in each instance. Then, as a part of the plan, I addressed a joint meeting of around eighty ministers of both groups on Monday morning at the Christian Church Homes of Kentucky. My theme was "The Deeper Spiritual Meaning of the Lord's Supper." In the open forum which followed there were many expressions of hope for closer fellowship. All of us were guests of the Homes at lunch, ending what proved to be a very worthwhile experience. I stayed over a day as the guest of the *Word and Work* brethren Janes, Boll, Clark, Jorgensen, and others. Janes' print shop was producing our *Christian Unity Quarterly* on a cost basis and it was a pleasure to form a personal acquaintance with this good man. He was largely responsible at this time for the development of the tragically weak missionary conscience of the a cappella brethren. He did not live to see the day when they were to excel in this important phase of the church's work. How he would have rejoiced in seeing his dreams come true!

Another rich experience was being the guest of E. W. McMillan and the Central Church of Christ, in Nashville, Tennessee. This was the leading congregation of the non-instrument brethren in Nashville (often called their "Jerusalem," with over a hundred congregations in the metropolitan area). In an unprecedented action on the part of the elders I was invited to offer the morning prayer at the Lord's Day service. More than a thousand people were in the audience. Then I was given the privilege of conducting the church's Monday morning devotional radio broadcast from the church's studios in the building. Brother J. W. Shepherd (who, with David Lipscomb, was responsible for the separate listing of the Church of Christ in the U. S. Government Religious Census) took me for a tour of the church properties which included modern dormitory facilities for single working men and single working women. We spent much time in the library which Shepherd was seeking to develop as the finest Restoration book collection owned by any congregation in the Brotherhood. I remember his gift of an autographed copy of his comprehensive and scholarly *Handbook on Baptism* which I have treasured through the years. A half dozen leading Church of Christ ministers and laymen entertained me at lunch in the Hermitage Hotel and afterward gave me a tour of the McQuiddy Printing and Office Supply plant where the *Gospel Advocate* was published.

The editor of the *Advocate*, H. Leo Boles, one of the bitterest opponents of our Unity Effort, was conveniently absent. Our reception by the management was most cordial. Indeed (and after many years it can be told), one of the McQuiddy brothers asked me to come into his private office. After he had asked me to be seated, he closed the door and said, "Brother Murch, I am glad to see you and Brother Witty engaged in your good work. I am praying for God to bless you. Of course, Brother Boles and his associates are using the *Advocate* to oppose you. This is the only thing they can do. If they approved your work thousands of our elders and college professors would rise up and boycott the *Advocate* and our company, which handles the major part of the book and supply business of our churches. We have to go along with their policy. I wanted you to know my personal feelings in the situation. We are delighted to have you visit us and to extend to you a hearty invitation to honor us by your presence whenever you are in Nashville. As far as I am concerned, I consider you a full brother in Christ. May the Lord bless you!"

It is impossible to describe the deep emotional experience of the trip with Brother Witty to Kentucky where we visited the scenes of the great Cane Ridge Revival. We sat in the old log meeting-house near Paris and talked and prayed about the unity of God's people. Then we visited the grave of Barton W. Stone in the nearby cemetery. In Lexington we visited the classrooms where J. W. McGarvey taught for so many years and then his burial-place in the Lexington Cemetery. There we had photographs taken which I have long treasured. We felt the moving of the spirits of "just men made perfect" urging us on in a work which often seemed futile but yet a work that must be done.

Then came a tragic development. A series of circumstances forced my retirement from the editorial staff of Standard (the story of which will be duly related later on). It became apparent that I could no longer command the respect and cooperation of all the brethren involved in the Unity Effort. It was mutually agreed that I should withdraw from leadership and someone else agreeable to the Standard management be chosen to work with Brother Witty. Another "National Unity Meeting" was soon to be held, using the facilities of Cincinnati Bible Seminary, and quick action had to be taken.

Standard chose Peyton H. Canary to succeed me. Canary was a highly-educated Ph.D. from Indiana University and well-equipped man for the position. He had held places of trust as an educator and a minister. Under his leadership he brought the Madisonville Church in Cincinnati to a membership of more than a thousand. Later he was to be president (and owner) of the ill-fated Southwest Christian Seminary at Phoenix, Arizona. Because of his temperamental eccentricities, however, I feared for the future of the movement. Plans went forward for the Cincinnati meeting and it drew a large attendance. Then an untoward incident occurred. Brother Witty and I had always agreed to the program personnel of the meetings and we always deferred to each other's ideas and opinions as to proper limitations in the conduct of the meetings. Canary had invited Ernest Beam (to whom reference has previously been made) to read a paper. At first Witty opposed his choice but later consented. Then Canary made plans to have the paper mimeographed and distributed following Beam's appearance, because he felt his views constituted a telling blow against the usually-accepted a cappella position. When Witty learned of the plan he promptly demanded that there be no distribution of any of the addresses. As I got the story, in his conversation with Witty, Canary acquiesced. But he secretly arranged for a group of CBS students to pass out the papers. When Witty learned of this he frankly told Canary he could have no further confidence in him and withdrew all contact with the Unity Effort. And that was that! There were subsequent gatherings of interested brethren in various sections of the country, but the movement lost momentum and finally died.

There is no question but that much good was accomplished in the "Unity Effort" and that the Lord used many of our plans and programs to His glory. This is a "continued story" and I shall have much more to say about Christian unity later on in my Memoirs. I recall, in this connection, an incident in Los Angeles in 1969. Following the Commencement address at Pepperdine College, as I was marching in the Academic procession, my partner suddenly remarked, "Brother Murch, this could not have happened in the days when you and Brother Witty were promoting your Unity Effort. The time was not ripe for it, but now the climate has changed in the Restoration Movement and all for the better." So mote it be!

I was just as deeply concerned about unity with those brethren who remained in cooperation with the International Convention, the United Christian Missionary Society, and other related agencies, as I was about the brethren to the Right. I was persuaded that at this time the great majority of our people were committed to the Christ of the Scriptures and to God's Holy Word. I felt, as I have previously stated, that we had no scriptural or ethical right to make the support of particular agencies a test of fellowship, or to build up a "middle wall of partition" that would keep men of like faith from cooperation in all matters that did not require compromise of basic and essential Christian doctrine. This position I took long ago, and to which I have adhered ever since, I believe to be scriptural and entirely within the will of God.

So when I was invited to become a member of the International Convention's "Commission on Restudy of the Disciples of Christ" I accepted with joy. I was not appointed on the original Commission, which was authorized at the Des Moines Convention in 1934. I was asked to fill a vacancy about halfway in the history of its existence. The meetings were held in the Marrott apartment hotel in Indianapolis, perfectly equipped for our purposes. The fellowship during the meetings was ideal.

It was not long until I was able to determine "who was who" right, left, and center in thought and practice in Commission personnel. It was apparent that there were (1) the Biblical exclusivists who accepted the Holy Scriptures as authoritative and normative, and were committed to the movement to restore the New Testament Church in doctrine, ordinances, and life; (2) the biblical inclusivists who were personally sound in doctrine but were ready to compromise their beliefs and their commitment to the Restoration plea to maintain a united front (which I call "the Disciples Establishment"); and (3) the liberal left wing who were committed to the rationalistic view of the Scriptures and all beliefs and practices that might be grouped under the banner of *modernism* or *liberalism*. ("Ecumenicism" had not yet appeared on the scene.)

Commission members that might be grouped under the third classification were led by the brilliant, irenic, and ecumenically-minded Charles Clayton Morrison and included Edward Scribner Ames, H. C. Armstrong, Eugene C. Beach, George A. Campbell, Charles M. Chilton, A. W. Fortune, W. E. Garrison, Henry G. Harmon, Edgar DeWitt Jones, Clarence E. Lemmon, and Willard E. Shelton.

Those of the second category were led by Raphael Harwood Miller, highly-intelligent and illustrious Brotherhood leader, respected by all of us. His associates were L. D. Anderson, George Walker Buckner, F. W. Burnham, Homer W. Carpenter, Abram E. Cory, Stephen J. England, Graham Frank, Claude E. Hill, Hugh B. Kilgour, William F. Rothenberger, M. E. Sadler, O. L. Shelton, G. Gerald Sias, George H. Stewart, and L. N. D. Wells.

Dean E. Walker was the most logical and succinct thinker and polemicist of the conservatives. (None of the groups had, so far as I know, actually chosen a leader. The men I am naming here as "leaders" were, to my way of thinking, the outstanding advocates of their respective schools of thought in the plenary sessions of the Commission and in the sub-committees which formulated findings and definitive statements.) Associated with Walker were F. D. Kershner, Edwin R. Errett, Robert M. Bell, Virgil L. Elliott, Joseph H. Dampier, Orval M. Morgan, T. K. Smith, William E. Sweeney, Robert S. Tuck, P. H. Welshimer, J. J. Whitehouse, and I.

In 1946 the Commission made a frank and honest report to the Convention in which it outlined the views of the three schools of thought on the character of the Movement, local church autonomy, conventions, Christian unity, baptism, faith and doctrine, and opinions and liberty (see pp. 264-267 in my book, *Christians Only*). Then in 1947 it reported on points of agreement to which a majority of the Commission members subscribed. This report was the highlight of the confrontations and read as follows:

"We find that the great body of Disciples agree that:

1. The acknowledgment of Jesus Christ as Lord and Saviour is the sole affirmation of faith necessary to the fellowship of Christians.

2. The New Testament is the primary source of our knowledge concerning the will of God and the revelation of God in Christ, and is the authoritative Scripture by which the will of God is conveyed to men.

3. Each local church is, under Christ, a self-governing unit; that organizations and agencies are in no sense governing bodies but may be useful instruments in carrying on Christian work and in fostering and expressing fellowship; that likewise congregations and individuals have the inherent right to initiate and carry on Christian work through directly supported enterprises without breach of the wider fellowship; and that the unity of the whole church in faith, fellowship, and service is to be earnestly sought.

4. In the proclamation of the gospel of Christ as the message of salvation to the affection and intelligence of men, we have found our largest unity. The Great Commission demands that to make this "one world" we must first make it God's world, by the universal acceptance of Christ as Saviour. This acceptance of Christ can be attained only by the recovery of the apostolic passion for the proclamation of the message, regarding the method as incidential. "That the world may

be saved" is our only hope of unity. The message of salvation in Christ is the only business of the Church.

5. The unity of Christians according to the program and prayer of our Lord, with Christ himself the center of that unity, by the restoration of New Testament Christianity, is necessary to the realization of God's program for human redemption.

6. Their historical position has given them practical insight into the New Testament fellowship which they desire to share with the whole divided body of Christ.

In the light of this body of unifying principles and sentiments of faith and practice, the Commission has come to the conclusion that we ought to take courage, and address ourselves to active endeavors to magnify our unity and rally our people to ardent advocacy of these central agreements. The Commission therefore proposes:

1. That, recognizing that the unity of the Church must be maintained by constant care, all who occupy positions of trust in both congregations and general work might well examine their work in the light of the above unifying center.

2. That we all seek opportunities of expressing our conviction that diversity of methods in Christian activities is no barrier to the fellowship of Christian men.

3. That we all magnify our agreement in belief of the Gospel — "in faith unity": here there must be unity; and all grant freedom in opinions and methods — "in opinions liberty": here there must be liberty; and in charity and Christian love each must seek to excel the other.

4. That, since the Word of God transmitted to us in the New Testament is of primary significance to the Church, we all give ourselves to a continuous study of the New Testament Church in respect to its origin and nature, its structure and function, its mission and hope.

In loyalty to Jesus Christ, we believe, lies the hope of unity for the whole Church of Christ. To accept, let alone advocate, division, would be, we believe, supreme disloyalty to our Lord. To give ourselves to advocacy of unity as encompassed above is, we believe, our mission in loyalty to our Lord (1947 *Year Book,* pp. 116, 117).

In 1948 the Commission asked to be relieved of its responsibilities and be dismissed, but it proposed that its findings be given wide publicity throughout the Brotherhood by publication in the church press and in ministers' meetings, conventions, conferences, and rallies where grassroots consideration of the issues involved might take place. I strongly supported the strategic proposal. But this was the last that was heard of this sincere plan to bring meaningful unity to the ranks of the "Disciples of Christ" in America. Someone or some coterie of leaders in the Establishment turned thumbs down on the idea and it was buried in the dust of the ages. If I had not resurrected the official pronouncements of the Commission and published them in my chapter on "Attempts at Reconciliation" in my history, *Christians Only,* the "powers that be" would have been able to get away with the lie they so assiduously propagated: "Conservatives would never sit down with us and sincerely seek to heal the wounds of division among us."

There are many personal memories of events which took place during my years on the Commission. I was asked to prepare the definitive paper on Church Polity which was presented at one of the plenary sessions. This assignment initiated my interest in the subject, which continued over many years and eventuated in my book, *The Free Church.* My paper was well received. In fact it made such a favorable impression on "Raphe" Miller that he asked for permission to print it in the *Christian-Evangelist.* I gladly consented. This was the first and only time I ever had a major article published in that journal.

When the day came for final adjournment of the Commission I was asked to have charge of the closing devotional. I think that this was the doing of Raphe Miller, because of our association in the Christian Action Crusade. I chose Colossians 3:1-15 as the basis of a brief expository appeal. I elaborated on the idea of our oneness in Christ and what was involved if we were to continue in that fellowship. Above all, I said in the words of the text, it is imperative that "forbearing one another and forgiving one another" we "put on love, which is the bond of perfectness and let the peace of God rule in our hearts."

Years afterward (1960) at the Louisville Convention, Dr. Morrison, editor of the *Christian Century,* "buttonholed" me in the lobby of the convention hall one noon and said, "I have always wanted to tell you how much I appreciated your devotional message and prayer at Indianapolis. It spoke the feelings of my heart then and still does."

My concern for Christian unity extended to our Baptist brethren. During the period in which so-called "official" negotiations were being carried on, the Northern Baptists were losing hundreds of churches and thousands of members to the Southern Baptists, the General Association of Regular Baptist Churches, and the Conservative Baptist Association of America. In these centrist Baptist bodies, and among brethren of like mind in the Northern Baptist Convention, there were individual pastors who were interested in rapprochement with Centrist Disciples. P. H. Welshimer and I carried on a rather extensive correspondence with such men. The problem of "baptismal regeneration" again appeared as the chief barrier to agreement and cooperation. In correspondence with Gabriel R. Guedj, then pastor of the famed Brooklyn Temple, I stated the generally held Disciples' view as follows:

Conservative Disciples believe the Bible teaches that salvation is basically by grace through faith in the atoning work of Christ. Faith, however, must be demonstrated (James 2:17; I John 5:2,3). Christ commanded baptism (Matthew 28:18-20) and was himself baptized to fulfill all righteousness. Peter, by the Holy Spirit, commanded baptism on the Day of Pentecost (Acts 2:38). In this sense Disciples believe that baptism is essential to salvation. The Bible teaches (I John 2:3-6) that refusal to obey a command of Christ is a demonstration of a lack of saving faith. The unimmersed are therefore denied membership in local churches of Christ. Without too much concern for systematic theology Disciples accept such Scripture texts as the following as buttressing their belief in the essentiality of baptism to salvation: Romans 6:3,4; Mark 16:15,16; I Peter 3:21; Galatians 3:27. They would object to any such view as expressed by Dr. Strong in his *Systematic Theology:* "(Baptism) is the appointed sign but never the condition of forgiveness of sins."

A number of conservative Baptists agreed that this statement could well be a basis for friendly discussions and that such a position should not necessarily preclude eventual unity. Closer relationships between these groups wait on aggressive leadership deeply concerned for the unity of the people of God.

Episode XI

Standard Publishing Company

My return to the editorial staff of Standard Publishing in 1933, while ostensibly to promote the Christian Action crusade, was, I have since been persuaded, in the thinking of the management, primarily for advancing the merchandise business of the company. This statement is not made critically, because they were most generous with me in placing their contacts and facilities at my disposal in the promotion of my "magnificent obsession." Had they not done this the success of Christian Action would have been delayed many years. But I had been designated "Book Editor" or "Literary Editor" (Standard at this time was not too particular about editorial titles) and I endeavored to render a service commensurate with my position.

The first product for which I was responsible was the preparation of the *Christian Ministers' Manual*. The Christian Churches and the Churches of Christ at this time had no adequate handbook of ministerial ethics, administrative guidance, forms for occasional and special services, marriages and funerals. I enlisted the aid of leading ministers who gladly assisted me in the preparation of a book which soon became the most popular and widely-used aid of its kind in the history of the Restoration Movement. It is at the time of this writing still a "best seller" in its field. Strangely enough it was voluntarily accepted by all three sectors of the Brotherhood and has been long in demand by Baptists and other "free church" communions.

I succeeded E. W. Thornton in my position. Because of failing health he had left much "unfinished business" on his desk which I endeavored to complete and process according to his plans. One of these items was a projected book of doctrinal illustrations of a distinctly Restoration flavor. He had collected about two hundred illustrations by contacting our outstanding "doctrinal" preachers, but they had not been classified or edited in any way. I saw the value of such a book and immediately opened correspondence with more than a thousand ministers to increase the number of illustrations necessary for an adequate volume. The response was most encouraging. J. Vernon Jacobs, of the editorial staff, was assigned the task of putting the materials in manuscript form. He did yeoman service and made it possible for us to complete and publish *600 Doctrinal Illustrations*, the only book of its kind ever produced for the distinctive use of the Restoration Movement. Several other book manuscripts in various stages of development and initiated by Thornton were processed in my early years in this position.

Growing out of the devotional emphasis in the Christian Action crusade

138

came the first daily devotional publications of Standard. They were annuals: *Altar Fires of Faith* and *Living for Jesus,* containing Bible readings and meditations. The first was authored by J. B. Hunley, who had contributed so effectively to devotional phases of our Christian Action programs. The second contained helps from 350 men who had been active in our crusade in various ways, their contributions being arranged under such general headings as: (1) Individual Life, (2) Home Life, (3) Social Life, (4) Business Life, and (5) Religious Life . Thus began a publications feature which has been continuously perpetuated by the company in various forms ever since.

I worked very closely with T. B. Booth, who was head of the Merchandise Department. All books and church and Sunday-school supplies produced by the Company had to have his approval before they went to press. Booth had come to Standard from the Christian Board of Publication and had a history of valuable contacts with the "trade," including such firms as Methodist Book Concern and Broadman Press. He saw the possibility of developing a monumental business in Sunday-school and non-doctrinal materials by expanding our market for these products throughout the Protestant world. Standard already had a good name because of its superior art collection and its incomparable offset color printing facilities. Booth strongly urged me to devote more of my time to creating new merchandise ideas in this field.

One of my first ventures was in gift booklets — 32-page collections of Bible verses, poetry, and commentary containing a wealth of full-color pictures from Standard's collection. The first was *Prelude to Prayer.* It was an immediate and long-run success, eventually reaching a circulation in the millions. Later came *Cheer Along the Way* designed for gifts to the sick and discouraged. It matched the first booklet in sales and was widely used by churches and Bible classes in their hospital calls. For many years the Salvation Army distributed thousands of them. Among other booklets in this series were: *Victorious Christian Living, The Call of the Church, Holy Matrimony, Discipleship, Bible Treasures, Precious Promises of God, Portals to Bible Study,* etc. During this period and long after I left the Company church publishing-house catalogs of all denominations carried pictures, descriptions, and prices of these booklets, which testified to a steady and ever-increasing demand for them. Through the years I have had thousands of people tell how much they have been helped and blessed by these booklets.

A stream of ideas for pins, badges, Special Day invitation post-cards, and other Sunday-school supplies were originated in my office and processed for the Merchandise Department. While I became a bit restive about having my time occupied with such minutiae, Booth was greatly pleased that someone on our staff had qualified as an "idea man." His sales soared and surpassed all former records in this field. Booth was a master salesman. As he made his periodic visits to the publishing houses he was "in his glory" when his products received enthusiastic acceptance. He would come home from his trips with a big, broad smile and say, "Well, what do you have up your sleeve for next season?"

There was a grave weakness, however, in the quality of Standard's educational books and books of methods available for use in the Sunday schools. Herbert Moninger had written *Training for Service,* which had phenomenal acceptance. It was still selling well in revised form — due to the fine work of C. J. Sharp. But there was little else Booth could offer "the trade." It was then I was able to create a whole new comprehensive series of training manuals based on my definitive textbook, *Christian Education and the Local Church.* This text was designed for use in Advanced Leadership Training courses and in elementary classes in Christian colleges, Bible seminaries and institutes. I had a hard time convincing the management that such an "advanced" book would sell. They said it was "too highbrow and intellectual" for the market. But in order to get the whole idea moving they reluctantly consented to publish it. I had to waive my royalty rights in the "bargain" we struck. Today that book is still in great demand. At one time it was the most popular text in its field in the evangelical training schools and colleges of more than thirty denominations. In the "bargain" I agreed to produce an 80-page digest of the book which we called the *Sunday School Handbook,* a best seller for many years. Around my book I built a set of training texts for each department of the school. Adult, *The Adult Teacher and Leader,* was authored by C. W. Brewbaker; Youth, by Mildred Welshimer; Intermediate, by Ross J. Griffeth; Junior, by Orval Ray Burgess; Primary, by Lillie A. Faris; and Beginner, by Evelyn Leavitt Grogg. Many new items in the way of special studies, such as *Through the Bible in a Year with Juniors* and Vacation Bible School texts, made their appearance. There were chalk-talk guides, object lessons, dramatizations, and other forms of so-called visual aids that flowed from the presses as we sought to serve the growing educational needs of the schools. There were life guidance books for adolescent boys and girls by Roscoe Gilmore Stott and Helen Welshimer. Also a considerable number of Sunday-school methods books or brochures such as *How to Build a Successful Men's Class* by Earl Hanson Fife; *How to Lead a Bible School* by W. E. Raffety; *Success with Intermediates* by Mrs. Owen Still, and *The Workers' Conference* by Henrietta Heron. "T. B." became one of my warmest friends and that friendship endured until his death. I never worked with any man at Standard who was more appreciative of my efforts and more cooperative in the achievement of high ideals for Church and Sunday-school publications.

I was never satisfied with our book publication program for the churches and the Restoration Movement in particular. Of course Standard had a great backlog of classic books in this field which continued to serve the needs of ministers, elders, and church workers, but I felt we were failing to keep abreast of current needs, and to reinterpret the Restoration plea in more relevant terms for our day. The actual publications in this field under my administration, besides *Christian Ministers' Manual* and *600 Doctrinal Illustrations,* were: *Concerning the Disciples* by P. H. Welshimer; *A Ministering Ministry* and *A Functioning Eldership* by W. R. Walker; *Training for Personal Evangelism* by C. J. Sharp; *Thomas Campbell* by W. H. Hanna; *A Popular Outline of Church History* by F. J. Gielow; *The Great American Revival* by Strickland, and *Great Songs of the Church* compiled by E. L. Jorgensen. I had plans for the development of a series of "workbooks" for use in Bible classes and midweek meetings, utilizing a new teaching technique just coming into use in the public schools. J. H. Dampier took the first assignment and produced the *Workbook on Christian Doctrine,* still widely used in our churches. The next I had in mind was a *Workbook on Acts* but did not get to carry through my plans. Other projects got no further than the dream stage: a series of *Classics of the Restoration Movement* including the "Declaration and Address," and "The Sermon on the Law;" *A Commentary on the Holy Scriptures* including all the books of the Bible, authored exclusively by our own best scholars; *A Comprehensive History of the Restoration Movement* (which I later wrote myself under the title *Christians Only*). Too, I had an idea for the development of a *Standard Sermon Quarterly* to meet the demand for the best in current homiletic material; something comparable to *The Pulpit* (a monthly which the *Christian Century* had recently launched). This phase of publication was always discouraged by the management in favor of profit-producing items for "the trade."

When I made my difficult decision to abandon promotion of the Christian Action Crusade as my major concern, Standard promoted me to "Managing Editor" or "Editorial Secretary," giving me editorial responsibility for all its publications with the exception of the *Christian Standard.* I had been quite critical of the quality of the Uniform Bible Lesson Series and the Standard Graded Lesson Series of quarterlies being provided for our Bible schools. I was immediately given *carte blanche* to make whatever changes I believed essential to provide "the finest true-to-the-Bible Sunday-school lesson materials" available from any publishing house in America. Standard had the facilities to do just this and I went to work with high hopes and great enthusiasm. I reviewed the products of all the major publishing houses in this field. I scanned the horizon for new writers, artists, and educational experts. I reorganized the editorial staff responsible for production, held individual and group conferences, and set up quarterly meetings of the editorial staff and writers. To make these meetings more impressive and meaningful they were usually held in formal surroundings at the Hotel Gibson. We usually had an imported speaker of note who dealt with the broader phases of our task, followed by an open forum. As an example, we had Rabbi Victor Reichert, Cincinnati's leading philologist, in an especially rewarding session. There were reports of progress in our publication program, exhibits of new art subjects and new catalog items. These meetings did much for morale and gave all our editors and writers a feeling of participation in a worthwhile enterprise.

The editors during this period were J. Vernon Jacobs, Adult publications; Fred J. Gielow and Mildred Welshimer, Youth; and Lillie Faris and Dorothy Poulton, Children; with associates Virginia Baley, Verda Bloomhuff, Alma Ingram, and Georgia Hubbell. Often participating in the meetings were Edwin R. Errett, Guy P. Leavitt, W. R. Boebinger, Mildred Covington, Maude Stevens, Dorothy Errett, and Helen Lyons, together with such members of the administrative and production staffs as might be concerned with the particular problems under discussion.

As we approached the huge undertaking of complete revision of the Uniform and Graded Lesson materials, I felt the necessity for a cooperative study in depth of the educational task of the local church school in the light of modern educational progress. Accordingly we took the key members of our editorial staff to Spring Mill Inn, a beautiful hostelry set in the midst of a thousand acres of virgin timber, near Mitchell, Indiana, for ten days of intensive study, conference, and planning. As a result of this historic gathering came not only the guidelines for our undertaking but a "Manual for Christian Education Advance" prepared by Fred Gielow, Guy Leavitt and me, which became the basis for a national educational campaign promoted effectively in the thousands of schools being served by Standard Publishing Company.

We first undertook the revision of the Uniform Series — the most important catalog item and the biggest money producer for the Company. The reader would not be interested in the details of the accomplishment. Suffice to say, we followed the "Manual" in the preparation of materials resulting in vast improvement in the educational value of our quarterlies, both teacher's and pupil's. But the most noticeable improvement was in format and graphic art. We took the Adult and Youth teacher's quarterlies, combined them, and produced a new publication called *The Standard Bible Teacher and Leader*. It was magazine size, printed on quality paper with a Bible art cover in full color. Then we took *Baby's Mother* and the *Home Department Quarterly*, combined them, and produced the *Christian Home Magazine*, likewise in color and in magazine size and quality. These were our feature items of the new series. In order to produce these modern eye-appealing "books" it was necessary to contract with Lakeside Press in Chicago, the printers of *Time, Life*, and other nationally-known magazines. (It is interesting to note that Donnelley's salesman who handled our job was James N. Johnson, who later became the President and General Manager of Standard Publishing.) The remainder of the items were produced in our own plant. Adult and Youth quarterlies for pupils were reduced to *Reader's Digest* format, pocket or purse size. Junior and Primary teacher's and pupil's quarterlies and class papers utilized Standard's superb Bible art subjects in color to make a tremendously attractive appeal. When this new series hit the display rooms of the religious bookstores across the country there was an

142

immediate increase in orders. I remember being in Boston about this time and paying a special visit to the city's largest religious bookstore on Beacon Hill. I asked to see a copy of the new *Standard Bible Teacher and Leader*. The saleslady threw up her hands and said, "We have only one copy, which you may see, but our stock is completely depleted because of the demand. This is the hottest item in the Sunday-school field today. We can take your order, however, and supply your needs immediately." Within the next few years all sales records were broken in the Uniform Series.

The revision of the Graded Series was next "on the boards" but my sudden departure from Standard precluded my finishing this very important phase of the undertaking.

Another project related to the revision was discovering modern artists who could produce Bible art that was relevant to the new day. Otto Stemler had done a marvelous job in his copies of much of the traditionally famous Bible art of the centuries and in originals which followed the style of the traditional schools. Standard would never have achieved its status as the leading collector of Bible Art in the religious publishing field if it had not been for Otto Stemler. We were good friends and worked together *en rapport* for many years. The reproducitons of his work by experts in offset color printing were rich and appealing with the result that Standard controlled the major portion of the Sunday-school publishing business in this field. At one time some thirty religious publishers were our clients. The salesmanship of M. Y. Thomas had much to do with this success. But the day came when Provident developed into a dangerous competitor, backed by the "International Council of Religious Education." Their art was of more modern style although they could not match Standard in color reproduction. I felt that the time had come to modernize our art style and produce a whole new series of subjects embodying the main incidents of the life of Christ. It was then that we discovered a young eastern artist by the name of Cleveland Woodward, who accepted an ever-increasing number of our assignments. He, with the aid of a number of men of his school, was able to bring our art collection again into the supremacy we had long enjoyed.

The Company had no "house organ" carrying news about its employees and information about its accomplishments. I proposed that we launch one and was given permission to do so. To enlist interest in the project we offered a prize for the best name for the new publication and set up a committee of judges to make the awards. The name chosen was *The Standpatter,* which is still being used. This attractive four-page monthly did much to promote employee morale. News representatives were chosen from each department of the business to provide copy.

My relations with the employees and heads of the various departments were such that many warm friendships were formed. During the Christian Action days I became a sort of "father confessor" for many of the clerks and secretaries who came to me with their personal problems. In the Music Department, J. E. Sturgis was a close friend; in the Printing and Production Department, Steve Spragens, John Post, and Roy Clore; in the Mailing Department, Oliver Bardon, Lew Sullivan, and Nelson Stahl; in the Art Department, Otto Stemler and his assistants; in the Proof Room, John Davis; in the Public Relations Department, Aldis Webb, Roy Linton Porter, and Harry Poll. Then there were Chester Allensworth, who was Superintendent of Buildings and Chief Engineer, and many others.

So close were these friendships and those with the editors during my administration that when death came I was asked to officiate at the funerals of such friends as E. W. Thornton, Roy Linton Porter, Fred J. Gielow, and Lillie A. Faris. The Hamilton County Baraca-Philathea Union asked me to bring the tribute at the memorial services for Henrietta Heron in Walnut Hills Christian Church. (Miss Heron was general counselor of the World-Wide Baraca-Philathea Union which has its headquarters at Mount Vernon, Virginia.) The families of several clerks and secretaries asked me to officiate at the funeral services of their loved ones. I deeply appreciated the opportunity to be of such service in this hour of need.

There were always "extra-curricular" activities engaging my attention. For instance, Standard paid fees to the International Council of Religious Education for the use of its Uniform Bible Lesson Outlines. We were naturally interested in what went on in the Council and, from our point of view, it was not good. The Council was controlled by liberals and its curriculum builders were liberals, committeed to the so-called "progressive" philosophy of education. They would have eliminated the Uniform system altogether if they could have had their way, but, thanks to Dr. John R. Sampey, Dr. Amos R. Wells, and influential friends, it had been kept alive. Nevertheless, liberal elements persisted in trying to determine the choice of Bible themes. As a result the Series gave constant evidence of the "progressivist" approach; "social gospel" teachings were given undue emphasis; the Scriptures were not chosen with historical, textual, or theological accuracy; the Outlines seldom dealt with fundamental Christian doctrine, and were lacking in evangelistic emphasis. We had frequently protested to ICRE leaders about these shortcomings but with little result. So we at Standard led out in canvassing evangelical publishers in an effort to secure a united protest. The response was most encouraging. Fred Gielow, Aldis Webb, and I were in a number of well-attended meetings in which strategy was mapped with encouraging results. We were always represented in the conventions of th ICRE and, when permitted, sat in as observers in sectional conferences where policy was discussed and formulated.

In 1942 or '43 the convention was held in Chicago in the skyscraper edifice of the Chicago Temple (Methodist). Aldis Webb and I were in attendance. The liberals were riding high and were unusually bold in their pronouncements and actions. I had been asked to prepare a report of the proceedings for the *Christian Standard* and our notebooks were bulging with information. One day Aldis was in a conference led by Dr. Wesner Fallaw (later Howard Professor of Religious Education at Andover Newton Theological Seminary). Fallaw was especially "rank" in his liberal pronouncements. His introductory speech had been mimeographed and it was about to be distributed when orders came from a higher authority to confiscate the copies. Aldis leaped to his feet, grabbed a copy, and fled to his room with it, making it possible for me to publicize accurately the following Fallaw quote, which caused a sensation in the evangelical Protestant world.

> We want youth to view Jesus as God's principal revelation of his nature. Jesus is not God, nor another god; nor yet the only revelation we have of God, the source and ground of existence. Our teaching becomes idolatry if it presents Jesus, the unique manifestation of God, as being himself a god. To my mind, one of the major faults of orthodoxy has always been the practice of confusing God with Jesus. We still have much to do in deleting from the prayers, hymns, and certain textbooks used with children evidences of Christ worship.
>
> . . . we shall continue to be aware of Bible fallibility, never accepting the Bible as a piece of work of uniform value. We shall be alert to inconsistency, to primitive error, discerning myth from historic fact. But in doing so, we shall teach more, not less, Bible. We shall keep in mind the Bible as living literature — to use Professor Bower's happy phrase. We shall use it to enrich the lives of our pupils young and old. We shall not permit the Bible ever again to become a fetish, for we refuse thus to desecrate its meaning and its truth.

This, with a particularly "juicy" bit from Dean Liston Pope of Yale urging the dissemination of the "social gospel" and church participation in "sociopolitical power politics," and the facts about "left-wing" decisions affecting future ICRE policy, made a report that was copied by the evangelical press in whole or in part throughout the nation. *United Evangelical Action,* the new official journal of the National Association of Evangelicals, reprinted the entire article, headlined it, and gave it front-page space in its next issue. The Fallaw bit was boldly denied but fortunately Aldis had heard it in the address and had the documentary evidence to prove it.

ICRE contacts during my years at Standard were to eventuate in important national repercussions that will be recounted in a later episode.

Always interested in history, I welcomed the move toward the organization of the Disciples of Christ Historical Society. I often met Claude E. Spencer, librarian of Culver-Stockton College, at conventions and inevitably we would talk and dream together about the possibility of establishing a library and museum worthy of the Restoration story. Spencer not only talked and dreamed but he was a man of action. Encouraging him at Culver-Stockton was Henry Barton Robinson, who had one of the finest private libraries of Discipliana anywhere. Together they persuaded President W. H. McDonald to permit the use of a section of the college library to house the collection of the nucleus of a Brotherhood library. Finally at the Kansas City International Convention a meeting was called to organize the Disciples of Christ Historical Society. Largely through my friendship with Spencer I was invited to be one of the founders of the Society, was elected a member of the Board (in 1941) and served in that capacity for more than twenty years. As I recall, among those initially interested and cooperating were Alfred T. DeGroot, W. E. Garrison, Enos E. Dowling, J. Edward Moseley (the first president), Eva Jean Wrather, C. C. Ware, Henry K. Shaw, Edgar C. Riley, and George L. Peters. As long as I was with the Standard Publishing Company I saw to it that two copies of every publication we produced went as a gift to the Society's library. Spencer made frequent visits to Standard's library which was then one of the finest collections of early volumes to be found anywhere in the country. I was able to add hundreds of books to the DCHS collection, credit always being given to the Company and not to me personally.

As far as my influence could be exerted, I urged that the services of the Society be made available to all segments of the Restoration Movement. This was Spencer's desire from the time he was made Curator until his retirement. We conceived of the Society as the servant of all the Movement and formed contacts with liberals, conservatives, and neutralists, all of which were immensely rewarding. It was this feature of Society policy that appealed so strongly to B. D. Phillips when he reached his decision to provide the Society with its million-dollar home in Nashville, the finest and most complete structure of its kind in America. I was glad to encourage Mr. Phillips in making that decision. Spencer was unquestionably the one man above all others who made possible the creation of the Society and guided it to successful operation. As a result of his prodigious labor and research, thousands of basic entries of Discipliana of priceless value were compiled.

In a later reference to my relationship with the Society, I shall deal with the Establishment's subtle efforts to dominate and control the organization, which was originally intended to be a "free agency" of the whole Brotherhood in the best and broadest sense of that term.

About this time I was deeply interested in the development of the National Association of Evangelicals. Many of the leaders in the new movement were connected with denominations that were among the best patrons of Standard services in color printing and imprinted editions of Sunday-school literature. Thousands of people had been alienated from the Federal Council of Churches because of its liberal policies. They had no medium to which they could turn that would provide essential interchurch fellowship and services. There was a yearning for "cooperation without compromise" of the great fundamentals of the Christian faith.

When a "Call" was issued for a meeting of these elements for exploration, discussion, and action in St. Louis in 1942, Edwin Errett, editor of the *Standard,* was one of the 147 signers. He was prevented by illness from attending, but the next year when a "Constitutional Convention" was held in Chicago, W. R. Walker, Aldis Webb, and I were there as observers. Our report to Standard management was favorable to participation, and for three years the Company gave the National Association of Evangelicals $1,000 a year for their work. I wrote a story of this history-making meeting which appeared in the *Christian Standard.*

Much more will be said about the NAE and its related agencies as my life story unfolds.

On a number of occasions Harry Poll, our minister at Westwood-Cheviot Church, had discussed with me an increasing number of religious radio programs. We noted especially the popular appeal of the Old-Fashioned Revival Hour and The Lutheran Hour, and felt keenly that the Restoration Plea should have an effective witness on the air. We shared our feeling with Ard Hoven, then minister of the Chase Avenue Church, who confessed that he had long been thinking along the same lines and would be interested in being the preacher if opportunity might offer. We had no funds but in great faith we began to pray and work for a radio broadcast. We soon enlisted the aid of others, set up an organization, and in 1942 prepared to air the first program under the nomen, "The Christian's Hour." Hoven prepared his sermon and the choir of the Westwood-Cheviot Church furnished the music. The first broadcast was over one small station WSAI in Cincinnati, and was a success. I asked permission to run a regular column in the *Christian Standard* in which we made a frank appeal for funds. The responses made possible the continuation of the work. With the expert professional advice of Bob Fleming we soon switched to WCKY, a station with greater power and wider coverage, and proceeded to add other stations. Roy Slifer assumed responsibility for opening an office and handling public relations. Later came Hugh Sensibaugh, William Harold Hockley, and others to assume responsibility for production and promotion until today some eighty stations carry the broadcast of The Christian's Hour, and millions of listeners hear the Gospel. The name of Preacher Ard Hoven has become a household word among our people and he has been instrumental in leading many to Christ. While I did very little of the actual work involved in the project, the brethren insisted that I remain on the board, a position I have held for 30 years. In this capacity I became responsible for relationships with the National Religious Broadcasters, Inc. Thereby hangs another tale which will be told in "Episode XV: National Religious Broadcasters."

It is now my painful duty to record the story of one of the most tragic periods in the history of my relations with the Standard Publishing Company. I shall begin with a little-known fact as background. As Russell Errett approached the end of his earthly journey, he saw that the next generation of his family was incapable of carrying on the great work initiated by his father, which he had developed into a mighty corporation seeking to serve the best interests of the Restoration Movement. Accordingly, he made a will creating a non-profit holding company, the net income from which would be devoted to the Cause he loved. Among the men he named as trustees were P. H. Welshimer, W. R. Walker, C. J. Sharp, Edwin R. Errett, and Stephen Spragens (head of the Printing and Publication Division of the Company). The holding company was to reimburse the Errett heirs in full for their lawful inheritances over a period of years and in the interim of settlement provide an adequate annual income for them on the basis of their holdings to be determined by the Trust Department of a leading Cincinnati bank.

When Russell Errett died in 1931 and the will was presented for probate, the family rose in violent protest. In long-drawn-out court proceedings testimony was given to prove that Russell Errett was mentally incompetent to make the will. Leaders in the protest were Harry Baird (husband of daughter Corinne Errett), John Errett (a son of Russell), and Willard Mohorter (secretary of the Company). To make a long story short, the will was broken and the Errett family retained possession of the Company. In a reorganization the following officers were chosen: W. R. Walker, president; Roy L. Slifer, vice-president; Willard Mohorter, secretary; and Harry Baird, treasurer. Baird was also named general manager, and Mohorter, assistant manager. In reality, a situation was created by which Baird and Mohorter "ran the Company" with Baird "calling the shots" in case of any disagreements.

All this happened while I was president of the Christian Restoration Association, but when I returned to the Company I became fully aware of the situation.

Many people in the Brotherhood thought, because of his name, that Edwin Errett, editor of the *Christian Standard,* was head of the Company. Edwin served the Company well for about thirty-two years. In 1912 he became office editor of the *Christian Standard* and held that position until 1918. From then until 1925 he served as a commentator and lesson writer for the Sunday-school publications of the Company and in 1925 was made editor-in-chief of these publications. Edwin was the son of W. R. Errett, a nephew of Isaac Errett and a cousin of Russell Errett. W. R. spent most of his life as a trust officer of one of Pittsburgh's leading banks and, upon retirement, in 1923, was made president of the Standard Publishing Company. This title meant little. He had no holdings (of his own) in the Company, and after about ten years of "fronting" for the real owners quit in disgust. Edwin, however, went on to become editor of the *Christian Standard,* the most influential journal of the Brotherhood.

Edwin Errett and I became very close friends. He was a graduate of

148

Bethany College and completed post-graduate studies in Yale. He was thoroughly committed to the Restoration Plea and, having been through all the bruising organizational battles leading to the break-up in Memphis in 1926 (see chapter VII), he came to the editorship of the *Standard* in 1930 with a scholarly understanding of the issues involved in the complex Brotherhood situation. He saw the fundamental objection to the liberal-controlled missionary agencies, "not that they are wasteful, or present a wrong method of doing things" but that "they have abandoned the plea and forsaken the movement." With his intelligently conceived and incisive editorials he dealt with this and all the other issues of the controversy in his day. Uncompromisingly loyal to the fundamental principles of the Restoration, he devoted his energies to the encouragement and promotion of such agencies, old and new, as he felt were committed unequivocally to the authority of the Scriptures. At the same time Edwin conferred courteously with all parties — right, left, and center — thus earning the suspicion and ill will of extremists and the respect of irenically-minded brethren everywhere. He participated enthusiastically and sacrificially in the work of the International Convention's Commission on Restudy and in many other conferences looking toward a better understanding and closer unity of the Brotherhood. In 1937 he became a delegate to the World Faith and Order Conference in Edinburgh, Scotland, and when that assembly took action to join in the conversations that eventuated in the World Council of Churches, he accepted a place on the continuing Committee on Faith and Order. He believed that he might be used of the Lord to bring to the attention of this world body the testimony of the Restoration Movement for Christian unity on the Bible and the Bible alone as the rule of faith and practice. When it became evident that the studies on faith and order were to be smothered in the plethora of World Council politics and the emerging Ecumenical Movement, Edwin resigned and told why. Both as editor and personal counselor in numerous areas of Brotherhood life, he gave himself unstintingly toward establishing a basis for unity in obedience to the Scriptures and in freedom from human ecclesiastical authority.

But there were extremist elements (the same people who had infiltrated the Christian Restoration Association in the last years of my administration) who "declared war" on Edwin and determined to have him eliminated as editor of the *Standard.* Mohorter was strongly influenced by these elements and began to exert pressure on Edwin to change his editorial policies. Articles reflecting the bigoted and sectarian ideas of these extremists began appearing in the *Standard* over the silent protest of its editor.

The office of the Assistant Manager, just opposite mine, began to swarm with "antis." Late in 1943 there was announcement of a "Call for Enlistment" and a "Committee on Action." Plans were being laid for a bitter onslaught on the International Convention and its associated agencies. The tone of the *Standard* articles was reminiscent of *The*

Touchstone, which had been edited by Robert E. Elmore. Documents drawn in the office across the hall were published as the work of major leaders of Brotherhood life. Signatories always omitted the names of Edwin Errett and James DeForest Murch. Then came an official statement from "The Executive Committee of the Standard Publishing Company, by Willard Mohorter, Secretary" that there had been a change in policy. The statement's high-sounding words meant that the extremists had taken over and no quarter would be given the enemy. A bloody fight was on.

Edwin's health was gravely affected by this turn of events. Finally, without public announcement, he was relieved of his editorial duties (although he remained in an anomalous position with the Company). In desperation he turned to his great and good friend, Will Irwin of Columbus, Indiana, who, failing in the use of his influence with friends of the Company to change the situation, decided to join Edwin in the publication of a new journal. Plans were being laid for it when word came from Indianapolis that Irwin had died suddenly of a heart attack in the citadel of his financial empire, the Indiana National Bank in Indianapolis. Seeing no hope for the future, Edwin, whose health failed rapidly, in 1944 became also the victim of a heart attack. Thus passed from the scene the Brotherhood's last best hope for reconciliation and renewal, while the *Standard* was delivered "lock, stock, and barrel" to the extremists.

The months following were filled with bewilderment and unrest. I began to lose confidence in the management. While nothing was done to interfere with my editorial program I felt an increasing coolness on the part of "the powers that be." Then came some revelations which were a shock to me. One day at the Optimist Club luncheon in the Gibson Hotel a friend asked, "Aren't you with Standard Publishing Company?" I said, "Yes." "Isn't that supposed to be a religious publishing house?" he queried. Again getting an affirmative answer, he laughed rather derisively and said, "I think I know your boss. How in the world did he ever get in that position? Did you know that he maintains a suite in this hotel where the motto is 'wine, women, and song' and where the hottest poker game in the city is carried on?" My embarrassment knew no bounds. I knew "the boss" made no particular religious profession but I had no idea his conduct was so flagrantly out of line with the Company's ideals. Then, too, as the new policy began to take shape I became the object of numerous insults from the extremists whenever I appeared in conventions and rallies across the country. I was branded as a "heretic" and a "compromiser." My close associates in the Company became increasingly resentful of these things. Meetings began to be held in the homes where working conditions were discussed and appropriate action was advised. There were whisperings in the offices and morale sank to low ebb.

Then one afternoon, Baird's secretary came into my office and said,

"The boss wants to see you." I immediately reported and found him and Mohorter in a belligerent mood. Baird said brusquely, "Sit down, you! Mohorter hired you and I am going to give him the pleasure of firing you!" At which the Assistant Manager, his face livid with rage, said, "You have become a dangerous influence here. You have outlived your days of usefulness and I am firing you. You have become too big for your britches. All you are, the Standard Publishing Company has made you, and now, after a few years nobody will know you ever lived! Your name will never again appear in our publications. Get out *now* and never set foot in this building again. If you do, we will call the police and put you where you belong!" (I am omitting the profane language used by both men.) I was not even given time to assemble and remove my personal belongings. I walked out and shortly afterward all my personal files containing many highly valued letters and manuscripts were destroyed.

In the *Christian Standard* for February 17, 1945, appeared a one-inch box containing this small paragraph:

> James DeForest Murch is no longer con-
> nected with the Standard Publishing Company.

This dismissal marked the beginning of a period of about fifteen years in which my name was boycotted and blacklisted by Standard and I became the subject of lies and misrepresentations almost beyond belief.

While I made it a point to avoid all contacts with those who worked with me, the furor raised by management's action had broad repercussions. Resignations were turned in during the next few weeks by J. Vernon Jacobs, Harry Poll, Aldis Webb, Mildred Welshimer, Dorothy Poulton, Verda Bloomhuff, and others, totaling fourteen in all.

How the news of my dismissal got out to the brethren, I do not know, but a veritable flood of protest came almost immediately from men like Welshimer, Trinkle, T. K. Smith, and Walker. There was talk of starting a new publishing house. Indeed, a meeting of about seventy brethren gathered, on somebody's call, in the Hotel Sinton in Cincinnati to lay plans for just such a move. (I was not invited to the meeting and of course did not attend.) Only promises of long-overdue changes of various sorts at Standard halted the contemplated action.

Letters from hundreds of brethren over the country — men of the right, left, and center — flowed in to me, which I have treasured through the years. They expressed sympathy and confidence and offered help. I discovered many friends I never knew I had.

I cannot describe the anguish my wife and I suffered for the next few days and weeks, but we put our faith in God and knew that He would provide. The Higley Printing Company pleaded with me to be their editor-in-chief. The Central Church, Huntington, West Virginia, considered me as their pastor. And then "out of the blue" came a telegram from Bishop Leslie Marston in New York City, asking me to fly there immediately for a conference with leaders of the National Association of Evangelicals.

What happened was undoubtedly the leading of the Lord who used what seemed to be a disaster to open the way for an undenominational ministry of national and world proportions during the next twenty years. Truly, "God moves in mysterious ways His wonders to perform."

Episode XII

United Evangelical Action (1)

Pursuant to Bishop Marston's telegram I arrived in New York City July 1, 1945, for a meeting with the Executive Committee of the National Association of Evangelicals to discuss the prospects of my becoming editor of the Association's official journal, *United Evangelical Action.* The meeting was held in the offices of the great modern highrise Calvary Baptist Church (the culmination of the dreams of the noted fundamentalist preacher, Dr. John Roach Straton). It began with prayer on our knees seeking the guidance of the Holy Spirit in reaching our decisions. Such prayer meetings marked the whole history of my relations with the Association — a marked contrast to the hard, cold, matter-of-fact business relationships that had characterized my previous ministries.

I was asked to give my personal testimony of my faith in Christ, was questioned as to my knowledge of the basic issues of the current liberal-conservative theological controversy and the aims and purposes of the NAE. Evidently I passed the examination satisfactorily because I was immediately offered the position as editor and manager of the magazine. One problem caused considerable discussion — my insistence that I remain in Cincinnati. The "Queen City" had been our home for years and both my wife and I had business, social, and church relationships which we did not want to give up unless it was absolutely necessary. The journal was being published at Boston, where the offices of the NAE were then located. However, there was considerable pressure being brought by its constituents for a move to some central city in the West. With but little difficulty I was able to convince the Committee to accede to my request and the details of our relationships were worked out with a sub-committee that very day. It was agreed that I should come to Boston for whatever time it would take to complete the details of the move and to assure the prompt and unbroken production of the magazine. When I took the plane back to Cincinnati that night there was a song in my heart and the deep conviction that the Lord had called me to the work that was to engage my time and attention for the next 14 years.

My interim stay in Boston was very pleasant and rewarding in many ways. I was ensconced in a modest but delightful room in a Beacon Hill hotel within walking distance of the NAE office, Park Street Church, and Tremont Temple.

I spent much time with J. Elwin Wright, then Executive Secretary of the NAE. He was, indeed, the founder of the organization in a very real sense. He was the inspired leader of the "New England Fellowship" which was formed in 1929. It was made up of many who could no longer find cooperative satisfaction in the apostate Councils of Churches. At Rumney, New Hampshire, under Dr. Wright's direction, summer conferences were held for pastors, women, business men, and camps for boys and girls. The fellowship was so delightful and rewarding that the organization naturally developed. Then came NEF-sponsored radio broadcasts, Christian education ministries in public schools, religious book stores, vacation Bible schools, and other united projects until the Fellowship became a major religious force in New England where unitarianism, liberalism, and Roman Catholicism had become so firmly entrenched. It was natural that Dr. Wright should become the national leader he was when I first met him. His vision, his faith, and his indefatigable energy kept the NAE alive and moving ahead for the early formative years of the organization. I sat at his feet in those Boston days until I had imbibed the spirit of the man, which I later tried to translate and transmit to evangelicals everywhere through the medium of the official magazine.

Another personality with whom I was privileged to associate closely during the Boston days was Harold John Ockenga, first president of the Association, and pastor of the historic Park Street Church. This was the church fronting Boston Common long known as "Brimstone Corner" because of its stand for the fundamentals of the faith. It was here that "My Country 'Tis of Thee" was first sung. The adjoining cemetery held the remains of early New England's most famous founders and patriots. Ockenga was a product of the great Princeton Seminary controversy. As a youth he took his stand courageously and sacrificially for the biblical and evangelical Christian faith. He possesses one of the most brilliant minds I have ever encountered and had a natural pulpit eloquence unequalled anywhere. I remember coming in to his office one morning while he was preparing a sermon. He had only one book before him — the Greek New Testament. He remarked "This and the guidance of the Holy Spirit are the only ingredients I have for sermon building." He had a genius for church administration which enabled him to build the largest and most prosperous Congregational Church in New England and the most popular and influential church in Boston. I remember one hot Sunday evening arriving late for the services and just barely squeezing into a seat on the back row next to two young Jewish students from Cambridge who had their notebooks with them and were scribbling wildly. Ockenga was preaching on "The Deity of Christ." After the service I shook hands with the two young men and one of them said, "We don't believe in Dr. Ockenga's premises and we don't believe in his conclusions, but we have the highest respect for his intellectual ability, his theological acumen and his reasoning powers. He was great tonight, wasn't he? We often come to hear him preach. There is no rabbi in Boston that can equal him."

One Sunday I spent with C. Gordon Brownville and the historic Tremont Temple, the largest Baptist Church in Boston. Some of the greatest preachers of the denomination had held its downtown pulpit and filled its large auditorium with magnificent audiences. At the time I was in Boston the Temple was experiencing financial and other difficulties. Yet Brownville was averaging around a thousand in his morning audiences. He was biblically expository and evangelistic in his messages and was carrying on in the fine traditions of this great church. There were responses to the Gospel invitation and baptisms at both services I attended.

I missed fellowship with Christian Churches and Churches of Christ. The old Roxbury church I once knew was gone. The congregation at Everett was a long way out from the center of Boston, but I managed to go there once or twice. At that time Spencer Austin, who was pursuing graduate studies in Boston University, was serving in an ad interim ministry. He asked to come down to my hotel for a visit one day and I was delighted. Spencer was one of the finest graduates of Phillips University and loyal to the faith. He brought with him a copy of a letter from an official of the United Christian Missionary Society offering him the position of National Superintendent of Evangelism. He was anxious to get my reaction. I questioned him about the freedom he would have in the development of a program. He assured me that he could "write his own ticket." Of course, one of the greatest needs of the Brotherhood, then as always, was an adequately aggressive program of evangelism and I agreed with him that it would be a great blessing if he could unite our forces in a great continuous campaign to win souls to Christ. But I pointed out to him the dangers of association with UCMS leadership which was largely liberal and apostate. I said, "I would be afraid that once in the hierarchal atmosphere of the Society your tendency would be to go along with its programs until your zeal for evangelism would be smothered and you would become more interested in promoting the machine then the message." He finally decided to accept and take the risks involved. Eventually Austin succumbed to the very influences that I had warned him against and became the enormously successful director of Unified Promotion, one of the greatest factors in the development of Restructure and the tragic schism in the Brotherhood. I am sure that neither of us had any idea of the seriousness of the issues and the portents involved in our conversation that day in my Boston hotel. It was a most enjoyable occasion and when we parted I sincerely wished him every blessing in his life work.

Another graduate student in Boston University was a frequent visitor at the offices of the NAE — Carl F. H. Henry. He and I often ate together and became very well acquainted. He had a background in journalism and we found much in common. At that time he was determined to prepare for a career as a theologian and seminary professor. We enthusiastically discussed at length the possibilities of a magazine that could be truly representative of the worldwide evangelical movement. He offered to make contributions to *United Evangelical Action* when I got back to Cincinnati and my new plans and policies had taken shape, which encouraged me no end. I little realized then that in later years I would be associated with him in the nation's capital in a project that would achieve our fondest hopes.

It was a thrilling experience to visit at my leisure many historic sites in the city and I availed myself of every opportunity to do so. There were Faneuil Hall, the sites of the Boston tea party and the Boston Massacre, Paul Revere's home, the old North Church, Bunker Hill, Charlestown, Dorchester Heights, Trinity Church where Phillips Brooks preached, King's Chapel the citadel of unitarianism, Cambridge and Harvard University, and scores of other places all testifying to the immense place Boston will always hold in the history of America. I felt I was walking on holy ground.

Finally the day came when all essential business and administrative matters had been resolved and all files, supplies, and office equipment had been shipped. I took my leave of the many friends I had made and flew back to Cincinnati. There I rented office space, (111 East Fourth which was to be my business address for fourteen years), made a contract with printers, hired a staff of workers, set up office routine for editorial and circulation departments, and proceeded to get out the first issue of the magazine in its new format. It may be of interest to know something of my plans because they were to have a considerable effect upon the evangelical movement, particularly upon its journalism.

My plans for the new magazine were based on two sets of principles which I perfected after careful research and study. I conceived it to be the advocate of historic Protestantism and a demonstration of its relevance to modern life.

The Protestant principles were: (1) Recognition of Christ as the sole and supreme head of the Church and Lord of all; (2) the Holy Scriptures as God's infallible revelation of His will and the ultimate authority of the Church in doctrine, ordinances, and life; (3) salvation by the justification of the individual soul through faith in Christ; (4) the universal priesthood of believers and the right of private judgment; (5) individual piety and social righteousness; evangelism as the chief task of the Church; (6) the separation of Church and State; and (7) the advocacy of universal education, freedom of speech and worship, and all the human freedoms which are the fruit of obedience to God.

The basic Christian doctrinal principles were: (1) The Bible is the inspired, the only infallible Word of God; (2) God is eternally existent in three persons: Father, Son, and Holy Spirit; (3) Jesus Christ is God's Son manifested in His virgin birth, His sinless life, His miracles, His vicarious and atoning death, His bodily resurrection, His ascension to the right hand of the Father and the promise of His personal return in power and glory; (4) the salvation of lost and sinful man is accomplished by obedience to the commands of Christ and regeneration by the Holy Spirit; (5) the Christian is enabled to live the godly life by the indwelling of the Holy Spirit; (6) there will be a resurrection of both the saved and

156

the lost, they that are saved unto the resurrection of life and they that are lost to the resurrection of damnation; (7) there now exists a spiritual unity of believers in Christ who are striving to do His will.

It was my belief that all those who held such views had an obligation to cooperate as far as possible without the sacrifice of sacred convictions, to the glory of God. This was the principle that had led to many forms of interdenominational cooperation. It was the departure from those principles which had made it no longer possible for evangelical Protestants to cooperate in the National and World Councils of Churches and had made it necessary to form the National Association of Evangelicals.

I felt that while our primary task was to glorify Christ and His Church we had to continually make clear to ourselves and to the whole religious world our reasons for separate existence. We could not cooperate with the Councils because: (1) They rejected an absolute minimum of Bible doctrine as a basis for fellowship; (2) they were controlled by a liberal theological and sociological hierarchy; (3) they were beginning to function as a Super-Church, threatening the freedom of brethren in Christ; (4) they were destroying distinctly Christian evangelism and evangelical Christian missions; (5) they were becoming more Catholic than Protestant; (6) they were encouraging leftist social revolution, meddling in national and international politics, thus imperiling the status of the churches and the peace of the world; (7) they were blurring the obligation of the Church Universal to maintain its spiritual unity and its apostolicity in doctrine, ordinances, and life by their emphasis on church union for ecclesiastical and political power and the building of "One Church for One World."

With these principles clearly in mind I began to recruit a group of outstanding evangelical leaders upon whom I might depend as "contributing editors." The result was a list of such distinguished men as Harold John Ockenga, pastor of Park Street Church, Boston; J. Elwin Wright, executive secretary of the NAE; Bishop Leslie Marston of the Free Methodist Church; Donald Grey Barnhouse, pastor of the Tenth Presbyterian Church, Philadelphia; Frederick Curtis Fowler, pastor of the First Presbyterian Church, Duluth, Minnesota; Stephen W. Paine, president of Houghton College; William Ward Ayer, pastor of Calvary Baptist Church, New York City; Paul S. Rees, pastor of the First Covenant Church, Minneapolis, Minnesota; Carl F. H. Henry of Northern Baptist Theological Seminary, Chicago; Clyde W. Taylor of the NAE's Washington office; Rutherford L. Decker, pastor of the Temple Baptist Church, Kansas City, Missouri, and others of like mind and heart.

United Evangelical Action had been issued in varied forms beginning with a four-page 10½ x 14½ bulletin-form monthly publication in 1942, then in an eight-column, eight-page newspaper format. This was followed by a newspaper tabloid issued twice a month, the format which I inherited in 1945. I conceived of the publication as a 24-page, fortnightly magazine and adopted that format with the first issue published in

Cincinnati. It contained thoughtful articles and editorials, feature stories, a wide coverage of evangelical news, and articles promoting the NAE and its associated agencies. It fell short of my hopes in many respects but it was enthusiastically received by evangelicals in all parts of the nation. It was my hope that the magazine would become "the voice of evangelical Christianity in America." I nailed that idea to the masthead and moved in that direction.

When I took over the magazine it had less than 10,000 circulation and much of that was "complimentary." It was not reaching American Protestantism as a whole — only the sector of it which was active in the NAE. The circulation was not sufficient to attract advertisers, a major source of financial income. These were problems for specialists in these fields, but because of limited resources I was saddled with the responsibility, not only of editing a magazine, but with supervision and promotion of circulation and advertising.

I was able to convince NAE leaders that the journal was the "life line" of the organization not only for the maintenance of constituency relations but for relations with its prospective members and the whole religious world. They saw the necessity for generous underwritings of a budget that would accomplish its mission, at least to a reasonable extent. In those days the U.S. Postal authorities were much more generous than now in their attitude toward second-class privileges for religious and non-profit organizations. We set up a plan which put the magazine in the hands of all the Protestant denominational leaders and a limited number of the ministers of local churches. The latter received the paper free for three months, then were given an opportunity to subscribe. We set up an exchange list which included all Protestant magazines. Under this plan our circulation moved up to around twenty or twenty-five thousand each issue. With this coverage we were able to "sell" increasing numbers of evangelical advertisers, particularly publishers and educational institutions. American Protestantism became aware of our presence in the journalistic field and we began to be quoted frequently both favorably and critically. Reprints of our leading articles and editorials reached hundreds of thousands beyond our circulation and eventually we were quoted in college and seminary seminars, and in official gatherings of denominational and inter-church organizations. We had arrived!

The word *Action* in our name became realistic through our aggressive policies. In 1952 when President Truman appointed an American envoy to the Vatican, Clyde Taylor and the Washington office led out in an NAE protest that shook the nation. I produced a special edition to back him up and wrote the lead article entitled, "Shall America Bow to the Pope of Rome?" I did a tremendous lot of research on the history of America's relations with Rome which proved to be of immense value to all leaders of the opposition. I was fortunate, through a friend in Religious News Service in New York, to get a photo of Truman's envoy (Myron C. Taylor) kneeling before the Pope and about to kiss his ring, just before the RNS was forced by Romanists to destroy the picture. This I displayed on the front page. So great was the demand for extra copies of this issue that we were forced to reprint the article in a twenty-four page brochure. We sold hundreds of thousands of these which were distributed in local churches of all Protestant denominations throughout America. The thrilling story of the part the NAE played in forcing Truman to discontinue this ambassadorial relationship is to be found in Chapter 11 of my history of the Association, *Cooperation without Compromise.*

In 1952 when the National Council of Churches launched its "Revised Standard Version" of the Bible, *Action* magazine was the first religious journal in America to print scholarly reviews of evangelical scholars (headed by Oswald T. Allis) both pro and con, an objective achievement which called forth words of appreciation from many of the religious leaders of the nation. We were instrumental in encouraging a movement in evangelical circles to achieve a more satisfactory translation. This movement, necessarily slow, is just now approaching realization. I remember, during the period when numerous unofficial conferences were held concerning our proposal, a meeting with American Bible Society leaders in New York City, headed by Eugene A. Nida, its director of translation. At that meeting I proposed that he and the ABC set up a committee which would engage the services of Bible scholars representing all sectors of the Protestant world to produce a Bible in modern English that would be universally recognized and accepted. I suggested that the ABS hold the copyright and be responsible for publishing the first editions. Nothing came of the proposal, but one result of the meeting was the recognition of the NAE as a member of the Society's Advisory Board. By action of our Board I was made the Association's representative and participated in the regular meetings in New York for several years.

One of the many services which *Action* magazine rendered its readers was its annual Book List. I set up an "Evangelical Book Committee" in 1945. We had begun to realize that Liberal philosophies had so infiltrated the religious book field that the average reader needed capable guidance in his reading. The first committee was headed by Carl F. H. Henry (later to be editor of *Christianity Today*) and consisted of twenty-seven intellectual leaders whose literary attainments qualified them to read and evaluate current literature and recommend certain books in two categories: (1) books of doctrinal soundness, and (2) other books which were of significance to evangelicals. This service was provided throughout my editorship. A by-product of this venture was the Evangelical Book Club, a privately-owned service, which selects a "Book-of-the-Month" and lists each month new volumes coming from the presses of evangelical publishers. It grew to be an exceedingly profitable business. Our Spring and Fall Book Numbers announcing and predicting the future publishing plans of bookmen often reached thirty-two pages and were well patronized by advertisers.

Episode XIII

Evangelical Press Association

As editor of *United Evangelical Action* I came in close contact with all the editors and publishers of the various denominations related to the NAE and those of other conservative houses. Only Concordia Press (Missouri Synod Lutheran) was producing materials of the highest quality. The rest were a shoddy lot, many of them issuing journals little better than high school papers. All of them faced common problems that needed solution if they were to improve their output. None of them was a member of the Associated Church Press, which while not organizationally related to the National Council of Churches, at that time frowned upon admitting non-Council editors. Its counterpart Publishers Association was, with a few exceptions, comparably exclusive. I felt that if we were to improve our situation and take our rightful place in the field of the religious graphic arts and effective journalism we had to organize and set in motion our own means of improvement. Accordingly, I shared my feelings with other individuals and found considerable encouragement. I was certain we had the potential. All we needed was "evangelical action"!

At the first convention of the National Sunday School Association (see Chapter XIV) in Chicago, October 1946, I called an informal meeting of editors in the Congress Hotel to discuss the situation. No action was taken. The seed was sown, however, and the following year (also in connection with an NSSA Convention, in Cincinnati), October 10, I invited a group of editors to my office, including Louis H. Benes of the *Church Herald,* J. H. Walker of the *Evangel,* and Carl L. Howland of the *Free Methodist.* We decided to proceed with a formal call to be issued all evangelical editors of record. Accordingly, on May 6, 1948, editors of some thirty-five denominational publishing houses met in Chicago. They chose me as temporary chairman and set up a temporary organization under the name "Evangelical Press Association," appointed a Constitution Committee, and called a Convention for April 4-6, 1949, to set up a permanent organization.

The Constitutional Convention opened in the Lakeview Covenant Church, in Chicago, on a Monday evening with William F. McDermott, former religion editor of the *Chicago Daily News* and widely-known publicist, speaking. The work sessions were held in the Electric Club with special conferences for editors of general denominational, Sunday school, missionary, youth, and children's publications. There was also a session devoted to the problems of religious publishers.

It was agreed that the field of evangelical publishing has a different base and outlook from any other. Secular standards and methods must be adapted, adjusted, and converted to fit evangelical needs. Furthermore, it was agreed that there was no hope for us in the NCC-oriented agencies.

Accordingly, a Constitution and Bylaws was adopted with the Statement of Belief of the National Association of Evangelicals as the theological basis of membership. After prayerful and thoughtful discussion it was unanimously agreed, however, that the EPA should not be NAE-related. The principles of freedom of the press, freedom of speech, wider evangelical coverage, and denominational responsibility were determining factors in the discussion.

The Purpose of the Association as set forth in the first Constitution was as follows (largely as I wrote it) :

"The purpose of the Evangelical Press Association is to promote the cause of evangelical Christianity and to enhance the influence of Christian journalism by providing Christian fellowship among the members of the Association, by rendering practical assistance and stimulating mutual helpfulness among them, by encouraging high ethical and technical standards in the field of Christian journalism, and by suggesting concerted and timely emphasis on important issues."

I was elected president; Robert Walker, editor of *Christian Life,* secretary, and Martin Eriksen, editor of the *Baptist Standard,* treasurer. I served in this capacity for three terms.

Since that time of formation, the Evangelical Press Association has grown with real life and vitality. Membership numbers over two hundred, representing publications of many denominations and publishing houses with a combined circulation approaching ten million. A very successful and interesting convention has been held each year. These conventions have been especially marked by the solid and helpful information which is given in lectures and in demonstrations by outstanding and recognized authorities in the field of journalism and editorial activity. Sectional meetings to explore the problems and interests of specialized publications are also a feature of each convention, and the emphasis is constantly on the practical presentation of information and "know-how" which will be essentially helpful to the members when they are back at work.

Sectional groups were organized to cover the following fields of religious publication: Youth Publications, Denominational and General Publications, Periodical and Book Publishers, Sunday School Publications.

The business of the EPA is administered under an official Constitution and is largely carried on during the yearly convention. During the interim, administration is by a Board of Directors consisting of the President, Vice-president, Secretary, Treasurer, and two Advisory Members. A full-time Executive Secretary is employed to carry out the directives of the administrators and to serve the needs of the members.

Membership in the EPA is by publication, not by individual. Publications may be represented at the EPA conventions by as many workers as desired, but each publication is allowed only one vote in business sessions. Press membership cards are issued by the EPA to all member publications, and additional cards are supplied to member publications for as many workers as requested.

At the 1954 Convention a Code of Ethics was adopted which is a guiding light for evangelical publications:

"The primary function of Christian publications is to advance the work and witness of Jesus Christ in the world. Our first responsibility is faithfulness to the truth and will of God as it is expressed in the Bible, which we accept as the infallible revelation of God, our only authority for faith and conduct. This dedicates Christian journalism to serve the highest welfare of mankind.

"As our secondary responsibility we recognize our duty to serve the 'principles, purposes, and policies' of the cause or organization our publications represent.

I

The freedom of Christian publications to publish the truth and to set forth the principles contained in the Word of God must be zealously guarded. Christian publications should be honest, and courageous, in all their presentations. Sincerity, truthfulness, and accuracy should characterize all Christian publications.

II

Readers of Christian publications have the right to expect that news items and articles published are written truthfully. Those responsible for the publication must exercise the utmost care that nothing contrary to the truth is published. It is the privilege, as it is the duty, of a Christian publication to make prompt and complete correction of its own serious mistakes of fact or opinion, whatever their origin.

III

Christian publications are conscious of their duty to protect the good name and reputation of others. Should it become necessary at any time to engage in controversy for the defense and maintenance of the truth, care should be taken to present opposing views honestly and fairly.

IV

Christian publications do not publish any material except with consent of the authors or owners. The editing of articles should not change the thoughts expressed by the author, without consultation with, and permission of, the author. Articles published in other magazines should not be reproduced without first receiving permission. Such articles should receive proper acknowledgment. Whenever previously published material is used, care should be taken to ascertain and acknowledge — if possible — authorship and source."

An amazing improvement has taken place in the style and content of all the participating magazines during the years. Each year plaques are awarded editors of journals showing the greatest technical progress and making the best contribution in the field of religious journalism. Evangelical publications now compare favorably with, and in some cases are superior to, similar Associated Church Press publications.

I remained active in the organization throughout my editorial career and upon my retirement from the managing editorship of *Christianity Today* was elected to an honorary life membership of the Board.

Episode XIV

National Sunday School Association

During my whole life I have been obsessed with the necessity of promoting the teaching function of the Church. I was always deeply impressed with the fact that Christ gave teaching major emphasis in the Great Commission. He said, "Go and *teach* all nations, baptizing them . . ." and with renewed emphasis he said "*teaching* them to observe all things whatsoever I have commanded you . . ." He himself was the Master Teacher and His ministry was largely a teaching ministry. When He built His church He gave teachers a prominent place in its leadership.

I have already hinted in previous chapters at the contributions I sought to make to the cause of Christian education, but there was nothing I have done in this field that has been more rewarding than the hours, days, and years I have given to the establishment and promotion of the National Sunday School Association. I am going to give a bit more space to this part of my life story because in a very real sense the NSSA in its beginnings was my creation.

From 1916 to 1940 there had been a steady decline in Sunday School enrollment in American churches. Clarence H. Benson of Moody Bible Institute in a review of U. S. Government statistics released in 1942 showed that Sunday School enrollment had decreased 12.6 per cent in that period. The Northern (American) Baptist Convention schools had slipped from 1,052,794 in 1926 to 892,872 in 1936. The Disciples of Christ saw their Sunday School numbers fall from 1,000,416 to 761,257 and the Methodist Episcopal Church from 3,796,561 to 2,515,181. This retrograde movement was nationwide among denominations which were experiencing the blight of liberalism. Only the Lutherans, the Assemblies of God, the Church of the Nazarene and other strictly evangelical communions were reporting increases in Sunday School enrollment.

With the abandonment of the strictly evangelical policy of the International Sunday School Association in 1922 there began to develop among evangelicals a definite dissatisfaction with that organization. This dissatisfaction increased with the advent of the International Council of Religious Education, with its so-called "inclusive" policy.

Evangelicals unfortunately failed to express themselves in a united policy and program. Some hoped to reform the ICRE. Some launched independent splinter agencies. Some altogether lost their interest in the Sunday School. This fact, coupled with the loss of denominational and interdenominational prestige and the lack of influential support, resulted in the dissipation of the forces of protest. The great Sunday School masses of America were unaware of what had happened at the top echelons of the movement. There was no medium through which they could be told.

One of the most apparent evidences of change was seen in the Uniform Bible Lessons Outlines. Protests were coming up from evangelical church leaders to publishing houses, with the result that around 1939 a group of so-called "independent" publishers called a conference to discuss the situation. I have previously alluded to this development. I was one of the Standard Publishing Company's representatives in this group which approached the ICRE with a catalog of our objections to the Outlines they were furnishing us. We said they were unsatisfactory because —

1. They gave evidence in theme, structure, aim and editorial comment of the "modernist" theological and the "progressivist" educational approach.

2. "Social gospel" teachings were given undue emphasis, and topical outlines were given a definite "liberal" and "social gospel" slant.

3. Many lessons were chosen on a topical basis with little regard for Bible context, resulting in the use of unrelated sections of Scripture to teach ideas other than those intended by the Bible writers.

4. There was a failure to provide a comprehensive view of the Scriptures historically, textually or theologically.

5. Topics were inadequate for instruction in fundamental Christian doctrine.

6. Scriptures suggested for printed texts for Primary children were often too short to provide an adequate basis for instruction.

7. There was a tendency to introduce a lesson plan (different rather than uniform Scripture texts for the various departments) which destroyed the strictly uniform lesson idea and made the lessons almost unusable in small schools.

8. Scriptures selected seldom dealt with evangelism or lent themselves to evangelistic emphasis.

9. The guiding principles in ICRE curriculum building were no longer clearly evangelical and Scriptural but basically humanistic in religious principle and naturalistic in application.

10. The Lesson Committee failed to establish any official consultative relationship with the evangelical editors and publishers who produced the majority of the Uniform Sunday School lesson literature of the nation.

After making repeated efforts through the ICRE to change this situation and failing utterly to achieve their purpose, a few of the publishers appealed to the National Association of Evangelicals Church School Commission for help.

In the fall of 1943 the NAE, in the meeting of its Board of Administration in New York City, considered the possibility of the development of a new evangelical system of Uniform Sunday School Lessons. At the December meeting of the NAE executive committee Clarence H. Benson was announced prematurely as chairman of a new lesson committee which never functioned.

April 12-17, 1944, upon the call of the Church School Commission of the NAE, a meeting was held in the Deshler-Wallick Hotel, Columbus, Ohio, attended by some two hundred Sunday-school leaders without regard to organization or denomination, independent publishers, denominational publishers, editors and denominational and interdenominational and undenominational organizations. Harold John Ockenga presided at the sessions. I acted as recording secretary.

All present were concerned about the apostasy of the International Council of Religious Education. It was here proposed that new Uniform Sunday School Lesson outlines should be produced and that *the task should be committed to a new national Sunday School association organized on strictly evangelical principles.* As an outgrowth of the Columbus meeting over 100 leaders in the field of Christian education gathered in the Stevens Hotel, Chicago, April 30-May 1, 1945, where a temporary organization of the National Sunday School Association was effected. Archer E. Anderson, pastor of the First Presbyterian Church, Duluth, Minn., was chosen temporary chairman and I was continued as secretary. The executive committee of the new organization called a meeting in the Central YMCA, Chicago, August 21 and 22 of the same year and appointed a committee to study the situation and nominate members of a new Uniform Bible Lesson Committee to be elected by the first convention of the NSSA. I was chosen secretary of this nominating committee. The Executive Committee also proceeded to make plans for the first convention.

Sunday School workers from thirty-five states and two provinces of Canada met in Chicago, October 2-6, 1946, in the first national (constitutional) convention of the National Sunday School Association. Meetings were held in Moody Church with audiences ranging from 400 in the mornings and afternoons to 1,000 in the evenings and 4,000 on Saturday night.

The delegates were of one mind concerning the necessity for the setting up of a new national framework of organization for the revitalization of the Sunday School. A constitution was adopted for the NSSA: officers were elected; the new Uniform Bible Lesson project was approved, and a program of expansion planned.

The NAE Statement of Belief was adopted, assuring the doctrinal future of the Association.

Work-study groups and departmental conferences were held morning and afternoon and were largely attended. Sankey Hall was filled with exhibits of denominational and independent publishers of Sunday School literature.

The first Board of Directors, elected at Chicago, consisted of Archer E. Anderson (Presbyterian USA), president; Clarence H. Benson (Presbyterian US), vice-president; James DeForest Murch (Disciples of Christ), secretary; Robert C. Van Kampen (Northern Baptist), treasurer; Jesse R. Hastings (Methodist); A. L. Brown (Free Methodist); J. P. McCallie

166

(Presbyterian US); J. R. Mumaw (Mennonite); Ralph M. Riggs (Assemblies of God); H. H. Savage (Northern Baptist); J. H. Walker (Church of God); J. Clair Peters (United Brethren); W. L. Surbrook (Pilgrim Holiness); A. L. Stewart (Canadian Presbyterian); Roy S. Hollomon (Southern Baptist). C. V. Egemeier was elected executive secretary. The Association was incorporated under the laws of the State of Illinois and Chicago was made permanent national headquarters.

Official relationship with the National Association of Evangelicals was through its Sunday School (Church School) Commission composed of the members of the executive committee of the NSSA.

It is interesting to note in passing that the old International Sunday School Association had its origin in the solution of a problem similar to that now posed to evangelicals. The Sunday School leaders of America had agreed to unite in the production of Uniform Sunday School Lesson outlines to be used by all Protestant Sunday Schools. The implementation of their plan required some overall organization representative of the schools. Accordingly the ISSA was organized in Indianapolis, Ind., in 1872.

The chief concern of the newly-formed NSSA was its uniform lesson project.

The Lesson Committee, which tackled the new job in 1946 consisted of Clarence H. Benson, chairman (Presbyterian US); James DeForest Murch, secretary (Disciples of Christ); Leslie R. Marston (Free Methodist); Henrietta Mears (Presbyterian USA); H. C. Mason (Free Methodist); Harry A. Ironside (Plymouth Brethren); H. H. Savage (Baptist); R. C. McQuilkin (Presbyterian); Stanley H. Frodsham (Assemblies of God) and R. H. Fritsch (Lutheran).

An Advisory Committee of One Hundred was also set up to work with the Lesson Committee. It consisted of educational leaders, pastors, local Sunday School teachers and leaders, editors, publishers, and lesson writers from practically every major Protestant body in America.

The Lesson Committee immediately adopted the Statement of Belief of the National Association of Evangelicals as the minimum basis of theological agreement.

A careful study of the history of the original Uniform Lessons since their inception in 1872 was then undertaken by the NSSA Committee. It gave much consideration to the work of the Uniform Lesson committees of the Old International Sunday School Association under whose aegis these lessons reached their widest acceptance. They sought to discover and utilize the wisdom, experience and methods of these evangelical educational leaders of the "Golden Age" of the American Sunday School.

The Lesson Committee finally adopted the following policy as a guide for its work:

1. The name of the new lesson series shall be the "Uniform Bible Lesson Series."

2. The curriculum shall be Bible-centered in content. The text for study shall be related to and in harmony with the context both in letter and spirit.

3. The supreme purpose of the series shall be the winning of every pupil to the Lord Jesus Christ and the submission of his life to the will of God.

4. The lessons shall be directed to the teaching and training of the pupil for Christian character and service.

5. Recognizing the limitations of the theory of gradual development as the solution of problems of character, the curriculum will keep clearly in view the important place of crisis, conflict and choice in the making of Christian character.

6. Each cycle will be five years in length.

7. Cycle content will consist of selections of Scripture approximately 40 per cent from the New Testament, 40 per cent from the Old Testament, and 20 per cent from both Old and New Testaments in a related study. One quarter each year will consist of related lessons on Christian doctrine and life. Thus three quarters will be devoted primarily to instruction in a body of Bible truth with the other quarter devoted to further emphasis on application.

8. The selection of lessons shall be determined by the nature and capacities of childhood with necessary adjustment to adolescent and adult life.

9. Topical lessons shall be limited in number and always grounded in Scripture.

10. The schedule of lessons shall be geared to major observances of the church year.

When the Constitutional Convention of the National Sunday School Association met in Moody Memorial Church, Chicago, October 2-6, 1946, the Lesson Committee was ready with its report. As secretary of the committee, I presented the project and it evoked such interest and discussion that the assembly decided to devote the entire morning to its consideration. When a final vote was taken the gathering expressed its unanimous and enthusiastic approval of the Uniform Lessons.

On Sunday, January 4, 1948, it was estimated that a million Sunday School pupils across the nation began the study of lessons based on the Uniform Bible Lesson Outlines prepared by the NSSA. It was a good beginning. Today some 4,000,000 pupils are using the new lessons.

But there is another side to the story. We had not proceeded far with our work before Dr. Benson resigned as chairman of our Committee. There were unfavorable repercussions from the Evangelical Teacher Training Association and from the Scripture Press, with which he was closely connected. Other members of the Committee encountered similar embarrassment and resigned. Independent publishers, like Standard, found that many Sunday schools in their constituency were so tied up with denominations officially related to the ICRE that they were not free to switch to other lessons. To adopt the new lessons and drop the ICRE outlines would entail considerable financial sacrifice, which they were not prepared to make.

In this crisis I was made chairman of the Committee. I had to bear the burden of reorganization and fight for the continuance of our program. Fortunately I was a free lance and the NAE fully approved of what I was doing. Fifteen publishers individually or in groups adopted our outlines and began production. They appealed to me for help when they realized the lack of supplemental materials. There was need for an annual general commentary similar to Tarbell's and Peloubet's. With the cooperation of Higley Printing Company (whose aid in the Christian Action crusade was so valuable to me) we launched the annual "Evangelical Sunday School Lesson Commentary" which I edited for several years. (Even today the book carries my name as "Founder"). A committee of publishers was able to prevail upon Standard to print color cards, rolls, and lesson papers on contract until they could produce their own line. We "muddled through" our next problems while many were prophesying failure. Leaning heavily on the Lord we were blessed with final victory. Faced with competition, even the ICRE Uniform Lessons took on a more evangelical stance. This was our bonus in the blessings which came our way. I served as chairman of the Lesson Committee until I was made managing editor of *Christianity Today* and am still a member of the Advisory Committee of One Hundred.

While the new lesson outlines were our major concern the parent organization, the National Sunday School Association, suffered. The second convention was held in Cincinnati but the attendance was quite disappointing. Offices had been opened in Chicago but financial problems beset us. C. V. Egemeier, William E. Kirschke and Russell T. Hitt came and went in rapid succession in the office of executive secretary. Denver, Colorado and Oakland, California, conventions were little more than regional affairs. I attended all the conventions except Oakland. I was startled on the closing day of that gathering to get a long distance call in Cincinnati. Victor Cory and H. H. Savage were on the other end of the line pleading with me to take the presidency. They insisted that I was the only one who could lift the organization out of its doldrums. I accepted, despite the fact that I was "loaded to the guards" with other obligations.

My first term was disappointing in many respects. My analysis of the failure of the association to "get off the ground" was (1) We had no roots — local, state, and regional organizations; (2) cooperating denominations had their own programs and saw little need of another; (3) publishers had their own clinics and conventions and wanted no additional competition; (4) there was no vision of future achievement on the national level; (5) financial underwritings for an adequate budget were difficult to secure; (6) evangelicals in the beginning days of the NAE had so many calls for time and money that NSSA was "one too many."

169

My solution was to get to the roots with our plea — to the common people in the local churches and Sunday schools and provide inspiration and services that they could not get elsewhere. We adopted as slogans, "Revitalize the American Sunday School" and "Revival Now through the Sunday School." We had never adopted an official constitution and bylaws. This was another case of "no roots." We determined to change that.

When the next convention came in Philadelphia, we were still operating without roots and the gathering was a disappointment. There were about 600 present in Town Hall. But we had our first reading of a constitution. There was born a vision of better things. We determined that Detroit, the following year, would be different. And it was.

I made a trip to the "Motor City" to see my old friend Merton Rice of the Metropolitan Methodist Church. (He had been interested in Christian Action.) He was also so disgusted with liberalism in his own denominational Sunday school literature that he had switched to Standard supplies. When his bishop rebuked him and ordered him to "return to the fold," he refused. The bishop said, "Don't you know that stuff teaches immersion?" "Yes," said Merton, "but I'd rather have our people accept that than the rank liberalism we get out of Nashville!" The pastor of the largest Methodist Church in Michigan stood his ground. He welcomed me into his office and asked what he could do for me. I said, "We want to use your auditorium (one of the city's largest) for our National Sunday School Convention and we want strong attendance support from your great Sunday School." "You can have both and it won't cost you a cent." Then I went across the city to see G. Beauchamp Vick, who claimed to have the largest Baptist Church and Sunday School in America (Temple Baptist). He knew me through the *Baptist Bible Tribune* which was always quoting my articles about ecumenism. He greeted me cordially. I told him about the Convention and asked for a great delegation from Temple Baptist on the opening night. He agreed. Neither one of these churches cooperated with the Greater Detroit Sunday School Association which was sponsoring the Convention. I encountered a little resistance to my "high-handed" methods but with "tongue in cheek" they consented to go along with the idea that we would aim for an enrollment of 3,000. *United Evangelical Action* got out a big special number promoting the convention. We broke all records at Detroit and the NSSA was on its way to become more than a provincial or isolationist body.

At Detroit we adopted our new Constitution and Bylaws. We laid plans for establishing metropolitan, state, and regional associations. (Some were already in operation.) We set up a Commission for Educators (professors of Christian education in the colleges) under the leadership of Harold Mason; a Commission for Denominational Secretaries under A. L. Brown; a Commission for Publishers under Victor Cory, and laid plans for enlisting the interest of outstanding laymen of

170

financial means. A new day was before us and everybody rejoiced in it.

When we went to Minneapolis the next year under the guidance of that prince of Sunday school leaders, Harold W. Erickson, and that super salesman for the American Sunday School, Clate A. Risley, we were ready to pack the great Municipal Auditorium and enlist the interest of scores of evangelical churches that had not previously been concerned with our movement. The whole city was impressed with our testimony for "the faith once for all delivered."

With the cooperation of an ever-increasing number of capable workers the NSSA was indeed "revitalizing the American Sunday School."

A free consulting service was set up at national headquarters. Problems were ironed out by Sunday School experts. A monthly bulletin of plans for superintendents was mailed to all member schools. So great was the growing demand for this clinical aid that the Association set up new Commissions dealing with every phase of Sunday School work. They produced helps which expressed in methodology the basic doctrinal position of the Association and acted as consultants with evangelical Sunday School leadership at local, regional and national levels.

Three basic emphases came to characterize the work of the NSSA: (1) the Bible, (2) evangelism, and (3) spiritual power. All these had been lost in the infiltration of "liberalism" into the Sunday School, beginning with the early 1900's. Largely through the work of the Association the following achievements were noted:

The Bible was restored to its rightful position as the textbook of the Sunday School. It is not only central in curriculum, but its teachings determine the principles and methods used in the educational and promotional process. Teachers are no longer ashamed to say, "We teach the *Bible!*" despite the sophistries of "progressive" educators about teaching *"the pupils."* Evangelical Sunday School leaders were united in believing that their great task is to indoctrinate boys and girls, men and women with the great revealed truths of the Word of God and apply them to life. This new generation of leaders discarded the antibiblical naturalistic and humanistic philosophies which were basic to the principles and methodology of "liberal" religious education. They now are in the process of building a new concept of the Sunday School's educational task which is true to the Bible. The natural result is a new generation of pupils who sing with the Psalmist: "O how I love thy word, O God; it is my meditation all the day. Thou through thy commandments hast made me wiser than mine enemies."

Evangelism was restored to its rightful position in the purpose of the Sunday School. Again it is being bravely said, "The purpose of the Sunday School is to *win souls to Christ,* teaching them the Word of God and training them in Christian character and service." Evangelical leaders equate education and evangelism as the twin objectives of the Great Commission and zealously promote them simultaneously. This is resulting in three things: (1) Enrollment and attendance are climbing

171

in schools which have caught the vision. The largest and most rapidly growing schools in America and abroad are of the strictly evangelical type. (2) People are being saved every Lord's Day as a result of the teaching of strictly Bible lessons. Every Bible lesson contains an "evangelistic emphasis" which enables the teacher to pin-point his instruction to win souls for Christ. (3) The churches fortunate enough to have Sunday Schools like this are reaching out in their communities constantly touching new lives for Christ. They are known as alive and "on the job," and as churches that act as though Christianity is a vital, full-time business.

Spiritual power was restored to the whole Sunday School operation. One of the reasons for this lies in the fact that the leaders in this new movement believe that the educational process involves crisis, conflict, and choice. This crisis involves the pupil's personal and individual acceptance of Jesus Christ as Lord and Saviour, his repentance, his obedience and his infilling by the Holy Spirit. If this is a truly valid experience it produces a regenerated and reborn person — a new creature in Christ Jesus. The old "progressive" educational philosophy was wedded to cold educational propositions, to methods and to programs which are purely naturalistic and intellectual in concept. They imparted no warmth and divine passion. They recognized no possibility of that spiritual influx by which God through the Holy Spirit breathes new life into the pupil. The evangelical concept gives spiritual dynamic for Christian growth, sharing and victory. In this new movement which is sweeping the land the Sunday School is being thought of as a divine institution with divine oversight, a divine program and a divine mission. Therefore it is becoming a dynamic spiritual power "winning souls to Christ, teaching them the Word of God and training them in Christian character and service."

Largely due to forces set in action by the NSSA a revival of Sunday School attendance and enrollment came to American Protestantism for a period of twenty years. It was a great joy and privilege to have had some part in it.

Today there is a fine NSSA headquarters building in Wheaton, Ill., with a capable staff of workers. The metropolitan, state, and regional associations and conventions are prosperous. I have covered the nation in speaking before these gatherings and conducting clinics and conferences. In 1965 I was surprised by being called to the platform during the national convention and presented with a plaque recognizing my services for the Sunday schools of America. I was further honored by being made an honorary life member of the National Board.

172

Episode XV

National Religious Broadcasters

My involvement with the Christians' Hour made it possible for me to render a valuable service in the movement to preserve and perpetuate the right of evangelicals to broadcast the Gospel over radio and television in America. As the official representative of the Christians' Hour, I automatically became eligible to participate in the affairs of the Radio Broadcasting Commission of the National Association of Evangelicals and later in those of the National Religious Broadcasters.

First a little background: Evangelicals were in the forefront of the forces of religion which recognized radio broadcasting as an effective means of propaganda. Their forebears had so recognized the printing press and had used it to disseminate the Gospel to the "four corners of the earth." Radio reached out everywhere; it carried its messages at a speed of 186,000 miles a second; it leaped over boundaries, penetrated walls, and touched people never before accessible to the Gospel.

Such aggressive exponents of Bible truth as John Roach Straton of Calvary Baptist Church, New York City; Robert P. Shuler of Trinity Methodist Church, Los Angeles, Calif., and Clinton H. Churchill of Churchill Gospel Tabernacle, Buffalo, N. Y., secured licenses and built their own radio broadcasting stations. Other evangelicals began to develop programs which were broadcast over a network of stations across the nation. Notable among these were Charles E. Fuller and the "Old-Fashioned Revival Hour," Walter A. Maier and "The Lutheran Hour."

It was not long until evangelicals were receiving a hearing across the nation that was mounting into the millions. They credited this wide acceptance to the drawing power of the evangelical faith. Thousands who had been denied Bible preaching by liberal ministers in their own churches rejoiced at the opportunity once again to hear the old Gospel.

Then complications began to set in. Religious racketeers began to use radio preaching as a medium of exploitation. Liberals were quick to identify these men as "fundamentalists." In the *Christian Century* a St. Louis clergyman took issue with "fundamentalist broadcasts" in language like this: "These programs and others of the same stripe have long been distasteful to liberal church leaders, to much of the listening public and to network officials." He went on to declare that the Mutual Broadcasting Company had "tolerated" programs like the Lutheran Hour because of the revenue which they brought to Mutual's treasury. He referred to these programs as "the network religious program racket, capitalized by independent super-fundamentalist revivalists." Then he appealed for the "elimination of paid religious programs" by Mutual, and failing in this, for a "rule of the Federal Communications Commission against the sale of time for religious broadcasting."

This was the beginning of propaganda by Liberals which resulted in an effort by the Federal Council of Churches to gain control of the broadcasting of religion. Under the leadership of Frank R. Goodman, the Council signed up fifty or more radio stations "with ironclad contracts obliging them to use the Federal Council approved programs and no other." It was his intention to extend this policy to include every broadcasting station and agency in the United States and thus effectually eliminate Gospel broadcasting.

One of the first victims of this drive was the Lutheran Hour which had the largest coverage of any evangelical broadcast. Dr. Walter Maier was an ordained minister of the Missouri Synod Lutheran Church, the most conservative of all the Lutheran bodies in the nation. He had a brilliant mind, held an earned Ph.D. from one of the leading German universities, was a professor in Concordia Theological Seminary, St. Louis, and was undoubtedly the greatest, popular pulpit orator of the times. He had a clear understanding of the basic theological and ecclesiastical issues of the Liberal-Conservative controversy. His broadcasts were tremendously effective and were causing deep trouble for the Liberals in every Protestant denomination in America.

I immediately rushed into print with articles and editorials condemning the Federal Council for its policy and the Mutual Broadcasting Company for its action. To my very great surprise I got a long-distance call from St. Louis one morning asking for a conference in Cincinnati with Dr. Maier and his business manager, Eugene R. Bertermann. We met in the Gibson Hotel for a full day, discussing every phase of the unfortunate situation. They were profuse in their expressions of appreciation for what I had written. The Lutheran Hour's files containing confidential correspondence with Mutual and the Federal Council were made available to me for use in further publicity. It was agreed that the National Association of Evangelicals would immediately contact all parties involved and "go to bat" for the Lutheran Hour, but, more than this, move for the organization of all evangelical broadcasters into an effective pressure group which could deal officially with all the broader and deeper problems involved. The services of the finest communications lawyers in the nation were retained and it was not long before the Lutheran Hour was given assurances that there would be no further interference with their rights to broadcast the Gospel.

As a result of this incident my personal relations with Drs. Maier and Bertermann and other Missouri Synod church leaders became most cordial and rewarding. I shall have more to say of this at the conclusion of the chapter.

The NAE laid its course to protect the rights of evangelical broadcasters in three areas: (1) The preaching of doctrinal sermons over the air. (2) The purchase of time for Gospel broadcasting over both na-

174

tional networks and local stations. (3) The right of representative evangelical inter-church organizations to their share of the sustaining time allotted to Protestantism.

Nation-wide resentment over Mutual's action had brought many repercussions. Outside the NAE there were evangelicals who held mass meetings and employed high-powered publicity through the press to castigate the FCC and the radio industry. Many of these impetuous evangelicals counseled legal action and bitter attack. The NAE leadership, on the other hand, felt that God was in His heaven and that those in positions of authority in both government and the radio industry were fairminded, public spirited, and most certainly not enemies of religion. They felt that once these leaders were acquainted with the facts of the situation they would listen to reason and deal justly with the demands of evangelicals. NAE's representatives were sane, judicious, constructive, consecrated, yet positive and insistent, with the result that the radio industry and the government agencies began to develop an increasing respect for them and their cause.

Upon the invitation of the NAE approximately 150 evangelical radio broadcasters gathered April 12, 1944, for a conference in connection with the second annual convention of the NAE in Columbus, Ohio. They agreed that a national organization was essential and moved to create one immediately. Accordingly a temporary committee was set up which voted to engage Louis G. Caldwell of Washington, probably the most capable communications attorney in the nation, as counselor in the preparation of a Constitution and Bylaws and a general policy and program. With his advice they made their report in Chicago at a duly called Constitutional Convention and the National Religious Broadcasters, Incorporated, came into being, September 21, 1944. I was chosen as a member of the board and of the Executive Committee on both of which I served for more than fifteen years.

I was appointed to the Committee which was charged with drafting a Code of Ethics for evangelical broadcasters and also a Statement to be mailed to all stations, networks, the industry, and the Federal Communications Commission, making clear the identity of evangelicals in the Protestant and general religious worlds. As often happened in situations like this, I was chosen to be the "scribe" and prepared the first "rough" and the final drafts of these historic documents. Because of this I am including them in my Memoirs.

CODE OF ETHICS

Recognizing the vital and increasingly important role played by radio broadcasting as an agency of mass communications, vastly extending the potential audiences of the church and the classroom, the National Religious Broadcasters believe that the propagation of the Gospel by radio is essential to the religious inspiration, guidance, and education of the public, to the enrichment of the national life, and to the full use of this blessing of modern civilization in the public interest. In furtherance of this belief and of its purposes to foster and encourage the broadcasting of religious programs, and "to establish and maintain high standards with respect to content, method of presentation, speakers' qualifications, and ethical practices to the end that such programs may be constantly developed and improved and that their public interest and usefulness may be enhanced," the Association has adopted, and each of its members has subscribed to, the following Code of Ethics:

I

Sponsorship of all programs broadcast by or in the name of the Association of any of its members shall be solely by a non-profit organization whose aim and purpose is the propagation of the Gospel.

II

The message disseminated in such programs shall be positive, concise and constructive.

III

The content, production, and presentation of such programs, including both music and continuity, shall be consistent with the program standards of the station or the network over which they are broadcast, and with the requirements of all Federal and State laws and of all regulations of the Federal Communications Commission.

IV

Persons engaging in the broadcasting of such programs shall, by prompt appearance, scrupulous conformity with the limitations imposed by physical, technical, and economic characteristics of radio, Christian courtesy, and otherwise, cooperate with the station or network management.

V

Appeals shall be of a bona fide character for legitimate religious purposes, and shall be presented in a dignified Christian manner. All donors shall be promptly furnished with receipts, and an accounting thereof shall be furnished the NRB Board of Directors upon request.

This Code became a veritable "Declaration of Independence" from radio racketeers on the one hand and ecclesiastical boycotters on the other. An official Statement addressed to the industry and the Federal Communications Commission, drafted later, read as follows:

A STATEMENT

Inasmuch as there exists among the Federal Communications Commission, radio network executives and managers of local radio stations an understandable misconception as to the situation within modern American Protestantism and its proper representation on the radio, we feel that it is incumbent upon the National Religious Broadcasters, Inc., an affiliate of the National Association of Evangelicals, to clarify the situation.

We believe that once radio broadcasting understands the issues involved it will be entirely fair to all parties concerned.

One misconception is that American Protestantism is one unified religious group, whereas in fact there are two distinct kinds of Protestants in America today. Each adheres to a particular form of teaching — the one the antithesis of the other.

One group believes the Bible to be the infallible rule for belief and conduct, whereas the other does not.

We believe it could be demonstrated that the majority of American Protestants belong to the former group. Yet this group is not given time or representation on the radio, either by the networks or by individual radio stations, in proportion to their numerical strength. . . .

National Religious Broadcasters, Inc., became essential when it was evident that existing interdenominational organizations, while claiming to be representatives of all Protestantism, were in reality representative of the point of view heretofore described — namely, that which rejects the infallibility and absolute authority of the Bible.

We stand ready to cooperate with the Federal Communications Commission and the radio industry in every possible way to ameliorate the present situation.

After many months of correspondence and conference, understandings were reached which fully protected the rights of all accredited religious broadcasters at national and local levels. The distinctively evangelical testimony was assured of a voice on the air. Means had been provided whereby the airlanes would be kept perpetually available for the preaching of the Gospel. The National Association of Evangelicals was given its proportionate share of sustaining time on all the national networks and evangelicals were recognized as having a valid claim to consideration at the local levels.

I am very definitely of the opinion that if it had not been for the National Religious Broadcasters the National Council of Churches would have taken over all Protestant time on the airwaves at the national level and that evangelical broadcasting would have been completely eliminated. The Christians' Hour, the Old-Fashioned Revival Hour, The Lutheran Hour, the Hour of Decision and other well-known broadcasts would have become the victims of Liberal imperialism and ecclesiastical tyranny.

NRB was guided by a group of capable and consecrated Christian gentlemen such as William Ward Ayer, Theodore H. Elsner, Myron F. Boyd, Thomas F. Zimmerman, and Walter Bennett, but we had one brilliant president who did us more harm than good. He was Clinton H. Churchill who served 1945-47. He headed the then immensely popular Churchill Tabernacle in Buffalo. Great crowds attended his services. The Tabernacle was quite a show place with a stage like a theater. His large evening audiences were entertained by musical groups, dramatic skits, and out-of-town lecturers. There was a strong evangelistic emphasis during periodic revivals. Churchill owned the million-dollar property and ran it like an extremely profitable business. He built the first and the largest radio station in Buffalo using the medium to effectively promote his interests. At the time we knew him, he was in legal difficulties over this station. It seems that he had leased it with the privilege of purchase and that the lessors had taken over the property. The contract called for a generous amount of free time each day for Churchill broadcasts. The management was seeking legal release from this feature of its agreement. Churchill had been shrewd enough to foresee such a contingency and had inserted a clause which would require the legal ownership to revert to him in case this free time was restricted in any way. NRB came on the scene at just the right time to give Churchill national prestige and status before the courts and the community. He won his case and title to this multi-million-dollar investment. We of the NRB executive committee were invited to Buffalo on several occasions and were entertained lavishly at Churchill's beautiful country estate where he lived in all the luxury of an English squire. All the facilities of his offices were made available to us in the promotion of NRB, along with his legal counsel (the best available in the field of communications media), all of which at that time considerably advanced our standing in Washington and with the radio industry. Fortunately we escaped the debacle which came some years later when Churchill became too prosperous for his own good. His followers in the Tabernacle lost faith in him as a religious leader. He got a divorce from his faithful wife of long years' standing and married a young actress accustomed to high life in New York society. It is said that Churchill became immensely wealthy and himself a devotee of the high life he once so profitably condemned.

After about ten successful years the NRB was faced with two problems which threatened its future. A number of the major broadcasters who were not members of the National Association of Evangelicals felt that this relationship was inimical to their acceptance in wider areas of Protestantism. They had not withdrawn but were increasingly lukewarm, not represented in the conventions, and neglectful in their financial support. The National Council of Churches, aware of this situation, decided to make a new move to take over complete control of Protestant broadcasting. Some of our loyal members, in a spirit of goodwill, had consented to become members of an *ad hoc* organization, along with NCC broadcasting and film commission members, to bring about "better understanding and closer unity" between all Protestant broadcasters. This move was of doubtful origin. I suspected it was initiated as a part of a new NCC strategy. In this crucial time (1956) I was asked to take the presidency of the NRB.

My first move was to strengthen the structure of NRB by enlisting the active interest of lukewarm members and making new contacts with groups like the Southern Baptists, Churches of Christ, and some inde-

178

pendents that hitherto had hesitated to associate themselves with us. I launched a monthly bulletin called the *NRB Radio-Tele-Gram* to keep everybody informed about new developments.

I felt that our position would be immensely strengthened if we could take our national convention to the Nation's Capital. This was the seat of the Federal Communications Commission and the lawmakers who could assure our constitutional rights to freedom of religion and freedom of speech on the airwaves. It was also the seat of the industry's National Association of Broadcasters and the leading trade journal of the industry, *Broadcasting* magazine. NAE's public relations offices were also in Washington ready to serve us in crucial situations. I felt we needed to be well and favorably known there. We voted to go to Washington and hold our convention in the prestigious Mayflower Hotel.

News began to infiltrate from several states that State Councils of Churches were initiating efforts to take over all Protestant broadcasting rights, under the clever ruse of opposing the "sale" of radio time for the broadcasting of religion. The propaganda was for "free" time to responsible broadcasters ("responsible" meaning, churches related to and/or approved by the Councils of Churches). Then the Broadcasting and Film Commission of the National Council came out boldly for this policy.

I immediately charged the Council with reopening the battle we had won a decade ago and laid down the gauntlet. Shortly thereafter the chairman of its Commission invited me to New York City to discuss the situation and assured me that the rights of evangelicals would be preserved in the new arrangement. He offered to pay my expenses. I accepted his invitation with the understanding that I would pay my own expenses so as not to be under any obligation to him. I also insisted we meet on neutral ground. Accordingly we met at the Prince George Hotel and spent an entire day from early in the morning to late at night discussing every phase of the proposal. After the usual amenities, our confrontation became a "battle royal." He was proposing that a joint commission be set up in which all elements in Protestantism would have representation to assure fairness in allocation of time. He said it would save our broadcasters millions of dollars. I pointed out that the NCC commission would have the right to determine the personnel of its own membership, the type and number of the programs aired, and that the commission would be officially related to the National Council of Churches and subject to its authority. I cited many instances of similar agreements between evangelicals and liberals, in the days prior to our open split with the Councils, which invariably resulted in eventual liberal victory and evangelical defeat. I assured him that the NRB would make no compromises and that we would immediately resume the battle to preserve, maintain and aggressively promote the rights and freedoms we had won ten years before.

This development gave us a *causus belli* that assured a great attendance

179

for our Washington Convention. We invited the chairman of the Federal Communications Commission, the president of the National Association of Broadcasters, and communications media experts from the National networks to speak. We set up workshops where technical problems could be discussed. We instituted a "Congressional Breakfast" to which our broadcasters invited their own senators and representatives as guests. We arranged a panel discussion of the BIG ISSUE. Exhibits for related agencies were permitted for the first time. We were able to get a reasonable amount of press coverage.

In this connection I want to tell the story of what happened with *Broadcasting* magazine. This is the "Bible" of the industry. I knew if we could get their endorsement of the "sale" of time for religious broadcasting as against "free" time controlled by the Councils, we would "have it made." Bob Fleming, the agency man who handled our Christians' Hour affairs, promised to get me an interview with Sol Taishoff, editor and publisher of *Broadcasting*. He and L. B. Wilson, the owner of Station WCKY in Cincinnati, were bosom friends. Fleming got Wilson to write Sol a very generous letter of introduction on my behalf. When I went into the offices of the magazine, just across the street from the Mayflower, I was given an immediate audience. After an exchange of the amenities I was asked to state my case. I told the story of the NRB and of the new National Council threat to the right of evangelical broadcasters to purchase time for the broadcast of religion. I said we would appreciate a word in our behalf in the columns of the journal. Sol leaned back in his chair and said, "Why can't you Protestants settle your disagreements amicably and make some sort of compromise on broadcasting policies?" I said, "Well, there are several kinds of Protestants and we are unwilling to give up our differing convictions for the sake of unity. May I illustrate? There are several kinds of Jews — Orthodox, Reformed and Conservative . . ." With a hearty laugh Sol threw up his hands and immediately retorted, "You don't need to argue your case any further. I know what you are talking about. You certainly have equal rights before the law and the sale of time is the easiest way to guarantee those rights." He then called in two of his best reporters and said, "Hear this man's case and pepper him with questions. Then, I want you to report the NRB convention for our next issue." When that number came from the press it contained not only a good news story but a boxed editorial championing our cause. The finest relations between the NRB and the magazine have existed ever since.

On the first day of the convention we had a fine luncheon in the Mayflower. I was presiding and in the preliminaries I read greetings from the President of the United States and other distinguished persons. The National Council of Churches had a table headed by my friend the chairman of its Broadcasting and Film Commission. He had always insisted that Councils did not seek to control Protestant broadcasting. It happened that one of the letters I was reading was from the manager of

180

Station KVOO, Oklahoma City. He said he was a Methodist layman and a member of the board of the Oklahoma Council of Churches and then proceeded to tell how he had openly opposed the efforts of the Council to control Protestant broadcasting in his state. He wished us well in our fight for our rights. I made no comment but the confusion at the NCC table was apparent to all.

The move to Washington proved to be tremendously beneficial. Assurances of support in our efforts to keep the airwaves open to evangelical broadcasting came from senators and representatives, FCC members, industry spokesmen, and others in highly influential positions. It was voted to return the following year. Thereafter the conventions were always held in the Nation's Capital.

Another important accomplishment came during my administration. The Voice of America, the U.S. Government's mighty shortwave broadcast beamed toward Russia and the Iron Curtain countries, gave a certain amount of time to religion. Billy Graham had frequently requested time on VA but was for one reason or another turned down. This was likewise the experience of other evangelical broadcasters. We investigated the situation and discovered that broadcasters of religion had to be approved as "responsible" by the Synagogue Council of America, for Jews; the National Catholic Welfare Conference, for Roman Catholics; and the National Council of Churches, for Protestants. The NCC simply would not approve of Billy Graham or any other evangelical. The NRB, with the aid of its legal counsel, finally initiated a formal plea for the recognition of evangelicals in general and the Billy Graham broadcasts in particular. After getting the proverbial "run-around" we threatened suit and gave our story to the press. It did not take long then to get action. We were invited to Washington for an off-the-record conference with the "top brass" of the Voice of America. It was quite a meeting with some twenty or twenty-five men, lasting for two sessions and finally resulting in Graham's being awarded time and the evangelicals' being recognized as having Protestant rights beyond NCC endorsement.

I introduced a new feature in our coverage — an organization of evangelical owners and managers of radio broadcasting stations. WMBI, Chicago, owned and operated by Moody Bible Institute was the finest example of this development in communications media. I asked them to assume the leadership in bringing these men together, which they did with an eventual membership of some thirty stations. While their problems were quite different from those of the founders of NRB, their aims and hopes were the same as ours, and we soon found them of invaluable aid in enabling us to maintain good relations with station and network managers. Their own efficiency was greatly increased and they enjoyed a rewarding fellowship with our members.

With the advent of television, evangelicals were quick to avail themselves of this medium in the dissemination of the Gospel. It is believed that the first televised service of worship in history was broadcast by a member of the NRB — The Lutheran Hour, over KSD-TV, St. Louis, Mo., January 1, 1948. Our own Eugene R. Bertermann, as director of radio for The Lutheran Hour, was responsible for this progressive step. Despite the high cost of televised programming a number of evangelicals launched out in this field with encouraging results. They asked for their share of sustaining time. They perfected television techniques and every method employed consistent with the Christian ethic.

Machinery for the effective utilization of radio and television for the proclamation of the Gospel and the support of the churches is now available to evangelicals everywhere, thanks to the foresight of the early leaders of the NAE. I was glad to have had a small part in that development. Without that vision it is altogether likely that evangelicals would today be without the means of challenging America with their radio-TV message.

Speaking of Dr. Bertermann, I want to pay tribute to this remarkable man and tell of our warm personal friendship over many years. When I came to the end of my term as president of the NRB I was asked to serve for another, but I declined. I was literally swamped with my duties as editor of *Action* magazine and the "extra-curricular" demands on my time. But, more than this, I had the conviction that a man of the stature of Dr. Bertermann in the field of electronics and mass media communication could do more for evangelical broadcasters than any man alive. He had served a term as president of NRB at a time when he was severely limited by NAE restrictions which had now been lifted. I felt that if we gave him *carte blanche* he could lead us on to higher and greater accomplishments. I was able to "sell" both Dr. Bertermann and our executive committee on this idea and as I write he is still the president of NRB, honored and revered by broadcasters, secular and religious, everywhere.

As I have previously indicated, Dr. Bertermann and I first met in Cincinnati, when Dr. Walter Maier and The Lutheran Hour were faced with elimination from the airwaves by the Federal Council of Churches. I was able to set up a chain of events which with the Lord's help saved the day for them. They became members of NRB, although their denomination (The Lutheran Church-Missouri Synod) was not related with any inter-church body. They became pillars of strength to us. The Lutheran Hour was and is the greatest religious broadcast in the world in number of radio outlets. It has offices all over the world where its programs are translated and managed. Its message is soundly orthodox in basic Biblical theology and of the highest technical quality. Much of this is due to Dr. Bertermann's administrative, theological, technological, and promotional ability. He was the moving spirit behind the organization of the Lutheran Laymen's League with chapters throughout America, the men who financially undergird the whole program of the broadcast. He has headed it for many years as its executive secretary. He holds an earned Ph.D. degree and speaks several languages. His writings and his research in electronics and mass media communication are highly respected by leaders in these fields. His knowledge gained in world travel and personal contacts with nationals in every land where The Lutheran Hour is broadcast enables him to advise with expertise those who manage this vast religious enterprise which, very largely, *he* has been able to build and maintain.

Whenever I am in St. Louis, where his headquarters is located, he insists on meeting me and hosting a luncheon or dinner with Missouri Synod leaders. I often ask him for personal favors and favors for the interests with which I am connected. For example, when I have been unable to get a hotel reservation on short notice, he has made arrangements for me to stay at the Missouri Athletic Club, the most exclusive in the city. When the North American Christian Convention first went to St. Louis, at my request he contacted the religion editors of the leading dailies and paved the way for excellent press coverage. The contacts he made for us gave veritable unknowns the respect of editors and reporters which has continued to this day. The same was true of radio and television coverage, largely due to the respect which is held for Concordia Theological Seminary's radio station in St. Louis. When our own "Disciples" were quietly seeking to boycott our NACC meetings in this city, it was a "denominational friend" who helped us overcome opposition in high places. We found a great deal in common in our mutual commitment to the inspiration and authority of Holy Scriptures, though we differed significantly in tradition and theological opinion.

It took a great deal of courage for Maier and Bertermann to do what they did for me. I recall, when I was president of the National Sunday School Association, we invited Dr. Maier to deliver one of the major addresses at our national convention in Cincinnati. He accepted and then ran into difficulties with denominational leaders who frowned upon his irenic action. Finally, he called me long-distance one day and said, "I regret this more than I can say, but my ecclesiastical superiors insist that the only way I will be permitted to deliver this address is for one of our Missouri Synod churches in Cincinnati to take over the entire convention platform that night and for their pastor and choir to conduct the preliminary devotional services using our Lutheran liturgy." He kept apologizing between sentences and assuring me that this was not his doing, but stated that he had no alternative. I checked with my associates and we agreed to the terms. Dr. Maier spoke before a packed audience in Emery Auditorium and the occasion was the highlight of our convention.

Through Dr. Bertermann's good offices I became closely acquainted with the management of Concordia Press, the Synod's official publishing house. It was through this connection that I was able to enlist their cooperation in the Evangelical Press Association. Concordia's superiority in the graphic arts was immediately recognized and their editors made a great contribution to the development of this important evangelical organization.

What a wonderful illustration of the Scriptural truth that when we cast our bread upon the waters it shall return to us with manifold blessing!

Episode XVI

Ecumenical Polemics

Timothy Dwight's great hymn expresses the actuating motive behind my voluminous writings on the Councils of Churches —

I love Thy kingdom, Lord, the house of Thine abode;
The Church our blest Redeemer saved with His own precious blood;
I love Thy Church, O God! Her walls before Thee stand
Dear as the apple of Thine eye, and graven on Thy hand.

For her my tears shall fall, for her my prayers ascend;
To her my cares and toils be given, till toils and cares shall end;
Beyond my highest joy I prize her heavenly ways,
Her sweet communion, solemn vows, her hymns of love and praise.

When I saw the efforts of ambitious Protestant ecclesiastics to create One Church for One World — a mighty religious behemoth comparable to the Church of Rome, I declared war against it. I realized that they were abandoning the authority of the Holy Scriptures and changing the very essence of Christian fellowship as it existed in the Apostolic Church; distorting and contradicting every thesis of basic New Testament truth; robbing rank-and-file Christians of all those freedoms implicit in Christ; and, by erecting innumerable ecclesiastical stumbling blocks, blocking the road to the achievement of the only unity for which Christ prayed. Furthermore, I realized that Liberals, committed to a completely humanistic and socialistic philosophy of life, dominated the leadership of the whole movement and were assuming the right to speak and to act for the whole Church in national and world affairs. I determined that at least one small voice would be raised against this attempted rape of Christendom.

United Evangelical Action gave me the medium through which I could speak and write. An examination of the files of the magazine during the fourteen years of my editorship will show that I majored in constructive matters that would build the Kingdom of God. I was committed to the principle of inter-church cooperation. I believed that the basic unity of Protestantism should be manifest in all forms of cooperation that did not require compromise of essential evangelical and biblical convictions. I believed that there were many ways in which all Christians should participate in communities of Christian forces to "do together what can be done better unitedly than separately." My record will show that I have been active in the leadership of many such enterprises. I expect to continue to participate in such cooperative effort all the days of my life.

There were some of our leaders in the National Association of Evangelicals who were opposed to a policy of speaking boldly against the apostasy of Liberals and against the shortcomings of the Councils of Churches. They were fearful that our movement might be confused with radical "Fundamentalism" or with the National Council of Christian Churches, headed by Carl McIntire. McIntire had created his organization primarily to fight the Councils and his journal, *The Christian Beacon,* was filled with attacks on everybody who disagreed with him, even the NAE. I was in thorough sympathy with these brethren and shared their fears but I felt there was a happy medium that could be maintained in *Action* magazine policy, which could allow for intelligent expression and confrontation of the issues involved in the ecumenical controversy. I felt we had to keep our own constituency and the public in general informed as to our reason for being a separate cooperative entity. I felt that we, like Paul, must speak boldly in defense of the Gospel and not shun to confront its enemies. By far the great majority of our leaders approved my policy and backed me loyally throughout my long term of service.

My first venture was a series of articles which was an apologetic for our movement. I first dealt with the basic principles of Protestantism and the "least common denominator" of fundamental Christian faith as revealed in the Word of God. Then came "A Study in Christian Cooperation in America" which gave the history of consecutive related efforts in this area. Next came an article on "How Federative Action Began in America" followed by "Why Evangelicals Cannot Cooperate in the Federal Council of Churches," "The Proposed National Council of Churches," "Adventuring in United Evangelical Action," and finally "Current Moves for World Christian Cooperation." So favorably was this series received across the nation that there were many requests for its issuance in brochure form for wider distribution. Accordingly, the booklet was published under the general title *United Action Now.*

Next came *Amsterdam 1948* which was a critique of the world gathering that voted the World Council of Churches into being. Its careful evaluation and analysis of what had taken place proved to be so accurate as to be almost prophetic. It had a wide circulation and prepared our people for an intelligent understanding of what was to come at the world level.

In 1950 the National Council of Churches came into being as successor to the Federal Council of Churches and seven other conciliar organizations. I reported it at the time but waited for two years and until all the facts were in before I undertook to write (1952) the critique, *The Growing Super Church.* This first appeared in continued-story form in *Action* under such titles as "Introduction and Background," "NCC Organizational Structure," "Its Theological Complexion," "NCC Super-Church Proclivities," "Its Leftist Social Doctrines," "Its Educational Inclusiveness," "Its Invertebrate Evangelism," "Its Betrayal of Missions,"

"Its Use of Political Power," and "The Evangelical Alternative." When the eighty-page brochure was published it was circulated by the thousands, not only in America, but around the world, and became among evangelicals and other Bible-believing Christians a veritable "Bible" on the subject. It continued to be distributed by the NAE until I wrote an up-dated critique of the Council in 1966.

In 1955 I wrote a similar critique of the World Council based on the actions of the "Constitutional Assembly" of the Council at Evanston in 1954. This was perhaps more authentic and exhaustive than the NCC brochure because I spent a week or more in Evanston and, as a member of the press, had access to all the most significant meetings scheduled there. I had the opportunity to meet and confer with such distinguished religious leaders as Bishop Eivind Berggrav of the Church of Norway; Dr. Charles Malik (then Lebanon Ambassador to the USA and delegate to the UN), a member of the Eastern Orthodox Catholic Church; Dr. Edmund Schlink, professor of systematic theology in the University of Heidelberg; and Bishop Hans Lilje of Germany. All of these men were evangelical in spirit and gave me many insights into developments within the Assembly.

As an example: Bishop Berggrav alerted me as to the efforts of Bible-believing leaders to get mention of the Holy Scriptures in the so-called doctrinal "Basis" of the Council which had omitted such reference in its original draft. The Bishop himself had assumed the responsibility for the fight to win this concession from "the powers that be." He said, "It is generally felt that the present Basis is lacking in clear expression of the very *basis of the Basis,* which as a matter of fact is to be found in the Holy Scriptures . . . What the WCC needs is a flying standard under which we all can march. This standard without the Bible is incomplete." He believed he would have no difficulty in convincing his comrades in the Assembly of the necessity for this change and when he was defeated he went home to Norway a sad, disillusioned, and disappointed man. He personally never had any fatih in the Council thereafter.

In my critique I discussed Evanston and the Council under the following heads: "A Bird's-Eye View," "The Ecumenical Device," "The Main Theme," "Faith and Order," "Evangelism and Missions," "The Social Order," "International Affairs," and "The Coming Great Church." The title of the last chapter was made the general title of the brochure. It had a tremendous circulation around the world and was translated in its entirety into the Korean, Japanese, and French languages. Chapters and excerpts were issued as tracts in some twenty foreign languages and dialects. Many evangelical colleges and Bible institutes used it as required reading for their students and for discussion groups, to say nothing of the thousands of evangelical churches which distributed it in quantities among their members and in their communities. Orders even came in from the offices of Councils of Churches, though the policy of Council leaders seemed to be completely "ignore both the author and the brochure" in all public meetings and communications. One Council secretary told me, "This document is the only one produced by the opposition that is even worth reading. It has some insights and reactions in it which we may consider in mapping future policies." I was asked by many evangelical journals to contribute articles on the Council. The popular Back to the Bible radio broadcast (Dr. Theodore Epp) asked me to contribute several chapters for its own brochure, *The Coming World Church,* which was widely advertised and distributed among its listening audiences.

In 1960 I went to St. Andrews, Scotland, to report the meeting of the World Council's Central Committee, which gave me new insights into the direction the ecumenical movement was taking. I shall report other experiences later.

In 1961 the NAE asked me to do an up-dated series of articles on the World Council in *Action* magazine. These were published later in brochure form under the title, *The World Council of Churches: An Analysis and Evaluation.* This received the same generous acceptance as its predecessor. It was translated in its entirety (for circulation in Latin America) in Spanish, Portuguese and French. As an example of these translations, the Portuguese was translated by an editorial committee of Livraria Editora Evangelica and issued under the title, *A Aventura Ecumenica: Uma Analise do Conselho Mundial de Igrejas.* I remember we had some correspondence about my allusions to Communism which were distasteful to the committee, and we agreed on revised statements. The brochure was distributed by bookstores in Sao Paulo and Sao Luis in Brazil. It was said to have had considerable influence on the attitude of Brazilian Protestantism toward the Council. As in the case of the previous WCC brochure, chapters and excerpts appeared in tract form in many languages and dialects, some of which are still circulating as I write.

In 1966 the NAE asked me to do an up-dated series of articles on the National Council of Churches. These were likewise issued in brochure form under the title, *The National Council of Churches: A Critique.* This came to be considered the generally accepted statement of the NAE's position on the Council, although no official action was taken to that effect. It still has a fair circulation as I write.

From those days until the present I have been in considerable demand as a writer and lecturer on modern ecumenicity. I have tried to keep well informed by reading everything published on the subject and by contacts with friends "behind the scenes" in the various manifestations of the movement.

In 1966 I was asked by Crestwood Books to contribute a chapter on the World Council to their symposium on the Liberal infiltration of the Protestant churches entitled, *Your Church — Their Target.* Among the other contributors were Kenneth Ingwalson, publisher of *Human Events;* Howard E. Kershner, editor of *Christian Economics;* Edmund A.

Opitz, director of the Foundation for Economic Education; Herbert A. Philbrick, former FBI counterspy; Charles S. Poling, founder of the National Committee of Christian Laymen; G. Aiken Taylor, editor of *The Presbyterian Journal;* and Rousas Rushdoony, editor of the *International Library of Philosophy and Theology.* This gave me entree to a wider sector of American conservatives, many of whom were prominent and wealthy laymen in the major denominations officially related to the Councils. This book marked the beginnings of a movement to withhold financial support for the leftwing socio-political programs of the Councils. So successful has it now become that both the liberal denominational leadership and the liberal conciliar leadership have been forced to retrench their budgets and reduce their staff personnel — a situation which is causing many to prophesy the early demise of the National Council of Churches in the USA.

Kenneth Ingwalson, Ed Opitz, and Irving Howard (of *Christian Economics*) shortly after the publication of the book, called me to New York City for a day-long conference on strategy for dissemination of the facts about the great "silent majority" of American Protestants who were outside the Councils. It was agreed that I should write a book on the subject which would be published and distributed by Crestwood Books. This eventuated in *Protestant Revolt,* a 350-page volume (in paperback and deluxe hardback bindings) which I consider the best thing I have done polemically on the Councils. Financially the work was backed by J. Howard Pew, founder and chairman of the board of the great Sun Oil Company ("Blue Sunoco"). I had several conferences with Mr. Pew and he collaborated with me in the writing of the chapter on "The Crucial Issue," which dealt with the separation of Church and State and the socio-political stance of the Councils. I did a tremendous lot of research in identifying the non-Council constituency in America, the facts and figures for which appeared in the appendices to the book. I showed that 37,303,793 Protestants were outside the National Council of Churches, against 31,077,536 inside its claimed membership. Here I listed the hundreds of non-Council Foreign Missionary agencies, the institutions of higher education, the Protestant periodicals and communications media. To my knowledge this was the first item-by-item exposure of non-Council strength ever given by responsible parties in the history of the ecumenical controversy. It was amazing to religion editors of the metropolitan press and to leaders in educational and religious agencies at all levels in the nation. As the title of the book indicated, most of its chapters had to do with the development of a strong revolt against liberalism and the Councils within the major religious bodies of the country. It was widely used to disseminate this information within these churches. For instance (largely due to the influence of Mr. Pew), the national Presbyterian Layman's League (United Presbyterian Church in the USA) reviewed the book on the front page of its monthly journal, *The Presbyterian Layman,* and successfully urged its chapters to buy the book in lots and distribute it to key lay leaders in Presbyterian churches in their respective areas. Several prominent businessmen underwrote an effort to place the book in all the major college and university libraries of the nation. Despite the efforts of Council advocates to boycott its sale and promotion, it has had and continues to have a wide sale.

A year or so after the book was published, *Moody Monthly* asked me to do a digest of its more significant chapters for six issues of that publication. Each installment was a virtual advertisement for the book and resulted in the sale of thousands of copies. I was in considerable demand to speak before laymen's groups such as the famous Freedom Club in First Congregational Church, Los Angeles, and the Thirty-third Degree Club of the Masonic order in the Cincinnati area. But calls for seminar and lecture work in evangelical churches and colleges were predominant in my speaking schedule.

It is interesting that my adventures in ecumenical polemics were the means of restoring good fraternal relations with conservatives in the Christian Churches and Churches of Christ, so rudely broken by my departure from the editorial staff of the Standard Publishing Company. I had been widely categorized as a "liberal," an "apostate," a "traitor," and everything else in the catalog of Satan, but my voluminous writings on ecumenicity and the Councils of Churches infiltrated the rank-and-file brethren in our local churches to such an extent that my enemies were forced to rethink their attitude toward me. The first break came in an invitation to conduct three conferences on the ecumenical movement at the Pittsburgh North American Christian Convention. There were many happy reunions there. Then came an invitation to give a series of lectures at Cincinnati Bible Seminary with more happy reunions. This was followed by lecture series in Midwest Christian College, Minnesota Bible College, Manhattan Bible College, Johnson Bible College, Lincoln Christian College, Pacific Christian College, Atlanta Christian College, Nebraska Christian College, and others until I had established relationships which gave me fellowship "in good standing" with all my brethren.

It was encouraging to see our churches, with their "isolationist" leanings, coming alive to the ecumenical threat to their very existence as free churches according to the New Testament pattern. Although they did not participate in ecumenical gatherings and programs at the national level, some of them were unknowingly involved at the local or regional levels. Some of our larger congregations with an irenic spirit had gone so far in this direction that they began to encounter serious problems. These churches in crisis situations turned to me for help and I was glad to respond. I will give two or three examples:

First Church, Canton, Ohio, our largest, urged me to spend a week with them advising with their leaders and holding public meetings of an educational nature. Under the leadership of P. H. Welshimer they had cooperated with the local Council of Churches in community "Preaching Missions" and special observances. Always, in these events, the auditorium of First Church was used because it was the largest in the city. P. H. always insisted that the speakers be evangelical in spirit and the Council had acceded to his wishes. But after P. H. had passed to his reward, liberal leaders brought in speakers who expressed doubts about the authenticity and authority of the Holy Scriptures. Our brethren were immediately up in arms at hearing heretical teachings like this being sounded forth from the pulpit which for many years was locally and nationally known for its loyalty to the Word. They called a meeting of the elders and then the general board and voted to withdraw from the local and the state Councils of Churches. This caused a sensation in Canton and statewide. Some of the members of the 6,000-member congregation were unprepared for such a radical step. They had not been indoctrinated concerning apostasy in the Councils. Some of their very best friends in the denominational churches of the city, who likewise were in ignorance of the true situation, prodded them to exert their influence for the continuance of the fellowship they had so long enjoyed. One of the most prominent and capable women of First Church was at this time president of the United Church Women of Canton. She and her closest friends opposed the action of the board. It was the unanimous desire of Harold Davis (then the minister) and the elders that I inform the church and the community as to the "whys and wherefores" of their action. They had made wonderful preparations for the meetings and under the circumstances it was not strange that more than a thousand people were in my audiences each evening. Our peak attendance was estimated at 2,500. Hundreds of people came from the denominational churches of the city to hear and to ask questions. (In such meetings I always conducted an open forum following the lecture.) Tapes were cut of all the lectures and made available at cost to all churches and groups in the area. The leading daily of the city, *The Canton Repository,* gave generous reports to its readers — one issue featured a full-page fair-minded interview in which my position and that of the Canton church was made clear to the community. Harold Davis told me later that scores of tapes were sold, one set going to far-off Burma. This meant that thousands of others heard the lectures in special group and regular church meetings throughout the Western Reserve. The church board met several times for briefings on special problems. They were so happy about the results of the meetings that they invited me to stay over for the Lord's Day and speak on "The Restoration Plea in an Ecumenical Era." These messages were well received and they ended the series on a highly constructive and fine-spirited note. A few families left the church because of their ecumenical convictions, but the great congregation as a whole moved forward in loyalty to the principles which had brought them into being. Our own ministers in the area were well represented every night and we usually went to some restaurant after the meeting for food and fellowship, often not adjourning until midnight.

They felt the series had been of information and blessing to our total constituency throughout the area.

First Church, Columbus, Indiana, had a somewhat similar problem. Housed in the finest ecclesiastical structure in Columbus, designed by Saarinen the noted Finnish architect, it was the leading religious force in the city. T. K. Smith, who had been in my classes at Cincinnati Bible Seminary many years before, was the well-beloved pastor and had taught, advised, baptized, married, and buried literally thousands of people in the area. The congregation had more than two thousand members. Everybody thought he would be the minister of First Church until he died. But the wealthy scion of the Irwin family (whose generosity had housed the church so magnificently) had been won over by the Liberal Establishment. He was given honor after honor by them and finally became the first layman in America to be president of the National Council of Churches. He was greatly embarrassed by the fact that the church of which he was a member and an elder would not support the Council and was committed to the "old Jerusalem Gospel" which (to his way of thinking) was completely *passe* in the modern world. He determined to do something about it. He called for T.K.'s resignation and the appointment of a committee to restudy the policies and programs of the church. He controlled most of the financial and industrial complex of the city and many members of the church were beholden to him for their livelihood. He used every device of Satan to force his will upon the congregation. For nearly two years the conflict raged behind the scenes, but so closely knit in the ties of Christian love and the "faith once for all delivered" were the people and their pastor that Irwin Miller finally withdrew fellowship from First Church and went with about two hundred members to form the North Christian Church in Columbus. All this had happened before I was approached to come for a week of meetings which would be explanatory of the basic issues involved in the stand of First Church on ecumenical issues. As in Canton, the church and the community were prepared to listen because of the situation. The meetings had wide publicity. We began with about five hundred people and the number increased every night until some fifteen hundred were present in the closing service. Most of our seventeen churches in Bartholomew County were represented each night. (It is interesting to note that every one of them had stood solidly by T. K. Smith in his "hour of Gethsemane.") I was given a most cordial reception throughout the week, with one interesting exception. Miss Elsie Sweeney, the wealthy and prominent daughter of the noted Z. T. Sweeney and Linnie Irwin, had remained a member of First Church after the Irwin exodus. She, like her cousin, had become the victim of Liberalism and was a generous supporter of the Councils of Churches. She had been in my audience every night. On Thursday night during the open forum she got up from her seat in the auditorium, boldly made her way to the pulpit lectern without permission of the moderator and told the people that I had been lying about the Councils. She said she knew all their leaders personally and that they were men and women of God. She said that her father was really a Liberal at heart and had his doubts about the Virgin Birth of Christ and other ancient myths of the Church. She called upon the church to repudiate me and put an end to the meetings. Everybody was stunned. Since no one moved to support her in her diatribe, I ventured to answer her. I first paid high tribute to her sainted father and mother. I said that if anyone had any doubts about the loyalty of Z. T. Sweeney to the fundamentals of the Christian faith, I would be glad to cite them to his manifold writings for proof. I said, furthermore, that all the statements I had made were the result of years of research and study and that I was prepared to stand behind every one of them with authentic proofs. The moderator then assured me of the support of First Church and called for a standing vote of approval in which it seemed everybody in the house stood except "Miss Elsie." An interesting reaction came after the service. I was approached by the minister and elders of the Nashville Church (county seat of nearby Brown County) which had been receiving generous support from Miss Elsie for many years. They said, "We had no idea she held such views. From now on we will reject any contributions she may send us. We would consider them 'tainted money.'" And they took such action in their next board meeting. The Sweeney incident served only to intensify the interest in the meetings and was probably responsible for the increase in attendance as they drew to a close. T. K. and the elders and deacons of the church were most generous in their appreciation of the service I had rendered. They believed that the church had been strengthened and given new status in the community as a result.

I could recount similar experiences in Indianola Church, Columbus, Ohio; Central Church, Portsmouth, Ohio; Broadway Church, Lexington, Kentucky, and many others. Truly the walls of partition that had separated me from many of our brethren for years were completely broken down and I was in position to render a unique and much needed service to them in a changing world.

I have had no illusions as to the ability of evangelicals to stop the modern ecumenical movement. In its present or some other form it is here to stay. It is the fulfillment of the hopes of many for a united front for non-Roman Christendom. It has prestige, money, power, and intelligent leadership within a growingly efficient and effective organization. Our hope as evangelicals is to be the agents of God in the preservation and perpetuation of a "Remnant" of those who seek to be true to the "faith once for all delivered." As I write, this Remnant is a considerable number high in the millions. We are determined that God will not be without a faithful witness in the earth as long as we have life and breath and if need be through our descendants until Jesus comes again. "Think ye when the Son of man cometh, he shall find faith in the earth?" Our answer is a mighty YES!

Episode XVII

Cincinnati Evangelicals

Although the offices of *United Evangelical Action* were located in Cincinnati, this was not because of any strong local or area organization related to the National Association of Evangelicals. The decision to locate there was a concession to my own personal wishes. Under the circumstances I felt a personal obligation to launch an evangelical cooperative program in the "Queen City."

Cincinnati has always been noted as a center of conservative strength in all areas of the social order. Its churches reflected that stance. The population was about 50-50 Protestant and Roman Catholic. Protestants were overwhelmingly conservative, though denominationally related to the Federation of Churches (later the Council of Churches) and, for want of anything else to enlist their inter-church concern, dominated by it. As in almost every metropolitan area in the USA, the Federation was firmly in control of the Liberal Establishment or *vice versa*. Protestants not in the Federation were "doing very well" in their "isolationism" and did not care to be disturbed.

When I began to agitate for an association of evangelicals I found very little response. The major exception to this attitude was the downtown Covenant-First Presbyterian Church. It was the "mother" church of Presbyterianism in Cincinnati and represented mergers of First Church (once pastored by the noted G. Campbell Morgan), Central Church, Sixth Street Church, and the Church of the Covenant. Problems of the "inner city" had forced the mergers and the resultant congregation was housed in the large, beautiful, and strategically-located Covenant property at Eighth and Elm Streets. In its membership were leaders in the business, professional, and social life of the city and as a result of the mergers and the gifts of wealthy families it was heavily endowed.

Under its pastor, Frank Stevenson, a brilliant graduate of Princeton in the days of Robert Dick Wilson, Oswald Allis, Benjamin Warfield, and J. Gresham Machen, its eldership had been made thoroughly aware of the basic issues of the Liberal-Evangelical controversy and had taken a strong stand for the fundamentals of the Christian faith. Stevenson had married into the wealthy and socially prominent Shillito family (then owners of the John Shillito Company, the largest department store in Southern Ohio), all active members of Covenant-First. It was through Stevenson that I had become acquainted with Dr. Machen, unquestionably the outstanding scholar of the then current evangelical movement in America. Stevenson was soon to go to Philadelphia as the president of Westminster Theological Seminary (evangelical successor to Princeton). While Stevenson was not himself too interested in seeing an evangelical association organized in Cincinnati, he encouraged his elders and other leaders to favor the move and cooperate in it. The facilities of this great downtown church were made available to us and many meetings were to be held there in years to come.

The first attempt to set up an organization came in 1947 when the National Sunday School Association decided to hold its convention in Cincinnati. The small group that responded to our call was in effect the local Convention committee. This effort gave us an excuse to arouse interest locally and demonstrate the need for such an organization. We adopted the name "Greater Cincinnati Association of Evangelicals" which has continued until today. I became its "executive secretary" and remained in that office for more than ten years. We planned monthly ministers' meetings and quarterly rallies open to the public and undertook various projects of mutual benefit to the evangelical community. Almost simultaneously, and because of the interest aroused by the Sunday school convention, we organized the "Greater Cincinnati Sunday School Association." The former was largely a minister's group, while the latter was mostly a lay (both men and women) group.

The first cooperative move of the GCAE to bring our presence to the attention of the city as a whole was the Billy Graham Crusade in 1950. Billy had broken into national prominence with his great revival in Los Angeles in 1949. The NAE had sponsored his meetings under a huge tent in the heart of the city. With the conversion of several prominent Hollywood and "underground" figures, he induced the editors of the Hearst chain of newspapers to give unprecedented national publicity to his work. From then on he was "made" as a national religious leader. Shortly after Los Angeles I got in touch with Billy to see whether he would be willing to come to Cincinnati for a Crusade. He was by this time getting so many invitations from cities with much larger evangelical constituencies that we stood little chance of any early date. Finally, after much prayer and a series of special deliveries, telegrams and long-distance telephone calls, he agreed to send his top promotion man to Cincinnati to "spy out the land" and, if he got a favorable report, he promised to give us a weekend (Saturday night, Sunday afternoon and Sunday night services). We passed the examination and the date was set with the proviso that we must get the entire Protestant community back of the project. Fortunately I had been able to interest a neighbor of mine, Fred Smith, vice-president and public relations man of the Powell Valve Company, and an outstanding civic leader, in becoming General Chairman. Several of his prominent Chamber of Commerce friends were "sold" on the project. **Smith was a strong Southern Baptist** and immediately elicited the enthusiastic support of the large Baptist churches in the "over-the-river" cities of Greater Cincinnati. We next tackled the Federation of Churches with only a lukewarm response, but when the executive secretary saw the list of distinguished business and professional men Smith had assembled on the committee, he notified us that the Federation would "announce the meeting" in its news bulletin and "not oppose it." Contacts were made with all Protestant denominational leaders with a generally favorable response. Financial leaders underwrote the entire cost of the crusade in advance (as Graham required) and we got fine advance publicity. The Cincinnati Gardens, the city's largest auditorium, was rented. A whole complex of sub-committees providing for music, ushers, etc., etc., was set up. It was a tremendous undertaking but it was well worthwhile. Graham lived up to our expectations and we packed the auditorium for the biggest local Protestant event of the time. The Greater Cincinnati Association of Evangelicals was prominently represented on the platform for every service and its leaders actively participated in the programs. There were several thousand responses to the invitations and a deep spiritual impact was made on the lives of all who attended.

I remember one outstanding incident that involved my friend Fred Smith. A strike had been called at Powell Valve, adding a tremendous load to his obligations during preparations for the Crusade. The strike dragged on for weeks. On the platform that last evening was O. E. Whitehouse, who headed the Union involved. Whitehouse was then an elder in our First Christian Church in Latonia. After the service Billy was made aware of this confrontation and in his own inimitable way he put his arms around both men and offered a prayer for the settlement of the strike. The next morning "capital and labor" reached a quick agreement on "Christian" terms fair to both parties.

Close personal associations with Billy Graham and his organization was formed in this Cincinnati event which were to last for many years to come.

Christian Churches and Churches of Christ in the area were highly critical of the Graham meetings. Indeed, most of them would not cooperate in the evangelical organizations we had formed. This stance was primarily due to their isolationist attitude toward "the denominations," but was accentuated by the boycott Standard continued to direct against me personally. Exceptions to this were Harry Poll and the Westwood-Cheviot Church, Ard Hoven and the Chase Avenue Church, Hugh Sensibaugh and the Lockland Church, and Joseph Hill and the First Church, Latonia. There were a few others who dared the wrath of "the powers that be," but I was made to feel terribly alone when it came to fellowship with my own kind.

What I was doing was in the best tradition of our Restoration fathers. Isaac Errett himself, founder of the *Christian Standard,* maintained relations with many denominational leaders of his day — men who were committed to the authority of the Word of God and the highest welfare of the Church universal. He was active in the International Sunday School Association and a member of its Uniform Lesson Committee. It was Errett who proposed the first series of lessons in the Book of Acts and drafted the basic outlines for that series. He frequently appeared in union meetings and spoke in denominational churches. Once he accepted the invitation of the Second United Presbyterian Church in Pittsburgh to give a series of sermons on the Holy Scriptures. He preached two of a series of sermons in Cornell University and frequently appeared in inter-collegiate interdenominational meetings promoting the welfare of Christian higher education in America. He saw nothing inimical to his advocacy of the Restoration Plea in such irenic relationships. Neither did I, nor *do I!*

One interesting backlash of the Graham encounter came with respect to our press relations. Most of the newspapers gave us good coverage, but there was a slip at the desk of the city editor of the *Cincinnati Enquirer*. A fledgling reporter was assigned to cover the Graham meetings. His brief story smacked of insolent superiority and downgraded the evangelist, his message, and the meetings themselves. He intimated that Billy was "in it for the money" and that his messages were little better than "cheap demagoguery." Fred Smith called me as soon as he had seen the morning edition and suggested that we go down to the office of Roger Ferger, the president and general manager of the paper, and register a formal protest. Fred had no difficulty in making the appointment. Ferger had not seen the story, but when he got a copy and read it he was furious. He called in his city editor and demanded that a "decent" story be written and carried next day in a prominent position. It turned out that Ferger was a convert of Billy Sunday's and a personal friend of the evangelist over many years. He knew what we were talking about and assured us that we could count on the *Enquirer* for full co-operation in our work in the future.

That "future" day came rather unexpectedly. Saturday's issue of the newspaper always carried a column written by the executive secretary of the Federation of Churches in which he discussed matters of interest to Protestants. Eventually he started to use this public forum to promote liberal socio-political doctrines. Conservative Protestants felt misrepresented by many of the things he said. One particularly disturbing column so aroused me that I called Roger Ferger and asked whether I might come down to his office and make a "Protestant protest." He graciously agreed to see me and we discussed at some length the whole Liberal-Evangelical controversy. I told him of our local evangelical organizations and my feeling that we should have an equal hearing with the Federation for our conservative views. He agreed and asked me if I would prepare such a column each week. This break was almost too good to be true. I began to write it at once and continued to do so until I moved to Washington. It was amazing how many friends I discovered for our point of view and how many doors of opportunity were opened to me in many areas of the city's life. The influence of the column spread throughout the region served by the *Enquirer* and I was in demand as a speaker for many occasions not only locally but in nearby cities and towns.

The problem of proper representation of Evangelicals in local radio religious programming also faced us. The Council of Churches controlled all sustaining time for Protestants. I felt that we were in a fine position because of the NRB agreements with the industry and the government agencies to negotiate for our share of free or "sustaining" time in Greater Cincinnati. The GCAE approached the managers of the local radio stations presenting a brochure setting forth (1) the story of the NAE and its working agreement with the radio industry; (2) the local organization, its purposes, personnel and program; (3) a listing of some 150 churches whose pastors expressed a preference to clear their radio time through the GCAE instead of the Council of Churches; (4) examples of other cities in which Evangelicals were receiving sustaining time from radio stations, etc. Negotiations were long-extended and difficult, but as a result we were able to acquire a weekly broadcast over both WCKY and WKRC. A committee was set up to schedule the appearance of speakers. The city was made regularly aware of the existence of the evangelical testimony and the GCAE was made an increasing power for good in the area.

Our success in the radio program attracted the attention of Milton W. Brown and his associates in "The Press-Radio Bible Service, Inc.," which had the rights to a broadcast on WSAI. Brown was a wealthy retired Presbyterian minister (formerly pastor of the old Central Church and later of the Westwood Church in Cincinnati) who had developed a service to over three thousand daily newspapers in the United States, furnishing a daily verse of Scripture for publication with a brief comment, generally used on editorial pages. He asked me to serve on his Board and at his death I became President. I undertook with the help of others to prepare the annual clipsheets and to direct the weekly radio broadcasts. Among those on the PRBS Board were G. J. Krumm, Irvin S. Yeaworth, Paul Sullivan (religion editor of the *Cincinnati Times-Star*), Dale LeCount, Charles P. Taft, Henry Hobson, J. Otis Young, and Frederick Giesel (manager of the *Cincinnati Post*). Mrs. Ethel Abbott handled the office work from 501 Keith Building for many years. Our motto was: "The Newspapers and the Radio — *Our Pulpit;* the World — *Our Parish.*" The Lord used this work in a marvelous way to touch and help people through His Word. A whole chapter could be written about its accomplishments in His name. When I moved to Washington the work was turned over to others who merged it with a similar syndicate and it lost its distinctive character.

Other evangelical agencies of long standing in the city were exceedingly cooperative in the work of the GCAE: The Virginia Asher Council (a women's Bible study group, a holdover from the old Billy Sunday campaign); the Association of Baraca-Philathea Bible Classes; and the Christian Business and Professional Women's Club. When we held our quarterly open meetings, rallies, and conventions, personnel from these groups were always glad to serve in important capacities. Our quarterly meetings presented such outstanding figures as R. G. LeTourneau, the earth-moving machinery magnate; Kenneth Keyes, Florida's leading realtor; Robert G. Lee, pastor of the great Belleview Baptist Church of Memphis; and Stewart Hamblin, radio songster, author of "It Is No Secret What God Can Do," etc., etc.

I cannot leave my memories of Cincinnati evangelicals without telling the story of how I helped Covenant-First Presbyterian Church get a sound evangelical preacher. After Frank Stevenson went to Philadelphia the church depended upon its staff of ministers to direct their work for a considerable time. They considered a number of candidates for the pulpit but the Cincinnati Presbytery, whose approval they had to secure under church law, favored only Liberals. One morning at my office I was surprised by a visit from the Pulpit Committee, headed by my good friend Elmer W. Miller, of the Miller Printing Company. They said, "You know a good many sound Presbyterian ministers across the country, whom would you suggest for our consideration?" It happened that I had only recently been with Irvin S. Yeaworth in a Bible Conference at Temple Presbyterian Church, Philadelphia ("The Wanamaker Church"). He had indicated to me that he felt his term of service there would soon end. I immediately put the committee in touch with him. They visited Temple Church and "fell in love" with Yeaworth. The next problem was getting this particular conservative minister called, and approved by Cincinnati Presbytery. They would not invite him. In this impasse the Committee again came to me for advice. I proposed that GCAE invite Yeaworth to be the main speaker at our next quarterly meeting which was to be held in the Norwood Baptist Church, and that the Covenant-Presbyterian session and other interested brethren turn out en masse to hear him. This they did (about two hundred of them), and to make a long story shorter, the church gave him a unanimous call. Philadelphia Presbytery (then a strongly conservative body) certified Yeaworth to be in "good standing" so there was nothing for Cincinnati Presbytery to do but approve him. This pastoral relationship lasted for some fifteen years. Through these years my ties with Covenant-First Church and its pastor were very close. I was frequently invited to participate in their services on special occasions.

It was in this church that Cincinnati Evangelicals gathered on August 15, 1958 to bid me "God speed" as I left the city for Washington, D. C. I still treasure a beautiful engraved leather desk set presented to me on that occasion.

Episode XVIII

United Evangelical Action (2)

It is impossible to give anything like an adequate review of the interesting and important happenings in which I was involved during my fourteen years as editor of *United Evangelical Action*. But to the record in Episode XII, I would add this "continued story";

Relations of the NAE with the United States government reached an all-time high in cordiality in 1953 when, on July 2, a delegation from the National Association of Evangelicals was received by President Dwight D. Eisenhower at the White House. The President discussed with NAE leaders the need for a moral and religious base for the guarantee and perpetuity of our American freedoms and affixed his signature to a document which called for a national reaffirmation of faith in God, the Author of man's freedom, repentance from sin and a new dedication to the task of bringing freedom to the world. Participating in the interviews were Paul S. Rees, R. L. Decker, Clyde W. Taylor, Frederick Curtis Fowler, Senator Frank Carlson, Representative Walter K. Judd, Herbert J. Lorber, F. O. Masten, Charles E. Kellogg, James Powell-Tuck and myself.

The President received our delegation in the famous Oval Room, shaking hands with each one of us. We were surrounded with security guards and were under strict surveillance every minute we were in the White House. Paul Rees, currently the president of NAE, presented our plea (although it had been cleared weeks before by the President's staff) and then the President signed the document, giving the pen to Dr. Rees. Photographers from the major news services were then admitted to take pictures. After that Mr. Eisenhower rose and began to chat with us informally. He referred to the fact that he had on many occasions boldly expressed his belief that a moral and religious base was essential to national and international stabliity, goodwill, peace, and prosperity. Then sitting nonchalantly on the edge of his desk he recounted an incident which took place after World War II when he headed an American delegation to Paris where he met with leaders of the new French government to plan for the rehabilitation of that war-torn land. Jules Mauch headed the French delegation. In their confrontation Eisenhower asked the French leader about the moral and religious health of his country. Mauch said he personally was an agnostic and had not given much thought to that. He expressed doubt that it had much relevance to the matters under discussion. At which Eisenhower replied, "Possibly the weakness of France in its hour of crisis is due to neglect of these basic matters."

I ventured that the Brethren in Christ Church (the church of his boyhood at Abilene, Kansas) was a member of the NAE. I said I knew many of its national leaders and had spoken in its Messiah College at Grantham, and at its national Camp Ground meetings, near Harrisburg, Pennsylvania. On these occasions I said I had met several families of Eisenhowers who claimed relationship to him. He was most appreciative and said, "Yes, these people were undoubtedly of the same family which came from Europe to American many years ago, settling in the Susquehanna River valley, and were all good members of what we called the 'River Brethren.' I owe a great deal to the religion of my parents."

When our time was up we were notified and left the White House promptly, fully appreciative of the willingness of our Chief Executive to make way for us on his busy schedule of appointments dealing with affairs of State. President Eisenhower's conduct during his years in office was a demonstration of his Christian commitment. When in Washington on the Lord's Day he and his wife were found in their accustomed pew in the National Presbyterian Church where his good friend and ours, Pastor Edward L. R. Elson, declared an evangelical and Biblical Gospel.

I made frequent trips to Washington during my tenure in office to work with Clyde W. Taylor, NAE's Public Affairs secretary, on various projects. Our Washington office kept closely in touch with developments in all factors of American life that affected NAE's constituency. Dr. Taylor wrote a page entitled "Capitol Report" for each issue of our magazine. He insisted that I be a member of the NAE's Evangelical Action Commission (at various times I was chairman) and act as its liaison with the Washington office. The record will show our vital expression of NAE opinion on crucial issues: Indian affairs, civil rights, public schools, immigration, labor, liquor, salacious literature, communism and fascism.

Taylor had a clear understanding of the difference between the NAE's concern with public affairs and that expressed by the National Council of Churches. I fully shared his views. The distinction is so important that I think it has a place here.

Evangelicals possess a dual citizenship. Paul said in Philippians 3:20 that "our citizenship is in heaven" and again in Philippians 2:15 that "we are sons of God, without rebuke, in the midst of a crooked and perverse generation among whom we shine as lights in the world." We are citizens of heaven and earth.

Earthly governments are ordained of God to do certain things. They are to control and direct the environment in which we live. They are to guarantee to men the rights and freedoms that are God's gifts. Governments fail when they conceive of these rights and freedoms as granted by men. They may, however, demand respect, enforce the laws, regulate society for the benefit of all. God gives specific instruction as to the Christian's relationship with his government. On the other hand in working out the relationship of religion and government we find abuses prevalent, even in the USA.

First, there are the efforts of the Roman Church to promote Church-State union with the Church dominant. This is best seen in the many efforts of the Roman lobby in Washington to secure federal aid for parochial schools; to get federal funds for Roman Catholic hospital building, and to participate as a Church in USA politics.

Another abuse is the effort of the agnostics, atheists, and misguided zealots who misinterpret separation of Church and State, to take all religion out of government, to take Christ's teachings, ideals and witness out of government. This they say is necessary to keep the church out of government. They seem to take for granted that it is possible for Christians to live in a nation and yet be restricted in the exercise of their faith and testimony in their daily occupation in government.

A third violation is caused by minorities in the name of freedom of religion abusing their rights to restrict the majority. We see the same agnostics, anti-religionists, and in a few cases those of the Hebrew faith opposing the distribution of the New Testament to students on the grounds that it is a sectarian book. This has been carried so far in most public schools that anything regarding Christianity is considered controversial and is ruled out of order by teachers. The study of and comment on any part of the Bible is in most states taboo.

Another minority abuse comes in the management of the public school systems. The Roman Catholics, while sending their own children to Roman Catholic parochial schools, seem to feel it their obligation to run for election to state and city school boards. Blind, indifferent Protestants help elect them and then mourn when the school system deteriorates under their management.

A different type of abuse in Church-Government relations comes through the activity of religious lobbies. There are a number of such lobbies registered in Washington and each one supposedly acts only to safeguard violations of its own convictions. In the main this is true. However, some lobbies are occupied in seeking special and generally illegal appropriations of funds for schools, hospitals and other basically religious activities.

There are abuses committed by Communists and Socialists in the government. The well-documented seditious advance of this subversion into government frightens serious minded Americans, as it indicates how easily they can lose their most precious earthly possessions.

There is also that abuse which by promoting government ownership of resources, industry and property would make US citizens wards of the state, placing them economically on the dole. Such a government by absolute control of the people grants or denies God-given freedoms and produces a nation of fatalistic or indifferent citizens.

Evangelicals live in this world and have a testimony to give and a duty to perform as citizens which cannot be shirked. As Christian citizens they can be, as was the Apostle Paul, *transformers* by spiritual processes but can also be *reformers* through active Christian citizenship.

In a republic such as the USA Christian citizens, if aroused to their duty, have enough strength to elect godly men to office. They, with Christian convictions voiced through the polls and to their representatives, can accomplish the unbelievable, but the great inertia of the average American often dominates the Christian and he fails to act because he is not sufficiently aroused.

There are, however, encouraging signs across the nation. Largely through the influence of the National Association of Evangelicals, under the leadership of evangelical men, many are already alert to the serious conditions in the nation. We look upon the Washington office of the NAE as a "watchman" in the nation's capital. Legislation bearing on church and evangelical activity around the world is reported. Evangelicals are urged to influence their Congressmen for the right.

The separation of Church and State is watched. Threatened violations are published. Cooperation is given through the Washington office with other like-minded groups in this field until today such violations are instantly detected and protested. A new respect is growing in the minds of those who propose to violate this basic doctrine.

Every division of government that has bearing on the American way of life is being watched by evangelicals. The Department of State with its great diplomatic service and its control over the movement of USA citizens is not to be neglected. Abuses are bound to occur in such a large agency. Discrimination sometimes takes place and a voice of protest is needed for the correction and control of any subversive action on the part of department representatives overseas. If need be evangelicals must apply the pressure for what is right to counterbalance the influence of the Roman hierarchy and other forces that constantly exert their maximum influence for their own interests regardless of the legality of their action. Government needs strong support to resist such pressures.

Evangelicals, as never before, are stepping into the breach and helping to furnish a moral conscience for the nation. The law of expediency has so taken control of the thinking of many leaders that God's moral law and what God may think of actions receive little attention. The result is that any act in the government interest is condoned. Evangelicals are beginning to assert their testimony against ungodly relations with militant atheism. Unless they let their voice be heard, their influence felt, a pagan conscience will prevail.

In this area of endeavor, evangelicals live in a shrinking world where the affairs of their brethren in Christ become their concern when their liberties are restricted. Evangelicals must not only appeal the case to Heaven, they must *act* when able to do so. The greatest weapons in this combat are diplomacy and the press. During the past ten years great strides have been made by evangelicals in maintaining such relations with the Department of State that every violation of religious freedom may effectively be called to the government's attention. Where it involves US citizens, they request action and generally get it. Where it involves

American interests, the State Department does what it can within its legal field of action. The press is an even greater weapon. Slowly evangelicals around the world are becoming more active in keeping the Washington office informed when they are persecuted or discriminated against. Slowly the American press is showing its willingness to print the news and public opinion is being moulded. Evangelicals have just started to use it in the defense of God's children. Evangelicals have the convictions and the means to exert great influence if they will shake off their traditional lethargy in such matters.

Much can be accomplished by reform, by vigilance, by using influence, letting the evangelical voice be heard, but to evangelicals there is still a better way. The better way is *transformation* with every Christian a transformer, being careful, however, to remember that this is not exclusive of *reformation*. Both methods may be used at once. Of course, in the Apostolic Church there was only one road open, that was *transformation* by saturation-evangelism. Amidst persecution and every form of violent opposition the Christian — everyone a witness, a personal missionary — went everywhere telling the Gospel. This was declared illegal but they obeyed God and pressed on. It took three hundred years, but the Gospel won. It took the Empire.

The twentieth century Christian in America has two ways open to serve His Lord and nation. He has a franchise, a moral responsibility before God to use his earthly citizenship for God's glory. Americans are a self-governing people. Either Christians who love the Lord are going to take Christ into the political life of the nation or the increasing infiltration of Roman Catholic power will take evangelical laymen into the political life of local governments. Evangelicals have demonstrated this time and again and have cleaned up local corruption.

Evangelicals do not want the Church in politics. They believe that only its members are US citizens. When the Church enters politics, it degenerates into another political lobby. The Church has a responsibility to inculcate in its members their responsibility as citizens and build the morality and ethics that control their lives through Christ.

In an increasing number of communities across the nation organized Christian lay leadership groups are promoting united evangelical action. This encourages evangelicals to take part in political life and run for office. These groups also supply evangelicals with information about candidates for office in ample time before city, county, state, and national elections so that they know the record, standing, and qualifications of each candidate regardless of party. Such groups expose corrupt political machines by giving the facts about the candidates who are machine controlled.

I was coached by Taylor to make appearances in hearings before committees and sub-committees of the Senate and the House of Representatives at which I read drafts of our position, which we prepared jointly, and answered questions. I do not mean to give the impression that I was the sole representative of the Association in these confrontations. Many others were used, but I was called to Washington quite often. All my presentations were recorded by court stenographers. Many times I was interviewed by reporters from the Associated Press, the United Press, the International News Services, and the Religious News Service. In extremely controversial matters the views I presented were given national publicity in the secular press.

One of these incidents had to do with "right-to-work" legislation. We took the position in the hearing that man had a right to freedom in determining his employment and his employers and whether or not he would accept membership in unions. Several minority religious groups took a similar position, including the Seventh-Day Adventists. The editor of their widely-circulated journal, *Liberty,* was so pleased with my presentation that he asked for the privilege of reproducing it in its entirety. He asked for a photo and requested that I pose with him before the Robert A. Taft memorial in front of the Capitol Building. This photo appeared in color on the cover of the next issue of his magazine. Later I wrote several articles on public affairs for him. Many contacts of this kind were made in this interesting phase of my work with the NAE.

Even after I left the employ of the NAE I was persuaded to continue serving as chairman of the Commission on Evangelical Action which had eventually absorbed the Commission on Social Action. In 1963 we held a history-making conference on Social Action at Winona Lake, Indiana.

Evangelicals, as a whole, have always been interested in the social implications of the Gospel. They give primacy to the saving power of the Gospel in the life of the individual and hold the chief concern of the church lies in the supernatural and spiritual realm. In their best tradition, however, evangelicals have been leaders in the application of the principles of Christianity to every aspect of life.

The eighteenth century Evangelical Revival in Great Britain under the Wesleys saw not only fasting, prayer, Bible study and revival but special ministries to those in prison and a strong stand against slavery in the Empire. The evangelicals of that time did far more for the masses than did the "liberal" elements in the Anglican church. J. Russell Bready in his book, *This Freedom — Whence?* piles the evidence mountain high in proof of this thesis.

During the "Great Awakening" of the early 1800's in America there was revival but there was also the inauguration of inter-church cooperation through the World Evangelical Alliance with consequent organization for reform by social action. In 1826 the American Society for the Promotion of Temperance was organized and became the forerunner of the Prohibition movement. Evangelicals were in the forefront of the battle to write into the law of the land the Christian attitude toward intoxicants. The injustice of slaveholding was recognized by the great majority of evangelicals and in the War Between the States thousands of them gave their life's blood to bring freedom to the Negro in America.

206

Evangelicals have a social conscience but they revolt at the idea of using the temporal power of the church to force world revolution according to any humanly-devised plan. They are particularly fearsome of such man-made ideas which have no adequate theological foundation.

It has been the conviction of most evangelicals that if a philosophy of social action can be formulated on the basis of an orthodox theology, once again the church will become a mighty force for righteousness and a mighty testimony for the full-orbed Gospel of Christ. Nothing less is adequate for the cultural crisis which has overtaken the Western world. Christians will then have a more biblical perspective of the needs of humanity and of the policies which our nation must follow if it is to remain true to its divine purposes and functions. They will then be able to speak with authority in such matters in a way in which Liberals could never speak because their concept of social justice was not based upon the revealed righteousness of a sovereign God.

I was able to "sell" the Commission and the leaders of the NAE on making a serious attempt to explore the issues and come up with a sound theological base for action. We decided to invite some 200 leaders representing a cross-section of the NAE constituency and other evangelicals beyond our orbit for a week of study, discussion, and decision. We took over all the facilities of Winona Inn and, despite some predictions to the contrary, we exceeded all our expectations in enrollment and results.

Among those who accepted places on our program were Oswald C. J. Hoffman, presenting the Lutheran theological position; Leslie R. Marston, the Arminian position; and Vernon J. Grounds, the Calvinistic position. Others of outstanding stature who presented papers were Carl F. H. Henry, S. Ritchey Kamm, Clyde W. Taylor, Gordon H. Clark, and Frederick Curtis Fowler. I gave the introductory paper and set forth guidelines for the proceedings. Following each paper an equal period of time was devoted to questions and discussion. Thanks to the generous provision of facilities from the studios of the Light and Life Hour at Winona Lake, everything of significance was taped and made available to the Executive Committee of the NAE together with manuscripts, correspondence and the conclusions and recommendations of our Commission. It is interesting to note that Dean M. Kelley of the Division of Life and Mission of the National Council of Churches was present as an observer throughout the sessions and made a very fairminded report for the *Christian Century*. *Christianity Today* and *United Evangelical Action* carried excellent reports. Our findings became the basis for future pronouncements and actions of the NAE in this field.

As editor of *UEA* I was invited to participate in almost every important meeting of the various Commissions of the NAE during the formative years. Their leaders were anxious to have my editorial support and to benefit from my promotional expertise. One of the most important of these was the NAE Commission on Education first headed by Stephen

W. Paine, president of Houghton College. He had an earned Ph.D., from the University of Illinois and was a highly capable educator and a princely Christian gentleman. I always enjoyed working with him.

I do not need to give background reasons for my special interest in this field. They have set forth *in extenso* in my voluminous writings on the subject in editorials, books, lectures, and contributions I have made to publish symposiums. I was "in" on the organization meetings when the Commission was first set up in 1945. It originally had sub-committees operating in five areas: (1) Liberal Arts Colleges, (2) Theological Seminaries, (3) Bible Institutes and Bible Colleges, (4) Secondary Schools, and (5) Christian Day Schools. Some of these eventually became separate Commissions and some withdrew to organize on a broader base to appeal to institutions not members of the NAE. I was a member of the group on Bible Institutes and Bible Colleges and the one on Christian Day Schools.

In 1946 a special Commission was set up to deal with the Christian Philosophy of Education and I was chosen to serve that group in an advisory capacity. It was headed by Frank E. Gaebelein, Headmaster of The Stony Brook School; other members were: Robert L. Cooke, Chairman Department of Education, Wheaton (Illinois) College; Ruth E. Eckert, Professor of Higher Education, University of Minnesota; Mark Fakkema, Executive Secretary, National Association of Christian Schools; Carl F. H. Henry, Professor of Theology and Philosophy of Religion, Fuller Theological Seminary; Harold B. Kuhn, Professor of Philosophy of Religion, Asbury Theological Seminary; Leslie R. Marston, Bishop of the Free Methodist Church, former president of Greenville College; Stephen W. Paine, president Houghton College; S. A. Witmer, president, Fort Wayne Bible Institute; Enock C. Dyrness, vice president of Wheaton College.

At the 1951 NAE convention in Chicago the Commission presented its final report in the form of a book entitled, *Christian Education in a Democracy,* published by the Oxford University Press. It did for evangelical Christian education what the famed Harvard Report, *General Education in a Free Society* (1945), did for secular education. The fact that the work bore the imprint of the Oxford Press gave it a prestige which compelled the attention of all educators. It marked a turning point in Christian education as carried on in evangelical institutions. Not only did the Report present basic educational philosophy from the Christian viewpoint, but it spoke boldly of areas of improvement in the evangelical educational program. It is today serving as a blueprint by which evangelical education is building for the new day.

Among my duties as an "adviser" on this project I was asked to prepare a tentative chapter on the local church school (the Sunday school) which finally appeared as Chapter 9, "The Church as Educator." More than half of my manuscript was used but the remainder was garbled to meet the theoretical ideas of the Committee — all of whom were college and seminary minded and knew as much about the Sunday school and the local church's educational situation as the proverbial "man in the moon." This has always been the "fly in the ointment" for me when I think of this great book. High praise is due to Dr. Gaebelein for the monumental task that he assumed in integrating all the material submitted by experts in various fields and in preparing the manuscript in final form for acceptance by the Commission and the Executive Committee of the NAE. He was also instrumental in persuading the prestigious Oxford University Press to publish and distribute the book. This was due to the fact that his sainted father was co-editor of the famous "Scofield Bible" which was copyrighted by Oxford and had made them "a mint of money." The Gaebelein "go" sign given to our book was enough to convince the "powers that be" in Oxford's New York office.

The standardization and accrediting of Bible institutes and Bible colleges was a problem early faced by the NAE Commission. The survey that was proposed by the 1943 convention revealed a complicated situation with problems not easily solved.

At their inception, Bible institutes represented almost a grassroots evangelical movement to provide once again for the Church training centers true to the Word of God and with a deep spiritual emphasis. These developed quite independently of one another in standards, interrelationships, or work. In later years there came, however, a definite spirit of cooperation in the field of Bible institute and Bible college leadership. Parallel with the development of the National Association of Evangelicals was the development of its affiliate, The North American Association of Bible Institutes and Bible Colleges.

This organization came into being in 1944 to provide a vortex of fellowship and work for Bible institute and Bible college leaders. Originally it also included the thought of providing a system of accreditation for schools in this field. However, in order to provide for a larger area of cooperation than would be permitted through an affiliate of the National Association of Evangelicals, it gave way to a new organization.

The Accrediting Association of Bible Institutes and Bible Colleges was organized in 1947 at Winona Lake, Indiana, following a call by Dean Samuel H. Sutherland of the Bible Institute of Los Angeles and other interested persons who believed that such an organization should be independent of inter-church control. The majority of the educators represented were active in the work of the National Association of Evangelicals and had participated in the establishment of the Commission on Education.

The AABIBC, completely independent of the National Association of Evangelicals or any similar body, has a large number of schools accredited on its rolls.

As at first conceived, periodic surveys kept the standards of the AABIBC ever before the member institutions. The first step in the accrediting process was to ask each school to evaluate itself in the light of the Association's criteria for collegiate division Bible Schools. These self-evaluative studies stimulated academic and spiritual leadership within each school and many excellent reports were produced. A set of detailed questionnaires was then filled out by each institution and these along with the self-evaluative report was placed in the hands of the examiners in order that they might compare the school's description of itself with their own findings after a two or three day visit to each campus.

On the basis of these written materials and the findings of their visit to the campus, the examiners prepared a fifteen to twenty-page report for each school and a list of fifty to one hundred specific recommendations. The examiners' report and their recommendations were used by the Executive Committee to determine whether the school's accreditation should be continued or whether it was to be placed on probation. In general it may be said that these surveys provided tremendous stimulation to the member institutions.

All appropriate federal agencies, the National Educational Association, the American Council on Education, the New York State Department of Education, and other educational bodies too numerous to list here eventually gave formal recognition to the Accrediting Association of Bible Institutes and Bible Colleges. The entire segment of Christian education represented by the Bible institutes and Bible colleges in the United States and Canada was greatly advanced by the progress of the Accrediting Association because many of its services were offered without charge to non-member schools and to educators and officials generally.

Because of my background in the development of Bible colleges among the Christian Churches and Churches of Christ I was frequently consulted by AABIBC leaders and urged to persuade our schools to apply for accreditation. The Standard boycott, however, made it exceedingly difficult for me to make acceptable approaches. Then, when I was in Minneapolis to speak at some kind of convention, I received a phone call at my hotel from Russell Boatman, then president of Minnesota Bible College. He asked whether I could come to the college and meet informally with a group of board and faculty members and present the accreditation program. I was glad to go and we had a very rewarding meeting lasting two or three hours. Our men asked every conceivable question to determine whether they would have to make any compromises of their personal convictions or of the standards and purposes of the school in order to enjoy the apparent benefits of accreditation. The major problem was the acceptance of the "Basis of Faith" required by the AABIBC. We went over each item carefully. Finally, it was agreed that MBC required acceptance of a statement of faith as essential to board and faculty relations and that the two statements did not conflict. The cordial reception given me by our brethren was heartening to me and I was overjoyed to learn some months later that Minnesota Bible College was to become the first of our colleges to be accepted as a member of AABIBC (later the AABC).

When my good friend S. A. Witmer became executive secretary of the Accrediting Association, he visited me in Cincinnati for a day's discussion of the Christian Church/Churches of Christ educational situation with the express purpose of making a special effort to enroll all our qualified institutions. We were frequently in touch from that day on and I was able to give him a vast amount of information which enabled him to enlist some twelve or fourteen of our schools. I tried to stay out of the approaches and follow-ups because of the Standard boycott, but the day was to come when I was again accepted in full fellowship by all our institutions. I was delighted to see several of our brethren assume responsibilities in the AABC, particularly President Earl Hargrove of Lincoln Christian College, who became especially active in its affairs and who served a term as president of the organization. On one occasion when I addressed the annual meeting of the Association in Moody Bible Institute, Chicago, I noted many of our men in the audience and after the session we had a reunion I will long remember.

But getting back to my relationships with other groups in the original NAE Commission on Education:

The Christian day school cause has become an American movement which stems from American evangelical life at the local level. The movement is marked with a vitality which is self-impelling and self-sustaining.

In 1947 the National Association of Evangelicals sponsored the organization of the National Association of Christian Schools to promote the establishment of new Christian Day Schools throughout America and to provide a united front and voice for schools of all evangelical denominations and groups. Mark Fakkema, who had given distinguished leadership to the Reformed school system, was chosen educational director.

Christian day schools can be divided into two distinct groups: (1) Christian schools sponsored and controlled by the local church acting in the name of organized (institutionalized) religion; (2) Christian schools sponsored and controlled by individuals, organized on a locally acceptable doctrinal basis serve the children of the constituency of its membership and such other children as the school board may admit.

Schools of the latter type were encouraged by the NACS and hundreds are now listed in its annual yearbook. I worked with Dr. Fakkema in many ways to advance his program and it gained wide acceptance by evangelicals. His successor, John Blanchard, a much younger man, was able to restructure the original organization into a much more representative and effective body which has been widely recognized for the high quality of its services.

When the U. S. Supreme Court ruled that prayer and Bible reading must be eliminated from American Public Schools new impetus was given to the movement. I recall that I was scheduled to speak at a morning session of the North American Christian Convention at Lexington, Kentucky, when the news of the Court's action was announced. I was so thoroughly stirred up about it that I took several minutes of my allotted time to excoriate the decision and announced that from now on I was unalterably opposed to all public education that had no moral and spiritual foundations. I urged the audience to go back home and start Christian day schools, and they gave me a tremendous round of applause. I have never quite been forgiven by the NACC leaders for this outburst, but I stand by my statement today with even greater conviction than the day I uttered it at Lexington. Shortly afterward, I was made a member of the board of the NACS and served several terms in that capacity. I wrote several articles for its official organ, *The Christian Teacher,* and have given its program support in many ways.

Our Christian Churches and Churches of Christ have been slow to enter the Christian day school field. I have been instrumental in encouraging in various ways the organization of schools in several of our churches, notably West Side Church, Springfield, Illinois; First Church and Lockhaven Church, Inglewood; and San Fernando and Golden West churches in Los Angeles, California. There will be more as the years pass and as the moral and spiritual inadequacy of the modern public school system becomes more apparent.

Through the columns of *United Evangelical Action* I backed the efforts of Clyde W. Taylor and J. Elwin Wright in, first, establishing relations with the World Evangelical Alliance in London, and, later, organizing the World Evangelical Fellowship. Important meetings looking toward more effective cooperation at the world level were held at Clarens, Switzerland, in 1948; at Hildenborough Hall, England, in 1950; at Woudschoten, The Netherlands, in 1951; and eventually a "constitutional convention" at Clarens in 1953, where the World Evangelical Fellowship officially came into being. It was my privilege to be a member of the United States delegation to Clarens that year and to participate in many of the meetings where definitive resolutions were drafted and the constitution and by-laws were formulated and adopted.

At St. John's school (an Anglican institution) overlooking beautiful Lake Geneva, evangelicals saw on July 27-31 the realization of the vision which had come to them in this identical spot five years before.

Some two hundred delegates and visitors from thirty lands attending the opening session heard Paul S. Rees, head of the USA delegation, call for a mid-century revival throughout the world.

The first half of the current century, said the American evangelical leader, has been marked by the challenge of Communism which has halted Christian missionary advance, one of the most severe economic depressions in history, the full flower of apostasy in the churches largely due to "liberal" theological infiltration, and a menacing materialistic state of mind throughout society in general.

Dr. Rees said that evangelicals faced the tremendous spiritual potential of the second half of our century with a surfeit of bickering, division and aloofness. He urged a repentant and humble waiting before God for His clear word for our day, quite possibly the word "Revival." He reminded his listeners that revival always comes from God and is not primarily the result of organization or highpowered advertising.

Preceding Dr. Rees' address the conference had been formally opened by Lt. General Sir Arthur Smith, WEF president, who made it clear that all those present were on business for Christ and in all things should exalt His name.

Six national evangelical organizations were received into full membership at the first business session — Singapore, Hawaii, Switzerland, Germany, France, and Holland. Seven had previously been received: Evangelical Fellowship of Ceylon, Gospel Workers Fellowship of Cyprus, Evangelical Alliance of Great Britain, Evangelical Fellowship of India, Japanese Association of Evangelicals, Taiwan (Formosa) Evangelical Fellowship, and the National Association of Evangelicals (USA). In addition, the following were granted "associate" membership: The Evangelische Contact Comite of Belgium, The Evangelical Fellowship of Cuba, The Evangelical Brotherhood of Greece, The Evangelical Alliance of Greece, The Chinese Foreign Missionary Union (Indonesia). Other applications were received. Terms of membership were broadened at Clarens to include "consultative members" and "individual members."

Commissions on Evangelism, Christian Action, Missionary Cooperation, and Committees on Literature, and Radio and Television were set up. A. J. Dain, of London, and J. Elwin Wright, of Boston, were made joint secretaries. Plans were laid for the development of rgional and national Fellowships which would be affiliated with the World organization. Since that day great strides forward have been made in covering the globe with effective evangelical cooperative organizations. History was truly made at Clarens and I have always been thankful to have had a part in it.

We Americans had a chartered flight under the direction of Fred Fowler, who, after Clarens, guided us in a tour of Switzerland, Italy, Austria, France, Germany, Belgium, The Netherlands and England. In London we saw the headquarters of the World Evangelical Alliance which would henceforth be shared by the World Evangelical Fellowship, and we had the inestimable pleasure of being entertained at the charming manor house of Lt. General Sir Arthur Smith just outside London. Smith was one of England's great heroes of the second World War. He had been Commander-in-chief of the military forces of London during the terrible Hitlerian bombing raids which destroyed so much of the great city. His bravery and ingenuity salvaged an unbelievable number of the great landmarks of history, made possible the salvation of millions of lives and the preservation of most of London's beautiful vistas. He had been the receipient of every honor his country could bestow. To meet him one was reminded of a modest but substantial English squire, but also a man of great faith with deep religious convictions who was thoroughly committed to his Lord. Now his great capabilities were dedicated to the cause of world evangelical cooperation. He and his good wife were generous hosts and made our stay a pleasurable experience none of us shall ever forget. He often expressed appreciation of *UEA*, each issue of which he avidly read. I had considerable correspondence with him through the years and our relationships were most rewarding.

Parenthetically, I would like to recall in this connection the only incident in my long flying experience covering hundreds of thousands of miles in which I experienced any fear. *The Lord has been good.* Back from London, we were flying out of Amsterdam headed for Iceland, Newfoundland and home, when suddenly out over the North Sea our plane began to turn back toward Amsterdam. Our landing gear would not retract. It was slowing our speed and our command feared there might be landing difficulties. However, we landed safely in Amsterdam, the plane evacuated its passengers, and we were made the overnight guests of the company in a Haarlem hotel. Cablegrams were sent to our "next of kin" telling of the delay. My wife still remembers the chill she had when she got that cablegram. Repairs all made, we took off late the next day and the remainder of the trip was accomplished without further serious incident.

In developing features for the magazine I made personal contacts with many of the outstanding evangelical leaders of America. For instance, I conceived the idea of a series of articles about the great evangelical churches of the nation under the general title, "Citadels of the Faith." Our Liberal antagonists had spread the word that Evangelicals had no truly outstanding churches and were pretty largely ignorant crossroads and small town people. Pastors of our larger churches were most cooperative. In many cases I visited their parishes and viewed their work first hand. In other cases they secured the services of outstanding local writers who prepared the manuscripts according to our guidelines. Among the churches and pastors featured in this series were: Moody Church, Chicago, Harry Ironside; First Presbyterian, Duluth, Minnesota, Frederick Curtis Fowler; First Baptist, Tucson, Arizona, R. S. Beall; First Christian, Canton, Ohio, P. H. Welshimer; Trinity Methodist, Los Angeles, California, Robert Shuler; Calvary Baptist, New York City, William Ward Ayer; First Covenant, Minneapolis, Minnesota, Paul S. Rees; Park Street Congregational, Boston, Massachusetts, Harold J. Ockenga; First Baptist, Pontiac, Michigan, H. H. Savage; First Presbyterian, Seattle, Washington, Mark Matthews; Tenth Presbyterian, Philadelphia, Donald Grey Barnhouse; Belleview Baptist, Memphis, Tennessee, Robert G. Lee; Central Baptist, Atlanta, Georgia, Paul S. James (the old Brougher church); First Presbyterian, Pittsburgh, Pennsylvania, Clarence E. MacCartney; and the Church of the Open Door, Los Angeles, California, Louis Talbot. The churches had from 2,000 to 10,000 members each. It made an impressive series and won us many friends in the areas covered.

All our NAE leaders were most appreciative of the services we tried to render through the medium of the magazine. Special numbers were

214

prepared to promote higher education, the Sunday school, radio and television broadcasting, stewardship, good literature, evangelism, missions, and other phases of the official program. Our convention numbers, used in large quantities to promote the NAE and the NSSA conventions, attracted many advertisers. When the Association faced a serious financial crisis in 1953-55 I was told repeatedly that if it had not been for *UEA* magazine the continued existence of the organization might have been despaired of. A word about this crisis may be in order.

The rapid growth of NAE and its expansion in too many areas of service, because of the insistent demands of our constituency, had overtaxed our financial capacities. Money borrowed to keep progressive programs moving had plunged the Association into serious fiscal difficulties. By 1954 the headquarters office was without an executive director and an adequate staff and several of the regional offices were leaderless. President Rees furnished magnificent spiritual and practical leadership in the crisis. An emergency committee headed by Wm. H. Lee Spratt, pastor of the Lorimer Memorial Baptist Church, Chicago, stepped into the breach. A special meeting of the Board of Administration was called The response was wonderful in this time of testing and gave proof of the essential solidarity of the Association. A new sense of faith in and dependence upon God came upon the entire leadership.

Henry H. Savage, pastor of the First Baptist Church (CBAA), Pontiac, Michigan, was persuaded to assume leadership of the Association in the midst of this critical period. Only his great love for NAE and his strong conviction that it had "come to the Kingdom for such a time as this" caused him to make the many sacrifices entailed. His great congregation released him from many of his responsibilities so that he could counsel, plan, pray, and work with the brethren at headquarters as they sought to meet the emergency. George L. Ford, who had served the Northwest Region as executive director and repeatedly demonstrated his abilities as an administrator and fiscal expert, was called to become "associate executive director." He proved to be God's man for the task. Financial retrenchment was ordered. New budgets were drafted. A "charter plan" was initiated for all regional offices. *Action* magazine was reduced in size and its budget integrated with that of the central office. Commissions were put on a self-supporting basis. A drive for funds to reduce the deficit was undertaken by a group of evangelical businessmen. Headquarters offices were moved from the high-rental district of Chicago's famous "Loop" to nearby Wheaton, Illinois. By the 1955 convention in Chicago a balanced program began to emerge and a new spirit of optimism pervaded the leadership. Through the crisis period morale on the field remained high and after 1955 the NAE was stronger than ever before in its history. *UEA* was given preferred status because of the services it had rendered during the crisis and we went on to do greater things in a better way than ever before. The magazine was now accorded a measure of prestige and influence in the field of religious journalism beyond what we had ever dared expect.

In this period I conceived the idea of writing a history of the National Association. There had been a grave neglect in preserving papers of historic value. There was no complete file of the magazine available anywhere. I was finally able, over a period of two years, to collect and bind all the issues. This lack of historical sense persuaded me that, out of my close and inner contacts with NAE people and agencies, I should bring together and document in definitive form the NAE story from its beginnings. Dr. Savage, Dr. Decker, and other leaders encouraged me in the project and the Wm. B. Eerdmans Publishing Company of Grand Rapids, Michigan, agreed to examine the completed manuscript with a view to publication. This was a monumental task in addition to my many other interests, but I undertook and completed it with the result that the 220-page work entitled, *Cooperation Without Compromise,* appeared in 1956. I have always been thankful that I made this contribution to the Association for no one else, even to this day, has produced anything comparable to it. (Bruce Shelley's splendid work, *Evangelicalism in America,* is not an "authorized history".) Someone should now undertake a revision of my work and update the record of NAE events and accomplishments. Scholars and researchers especially require a new and more adequate volume.

In the midst of my happiest and most rewarding years with the Association I was called to Washington to be managing editor of *Christianity Today.* More will be said later of this episode in my life. I merely mention it here. My associates urged me to remain in the chair I had occupied for fourteen years, but I felt the Lord had called me to a position of greater influence for His kingdom.

At the Los Angeles convention in 1959 my friends arranged a banquet in my honor in the Statler Hilton Hotel, attended by over three hundred diners. Charles Seidenspinner presided and tributes were given by a number of NAE leaders past and present. It was in a way a most embarrassing experience but immensely rewarding. A beautiful painting of a scene in the Loire River Valley by a noted French artist was presented to me in appreciation of my services and we have ever since that time given it a prominent place in the living room of the residences we have occupied. A table of ten ministers of the Christian Churches and Churches of Christ in the Los Angeles area, who joined in the tribute, especially gladdened my heart. This marked a change in the climate in my own ministerial fellowship and was to be a token of a new day in years to come.

When I returned to Los Angeles in 1967 for another national convention (the "Silver Anniversary Convention"), the NAE not only honored me with a beautiful plaque, "A Citation for Meritorious Services," at one of the evening sessions, but I was tendered a reception by our own ministers which pleased me even more. On the Lord's Day I preached before an audience of nearly 1,000 in the Crenshaw Boulevard Christian Church (thanks to the invitation of my good friend James Merle Appelgate, the minister). On Monday I spoke to our area ministers and conducted an open forum dealing with the modern ecumenical movement. Never have I had a more cordial reception and greater expressions of appreciation.

The problem of securing my successor as editor of *UEA* hung fire for months. I instinctively knew the man who should be called, but there was opposition from some sources in our leadership — men who were unacquainted with him and his abilities. He was W. Stanley Mooneyham, then executive secretary of the National Association of Free Will Baptists and editor of their official journal. Finally, in the providence of God, my suggestion was approved. He developed into one of the greatest evangelical leaders of our time and served for several years as editor with great distinction. He later attracted the attention of Billy Graham who gave him a high position in his world organization. Among his contributions to world evangelism was his development of the significant Asian Conference on Evangelism in 1968. When he was, for reasons of health, unable to endure the heavy pressures of constant travel, he was made president of World Vision, Inc., to which he is now devoting his immense administrative and promotional abilities.

Since my editorial years with *UEA* I have written much for its pages. My relationships with the commissions I formerly served have been continued. I still am consulted by the important Resolutions Committee and often write first drafts for its consideration. I am warmly in favor of the services which the National Association of Evangelicals renders evangelical Christendom. I would hate to think of what our situation would be if we did not have such an organization in a high-pressure world like ours controlled by Liberals in almost every area of life.

My word for the future of the NAE is the same today as that which I expressed in the closing paragraphs of *Cooperation Without Compromise:*

We need to lift our sights above old non-biblical concepts, accept the valid discoveries and worth-while advances of modern life and think, plan, and act accordingly. We need to abandon our isolationisms, provincialisms and traditionalisms which are obsolete and which might keep us from a realistic approach to the actual problems of men in our day and time.

We need to realize that the Christian world is in a state of flux. Many of the old lines which used to separate us have little meaning in a modern frame of reference. Men who were "liberals" yesterday are not so sure of their ground today as they face an atomic world and the possibility of the utter destruction of civilization and the human race. Evangelicals who were anti-cultural, anti-scientific and anti-educational yesterday are realizing the necessity of living effectively in a bigger, wider world than they even knew existed. While, as we have said, the great eternal facts and truths of Christianity are unchanging, men and institutions and science are changing and we must meet them, challenge them, and help them grow in the direction of God and the Gospel. We must not condemn sincere thinking and growing men or refuse to meet with them (because of some preconceived notions about them) and talk and pray with them and teach them.

We need to examine ourselves, not only to determine whether we are in the faith, but to see whether we are guilty of self-righteousness and pride. We need to humble ourselves and pray and seek the face of God in new and vital spiritual experience. We need a new endowment of the Holy Spirit and a new willingness to follow His leading.

We need to restudy the Bible itself. The dogmas and creeds of men, however noble and inspiring, however enlightening and strengthening, however purposeful in grounding our minds in fundamental doctrine, can never take the place of the Bible as the direct revelation of God and the infallible authority in all that pertains to faith and life. Fresh touch with the living, written Word can under God give evangelicals a new birth of freedom of thought and launch us upon a movement of such broad proportions that it can sweep the world.

We need to rise above all organizations of men in a bigger and broader fellowship, as big and as broad as the eternal Church of God. God has blessed some of us in our bold and uncompromising stand for the "faith once for all delivered" in the midst of doubt and apostasy. We have built great churches, great Bible institutes, colleges and seminaries, missionary enterprises that span the world, publishing houses, radio ministries and inter-church agencies that show every mark of the blessing of God. But if we are going to allow these works of our hands to bulk so large in our thinking as to cut us off from fellowship with others of like mind and heart, we are failing Him who made it possible for us to achieve great things for Him. We need to see today's religious problems from the viewpoint of God and be as big and as broad in our concerns as He is. Any barriers that we allow to keep us from having a love for mankind as wide as the love which our Lord Jesus Christ demonstrated on Mount Calvary should be pulled down *now!* Tomorrow may be too late in the schedule of God's plan of the ages.

We need to mobilize all our evangelical forces, endowments and personnel in the local churches, in inter-church agencies, in education, in evangelism, in journalism, in radio and television, in missions — in all fields and spheres of Christian service — for a movement of such proportions that God can take it and use it to the accomplishment of His ultimate purposes. This will call for the absolutely complete and unwithholding surrender of our intellectual, material, and spiritual resources and a wholehearted determination to match and exceed the highest and the best that liberalism, humanism and paganism have to offer.

Dr. Harold J. Ockenga at St. Louis in 1942 said that an organization of evangelicals should be launched which "will be the vanguard of a movement" which will have "repercussions in every phase of life" to the glory of God. That organization was realized in the National Association of Evangelicals, which has rendered and is rendering yeomen services in inter-church cooperation. But let us not lose the vision of Dr. Ockenga. Let us think of ourselves as "the vanguard of a movement" that shall achieve God's purposes in our time and literally "turn the world upside down" for Him.

If evangelicals cannot measure up to a vision, a dedication, a purpose, and a program superlatively adequate for our day, the God who gave us the torch of Faith two generations ago will take it from our hands and pass it to some new Company of the Saved who can and will carry it to victory.

Episode XIX

Westwood-Cheviot Church

Now to change the tempo of my story: Most of my life span has been given to service for Christ and the Church at the national or regional level. During all this time, however, I was conscious of the fact that the local church is the foundation of all larger Christian endeavors. I was not of that breed who confined their contacts to the higher echelons of leadership, built theories on philosophical ideas, lived in isolated ivory towers and plush executive offices, and devised patterns and programs that were bound to prove impractical to local congregations. I tried to keep close fellowship with local church leaders and workers by being one myself, understanding their needs and problems, and seeking to lead them to greater accomplishment in terms that were meaningful and attainable for them.

This was one of the factors that led me to serve for some eleven years in a part-time rural and village ministry (see Episode VIII). When my responsibilities with Standard Publishing made it necessary to terminate that phase of my work, God provided an opening for a continuing ministry of a different sort with the Westwood-Cheviot Church of Christ in Cincinnati.

In the 1930's we were living in Westwood. I had kept a nominal relationship as elder with the Western Hills Church (located in Price Hill). Olive was teacher of the women's Bible class, the largest in the Bible school. Our son had his school and social life in Westwood and we had often discussed the advisability of transferring our membership to the Westwood Church on his account.

At this time we had a very happy relationship with Westwood people. Olive had been elected president of the Westwood Woman's Club and I was active in community organizations. We knew most of the leaders in the Church of Christ. In fact, I had had contacts with its ministers and workers from its beginnings.

Its first resident minister was B. W. Carrier whom I had known as a boy in Highland County, Ohio. At that time we lived in adjoining school districts and attended the same rural churches. He was a graduate of the Old Phillips Bible Institute at Canton and a great admirer of P. Y. Pendleton, one of his old teachers. Under his ministry the first frame church building had been erected at Glenmore and Meadow and the membership grew rapidly. We had fine fellowship and I was frequently invited to speak on special occasions. Burley was eventually called to the Hessville Church in the Chicago-Calumet district of Indiana-Illinois and had an outstanding ministry there.

Then came George Wise, who had a good ministry but was so closely allied with the Indianapolis Establishment that he could not enlist the total membership in his program. When he resigned, L. G. Tomlinson succeeded him.

I believe I have already written of L. G. I had a great deal to do with the call given him by the Westwood Church. C. D. Saunders, John Bentel, Paul Dornette, and William Busch — the key elders — came to see me about a successor. Upon my recommendation they secured a unanimous invitation from the church. I had urged his choice because of his ability as a preacher, Bible teacher, and evangelist. He had committed most of the New Testament to memory and usually read his Scripture lessons standing in front of the pulpit. At that time I was not aware of certain personal proclivities that eventually made his ministry a disaster. At first he drew capacity audiences and had additions at every service. The church was doubled in membership in a very short time and plans were made to erect an adequate new building. The problem was that L. G. had to have his own way about everything. He ran roughshod over the elders, deacons, and other church leaders. When he was outvoted in board meetings, he would go home and pretend to be "at death's door" until the "offending brethren" came and prayed with him and promised to do things his way. Finally he singled out his "enemies" and demanded their expulsion from the church. Twice he engineered such a "purge" with the result that the Westwood Church lost many of its leading members to other churches in the community. The financial ability of the congregation was so crippled that it was necessary to build only two units of the new building — a basement auditorium and one wing of the education building. By dedication day a third split impended. Shortly afterward, the Bridgetown Church was formed and L. G. went West to seek a new field of service. Parenthetically, it may be noted that he organized a new church in the Los Angeles, California, area. He devised a constitution and bylaws that gave him full and final authority in all matters. He bought property and built a church building, vesting the title in his own name. With everything under his control he had a lone-wolf ministry of many years which was quite rewarding according to his strange standards.

While Burley Carrier and George Wise had frequently invited the Murches to join the Westwood Church, it was fortunate that we had not acquiesced. I believe that this was of God's guidance, for we avoided participation in a series of events that put the cause of Christ in the community in such disrepute that the church was set back twenty years. We also kept the respect of many good people in each of the three factions that had split the congregation but who had remained in the area.

Into this discouraging situation came Ira Matthews, a student minister at Lawrenceburg, Indiana, who was enrolled in Cincinnati Bible Seminary. He had made his decision to enter the ministry rather late in life and had the maturity to commend him to the remnant congregation burdened with a huge building indebtedness. Ira rendered a yeoman service. No one knows the tremendous burden he carried uncomplainingly. He spent much time in Bible teaching and indoctrination, but more in healing the wounds of division and creating a new spirit of hope for the future. It was Ira who convinced the Murches that they were needed in the Westwood-Cheviot Church. He knew my deep concern for the cause of Christian education in the local church. In fact, he had sat in my classes at CBS and imbibed something of my spirit in this field. He promised that if we would come into the fellowship he would see to it that I was given *carte blanche* as Superintendent of the Bible School to work out my ideas in practical ways. We felt the Lord's leading in the matter and soon were active in this new ministry.

Together Ira and I were enabled to bring back some of the former leaders of the congregation — men who became bosom friends and were to furnish the moral and spiritual abilities, the financial backing, and downright hard work needed to build a great church in the years ahead. A new spirit of cooperation began to take hold of the people, though it was to be many years before the community as a whole was to be persuaded that Westwood-Cheviot Church of Christ was again worthy of its respect. When Ira was called to another field, Harry Poll entered upon a ministry that was to be marked by great progress under difficult circumstances.

Harry Poll was born in England of poor parents. As a child he worked in the potato fields around Boston for paltry wages. Seeing little hope of improving their condition in Boston, the family emigrated to Minnesota. Here Harry was able to work his way through high school. Called to the ministry, he later graduated from Minnesota Bible College. His remarkable talents in the pulpit and all forms of Christian work gained him recognition in high places. He became minister of First Christian Church, Austin, Minnesota, where the nationally famous Hormel meat-packing company is located. The impact of his ministry in the community was so great that at one time he was elected Mayor. In state church work he became president of the Minnesota Christian Missionary Society and was later given positions of responsibility in the International Convention. Faced by the rising tide of liberalism in the Disciples of Christ, he determined to break with "the powers that be." It was at this point that Westwood-Cheviot Church contacted him and gave him a call to its pulpit. It was a mutually happy experience for both church and minister. Harry became the "man of the hour" for us and he found himself in Cincinnati — the center of the conservative movement in the Christian churches of the nation. We became lifelong friends. During his lifetime he was probably my closest friend in the ministry.

Harry led in the complete reorganization of the church and the development of a new leadership. His high ideals in moral and spiritual matters began to impregnate the whole congregation. His sermons on Christian stewardship and tithing, coupled with his advice on fiscal matters, gave us a new and solid financial base for the demands that were to come in the provision of adequate building facilities. He was accepted by the community as an outstanding leader. The past was forgotten and he built great hopes for the future in the minds and hearts of us all. His ministry marked the turning point for Westwood-Cheviot.

Now began my effort to set up a Church School worthy of the name. The obstacles were immense. Our building was totally inadequate. The past history of the school was discouraging. The first Sunday when I took over my duties we had, as I recollect, only 128 in attendance. This was about average for the year. I am not going to recount in detail the changes that took place over the seventeen years I served in this capacity. Reference to my textbook in this field, *Christian Education and the Local Church,* will give the graded blueprint by which we built.

We established close liaison with the elders of the church, who ideally have responsibility for the educational development of the congregation. We had their approval for the choice of all leadership, especially the teachers. It took several years to develop an adequate teaching staff and a "Cabinet" charged with supervision, administration, growth, and development. In the process we were able to create a "family" spirit. Once a month we met in one of the homes, adopted goals, prayed together, heard reports, laid plans for action, and dreamed dreams of what was to be. After the meeting we served refreshments and "talked shop." I never knew a finer group of people with whom to work. Their complete and enthusiastic cooperation brought results far beyond our expectations.

We did a lot of things that "orthodox" religious educators would disapprove. We had contests, special days, banquets, picnics, outings, retreats, organized choirs, bowling teams, baseball teams and the like. In doing these popular things we did not give one inch on the main business of the school; in fact, I think we used them to accomplish far more than the average school in Bible teaching and training, in building Christian character, in meeting individual and social life challenges, and in winning souls to Christ.

Among the new educational features we introduced were classes for young married couples, graded choirs, junior church, vacation Bible schools, and evening schools.

We were faced by the loss of many young people after high school — folk who never came back to the church. We decided that we needed young married couples' classes to bridge the gap and reclaim our youth for the church. Among the teachers we had for these classes were the brilliant Fred Gielow, J. Vernon Jacobs, David Lange, and Ed Eldridge. So interested did these groups become that they added Saturday night get-togethers to their normal Sunday sessions. The Saturday event consisted of smorgasbord, games, and a "bull-session" where all sorts of life problems were discussed. There was a closing prayer meeting which left everybody in the mood for Sunday morning.

223

Our first venture in the music field was the organization of a chorus for high-schoolers. We brought in Professor W. B. Rimanoczy, who was in charge of music for Western Hills High School, to organize and lead the group which we dubbed "The Bethany Chorus." It soon reached an enrollment of around fifty and gained such a reputation in the community that many new young people were enrolled in our classes and won to Christ. This success led us to project a graded choir program. We added a Junior Chorus and an Angel Choir which, with the Bethany Chorus and our Chancel Choir, made a tremendous change in our church music situation. We were fortunate in having David Lange, one of the city's most prominent musicians, leading our Chancel Choir, thus giving Westwood-Cheviot an enviable position in this area of church life.

The vacation Bible school began with an enrollment of less than one hundred and was built through six successive summers to more than three hundred. Classes were offered in all Children's Department grades. On "Demonstration Night" there were exhibits of handwork and Bible drills which drew a packed house of fathers, mothers, uncles, aunts, and friends with an offering that more than paid for school expenses.

The night school was a pet idea of mine, patterned after the very successful Southern Baptist B.T.U. system. We set up a mainly youth and adult system of classes (with a nursery school) meeting on Sunday evening and covering such themes as the Christian Home, Studies in Christian Living, Personal Evangelism, studies in special books of the Bible, Missions, Church History, and the like. This came late in my administration and we were not able to develop it completely, but during its short life it had many fine results.

Our visual aids department was developed with very high standards. We purchased much valuable equipment. We trained capable operators and set up a visual-aids library. In this area, as well as in other new educational discoveries, we aimed to keep abreast of the times.

Did the school grow? We moved to an average of 200 and then to 300 in the old building, our quarters often being jammed to the doors on special days. By this time we had the organization and the personnel to shoot for 400 and 500, but it became evident that we first had to have an adequate sanctuary and an efficient education building. My part in this development will be told later in the story.

As I have already indicated, our minister Harry Poll proved to be a leader par excellence. He worked night and day to advance the Gospel and was rewarded by additions almost every Lord's Day. His health was always fragile and he had a tendency to overwork. He was afflicted with diabetes. I remember one night when he was in the midst of an evangelistic meeting at Westwood-Cheviot that he had a fainting spell just as he was beginning to preach. As he felt it coming on he gestured to me as I sat in the congregation and said, "J. D. will finish the sermon!" As the brethren assisted him from the auditorium I took the pulpit not knowing how I would handle the situation. Praying for strength and guidance I took his theme and preached about twenty minutes. At the invitation two young people confessed Christ. That was the shortest notice I ever had for a preaching engagement.

Harry's popularity and good reputation among the churches made him the most likely candidate for an important public relations position with Standard Publishing and upon my recommendation the management gave him a call with an increase in salary that he could not turn down. We were sorry to lose him at Westwood but rejoiced with him in his larger opportunity for service. He and his family remained in our membership and he continued as an elder.

At the request of the elders I recommended a replacement, suggesting Floyd Pence, minister of the First Christian Church, Springfield, Ohio, as Harry's successor. Floyd was one of our Highland County, Ohio, boys whose family I had known for years. He was a graduate of Cincinnati Seminary and had done an outstanding work at Springfield. He took the church there when it was meeting in a hall and built it into a fine working body. When a splendid well-located and well-equipped modern church building was made available through the merger of the Congregationalists and the "Christian Connection" brethren, he led in its purchase. The name "First Christian Church" on the cornerstone was not even changed, so completely did the facility meet the needs of the congregation. The church grew rapidly under his leadership and became one of the finest in the state.

Our Westwood brethren welcomed Floyd and his family enthusiastically and he started his new ministry with great prospects. He was a strong believer in the Bible school as an evangelistic agency and we worked together with splendid results. Under his guidance we adopted a new church constitution and bylaws which served for many years. The building problem kept staring us in the face and he guided us in laying plans for a new sanctuary, although he encountered considerable opposition from a small group who felt we were not financially able to undertake such a venture.

Then came my tragic separation from Standard Publishing. I took the matter to our board of elders and suggested that if my leadership in the Bible school and in the eldership might prove embarrassing to the church or the minister, I would resign. I was greatly encouraged by their unanimous decision to keep me in those positions and back me to the limit. The whole congregation rallied to me in a remarkable expression of Christian understanding, love, and compassion. I strongly advised that the school continue using Standard literature when it was proposed to drop it. Floyd went along with the situation, but it became evident to me that he was being strongly pressured by the "powers that be" to rid himself of the "contaminating influence of Murch" if he expected to retain his position in the brotherhood. Shortly afterward he resigned and accepted a call to First Church, Michigan City, Indiana, in the Chicago-Calumet area. This was a congregation of around a thousand members with a splendid new building and a situation which constituted a fine promotion for Floyd. He did an outstanding work in Michigan City. We continued to be and have always been friends. When his health failed and he went into semi-retirement in Highland County, Ohio, I often visited him in his beautiful home in Hillsboro. I continue to have the highest regard for his remarkable abilities.

Harry Poll was also put in a difficult situation by the happenings at Standard. He was called in by the management and told that he must sever all relations with me as the price for his continuance on the payroll. This he refused to do and prepared to leave their employ without any idea of what his future might be. When our elders at Westwood-Cheviot heard about his dilemma they immediately voted to give him a call to return to his old pulpit. He accepted and entered upon a most rewarding second ministry with us.

The first great achievement in this ministry was the burning of the mortgage on the church property which had been a "white elephant" for so many years. We then moved to appoint a Building Committee and make contacts with architects, but the same "wrecking crew" that opposed Floyd Pence's efforts in this direction wheeled into position and blocked every effort to finalize definite action on the project. Again, as in Harry's first ministry, we had additions almost every Lord's Day, financial support grew, the general spiritual tone of the congregation was raised to unprecedented levels. But Harry knew that if we could not soon build an adequate church home, his ministry would be severely limited in the days ahead. So when the great 3,000-member Englewood Christian Church, in Indianapolis, Indiana, gave him a call he accepted. This was our largest congregation in the state. Located in the capital city it had great influence far beyond its borders.

In this historic ministry Harry led his people in the erection of a large education facility. I was invited to dedicate it. In fact, Harry and his leaders often gave me the privilege of speaking on special occasions — a relationship that existed for many years after he had moved on to larger fields of service. He was elected president of the North American Christian Convention and made a great contribution to its growth and effectiveness. Later he became Dean of the Midwest Christian College, at Oklahoma City; then President of his Alma Mater, Minnesota Bible College, at Minneapolis; and still later Dean of Atlanta Christian College, Atlanta, Ga. Hundreds of young people in full-time Christian service give him credit for the marvelous contribution he made to their lives. Everywhere he went was home to me and I had frequent invitations to have fellowship in his ministries. He developed into one of our greatest leaders and had the utmost respect of the brotherhood until his untimely death in Atlanta.

After Harry's departure for Indianapolis our elders and our people in general were greatly depressed about the future of Westwood-Cheviot. After canvassing the possibilities for securing a new leader with little success, three of our elders visited me in my home one evening. The spokesman said, "Brother Murch, it is the consensus of our board that you are the only one who can solve this building impasse for us. You have the regard of all our people and if anyone can convince the opposition that we must build and *build now,* you are that one. Will you accept an interim ministry with that purpose in view?" I wrestled with the proposition for several days. I had a schedule which seemingly called for the exercise of my total physical and mental strength. But after prayer and many personal assurances of aid I accepted on a part-time basis and began one of the most rewarding experiences of my life. I was also appointed chairman of the Building Committee and immediately began to lay plans for raising necessary funds to enable us to obtain a loan. Giving was sacrificial and abundant with the result that we were soon able to negotiate with local banks and lending institutions. However, the shoddy handling of financial matters in connection with the old structure, coupled with the well-known divisions which had taken place under the Tomlinson ministry, made it impossible for us to get a loan locally. I finally convinced our men that the only hope lay in a loan from the Board of Church Extension of the Disciples of Christ. We were not supporting Disciples agencies, but we had been told that the BCE was loaning funds without regard to such support. We were cordially received at Indianapolis and assured that we could obtain the desired loan if our final architectural plan and our construction bids were satisfactory. We were assured that there would be no interference in any way with the internal affairs of the congregation and that we would be free to carry on our work according to existing policies and leadership. This move brought a great deal of criticism from extreme "independent" ministers and churches, but our people accepted the plan without any serious dissent. Indianapolis kept faith with us and we had no regrets.

Then ensued the difficult series of final decisions regarding architectural plans, construction bids, and various procedures. I asked for and received from the church board a wide range of powers for the Building Committee with the understanding that our full and final report should be approved by the congregation. There was never a unanimous decision in the board, but our whole committee backed me in a determination to go ahead regardless of the opposition, hoping and praying that we could win eventual support from all our people. The A. M. Kinney Company of Cincinnati were retained as our architects — one of the best architectural firms in the nation. Leading construction companies gave us reasonable bids and then came the final showdown. I made personal visits in the home of every family that opposed immediate construction and finally whittled down the opposition to three families. The key man of this group was an executive of a large electrical firm. I spent a whole evening with him and finally convinced him with a series of facts-and-figures charts that the church could successfully undertake the project. I said to him, "I want to use these charts in my presentation to the final congregational meeting. Can you get me slides and operate the lantern to show them while I speak?" To my amazement he consented. But I was not any more surprised than the hardcore opposition when he took the platform with me that night and carried out his promise. The vote, after a moving prayer by one of our most respected elders, was almost unanimous. Only three people stood in opposition and they were engulfed in the spirited singing of "Praise God from Whom All Blessings Flow" that rose spontaneously from our people. Threats of a few to leave the church if we went ahead with the building program were never carried out.

My assignment was completed except for the responsibilities that remained for me as chairman of the Building Committee. But I must tell about the new spirit in the life of the church that came as a result of my interim public and personal ministry. I preached, taught, called, baptized, married, buried, and counseled our people for nearly a year. My sermons were mainly of the Christian Action type (see Episode IX) and were eagerly received. Our auditorium was packed every Lord's Day morning (I begged off preaching at night because of the drain upon my strength). We kept the baptistery wet. We began to see some of the old leaders who had left the church in the Tomlinson days back in their accustomed places. One of these, now the wealthiest man in the congregation, who had vowed he would never darken the doors of the church again, heard all my sermons and was restored. Today he is one of our honored trustees. Among those who placed membership with us are some of the most respected leaders of the church today.

I was eager that the old-time favorable image of the church, in the days before its schisms, be restored in the community. To this end I invited noted men to speak on special days. One of these was my friend R. G. LeTourneau, the multi-millionaire inventor and manufacturer of earthmoving machinery (the "God-is-my-Partner" man). I explained our situation: told him we met in a basement auditorium but were moving toward bigger things. He readily accepted our invitation, flew over from Peoria, Illinois, in his private plane with a company quartet that furnished special music for the occasion. We advertised his coming and we got an amazing turnout of Westwood-Cheviot businessmen to hear his "success story." Another such speaker was our fellow townsman, the noted Senator Robert Taft, who gave us new community respect. When our beautiful new sanctuary began to take form we were definitely "in" again, the past gone and forgotten.

The A. M. Kinney architects were most cooperative in carrying out our wishes with regard to the new sanctuary. We wanted it to be symbolic of the spirit and program of the Restoration Movement. Fortunately, one of our elders and member of our Building Committee was Val Heinold, a valued member of the architectural staff of the company. Our committee gave Val and me *carte blanche* in developing the plans.

228

Val handled the architectural problems involved and I suggested the symbolically interpretive features.

We were agreed that the architectural style should be "contemporary American," since the Movement had its origins in America and sought always to keep abreast of the times in its national development. There was to be a beautiful simplicity about every feature of the interior. The lines employed were straight, and rectangular, with a high vaulted ceiling giving immediate uplift and worshipful stance to the beholder. Five hundred were to be seated on the slightly-tilted main floor with a hundred more in balcony and choir loft. We planned a center-aisle seating arrangement. The wide aisle proved ideal for wedding processions and the choir's processional and recessional. The side aisles were to be hidden by square pillars running the full length of the room. Between the pillars were to be cathedral-type pendant lighting fixtures. The windows on both sides were high, composed of simple panes of variable rainbow glass blending into the wholeness of the sanctuary and not distracting to the worshiper. The front of the worship area was ideally planned. Above the choir we placed the baptistery with a high bordered proscenium alcove featuring an appropriate painting in the background and topped by a lighted cross. Behind the scenes were several well-equipped cubicles for robing purposes. The choir facility surrounded a hidden organ console and seated fifty singers. On either aside behind webbed walls were accommodations for the eventual installation of one of the finest organs in Cincinnati. On the third level and central in congregational view was the pulpit for the reading and preaching of God's Word. Below and also central to congregational view was to be the Lord's Table. It was placed on the audience level to portray the fact that it was in no sense an altar but rather a simple medium through which our Lord is to be in the midst of His people on the Lord's Day when according to His wishes they remember His death and suffering for their redemption and the promise of His coming again. This plan constitutes one of the most worshipful and meaningful arrangements I have ever seen anywhere in Christian Churches and Churches of Christ. The spacious front foyer and lobby space on two levels gave adequate access to the whole structure. Later refinements of the sanctuary have made it even more attractive in its worshipfulness, simple dignity, and beauty.

Bids were received and the contract let to the Penker Construction Company, one of the best in the city in that day. They were most cooperative in carrying out our wishes and those of the architectural engineers. The next step was to set a day for the Groundbreaking ceremonies. It seemed almost unbelievable that, after so many frustrating delays through the years, we were at last to see our dreams come true. It was to be a day of rejoicing and victory.

In the providence of God it was also to be the day of the installation of our new minister, the man who has guided our destinies so masterfully and effectively from that day to this — William Harold Hockley. Our

Pulpit Committee, after a long search, discovered a young Canadian who was just finishing his graduate work in the School of Religion at Butler University, and preaching for the congregation at Windfall, Indiana. Their recommendation to the congregation was accepted unanimously. It proved to be a wise decision.

Every day I was in Cincinnati during the construction period I went to the building site to see the progress being made and to assure myself that the quality of the building material and the workmanship were according to our contractural arrangements and the wishes of our people. I was "on call" night or day when problems arose. And I enjoyed every minute of it.

We dramatized every step of the construction. One big event was the laying of the Cornerstone. The flat roof of the old basement was our platform. We invited the Mayor of Cheviot to speak and the Masonic order of Knights Templar in their resplendent uniforms to lay the cornerstone. Our robed choir and an orchestra furnished music and the minister and elders provided the devotional hour. A throng filled the Meadow Avenue side of the property. Cheviot police managed the through traffic on Glenmore and rerouted cars during the services. It was a happy occasion.

When the time came to plan our Dedicatory Services, I urged that my good friend P. H. Welshimer, pastor of our greatest church in America, be invited to preach the sermon. He was seldom away from Canton on the Lord's Day, but with a little urging on my part he consented to come. It was an unforgettable day with the largest Bible school attendance in our history and standing-room-only audiences in morning worship and afternoon exercises.

I have an understanding sympathy for those who say that a building should make no difference in the growth of a church. I agree with them in theory but human nature being what it is few people are going to worship God in a "hole-in-the-ground" basement when more favorable surroundings are available elsewhere. After the completion of our new sanctuary, audiences zoomed and contacts were made with prospective members far beyond anything Westwood-Cheviot had experienced in its history. Our people responded to the whole church program with a new loyalty, generosity, and enthusiasm. We had arranged our mortgage loan for ten years, but we paid it off in five.

I was aware all along that we were doing something which, while of first importance to the church as a whole, was not anything that met the desperate educational needs of our Church School. Our people saw this as we labored to build a great school without adequate facilities. When I began to agitate for a new education building which would cost more than the sanctuary had, I expected resistance. However, there was virtually none. Everyone seemed to believe that we had done it before and that there was no reason on earth that we couldn't do it again. Almost immediately after the mortgage burning we moved toward the erection of a facility which, with what we already had, could accommodate a school of 1,000. The church board appointed me chairman of the new Building Committee and things began to roll. Harold was most cooperative and entered into the planning with great enthusiasm. I found everything easier in the new project because of his eager helpfulness, his intelligent counsel, and wise guidance.

When the problem of financing arose Harold and I decided to make a trip to Indianapolis to request another loan from the Board of Church Extension. We were cordially received. They said our record in repayment of the former loan was the best of any church in their history. However, they said the amount of our loan was much greater than they normally approved and that the interest rate would have to be raised. We were put on their "waiting list." Then a providential thing occurred. I met my friend Walter Eckert of the Cheviot Building and Loan Company on the street one evening. Said he, "Where are you going to get your loan for the new building?" I told him, "Indianapolis, I guess, but we are on their waiting list and will have to pay a higher rate of interest." "Why do that?" he asked, "Maybe you can get the money immediately and pay no more interest than you did before." I knew at once that he would "go to bat" for us with his bank. He said, "Why don't you and Brother Hockley come over to our house tomorrow night with your plans and we will see what can be worked out." We did. He did. And we were "in business."

We were most fortunate in securing the architectural services of Carl Schmuelling in the planning of the new building. I had the ideas and he had the know-how so we worked together beautifully in producing what we have today. It is not ideal, because we were limited by our building space and by the old ill-planned unit we had to incorporate in the structure as a whole. Our task involved remodeling and completely new construction under the direction of R. B. Witte and Son. As a result we had these new facilities —

A fellowship hall for social events, plays, special assemblies, dinners, and recreational purposes. It seats on occasion nearly 300. On the ground floor, with good light and air, were the Nursery, Beginner, and Primary Departments with all modern equipment for the little tots. Here, too, the Bible-school offices. On the main floor were the church offices, the Adult Department classrooms, and quarters for the Junior Department. Every entrance door was numbered and labeled for easy access. Also on this floor was the spacious Church Parlor to be beautifully furnished and with an adjoining kitchenette for use for social events, small wedding receptions, and the like. When converted for use on Sunday mornings with the aid of folding partitions, it was to serve as assembly rooms for the two ladies' Bible classes. On the top floor were the adjustable areas for use of the Junior High, Senior High, and College and Career Bible classes and assemblies. Here too, was the assembly area for the Junior Church. Space fails me for a further description of the facilities and furnishings which in that day were the finest that money could provide.

When Dedication Day came we had another record-breaking attendance in Bible school (nearly 800) and in the months immediately following our average attendance approached 600. Ard Hoven, then minister of Broadway Church, Lexington, Kentucky, (now with First Church, Columbus, Indiana) brought the dedicatory message. Ministers of many of our churches in the area were in attendance. The tour of the building which followed brought "Ohs" and "Ahs" from our neighboring brethren. It was agreed that at that time we had the largest and the finest facility of any of our churches in Greater Cincinnati. What a far cry from the little basement church we once knew! I thanked God that I had been privileged to have a part in this remarkable story of church growth and in the blessings He was showering upon us.

We then launched upon an enlargement program for our Bible school. There was a complete reorganization of the graded system in our new facilities. We projected new areas of service for the school. We began training a new generation of officers and teachers. One of these prospective leaders was Jack Eick, a rising young executive with General Electric. His capable and lovely wife, Georgi, credits me with having first interested him in Christ and the Church and finally getting him actively involved in the work of the church as assistant superintendent of the school. He developed all the qualifications for leadership and was to figure largely in the future growth of the congregation (superintendent of the Bible school, an elder, and chairman of the Church Board).

Then just as we were ready to launch a new drive forward in every department, I was suddenly called to service in Washington, D. C., as Managing Editor of *Christianity Today* — an area of service of which I shall have more to say.

My good friend Henry Follmer, whom I had received into the church during my interim ministry, set up a voluntary committee and proceeded to lay plans for a big farewell Testimonial Dinner. Henry had been an outstanding lay-leader in the historic Ninth Street Baptist Church, had been elected elder and was a leader in the Mr. and Mrs. Bible class. The occasion was long to be remembered by the Murches. We were presented with a portfolio of tributes from ministers, educators, and editors all over the land. Our own local leaders were present and were most generous in their friendly words of farewell. We received a beautifully initialed set of leather luggage and amid tears, smiles, and good wishes we were sent on our way to our new home in the Nation's Capital.

A footnote: Eight years later when we retired from active service we came back to Cincinnati to make our home in the Hammond North. On the very first Sunday in the city we went back to Westwood-Cheviot Church and "placed our membership" during the singing of the first stanza of the invitation hymn. We were "back home" indeed. Since that hour, which was replete with the welcomes of scores and scores of our old friends, we have been happy in our continuing fellowship. Harold Hockley and his precious wife May had led the congregation into ever-enlarging fields of usefulness. He had attained notable national status as a preacher of the Gospel. The membership had increased to 1,100 and two morning worship services were necessary to accommodate the audiences. The choirs had achieved note as among the best in the city. Additional property had been purchased providing a new Youth Center, parking facilities, and an open-air assembly ground. The whole property represented an investment of over half a million dollars. Harold had been chosen as president of the North American Christian Convention and honored with leadership in many of our voluntary agencies, not the least of which was his chairmanship of the Board of Trustees of the new Emmanuel School of Religion.

Now as we sit in the Lord's Day worship services, as the Lord gives us strength to attend, our cup of joy runs over. "Surely goodness and mercy shall follow us all the days of our lives and we shall dwell in the house of the Lord forever."

Episode XX

Sale of Standard Publishing

Who was I to be a determining factor in the sale of the Standard Publishing Company in Cincinnati — a business transaction that could to a large degree influence the future course of the Restoration Movement in America?

I was *persona non grata* with its management and with most of its owners and editors. Even more: I had been ordered never to set foot in its buildings and offices. I had been made the subject of vicious attacks on my loyalty to the Restoration Plea and my personal character. My name had been eliminated from the thousands of copies of publications I had helped produce over a period of thirty years. I had been placed on the "black list" of all the journals it published and my name was not allowed to appear even in items of news.

Yet the Lord had a role He expected me to play in this crucial situation. I have never experienced in all my life a more convincing proof of the fact that "God moves in a mysterious way His wonders to perform." This is the story:

One afternoon as I sat in the editorial offices of *United Evangelical Action* in Cincinnati, I received a phone call from the Hoffman Realty Company, asking whether the president of the company could see me within the hour on a matter of extreme importance. I did not know the man, but I agreed to see him.

Upon his arrival he told me that he had come at the suggestion of his secretary, who was a member of the Christian Church and whom as a girl I had baptized some years before. Then he shocked me with the question, "Would you be interested in buying the Standard Publishing Company?" I am afraid I laughed at his suggestion. I said, "Is this some sort of practical joke?" Then I explained to him that, even though I might be interested, I was totally incapable of raising the funds necessary for such a transaction.

I could scarcely believe the firm would be for sale. I knew it was a multi-million-dollar corporation, with a super-excellent credit rating, and was a virtual "gold mine" for the Errett family. It was the type of concern that was virtually unaffected by the rise and fall of the stock market and by the fluctuating economic conditions of the nation. The churches and religious leaders patronized it "rain or shine" and it was one of the leading houses of its kind in the world. "I did not even know the Company was for sale," I told Hoffman. "Why would the Erretts want to sell a successful 'gold mine'?"

234

The noted realtor was surprised that I had not known that the Company was on the market. He showed me copies of the *Wall Street Journal* in which the offering was advertised, and copies of the elaborate prospectus detailing full information concerning the business, which had been prepared for prospective buyers.

I then asked whether approaches had been made to wealthy members and/or institutions of the Christian Churches and Churches of Christ. These, I felt, would be the natural and most appropriate buyers. Under questioning he volunteered the following information:

The Phillips Gas and Oil family of Butler, Pennsylvania, whose ancestors had helped establish the *Christian Standard,* were approached but turned down the offer on the ground that this was not the type of investment they wanted.

Kieth Kindred, of Chicago, the wealthy son of C. G. Kindred, long minister of the Englewood Christian Church in Chicago, was interested but he would offer only two million dollars.

Small groups of our conservative Christian ministers and businessmen had met to consider creating a tax-free corporation which might buy it, but they were unable to raise the necessary funds to warrant an offer.

The property had then been offered to The Christian Foundation of Columbus, Indiana. This was the multi-million-dollar fund set up by the Irwin family and their friends to advance the cause of Christian education among the Disciples. Originally its board was sound in the faith but then, under the management of J. Irwin Miller and his associates, it had been taken over by the Liberals. It was later the major financial supporter of the left-wing Christian Theological Seminary of Indianapolis. The Foundation was not interested.

An offer had been made to Texas Christian University — an avowed enemy of the *Christian Standard* and all it stood for — the wealthiest educational institution of the Disciples of Christ. According to Hoffman, TCU had almost bought the Company, lacking only one vote in its Board for approval of the deal. Other offers had been made to Disciples' schools but without any results.

I expressed amazement at this utter disregard for the preservation and perpetuation of the traditional policies of the Company, and under pressure Hoffman said, "The Standard management will sell the firm to anybody — and I mean *anybody* — who can come up with five million dollars, their minimum asking price. The majority of the Errett heirs are determined to get out of this type of investment and seek more lucrative returns for their money."

After nearly two hours of very enlightening conversation, Hoffman said, "Is there anyone anywhere you know who might be interested in taking over this Company?" Sadly I shook my head and said, "Nobody whatsoever." "Well", he said, "if you can come up with any prospects later, get in touch with me immediately." The whole incident upset me

235

so completely that I left my desk, walked out of the office, and went home.

That night I was unable to sleep. I prayed earnestly for guidance if, perchance, there was anything under God that I could do to avert the catastrophe that seemed to impend. Suddenly, about three in the morning, there came to me the realization that I knew several multi-millionaires who might be persuaded to finance a purchase. None of these was a member of the Christian Church or Church of Christ, but they were wonderful evangelical Christians who loved the cause of Christ enough to do whatever the Lord might lead them to do. I got up and jotted down their names and addresses:

John Bolten of the Bolta Corporation, Boston and the General Tire and Rubber Company of Akron.

R. G. LeTourneau of the giant earth-moving-machinery manufacturing company at Peoria and around the world.

C. David Weyerhauser of the Weyerhauser Lumber Company with headquarters in Tacoma and Seattle.

H. J. Taylor of "Club Aluminum," Chicago, and at that time international president of Rotary.

Charles E. Fuller of the "Old-Fashioned Revival Hour" and (with his wife) a businessman of distinction.

Kenneth Keyes of Miami, Florida, the "real estate king" of Florida and the Southeast.

Early that morning I went to the office, contacted Mr. Hoffman, and within minutes we were deep in plans to interest these men in a deal. It was agreed that I should write a personal letter to each one containing essential information and making a personal appeal on a religious basis. This letter marked "Personal" together with a copy of the Standard prospectus was sent by insured air mail, special delivery, that same day.

I heard from all but one of these men within the week. They wrote in a wonderful spirit to tell me that, for various appropriate reasons, they would not be able to consider the offer. They expressed an interest in the situation and asked me to keep them informed concerning the outcome of my efforts. The one man who did not reply immediately was John Bolten.

The next week I had to go to Portland, Oregon, to speak at the annual convention of the National Sunday School Association. I flew in toward evening and went to my hotel to check in. The bellboy asked me if I expected any mail. I told him "No" but he said, "Maybe I better check." He did and came up with a telegram which I hastily opened and discovered it was John Bolten's reply. He said he had been out of the country, but was interested. He asked that I be available for a long-distance telephone conversation next morning at six o'clock.

Promptly at six my phone bell jingled and I heard John's voice. He apologized for not answering my letter sooner and said he had been in South America on a business trip. "Now," he said — speaking clear across the nation from Andover, Massachusetts, to Portland, Oregon — "this is a four-way call. I have my secretary and my attorney with me here, our conversation is being recorded, and I hope you can give us informative answers to a lot of questions." Then he began and for *two hours* he almost "pumped me dry" about Standard Publishing. Fortunately I had the answers he desired and upon which he made his decision. "I will contact Mr. Hoffman at once and begin negotiations." I warned him, as I had Mr. Hoffman, that my name should not be mentioned at any time; that to do so might terminate relations immediately.

Who was this man Bolten? There may be some of my readers who have not been so fortunate as to learn of his abilities and accomplishments in many fields of endeavor. He was born in Germany, the son of a British Plymouth Brethren missionary, and his wife, the daughter of a German family of distinction. He received the best education that could be provided in European schools. He learned to speak several languages. He was a musician of note who specialized in the works of Bach, loving to sit down at a piano and play from memory for his friends almost any opus desired. He was always a devout student of the Bible and gained from his father the equivalent of a theological seminary education. He could early in life speak and preach in the Plymouth Brethren assemblies and has continued all his life to "do the work of an evangelist." But his natural bent led him into the field of business.

When first I knew him he had reached maturity and had immense investments in business corporations in several lands. He had a factory in Nuremberg, Germany, which manufactured optical lenses — the entire product of which was contracted to Sears; factories in America manufacturing vinyl products, including the widely advertised "Bolta cloth"; sales rights for Coca Cola in many nations of Latin America, and exclusive vinyl manufacturing rights in these same nations. He was one of the five leading stockholders in and was a member of the Board of the General Tire and Rubber Company and had investments in many similar enterprises. He had oil interests the extent of which I never knew.

A good steward of the blessings with which God had endowed him, he gave liberally to his church (Park Street, Boston, where he was for years its treasurer), to many missionary projects and educational institutions. He virtually underwrote the work of the Inter-Varsity Christian Fellowship International and the Student Foreign Missions Fellowship. He was a great friend of Billy Graham and gave freely to all his projects and enterprises. When the National Association of Evangelicals was formed he was one of its first supporters. It was in this area of service that I became acquainted with him in the realization of some of his ideas. He served on many boards such as that of *Christianity Today*.

After Portland I became deeply involved with Mr. Bolten in his efforts to purchase Standard Publishing lasting over a period of more than a year. There was seldom a week that went by without lengthy long-distance phone calls and conferences in Boston, Chicago, Washington, Philadelphia, New York and (many times) Cincinnati. He was generous in paying all my expenses and entertained me lavishly. There were many, many problems involved and he shared them with me in the hope that I along with many others might give him helpful ideas and advice. He finally came to the place where he was really obsessed with the idea of owning and operating Standard as a service to the evangelical cause nationally and worldwide. Often in his hotel suites he would ask me to join him in Bible study and prayer for the consummation of the deal. He had a deep and abiding faith that he would be the eventual buyer and that faith never faltered.

One of the problems was financing. He expected to borrow to the hilt of his credit without endangering any of his vast holdings. He would tell me about his negotiations with Aetna, Axe-Houghton, Little and Little, Talcott James, and banks in Boston, Chicago, New York and — all along — with First National of Cincinnati. The latter institution had been banker for Standard for many years, knew the condition of the Company, its high rating, and its prospects for the future. As time went on it would seem that any one of these contacts would result in the kind of loan he desired and then something would occur to halt negotiations. Finally it was our local bank that granted him what he wanted, or *almost!*

Another ideal he "shot for" was reorganizing Standard's whole structure to make it a corporation not for profit. He was in touch with corporation lawyers and government agents submitting idea after idea and being turned down time and time again. It was in this area of the deal that I was frequently called upon to pass on the feasibility of plans as far as the Christian Churches and Churches of Christ were concerned. One day John came up with the idea that the National Association of Evangelicals might be the medium through which his ideas could be realized. He was on the NAE Board of Administration and he asked me to form a wedge of support and carry the proposition to conferences and a final vote. I was not very enthusiastic about the idea because I foresaw complications that could be dangerous both for the NAE and for us. Yet I went to bat, did my best, even to endangering some of my close friendships within the Board, but the proposal finally failed of adoption. I was not too unhappy, although John was. From that day on he was only a lukewarm supporter of the NAE. Even after the purchase he would not give up the idea of a non-profit corporation and tried a number of unsuccessful organizational ventures in which the management of the Company participated.

Another problem was staffing the editorial and business divisions of the Company. He insisted that I become responsible for editorial and always planned with that in mind. He had in his own organization the personnel which he believed could effectively set up the business end of the Company. We often talked about possible developments but came to no conclusions.

One of the matters on John's conscience was his church relationship.

He felt he should be associated with the religious communion which the Company served in its major operations, yet he was not willing to compromise his own religious beliefs to accomplish that end. I will always remember a phone call I got one afternoon asking me to come to Chicago for a day of study and discussion on this subject. I went, at his arrangement, to the exclusive Ambassador East (home of the famous "Pump Room") where he had a suite. I called him and apologized for arriving so early in the morning, but he said, "Come on up. I'm shaving but we can talk." He ordered breakfast sent in. We had a Bible reading and prayer before we ate. Almost immediately he manifested his eagerness to hear me recount the beginnings of the Restoration Movement in America and the reasons for its advent in an already well-churched nation. I need not recount the story as I told it, together with instruction in fundamental New Testament doctrine. Most of my readers will be familiar with my views. John responded with enthusiasm. "Why," he said, "this is essentially comparable to the story of the Plymouth Brethren in whose faith I was reared as a youth. It, too, is a free church movement seeking to restore the New Testament church in doctrine, ordinances, and life." He would frequently interrupt me to ask questions and make favorable comments. The morning passed swiftly. After lunch we went back to the suite for more discussion. Early in the conversation he said, "Jim, I see no reason at this moment that I should not identify myself with one of your churches, but I want to explore some possible consequences." So, the afternoon passed until the time came for my departure for Cincinnati. "What church would you recommend that I join? We have very few if any in the Greater Boston area." Then I proposed, since he would, hopefully, be in Cincinnati a great deal of his time, that he place his membership with either the Westwood-Cheviot Church or the Lockland Church there. I left him in the full assurance that when the time came he would be "one with us" in a common cause.

As the sale of the Company continued to be delayed, due to the fact that there was no offer in the five-million-dollar range, my friend Hoffman kept me informed of the more promising offers. One of them was from the Kresge Foundation in behalf of Albion College. Albion was a left-of-center Methodist institution in Michigan. It had fallen upon hard times but had found a warm friend in ardent Methodist business tycoon Sebastian Kresge. It mattered not to Standard's management that such a sale would not only bring Methodist control but Liberal control as well. For some reason, after several months of negotiation, the offer fell through. There were other equally strange negotiations all of which would have endangered Standard's historic relationship with the Restoration Movement. I could list them, but to no purpose.

Then came a much more dangerous trend in the sales situation with offers from firms noted as ruthless liquidators. They were tax racketeers who used indebtedness and non-taxables as blinds to cheat the government and get rich quickly. The "woods are full of them" even today. The particular firms and associations which entered the Standard picture were headed by Jews and by others of no religious faith. There were also prospective purchasers in completely secular insurance fields, such as Woodmen of the World with headquarters in Omaha.

At long last, the Bolten interests had put together a final offer which was close to the five-million-dollar price, backed by a substantial loan (at that time the largest ever made to a private corporation) from the First National Bank of Cincinnati. The Standard management appointed a date at which time the Bolten offer and another of the liquidator type mentioned above would be presented to the stockholders for final action. The management favored the latter and recommended the refusal of the Bolten offer.

At this point I decided on a daring move. One of my best friends in the world was Roy Slifer, vice-president of the Standard Publishing Company. Roy had married Hallie Errett, a daughter of Russell. At his death she inherited a large share of the family-owned stock. She, too, died and Roy was left with an important place in the Company. He was also the trusted representative of a bloc of stockholders. Roy was not of an aggressive nature and became a virtual "yes-man" for the management. It was assumed that Roy would join the management in its decision on the sale. He was not even told the nature of the proposition or the character of the proponents. He was just expected to "sign on the dotted line."

For years we had eaten together at the noon hour in the Florentine Room of the Gibson Hotel. Even after my break with Standard this close relationship existed, based on a common concern for the Restoration Movement and a common interest in the Christians Hour, our national radio broadcast; several of our independent mission enterprises; the Disciples of Christ Historical Society, and our local church affairs. (He was a long-time elder in the Madisonville Christian Church.) My wife and I were frequent guests in his home and he in ours before and after Hallie's death. We thought alike and acted alike in many situations — social, political, and religious. In order to preserve our friendship we mutually agreed that we would not discuss Standard matters, and we had kept our pact inviolate up to this time.

I decided that I must talk to Roy about the sales decision he was about to make, since it was to involve a matter that was of far more importance than our personal friendship. Accordingly, at one of our noon get-togethers I said, "Roy, I want to talk to you about a very important matter in which you are involved. It pertains to the Standard Publihsing Company." He was startled, but he said, with a look of amazement, "Certainly, J.D. Let's go over to my office."

I began with a recital much along the lines of my story in this chapter. He listened with rapt attention and with a friendly attitude that grew to intense interest and concern. Then he asked scores of questions. We were together for most of the afternoon. Finally, he said, "This comes as a great shock to me. I am glad that you have brought these matters to my attention. I will certainly make my own investigations and pray about your advice. I am aware of the fact that my decision might well determine the stockholders' action. I will do what I think best for the cause we both love."

After the sale had been made to the Bolten interests Roy told me what happened at the historic meeting. The management made its statement to the stockholders and then signed the contract for sale to another concern. The document was passed over to Roy for his expected signature, but he refused to sign. Several other stockholders followed his example. The general manager and treasurer then in anger demanded to know why this resistance to company policy. Roy made a brief speech telling why he had made his decision and then offered to sign the Bolten contract. His brother-in-law then cursed him and swore at him and threatened never to speak to him again if he did not go along with the management. But Roy nobly stood his ground and the Company was sold to Bolten. I have often tried to picture the situation. It was so out of character for the mild-mannered Roy, but his adamant stand saved the day.

Afterward Roy said to me, "J.D., you have saved the Standard Publishing Company for many more years of service to the Restoration Movement." And I replied, "No. I had no authority in the matter. It was you who did it and our people should be everlastingly grateful to you for your unselfish and courageous stand!" We remained warm friends to his dying day. In his personal effects was found a note to the effect that "If Dr. Murch should outlive me, I request that he shall have charge of my funeral service."

Completion of details for the final take-over of the Company by the Bolten interests took around another year. In the interim the old management continued in charge and editorial and publishing personnel remained the same. John Bolten kept in touch with me and repeatedly assured me that I was to become vice-president and executive editor in the new set-up. As the time for the take-over approached I received a call to come to Washington where I met John and his senior attorney. We spent a morning and afternoon together in his suite in the Mayflower Hotel, where we talked over every angle of our agreement as to policies, programs, and plans for the future. I never knew John to be happier about Standard than that day in Washington.

But it was not to be. When my name was mentioned as the incoming executive editor, the management blew up. One of the men said, "If Murch comes in here it will be over my dead body!" The other said, "If Murch comes in everybody in the editorial department will leave. You will have the biggest strike on your hands that you have ever seen." There was much more that might be said about the effort to bring about a peaceful understanding on the basis of my incumbency, but it was to no avail. Then, rather than precipitate a situation that would make it very difficult to operate the Company successfully, the Boltens acquiesced to the status quo with only such personnel changes as were necessary for the structural and fiscal reorganization of the Company. John accepted the inevitable with tears in his eyes and assured me that the old boycott against me would eventually be ended and cordial relations restored. Said he, "Maybe the Lord has something better in store for you!" John was right and spoke prophetically, though I was not in the mood to believe him at that time.

This was not the only disappointment John had in his plans for Standard. He failed to get government approval for setting up a corporation not for profit, despite all the plans presented and all the commendations he received from evangelical leaders throughout the nation. So he said, "If *not for profit,* then *for profit!*" With the superb aid of his son-in-law, Daniel Hogan, and their associates they organized Standard International which embraced all his interests at home and abroad. It became a stock company with offerings on the New York Stock Exchange and the approval of the U. S. Securities and Exchange Commission. Today it is one of the major conglomerates in the nation. Standard Publishing is a division of Standard International. With it all John has insisted that the integrity of the Christian Church and Church of Christ publications be maintained and perpetuated.

There are many, many more stories I could tell about this episode in my life (such as the story of why John Bolten never identified himself with the Restoration Movement which had Campbellian origins in America), but maybe the telling would do more harm than good, so I hereby cease and desist.

I have kept in touch with the development of Standard International and rejoiced in its high attainments. John, in the beginning, had no idea of expansion beyond the publishing company. He was literally forced into creating a conglomerate. In the last seventeen years they have made 45 acquisitions under the exceptional direction of Dan Hogan. As I write, the corporation reports current sales of $125 million with earnings of $5.5 million. Unlike many other conglomerates Standard International is now in a highly liquid position with about $50 million in marketable securities. It has a debt to capitalization ratio of approximately 25 per cent. Internal growth has been significant. Standard Publishing had annual sales of only $4 million in 1955. Today they have risen to $22 million. One factor in this growth is its chain of 25 Berean religious retail bookstores strategically located, in centers of major sales coverage, from coast to coast.

After a few years elapsed I began to get feelers for the renewal of friendly relations with Standard. At this time Burris Butler was vice-president and executive editor. He had been with the Company for a number of years and was widely respected. We were to have many friendly associations until his retirement in 1971. I was first asked to prepare some gift brochures. Then I received a huge assignment to make a comprehensive survey and critique of fifty-some publications of the Company, mainly in the field of Bible-school literature. More concerning this later.

Then came the publication by Standard of probably the major book of my career — *Christians Only* — a history of the Restoration Movement in America with particular concern for the growth and development of Christian Churches and Churches of Christ. It has had and still has a wide circulation and is the major textbook of its field in our conservative colleges and seminaries.

From this point on the most cordial relations developed. At the suggestion of my good friend, Edwin V. Hayden, I became a staff contributor to the *Christian Standard* with a regular page, "Today in Christendom." I reported all the crucial conventions of the Disciples of Christ during the "Restructure" years and was given carte blanche in expressing opinion-forming comment on that tragic development in our Brotherhood life.

With the chief sources of vindictive animosity toward me and my life work virtually eliminated, I was able to enjoy a peace of mind that had not been mine for many years. I learned that a man's enemies have no power to harm him if he is true to himself and loyal to the Lord Jesus Christ. In every instance when there was intent to harm and destroy me, God lifted me to new heights of attainment and Christian service, as we shall see in later chapters.

As I write, my good friend of many years, Ralph Small, occupies the important position of Vice President and Executive Editor of Standard Publishing. He is the son of J. Marion Small, who was one of our most effective evangelists when I was president of the Christian Restoration Association. The rapid growth of the company indicates its mounting favor with the Christian Churches and Churches of Christ, and evangelicals everywhere. It is a real pleasure to make some small contributions from time to time to the on-going success of Standard — "my first love" in the field of journalism.

Blessed is the man that endures persecution, for when he is tried he shall receive a crown of life, which the Lord has promised them that love Him. That is the divine assurance. It begins with man, it ends with God. It begins with earth, it ends with heaven. It begins with struggle, it ends with a crown. The man that, with the help of God, stands up under trial, resists and persists, conquers. To him inevitably come new wisdom, new strength, new joy, and in the end eternal life.

Episode XXI

Christianity Today

John Bolten's observation, "Possibly the Lord has something more important in store for you," came to fruition in 1958 when I was called to Washington, D. C., to become Managing Editor of *Christianity Today*. This undenominational fortnightly magazine was at that time the universally acknowledged leader in evangelical journalism and the thought and life of American evangelicals.

I had some small part in its launching, after this wise: As editor of *United Evangelical Action* for more than fourteen years, I had finally come to the conclusion that we were too limited in our appeal to the total evangelical constituency in the churches. We did not have adequate funds for subsidizing a magazine of outstanding quality. As the official organ of the National Association of Evangelicals, we were severely limited in our ability to enlist total evangelical appreciation and cooperation. We could not produce the quality-type magazine that would have effective appeal to the highest and best evangelical scholarship and inspire our best writers to contribute to its pages.

This situation was hindering the progress of the evangelical cause as a whole. The well-subsidized *Christian Century* of Chicago commanded almost total liberal support and had occupied a position of prestige and power as America's leading religious journal. It was widely considered the voice of American Protestantism. Evangelicals had nothing to match it. This, in face of the fact that surveys had shown that seventy-two percent of American churchmen were either fundamentalist or conservative in their theology.

I became so deeply concerned about this situation that I was led to write Billy Graham, then in an evangelistic crusade in New Orleans. I enclosed in my letter a skeleton prospectus of a journal I felt would meet the need of the hour. I told Billy that I believed he was the only evangelical who could command complete responsible evangelical support for such an enterprise. I received an immediate reply indicating that he and others were already attacking the problem and that an announcement of a new journal would be forthcoming in a few months. This is another example of how the Lord moves in the hearts of His people in widely separated places to bring His purposes to pass. Billy was a friend of the NAE and assured me that *United Evangelical Action* still had a vital part to play in the evangelical cause.

In 1956 *Christianity Today* made its appearance in answer to our prayers. The chairman of its board of management, Harold John Ockenga, stated its basic theological beliefs and announced its future

244

objectives: "Evangelicals have general objectives we wish to see achieved. One of them is the revival of Christianity in the midst of a secular world . . . We wish to retrieve Christianity from a mere eddy of the main stream into the full current of modern life. We desire to win a new respectability for orthodoxy in academic circles by producing scholars who can defend the faith on intellectual grounds. We hope to recapture denominational leadership from within the denominations rather than abandoning these denominations to modernism. We intend to restate our position carefully and cogently so that it must be considered in the theological dialogue of the times. We intend that Christianity will be the mainspring in many of the reforms of the societal order. It is wrong to abdicate responsibility for society under the impetus of a theology which overemphasizes the eschatological."

Carl F. H. Henry assumed the editorial chair, coming from the faculty of Fuller Theological Seminary in Pasadena. We had been friends since the days in Boston where I had gone to assume the editorship of *United Evangelical Action*. He had earned doctorates from Northern Baptist Theological Seminary in Chicago, Boston University, and New College, Edinburgh. He had a natural flair for journalism, having earned his spurs as a youngster on the reportorial staff of the *Detroit Free Press*. He was undoubtedly the man for the place.

The necessary financial underwriting for such an enterprise had been provided through the persuasive powers of Billy Graham. He and his father-in-law, Dr. L. Nelson Bell, got an initial gift of $50,000 from J. Howard Pew of Sun Oil Company. Other big gifts came from Maxey Jarman of Genesco, John Bolten of Bolta Corporation, and other multi-millionaires of evangelical persuasion. These men and a few outstanding clergymen formed the Board of Management, thus assuring generous subsidies for the future. No expense was spared in setting up an adequate suite of offices in the Washington Building, across the street from the U. S. Treasury, and furnishing it with the latest equipment for the operation of a first-class magazine. With a "controlled subscription list" the journal from the first went automatically to more than 200,000 Protestant clergymen and all the leaders of religious life in America. *Christianity Today* became at once an outstanding advocate of the "faith once delivered," a challenge to liberalism, and began to move toward eventual leadership in religious journalism.

The first intimation I had that I was being considered for the managing editorship came from Walter Bennett, successful Chicago advertising man. Walter handled all Billy Graham's promotional ventures, including his radio program, "The Hour of Decision." I got acquainted with him when I was president of the National Religious Broadcasters and had great respect for his ability. One day we met and he said, "J.D., you will be hearing some interesting news from Washington one of these days. Billy has his eye on you for the staff of *Christianity Today*."

In due time I heard from Dr. Ockenga and from Carl Henry. Carl made a trip to Cincinnati for a mutually satisfactory conference. Dr. Ockenga wrote, "Your coming to *Christianity Today* will be a fitting climax to your distinguished career in religious journalism. We are hopefully expecting your acceptance." I was thrilled with the prospects of a larger service for Christ and the Church. I agreed to become Managing Editor, resigned my editorship of UEA, and began making arrangements to sell our property in Cincinnati and relocate in Washington. The move represented quite a change for the Murches after some forty years in the "Queen City." The breaking of long-time social and religious ties was no easy matter.

We enjoyed a series of testimonial gatherings — the Westwood-Cheviot church, the Greater Cincinnati Association of Evangelicals, the Greater Cincinnati Sunday School Association, the National Association of Evangelicals (a dinner at the Statler-Hilton in Los Angeles attended by more than three hundred), and a dinner at the Cincinnati Country Club at which many of our friends prominent in the social and community life of Cincinnati were present. We had not realized that we had so many friends. They all wished us happiness in our new relationships.

I realized that our adjustment to Washington would be easier if we found a delightful place to live in a section of the city near one of our Christian churches. This I was able to secure at 4711 Trent Court in Chevy Chase, Maryland, just over the District line. The modern nine-room house was located on a beautifully landscaped half-acre lot. It was situated on an elevated cul-de-sac with a view of the entire length of Trent Street. In spring we had a panorama of two rows of Japanese cherry blossoms stretching as far as eye could see. This particular part of Chevy Chase was incorporated as the "Town of Somerset," with restrictions assuring ideal community surroundings. Our house was within walking distance of Bethesda Christian Church, about which more anon. At nearby Wisconsin Circle we had access to a comprehensive shopping center which included Lord & Taylor, Saks Fifth Avenue, Woodward & Lothrop, and Bonwit Teller. Here we could get public transportation to downtown Washington and the entire Northwest sector of the city. Although we had little use for their facilities, we were "next door" to all the city's plush country clubs — Chevy Chase, Burning Tree, Congressional, Kenmore, and Columbia. These and the neighboring Potomac horse farms helped make our investment a wise one, as our later experience proved.

My associates on the editorial board of *Christianity Today* were: Carl F. H. Henry, editor; L. Nelson Bell, executive editor; J. Marcellus Kik, associate editor; Frank E. Farrell, assistant editor, and David Kucharsky, news editor. Two other assistants who worked closely with me were John A. Johanssen and Marian Cain. I was primarily responsible for editorial planning, format, and the general development of the magazine. Everything went over my desk before each issue was made up and then to John Johanssen, who was an exceptionally good layout man. He was a Methodist minister born in Sweden and former employee of the American Bible Society. It was always a pleasure to work with him and we became close friends. I contributed my share of editorials, feature articles, and news stories and had a voice in determining policy and program.

One of the first weaknesses I detected was the lack of any effective book section. There was a book review department, but the magazine was not setting a high standard either in its relations with book publishers or in the quality of reviews. Ministers and Christian leaders could not find guidance in their reading programs by reference to our pages. I immediately got in touch with all the major book publishers in the United States and Great Britain. They were delighted to cooperate and we were flooded with review copies. We then organized a group of reviewers who were specialists in various phases of religious life. Assignments of books for review purposes were made by our editorial board. We set up two major issues as Book Review numbers, one in the spring and the other in the fall. In these issues we were able to forecast six months in advance the major new titles coming from the press. We suggested "must" books for librarians and the personal study of pastors and teachers. Never have I had finer relationships with bookmen — a truly rewarding experience.

In this connection I might mention my success in getting *Christianity Today* accepted for indexing in the prestigious *Readers' Guide to Periodical Literature.*

Another weakness in the magazine was its failure to secure adequate advertising. There had been two advertising managers before I arrived. These were good men but they seemed unable to understand and to sell the peculiar advantages of representation in our columns. A new man, Clair Burcaw, arrived shortly after my coming. He was a high-type Christian layman who had been immensely successful as the sales manager of a large New England textile firm. He had lost his job because he was unwilling to lower his moral standards to sell goods. He knew next to nothing about selling advertising for a religious journal. I took him under my wing and taught him the techniques of his new trade. I arranged with our business manager to make several field trips with Clair, introducing him to key men in the firms who were potential advertisers. Between my years with Standard and *Action* magazine I knew almost all of them personally. This was all Clair needed to become one of the finest religious advertising men in the business. His success contributed immensely to the strengthening of the financial prosperity of our journal.

I had fine relations with David Kucharsky, our news editor. I knew that a religious news feature in terms of *Time* and *Newsweek* style and coverage would have a great deal to do with the readability of our magazine and its appeal to people of all denominational persuasions, both liberal and conservative. David was a graduate of the University of Pittsburgh with a major in journalism. He had a natural "nose for news" and was able to get the facts in first-hand contacts with persons "in the know." He "covered the waterfront" and many is the "scoop" our pages carried. David made a fine impression on the secular newsmen of the "fourth estate" (AP, UP, and INS) and the RNS. CT soon had "status" in this field. I was able to get increased space for David in our format until our theologians said "thus far and no farther." Today he is Managing Editor of CT and well deserves that important position.

One of my first exploits in feature articles was the coverage of the merger negotiations going on between the Congregational Christian Churches and the Evangelical and Reformed Church. I was well acquainted with the conservative leaders of both denominations and was able to write a four-page definitive story angled against the liberal elements who were bent on destroying all the best in each body to attain ecclesiastical control and hierarchal power to achieve their liberal goals. Much of the information in my story was publicized for the first time and it had national repercussions. Immediately our conservative friends called for extra copies for wider distribution. We quickly exhausted our supply and had to reprint several hundred thousand copies of the story itself to meet the demand. More than three thousand churches refused to enter the merger. Many of the conservative ministers and churches, especially in the Congregational-Christian fold, became my warm friends over the years and we still continue that relationship. I think especially of Henry David Grey of First Church, Hartford, who took almost as great interest in our Disciples' Restructure experience as in his. He made a great contribution in rebuilding the national fellowship of conservative Congregational churches in his latter years.

In 1960 I was chosen as a delegate to President Eisenhower's Golden Anniversary White House Conference on Children and Youth; also I was given press credentials for reporting the event. The 7,000 delegates were chosen from various fields such as education, religion, medicine, psychology, business, social work, letters, economics, and anthropology. Scores and scores of graded conferences meeting simultaneously in a dozen or more hotels and auditoriums around the city considered a multiplicity of phases of three major matters concerning the nation's children and youth: (1) The Family and Social Change; (2) Development and Education; and (3) Problems and Prospects. We heard papers, panel discussions and addresses and then appointed committees to express consensus on all the matters considered. The conference as a whole was in control of educators committed to a humanistic philosophy of life, but in the sections there were many profitable results. In my notes I find a very good statement on "Religion in American Life" from which I quote:

Parents and families have a distinct role to play in the reestablishing or the perfecting of moral standards, religious convictions, and ideals. Reconstituting themselves as the primary teaching unit and basing their instruction on the eternal verities which have stood the test of time, parents can contribute to favorable circumstances wherein their children can achieve their greatest potential . . . Parents are urged to return to the observance of family religious practices. Family prayer has been promoted widely in the United States in recent years with encouraging results. It is not sufficiently promoted, however, to have a telling result on the spiritual climate of our society. The reading of the Holy Scriptures by members of the family presents a doubly favorable impression. Presenting the counsel of God through the pages of Scripture will not be lost on the minds of the children who are looking for a way of life with authoritative endorsement. Worshiping as a family unit in churches and synagogues contributes to the integrity of the family. This, in turn, enables its children to withstand the forces contrary to the highest good in life.

My report of the White House Conference can be found in the pages of *Christianity Today*.

The 1960 presidential election campaign was a thrilling time around our offices. We early decided to take no overt action politically but to deal with the Church-State issue which had become pertinent in the candidacy of John F. Kennedy, a devout Roman Catholic. We determined to avoid accusations, charges, and emotion. We recognized the issue and called on the Roman Catholic church to repudiate the view of the "Syllabus of Errors" and *"Immortale Dei"* on the doctrine of Church and State. We said the Roman Catholic leaders in America needed only to democratize or Americanize their Church in the nation to eliminate this issue from the election. We asked them to admit that we have a pluralistic society with a constitutional wall of separation of church and state and then let the people elect a President strictly on the basis of personal merit and his position on national issues. As election day approached, Daniel A. Poling, editor of *Christian Herald,* and Norman Vincent Peale, pastor of the Marble Collegiate Church in New York City, called a meeting in Washington to see what could be done to break open the anomalous position of indifference to the campaign on the part of Protestants. Southern Baptists had officially opposed the Kennedy candidacy. So had the Episcopal bishops, the Presbyterian ministers, and inter-church organizations such as the National Association of Evangelicals. But the Methodists and the Councils of Churches were mute. The Poling-Peale conference call for action was supposed to be *sub rosa* but some alert Washington newsman "got onto it" and it hit the headlines across the nation. I was asked to be the unofficial representative of CT at the affair which was quite a success. But then the giant Roman Catholic boycott apparatus swung into action. Peale, who had a lucrative income from his syndicated articles in the press, was told to call off his proposed drive or his features would be eliminated. Poling got his "walking papers" from his board. In a small way CT was affected. We had a feature article scheduled for the week before the election by a noted German scholar on the up-dated status of Roman Catholic Church-

State doctrines. It was set up in type when we got the word from prominent members of our Board that it was to be canceled or else.

I personally "met my Waterloo" as a newspaper columnist as a result of my opposition to Kennedy on the Church-State issue. For several years I had written a column for the *Cincinnati Enquirer* in which I attempted to state the evangelical position on current issues and events. It appeared every Saturday on the Church page. It seemd to me altogether appropriate to state that position as something relevant to the coming Presidential election. The column appeared but the next Monday I was attacked in a three-column-head article by the senior priest of St. Mary's Church, Hyde Park, one of the wealthiest and most influential Roman Catholic parishes in Cincinnati. He attempted to answer my statements item by item and then deplored the fact that bigotry and sectarian prejudice still existed in an enlightened society. I answered him factually and in all good spirit, but my effort was in vain. My answer was not published and shortly afterward I was notified that the *Enquirer* had no further need for my column.

From the time of Kennedy's election to the present time, Protestantism in America has been impotent as a political force. Many people say to me, "Well, Kennedy was a Roman Catholic president but he proved that we have nothing to fear from Rome." I reply, "Look at the growing Federal bureaucracy with its predominantly Romanist personnel appointed by the Kennedy administration. Rome worked while others slept."

In 1960 the Central Committee of the World Council of Churches was to meet in St. Andrews, Scotland. At nearly the same time (August 2-7) the World Convention of Churches of Christ was to have its assembly in Edinburgh. It was agreed that I should attend both meetings and report them for *Christianity Today.*

Our own gathering at Edinburgh was an eye-opener to Scotland. It introduced the Scots to a movement with which they were largely unfamiliar. Our constituency in Scotland was negligible. But the press gave us wonderful coverage including intelligent articles on our heritage and biblical position. There were more than 4,000 conventioneers at Edinburgh coming from twenty-six of the thirty-four nations and areas where we have churches. The fellowship was not unlike the fellowship of the New Testament Christians in the first century as they sang together, prayed together, ate together, and showed concern together for the cause of Christ. One of the impressive events to the residents of Edinburgh was the Garden Party tendered the delegates by the Lord Provost of the city. Forty-seven buses were provided to take the delegates to Lauriston Castle on the sea, but even the Transportation Corporation of Edinburgh was not able to accommodate us all. It is estimated that 1,400 of our delegates were unable to get transportation to the biggest social event of the convention. The high point was, as always, the Communion service in Usher Hall, Edinburgh's largest auditorium, where we remembered together our Lord's death and suffering for our redemption. The attendance was so great that an additional service had to be provided in the great Lothian Road Church of Scotland. As always, we enjoyed the fellowship of the brethren.

Olive was with me and between the meetings we toured Scotland, always her delight because of her Scotch ancestry and direct descent from the Cameron clan.

CT was primarily interested in the St. Andrews meeting because of its significance to all of Christendom. We arrived a day ahead of the opening and registered at Hotel Athol. The desk clerk asked me, "And who is your partner?" He was disappointed to learn that I had not come to play golf. I then realized that I was on ground sacred to all the golfers of the world. Our windows overlooked the old course of the Royal and Ancient Golf Club of St. Andrews, founded in 1754 to preserve, protect, and perpetuate the "holy place" where, according to tradition, golf was first played in the history of man. I was never a devotee of the game, but if I had had any bent in that direction I certainly would have remained in St. Andrews long enough to learn it. I would then have been the envy of all my brethren who find it such a pleasure. The Royal and Ancient, whose clubhouse we "inspected," was erected in 1840 and houses the premier club of the world. The Royal and Ancient is the supreme authority in golf; it frames and revises the rules; and its decisions are accepted by clubs in every nation except the USA.

But we were in St. Andrews to report the meeting of an ecclesiastical body which had as its aim supremacy in Christendom. It was framing and revising the rules for a World Council of Churches and hoping that its decisions would be accepted by all the churches of the world. That report appeared in *Christianity Today* and it is not necessary to repeat it here. It was one of the most cordial and friendly critiques of the Council that I ever wrote. I thought I saw glimmers of hope in it, but they have long since been dissipated. It was a pleasure to meet privately and talk with many of the more conservatively-minded delegates.

Ernest A. Payne of Great Britain was my favorite. He was a former president of the Baptist World Alliance and was held in high esteem by Baptists everywhere. He was at that time head of the WCC Commission on Faith and Order. In those days the Commission was what its name implied. It was concerned with fundamental Christian doctrine and was seeking a biblical theology that would form a basis for ecumenical agreement. Dr. Payne's views, as expressed to me, were most heartening. But since that day the Commission has become a blind behind which clever ecumeniacs plot mergers for the building of a world hierarchy. As I write, Dr. Payne is one of the six presidents of the World Council.

Hans Lilje of Germany conversed with me in fine English. He told me of the problems being faced by the German churches because of the unfortunate East-West division of the nation. I was impressed that he was basically sound in the faith. I went to hear him preach in one of the churches in St. Andrews and was further convinced. Later I asked him for an article for CT and he gladly agreed to send it shortly after his return to his native land. He did so, and we had a "scoop" of some importance.

Jesse Bader (general secretary of our World Convention) and Stephen England (a member of the WCC Commission on Faith and Order), our own brethren from the USA, were invited to eat with us one day in our hotel dining room. Both accepted and we had a delightful talk — mainly about the possibilities for unity in our own Movement in America. I wish they had remained as irenic in their attitude in the years that were to come, as they seemed to be that day in St. Andrews.

Angus Dun, the Episcopal bishop of Washington, and John Mackay, former moderator of the General Assembly of the Presbyterian Church in the USA and president of Princeton Theological Seminary, had their assigned table in the dining room next to ours. One day we ate together. On that occasion I spent most of my time answering their questions about *Christianity Today*. They were deeply interested in the amazing progress we were making in the field of religious journalism and I "recommended CT most highly."

By the way, our hotel room was next door to that occupied by Martin L. Marty, who was reporting the meeting for *Christian Century*. He was the most indefatigable typist I ever knew. He was writing day and night — *especially night!* — until the wee small hours, to our disgust and rest-less-ness. However, we exercised our Christian consideration to the point that we did not complain to the management. Marty and I occasionally compared reporter's notes but we never agreed about anything. That disagreement with this brilliant liberal pundit continues to this hour.

The most significant event of the Council's meeting was the appearance of two unofficial representatives of the Moscow Patriarchate of the Russian Orthodox Church. Professor Vitaly Borovoy and Mr. Victor Alexcey bore a cordial greeting to the committee from His Holiness the Patriarch of Moscow. They were accorded generous time on the platform and submitted to questions about the prospects for future accord with the Council. Little did I realize that these men were the forerunners of the official Soviet delegation that was later to visit Buck Hill Falls and get the "go sign" for acceptance into full membership by the New Delhi (India) Assembly in 1961. This marked the beginning of the complete dominance of the Council by liberals and Communists which continues to the present day. Today the Council is the chief exponent of cooperation with Communists and the chief defamer of anti-Communism as willful, inhuman, and unchristian. This doctrine is disseminated in all the churches related to the World Council including all the "kept" churches behind the Iron Curtain.

The mention of Angus Dun recalls a most significant incident which occurred while I was managing editor. One Monday morning I read a news story in the *Washington Post* about a unique Communion observance in the Washington Cathedral on Mount Saint Albans. It occurred on Septuagesima, the third Sunday before Lent, and was billed as "The Communion of the People." This was not some every-Sunday Communion service as was usually held in one of the chapels of the Cathedral, but took place in the great sanctuary in a complete liturgical setting. Instead of the altar service which usually marked High Communion, the Communion table was set up in front of the altar rail on the floor adjacent to the congregation and lay ordinands — not the priests — presided and administered the emblems to communicants in the pews. I was so intrigued by this seemingly non-episcopal procedure that I wrote Bishop Dun asking an explanation. I identified myself as "a minister of the Christian Churches (Disciples of Christ)" and told him this was also our custom. He wrote me immediately in a very cordial two-page letter. He said he was familiar with our custom of every Lord's Day Communion and said the Cathedral provided such a service to all Christians. Then he launched into an historical survey of Communion customs of the Anglican Church from the earliest Reformation days in England. He said that for the first 200 years of its history, the type of service just held in the Washington Cathedral was the universal practice of his people on the ground that it was a practice of the New Testament Church. He also said that in two of their American theological seminaries the "Communion of the People" was accepted as the preferred form of observance. He expressed the hope that the basically common belief and practice of our two church bodies in this matter might eventually be accepted by the whole ecumenical church.

I was frequently invited to participate in consultations and conferences at high national levels dealing with issues and problems facing the Church and the nation. As an example, I was asked to participate in a Consultation on the Church in a Secular World, directed by H. Phillip Hook and Arthur Climenhaga. Some forty invited leaders gathered for three days at the beautiful retreat of the Maranatha Fellowship Deaconry (Lutheran) at Elburn, Illinois. This quiet setting was an ideal place for study, meditation, and fellowship. Papers were presented by Edmund Clowney, president of Westminster Theological Seminary ("Working Definitions of the Church"); Vernon Grounds, president of Conservative Baptist Theological Seminary ("Evangelicalism and Ecumenicity"); David Moberg, of Bethel College ("The Church and Society"); Harold Lindsell, then of Wheaton College, now editor of *Christianity Today,* ("The Church, Government, and Politics"), and others of outstanding capabilities. After the papers were presented, written responses were received and afterward groups met for discussion. The final presentation was by Dr. Grounds on "The Unity of the Church." The gathering was stimulating and profitable in every way. It introduced me to the thinking of Bible-believing evangelicals in various denominations on themes which I had previously studied only in the limited fellowship of the Christian Churches and Churches of Christ. I agreed with much that I heard and, of course, dissented to some degree. I recall that copies of a statement I made about the nature of the church were eagerly sought. It read as follows: "The Church of Christ is the society of born-again believers in Jesus Christ who seek to do His will in all things as it is revealed in the New Testament. It functions in individual lives and in free autonomous groups under Christ's guidance in worship, fellowship, education, evangelism (or witness), nurture, and benevolence. Its unity is described in Christ's prayer John 17 and is sealed by the living presence of the Holy Spirit." Many believed this. We all need more experiences like Elburn. Here there was no attempt to convert anyone to some opinion, but only freedom to express oneself, study, meditate, and discuss, with the Bible as the ultimate standard for decision.

I was invited by Oswald J. Hoffman of the Lutheran Church-Missouri Synod to become a member of a *sub rosa* Protestant discussion group that met in Washington twice a year to deal with matters of Church and State. It had no name. It kept no official records. It was composed of men in the high official echelons of most of the major denominations from Episcopal to Baptist. Here men felt free to express their own opinions and seek understanding. Their views were not to be quoted without their permission beyond the walls of the assembly hall. I was the only member from Christian Churches and Churches of Christ. Often when a consensus was reached it was interesting to read in the press and other communications media weeks later that a similar position had been taken by major religious bodies. I recall that after the Supreme Court's decision on prayer and Bible reading in the public schools we had quite a warm discussion in this distinguished body. Most of the men favored the decision. I did not and I vigorously expressed my reasons. I had studied the best thought of the judiciary on the constitutional right of "the free exercise of religion." I had been privileged to attend sessions of the Supreme Court during the debate over Engel vs. Vitale, the New York State case, and Abingdon School District vs. Schempp, and I thought I knew what I was talking about. When the time came to decide on a paper for presentation at the next meeting there was unanimous agreement that I should prepare a document presenting my views and field questions afterward. Accordingly, I came up with a paper on "The Free Exercise of Religion in Civic Life." It was a "shocker" and I was on my feet for two hours answering questions and attempting to sustain my position. It was shortly after this that a good Lutheran senator, the Honorable Everett Dirksen of Illinois, presented his bill, D.J.R. 148, to amend the First Amendment to insure our constitutional guarantees of religious liberty and restore prayer in the public schools. I was invited to present testimony in the hearings on this bill. As I write, years afterward, there are big headlines in our newspapers that seem to indicate that such a bill will finally pass both House and Senate and an Amendment will be submitted to the states for their approval. The ecclesiastical lines are still drawn for and against, about as they were in the *sub rosa* meeting at which I spoke. The National Association of Evangelicals asked for my manuscript and it was published and widely distributed. I firmly believe that there are dangerous forces at work in our American life to destroy the foundations of religion and morality that have undergirded our nation from its beginnings. Unless positive action is taken by our churches, it appears likely that a small group of atheists and anarchists may succeed not only in abolishing religion in national life but in establishing the religion of secularism. They will continue in the name of religious freedom to subject the majority to the will of the minority. I attended these *sub rosa* meetings as long as I remained in Washington and look back upon them as one of my most rewarding experiences.

Another group of religious leaders called "The Remnant" met in Washington twice a year for study and fellowship. I was honored by election to membership in the group through the kindness of Edmund Opitz, a former Congregational minister, who was a senior staff member of the Foundation for Economic Education and book review editor of *The Freeman*. "The Remnant" is a nationwide fellowship of ministers predominantly conservative or libertarian in their political and economic outlook. Our speakers and/or study leaders dealt with various economic and social problems in American society, seeking religious orientation and the application of religious principles in practical action. It was a real privilege to become acquainted with some of the nation's outstanding religious personalities in these meetings and to have the benefit of their insights. I am still a member.

Invitations to speak in churches and schools of all denominations (even in a Conservative Jewish Synagogue) came to me constantly. This was a tribute, not to me personally, but to the magazine I had the honor to represent. I was growingly amazed at the influence of *Christianity Today*. At last, evangelical Christianity in America had a voice which was respected not only in the churches but in the communications media, in fraternal and commercial circles, and in the precincts of government at home and abroad. In later episodes I shall elaborate on my own experiences at some of these levels. As I write, the paid circulation of CT is three times larger than that of the *Christian Century* and, I believe, it has an influence for good in like comparative proportions. Thanks be to God for His enabling power. To Him be the glory!

When I reached the age of seventy I retired from the managing editorship, loath to give up the happy relationships I had with my editorial associates, the board of management, office helpers, and a wide circle of friends. On my last day in the office I was presented with a copy of the New Testament of "The New English Bible," which had only recently come from the press. In it were inscribed the names of those I had worked with through the years: Carl F. H. Henry, L. Nelson Bell, Frank E. Farrell, David Kucharsky, Irma Peterson, Marian Cain, John J. Johanssen, Louise Pleines, Clair L. Burcaw, Carolyn W. Bateman, Roland E. Kuniholm, Janet L. Thompson, Donna J. Pitts, Effie Hanna,

255

Lewellyn L. Bunton, Juanita McVeigh, Faye Truitt, Martha Kielman, Florence Beard, Marilyn Shearer, and Art Noll — with the words: "This is a token of appreciation from your colleagues and associates in the ministry of Christ, with every good wish for the best of years ahead in the common bond of the Saviour's love." Then Clair Burcaw gave me, amid laughter and tears, a de luxe portfolio and an umbrella — the symbols of Washingtonian distinction.

This chapter would not be complete without a special tribute to one of God's noblemen — J. Howard Pew.

Mr. Pew inherited from his father a great industrial complex but chose to begin his career at the lowest rungs of the ladder of success and climb to the top on the basis of sheer merit. As president of Sun Oil Company he initiated plans and programs which were imaginative and remarkably successful. Everybody knows about "Blue Sunoco" and about everybody has bought it or its products at some time or other. For many years he and his family have been the largest financial supporters of the Republican Party and have labored for the highest and best in American life.

J. Howard Pew, as a Presbyterian elder, was always active in church affairs. He was an outspoken biblical conservative and was a pillar of strength to the evangelical elements in his denomination. He was one of the chief financial supporters of the educational, benevolent, and missionary enterprises of his church. He was long president of the board of trustees of Grove City College where he built the beautiful chapel in memory of his wife. He was president of the board of trustees of the Presbyterian Foundation until his death.

Honored by election to the presidency of United Church Men, prestigious arm of the National Council of Churches, he took his duties seriously and launched a survey of the programs and policies of the Council. When he became convinced that it was an enemy of orthodox Christianity, he published a 500-page report that was highly critical of the Council and resigned his position. He took this drastic action only after he had done everything within his power to correct its shortcomings from within the organization.

It was not long after this that Mr. Pew was approached by Billy Graham and L. Nelson Bell asking his aid in launching *Christianity Today*. It was Mr. Pew who really made *Christianity Today* possible. Throughout its history he was its staunchest supporter, assuring the subsidy necessary to the perpetuation of this type of religious journalism. In this respect he did for evangelical Protestantism what the Hoover family and the Irwin-Miller family did for the *Christian Century,* the outstanding advocate of ecclesiastical and liberal ecumenism.

At *Christianity Today* I became personally concerned with several enterprises Mr. Pew supported. One of these was the Christian Freedom Foundation, the publisher of *Christian Economics.* When I was asked to write my book, *Protestant Revolt,* Mr. Pew became deeply interested in the project. He collaborated with me in the writing of Chapter 3, "A Crucial Issue." When the book was published he sent complimentary copies to many of his lay brethren in the Presbyterian Church and helped provide a fund to place the book in the libraries of all the major colleges and universities of the nation.

One of his later activities was encouragement of the organization of the Presbyterian Lay Committee, Incorporated, a voluntary agency working within the denomination for the achievement of certain high objectives. Among them: (1) Greater emphasis on the teaching of the Bible as the authoritative Word of God in seminaries and churches; (2) A demand for the preaching of the Gospel of Redemption with evangelical zeal; (3) Encouragement of ministers and laymen alike to take their places *as individuals* in society and, as led by the Holy Spirit, to become involved in such social, economic, and political problems in which they have proper competence; (4) Discouragement of public pronouncements of church leaders, speaking for the church as a corporate body, either specifically or by implication on political, economic, and social questions, unless there are spiritual or moral issues involved that can be supported by clear-cut biblical authority; (5) Provision of adequate and reliable sources of information on all significant issues confronting the Church. In this latter connection the Lay Committee publishes a monthly journal, *The Presbyterian Layman,* which has a tremendous influence for its announced objectives in Presbyterian churches everywhere.

Shortly before his death Mr. Pew wrote an article which appeared in *Reader's Digest,* entitled, "Should the Church Meddle in Civil Affairs?" which had a worldwide circulation. Today his pen is stilled and his activities in behalf of evangelical biblical Christianity have ceased, but he has set in motion currents of faith and life which will have repercussions for truth and righteousness for many years to come.

Parenthetically, I might mention that several greatly appreciated honors came to me at about this time: The Evangelical Press Association made me an honorary life member of its board; Milligan College conferred on me the honorary degree of Doctor of Letters (Litt.D.); Ohio University my alma mater, gave its Distinguished Service award for "attainments in the field of religion"; the O.U. chapter of Sigma Delta Chi (honorary journalism fraternity) granted me a life membership, and I was made a fellow of the International Institute of Arts and Letters.

I was to stay on in the national capital for several years more, basking in the afterglow of a rich and rewarding experience. I was "retired" but I discovered that the Lord still had work for me to do.

Episode XXII

Red, White, and Blue

On my first Saturday in Washington I stood at the corner of Pennsylvania and New York Avenues witnessing a massive parade of some 30,000 Shriners who were in the city for a convention. In the background were the Treasury Building and the White House with the top of the Washington Monument looming in the distance. As wave after wave of the glittering spectacle passed with its plethora of noted bands and American flags, I got a great big lump in my throat and tears came into my eyes. I realized, as never before in my life, that this was the throbbing center of the United States of America, the greatest nation in the world. And I was there!

Amid the sounds of the "Washington Post March," "The Stars and Stripes Forever," and "The Star Spangled Banner," the words of the first patriotic song I ever learned came to me with new meaning —

> *Let music swell the breeze*
> *And ring from all the trees*
> > *Sweet freedom's song;*
> *Let mortal tongues awake,*
> *Let all that breathe partake,*
> *Let rocks their silence break*
> > *The sound prolong.*

> *Our father's God to Thee,*
> *Author of liberty,*
> > *To Thee we sing*
> *Long may our land be bright*
> *With freedom's holy light*
> *Protect us by Thy might*
> > *Great God our King!*

Though I had not come to Washington primarily to serve my country I was soon caught up in a series of circumstances and experiences which made that possible.

I had hardly landed until I received an invitation to attend a formal dinner of the Sons of the American Revolution at the Army and Navy Club. It seemed that two of my good friends in the Ohio Society, former presidents general of the National Society, Charles A. Jones (for years Senator Frank Willis' executive assistant) and Charles A. Anderson, M.D. (noted urologist and elder in Central Christian Church, Warren) had tipped off the District of Columbia Society that I was coming to Washington and that they should get me involved in their organization. This statement calls for a little background:

The Cincinnati Chapter of the SAR had persuaded me, back in 1937, to apply for membership. I was required to trace my ancestry back to a soldier in the Continental Army in the American Revolutionary War. Thanks to a thoughtful great-great grandmother, Margaret (Brown) Mallory, I had a memo which proved that I was a direct descendant of Joseph Brown, "soldier in Connecticut Troops, a member of the Fourth Company under Lieut. J. Seymour of Hartford, Connecticut." It seems that Brown was taken prisoner by the British, confined in New York, and upon his release cited for bravery.

Active in the Cincinnati Chapter, I was eventually made president. With the splendid cooperation of my compatriots we were able to achieve some unusual goals. We produced and published a 546-page "Lineage Book of the Cincinnati Chapter SAR" — one of the finest of its kind in the nation. We made "Constitution Day" a great city-wide celebration, instead of a chapter event. The year I was president over 500 sat down for a luncheon in the Hall of Mirrors of the (then) Netherland Plaza Hotel and heard an address by Clarence E. Manion, former dean of the Law School of Notre Dame University. L. D. Warren, the noted cartoonist of the *Cincinnati Enquirer,* produced his famous "We the People" cartoon in honor of the occasion and dedicated it to me. (I have the framed original on the wall in my study as I write.) The Mayor of the city made a special proclamation urging all citizens to fittingly observe the Day. In many other respects our Chapter achieved wide recognition.

Among the prominent citizens of Cincinnati who were active in our chapter at this time were: Senator Robert A Taft, Governor Myers Y. Cooper, President Raymond Walters of the University of Cincinnati, Richard S. Rust and John A. Lloyd of the Union Central Life Insurance Company, James H. Garrison and Alfred L. McCartney of Procter and Gamble, and many others I might mention. Later I became Chaplain of the Ohio Society and continued in that position until we moved to Washington.

Now, back to the District of Columbia Society. This organization was unique in that it was both a Chapter and a Society with rank equal to the states in the National Society. The D. C. Society maintained offices in the Heurich Mansion with a paid staff. It had a membership of between 600 and 700 men many of whom were high in military rank and prominent in the life of the city. In my time we had such prominent military figures in our active membership as Rear Admiral William R. Furlong, Generals Guy O. Kurtz, Louis J. Fortier, John L. Strauss, and George F. Wooley, Commanders W. Harvey Wise, Charles T. McDonald and Donald R. Osborne, and Colonels Harold D. Krafft, Thurston H. Baxter, Walden F. Woodward, Calvin J. Kephart, George D. Webb, Pinckney G. McElwee, Howard D. Criswell, Samuel Pierce, Jr., Willis Bergen, and others too numerous to mention. In the field of business we had Glenn

Mayfield Goodman, of the Federal Reserve Board; Grahame T. Small-wood, TWA's Washington representative, and W. Rodney Adams, corporation executive. In the cultural life of the city we had such men as Dr. Louis B. Wright, director of the Folger Shakespeare Library and president of the Cosmos Club; Dr. Elmer Kayser, Dean of George Washington University; and Dr. L. Nelson Bell, executive editor of *Christianity Today*. Honorary members included such distinguished names as President Dwight D. Eisenhower and Associate Justices of the Supreme Court Potter Stewart and Thomas C. Clark.

Among the distinguished military men I came to know quite well was Rear Admiral William Rea Furlong of the United States Navy. Early in his career he was on the staff of Admiral Fletcher during the landings at Vera Cruz in 1914. He was steadily promoted because of his experience in gunnery. During World War I he was first attached to the British fleet and later served as chief gunnery officer of the U.S. Atlantic Fleet. Great Britain honored him as U.S. gunnery observer in the review of the Grand Fleet of its Navy in the North Sea, at Scapa Flow and the Firth of Forth. After the War he was made chief gunnery officer of the Pacific Fleet, and then made Rear Admiral and Commander-in-Chief of the U.S. Bureau of Ordnance in Washington. World War II found him engaged in the defense of Pearl Harbor, when his flagship U.S.S. Oglala was sunk. He continued as chief commander in charge of Pearl Harbor until it was cleared of the wreckage caused by the infamous Japanese air attack which changed the course of the War. Wherever Furlong went in his retirement years he was accorded the highest honors as a naval hero and as a gentleman of sterling worth and integrity. The U.S. government chose him to direct and complete the most exhaustive study and research ever made concerning the origins and history of the U.S. Flag, which is now contained in a four-volume work that will ever be a monument to his constructive patriotic abilities. The hours I spent with him were always rewarding. We saw eye to eye on the fundamental principles of Americanism and on a number of occasions I served with him on S.A.R. projects designed to advance those principles.

Serving as the Society's Historian, Chaplain, third, second, and first **Vice President I** was eventually elected President and later became the Society's representative on the National Board of Trustees. As I look back on this relationship many things clamor for a place in my memory. I note a few:

My experience with the observance of Constitution Day in Cincinnati led me to propose changes in the Washington tradition. For many years the Society had gone to the auditorium of the Archives Building (where reposes the closely-guarded original document itself) for a poorly-attended observance. The Daughters of the American Revolution had a similar observance across the city in one of the governmental department buildings. I proposed that we join forces and together with the Children of the American Revolution put on a celebration of unusual significance in the form of a Constitution Day luncheon at the Shoreham Hotel. The United States Army chorus of forty-three vocalists, under the direction of Lieut. Allen Crowell, provided a musical program. Dr. Elmer Kayser and I made brief addresses. Honors were awarded. Distinguished officers of the national Societies were guests. The largest dining facility of the hotel was filled and some had to be turned away. Since that day this pattern of observance has been followed by the District societies.

In my files I find a copy of some excerpts from my address on this occasion, which our monthly *Bulletin* carried in response to many requests:

> We live in perilous times. This is a cliche, but the very fact that it is a cliche means that millions of people believe it. We live in a day when a growing number of our citizens no longer believe in the USA. They no longer regard our institutions and our traditions with respect. They seek learning without effort and wages without work. Too many of our people have become hedonistic and pleasure oriented; they accept payola as a part of life and defend union goonery and bureaucratic imperialism as rights to be maintained. Truly the nation is in danger.
>
> We who are met here today are committed to the American way of life in the tradition of our founding fathers so well expressed in the Declaration of Independence and the Constitution of the United States. The SAR, the DAR, and the CAR represent minorities, but thank God for patriotic minorities. The choice heroes of the earth have been in a minority. There is not a social, political, or religious blessing that we enjoy that was not bought for us by the blood, sweat, and tears of a minority. Yes, we are in a minority in America, but let us here today highly resolve that we will stand in the van of those who believe in God and in the great moral principles of the Judeo-Christian tradition; that we will support and defend the ideals set forth in the Declaration of Independence and the Constitution of the United States; that we will risk our lives and our sacred honor in behalf of all that is noble in American history and go forward to the achievement of yet greater things in the land that we love.

The sentiments expressed here are some of the reasons I have been willing to give so much of my time and strength through the years to patriotic endeavors.

Among the other patriotic observances at which I presided were:

The annual (1964) celebration of the birth of Thomas Jefferson at the beautiful National Jefferson Memorial overlooking the cherry blossom rimmed Tidal Basin. Traditionally the District Society of the SAR was in charge of this event in cooperation with the National Park Service, National Capital Region, and U.S. Department of the Interior. On this occasion the Secretary of the Interior, Stewart L. Udall, was our speaker. Our music was provided by the United States Army Headquarters Command Band. An Armed Services Honor Guard consisting of representatives of the U.S. Army, Marines, Navy, Air Force, and Coast Guard was responsible for all protocol for the occasion. Commemorative wreaths were laid in formal presentations by the President of the United States, Lyndon B. Johnson; the Department of the Interior; the National Park Service; the National Capitol Region; the Board of Commissioners of the District of Columbia; the National Society Sons of the Revolution; the District of Columbia Society SAR; the National Society of the Daughters of the American Revolution; the District of Columbia Society of the DAR; the National Society of the Children of the Revolution; the District of Columbia Society of the CAR; the National Hugenot Society; the Order of the First Families of Virginia; the National Council of the Sons and Daughters of Liberty; the District of Columbia Society of Founders and Patriots of America; District of Columbia Society of Daughters of 1812; District of Columbia Chapter, American Red Cross; The Society of Mayflower Descendants; the American War Mothers; the District of Columbia United Daughters of the Confederacy; Military Order of the Loyal Legion and a number of others too numerous to mention.

Washington's Birthday was always celebrated by a luncheon. The year I presided at this event it was held in the Statler Hotel and was addressed by Associate Justice of the U.S. Supreme Court Thomas C. Clark.

For the Fourth of July observance during my incumbency, I proposed that all the church bells in Washington be rung at high noon, reminiscent of the ringing of the Liberty Bell in Philadelphia announcing the signing of the Declaration of Independence. I approached my friend Bishop Angus Dun of the Washington Cathedral asking him to set the example. He not only agreed but also offered to present a patriotic concert on the bells of the magnificent new Cathedral carillon only recently dedicated. When his decision was announced we enlisted our compatriots in making personal contacts with churches throughout the District with a most encouraging response. The traditional SAR event for Independence Day was a wreath-laying ceremony at the grave of Elbridge Gerry of Massachusetts, the only signer of the Declaration buried in the District of Columbia. I was asked to give the address in Congressional Cemetery to representatives of a number of patriotic societies. Gerry is usually thought of only as the originator of the questionable political practice of "gerry-mander," but he was really a courageous and honorable public leader in his day, also serving two terms as governor of Massachusetts and later as vice-president of the United States. He died when he was on his way to preside at a session of the U.S. Senate. My research gave me a new respect for the man, which I tried to convey to the great assemblage that day.

Our annual wreath-laying ceremony at the monument to the memory of General Casim Pulaski, of Revolutionary fame, in downtown Washington, was addressed by Rep. R. C. Pucinski, of Chicago.

One of the most rewarding features in our calendar of events was the

Monthly Luncheon at the Army and Navy Club. It kept up a continuity of interest in the Society and offered a meeting place for fellowship of like-minded compatriots. Among the speakers I remember at these affairs were Strom Thurmond, J. Edgar Hoover, W. J. Bryan Dorn, Archie Roosevelt, Ulysses S. Grant III, retired U.S. Supreme Court Justice Stanley F. Reed, and Judge George William Washington of the U.S. Court of Appeals (District of Columbia Circuit). Judge Washington was a direct descendant of Colonel Samuel Washington and thus related to the family of George Washington. I remember presiding at a luncheon when we had as our speaker John B. Layton, chief of Metropolitan Police for the District of Columbia, and presenting him with a Medal of Honor in recognition of an outstanding contribution to good citizenship and community welfare. The privilege I had of meeting these men, chatting with them, and getting personally acquainted with many of them was a privilege that could come only to one who lived in Washington and had such a channel of rapprochement.

Another feature of similar advantage was the Annual Pilgrimage. We selected an historic site within driving distance of the city, arranged a luncheon nearby, and then enjoyed a briefing on persons and events at the site. Among the pilgrimages I enjoyed were Gunston Hall, the home of George Mason, Virginia's advocate of the separation of Church and State; the old State House at Annapolis where George Washington surrendered his sword and resigned his commission as Commander in Chief of the Continental Army; and Mount Vernon, Washington's magnificent home on the banks of the Potomac. Historic spots abound in the Capital Area and there is no end to the potential for these enjoyable and instructive occasions.

I was pleased to be the medium for reconciliation between the District of Columbia Society and the National Society. Not that we were ever alienated in the discharge of our mutual responsibilities, but a coolness existed which puzzled me. I finally discovered that it stemmed from the elimination of the District offices from the National Headquarters building when headquarters were moved from the old building, near the national headquarters of the National Education Association, to the General Patrick Hurley Mansion on exclusive "Embassy Row" (Massachusetts Avenue). It occurred to me that it would be a conciliatory gesture to arrange a formal reception for the new President General Harry T. Burn, and his entire official retinue in the Ballroom of the Mayflower Hotel. This we did with all the pomp and ceremony worthy of such an occasion. The plan was successful. Such a reception for the President General has now become an annual event.

When I was elevated to the post of National Trustee I was made aware of the fact that there was on foot a *sub rosa* plot to move our national headquarters from Washington to some other "more advantageous" location. Under consideration were Philadelphia, Yorktown, Williamsburg, Valley Forge, or a site above New York City on the Hudson River.

The plan was originally proposed by a group of Southern compatriots who feared the encroachment of the rapidly increasing Negro population of the Capital Area. At the next meeting of our District Board of Management I sprang the news on our compatriots and there started a regular riot of protest. The Board appointed me as chairman of a committee to oppose the move and voted funds to contact every chapter and society in the nation. Then ensued a fight which continued for some two years. We made it clear that the national headquarters building on Embassy Row enjoyed the same zoning restrictions as the embassies of foreign lands surrounding us. We were further protected by contiguous contact with restricted areas of Rock Creek park. We stressed the idea that such a move would separate us from close contact with the national offices of the Daughters of the American Revolution and the Children of the American Revolution at the center of the nation and interfere with the spendid effective cooperation of these closely-related patriotic agencies which had existed for many years. We got the national officers of the DAR and the CAR to go on record as deploring such a move. To cap the argument we discovered that the Act of Congress in 1906 chartering the SAR provided that headquarters of the corporation should be permanently located in Washington. When the Annual Congress of the National Society met in Williamsburg, Va., the crucial decision was to be made. I was asked to appear on the platform representing the opposition to the move. My presentation was enthusiastically received and soon afterward an overwhelming vote to stay in Washington was recorded. As I write, plans are being made to double the admirable facilities of the Massachusetts Avenue property, to the immense satisfaction of compatriots everywhere.

My last official contact with the annual congresses came at Groton, Connecticut, the year I left Washington. Groton was historic ground to our compatriots, as well as noted New England resort country. Here I had my first and only experience of riding in a submarine. My good Methodist friend Dr. H. R. Carson of Indianapolis, then Chaplain General, but in failing health, asked me to offer prayer in an early session and later approached me with a high official of the Society asking whether I would allow my name to be presented as his successor. I declined on the ground that my time would be fully employed in efforts to forestall the drive for Restructure among the Disciples of Christ. They expressed regret and the high official then remarked, "It's too bad, Dr. Murch, that you are a preacher. Otherwise, we might have elected you President General in a year or so!"

Speaking of the chaplaincy, it might be interesting to know that I have offered prayers and benedictions on literally hundreds of patriotic occasions. In such a position there is a temptation to fall into the habit of praying the same prayer until the words become meaningless and without heart-felt significance. On special occasions I usually write the prayer beforehand. I kept the prayer I offered at Groton at the Annual Congress, as an example of something appropriate to the occasion:

Our Father's God, to Thee we again lift our hearts in prayer and supplication. Again we acknowledge Thee as our Creator who has endowed mankind with certain inalienable rights including life, liberty, and the pursuit of happiness.

We thank Thee for Thy providential guidance under which our nation has been conceived and ordered and brought to this good day. We thank Thee for that measure of prosperity and moral and spiritual strength which has made us great among the nations of the earth.

We humbly beseech Thee that we may always prove ourselves a people mindful of Thy favor and glad to do Thy will.

In these times of crisis, when men's hearts are failing them for fear in the face of atheism, materialism, and the rise of totalitarian communism, give us a rebirth of faith. Help us to dedicate ourselves anew to Thee and to Thy principles of morality, justice, and freedom which our forefathers so nobly upheld.

Endue with the spirit of wisdom those, to whom, in Thy name, we entrust the authority of government. May they turn to Thee for guidance at all times and especially in days of trouble. May they obey Thy Law in all things, so that this nation, under God may continue to show forth Thy praise among all the nations of the earth.

And, unto Thee we will ascribe all glory and praise through Jesus Christ Thy Son and our Saviour, Amen.

I notice that many modern clergymen often omit reference to Jesus Christ in concluding their prayers on such occasions. They do this in deference to agnostics and devotees of other religions. I have never bowed to this compromise of the "faith once delivered." If questioned, I say, "I am a Christian minister. That's the way I pray. If you want some other type prayer, get yourself another chaplain."

I have often wondered how much attention an audience on patriotic occasions pays to the prayer message. But through the years an amazing interest has been shown in the sentiments I have expressed. I remember when I offered the opening prayer on a state occasion in the Ballroom of the Fort Hayes Hotel, in Columbus, Ohio, that Senator and Mrs. John W. Bricker came to me after the program, expressed appreciation for the prayer, and asked whether I could furnish them with a copy for use in their own private devotions. Fortunately, I had a copy which I was glad to give them. I feel it is a great privilege and opportunity to serve in such a capacity and that all ministers should welcome invitations to participate in like occasions.

Among the opportunities that came to me as a resident of Washington to serve in expressing the views of evangelical Christians in governmental circles, was the invitation to become chairman of the influential Commission on Evangelical Action, of the National Association of Evangelicals. The NAE maintained a well-staffed office of Public Affairs in the Western Union Building in downtown Washington. It was headed by Clyde W. Taylor, whom I have previously mentioned. I was frequently asked to appear in my capacity at committee hearings in the Senate and the House of Representatives. During my stay in Washington I expressed the NAE view on various phases of such matters as Indian affairs, civil rights, public education, immigration, liquor, salacious literature, right to work, communism, government regimentation, and bureaucratic controls. I was frequently quoted by the press and occasionally on TV news reports. (Refer to Episode XVIII.)

I have often been asked why I am so critical of the Councils of Churches for becoming involved in political matters, when the NAE seems to be just as guilty. At the risk of repetition let me say that our philosophy is uniquely different from that of the Councils. We believe that evangelicals live in two worlds. Their primary duty as Christians in the Kingdom of God is to transform individuals by the spiritual processes laid down in the New Testament. But we also have social obligations as Christian citizens of our nation which we must perform. In the former relationship we are *transformers;* in the latter, *reformers.* We believe that the Christian way of life must be made known and that exponents of that way should be elected to office. We believe that evangelicals as individuals, not as *The Church,* must fight for their rights — their God-given freedoms — and should voice their protests for the correction and/or the control of all evil or subversive influences and actions in our national socio-political order.

Washington was also the location of the headquarters offices of Americans United for Separation of Church and State (formerly POAU). I had long been a member of the Cincinnati chapter and had served a term as its president. Several years before my move to Washington I was appointed a member of the National Advisory Board. When the famous North College Hill public school case was in the Ohio courts I was active in advocating the separation position. Our forces won in a close election that finally eliminated Roman Catholic teachers and Roman Catholic controls from the public schools of that community. So when I went to the offices of Americans United I received a warm welcome from executive director Glenn L. Archer and C. Stanley Lowell his associate. It was a privilege to work with these men as my time allowed. I prayed for them at their annual Church and State rally in Constitution Hall, in their Board meetings, and I contributed to their magazine, *Church and State.*

I recall that I was invited as Managing Editor of *Christianity Today* to appear before their annual Board meeting and express our view of their work and make suggestions for improvement. Among other ideas I proposed was the preparation of a study book for use in churches, lodges, community groups, and in chapter meetings dealing simply and essentially with the Church-State problem as it exists in America today. I said it should be factual, tolerant and just, and manifest goodwill toward all elements involved but boldly champion the principles set forth in the Constitution of the United States which are so vital and essential to the cause of American freedom. I held that there was an amazing ignorance on these matters even among our most ardent supporters. Later on in the meeting Dr. Charles Clayton Morrison, editor of the *Christian Century*, and usually credited with the authorship of the historic "Manifesto" that led to the organization of POAU, arose and said, "I would like to endorse Dr. Murch's idea of a study book. I think we need it, and I would like to move that we invite him to become its author." The motion passed unanimously and I later produced the 72-page volume, *Church-State Relations: The American Way*, which has been so widely used across the nation.

As I recall, there were present that day, besides Dr. Morrison and the POAU staff, John A. Mackay, Louis D. Newton, J. M. Dawson, Clyde W. Taylor, Frank H. Yost, W. Stanley Rycroft, Harold C. Fitz, Elmer E. Rogers, E. H. DeGroot and a group of advisers — a curious combination of liberals and fundamentalists, evangelicals and neo-evangelicals, Jews, and Council of Churches leaders, but they were "Americans united" when it came to advocacy of the preservation and protection of the great Constitutional principle of separation of Church and State. It has always been a pleasure at that level to work with these men.

I would like to pay tribute, especially, to Dr. Archer, who has so capably and wisely directed the affairs of Americans United through more than twenty-five years of its history. He took his place (coming from his position of Dean of the College of Law of Washburn University) when the future of POAU was precarious and the organization was lacking in financial security. He erected a non-profit corporation so skillfully fashioned that it today gives every evidence of permanence in structure, in accomplishment, and in financial integrity. It is housed in a beautiful modern thoroughly adequate headquarters in Silver Spring, Maryland (just over the border from the District of Columbia). It has functioning branches in every important metropolitan area of the land. It is recognized by every power element in American life as a factor to be respected in all matters pertaining to Church and State. In fact, I would say, if it had not been for Dr. Archer and Americans United we would not today have these freedoms guaranteed us by the Constitution of the United States. They deserve the support of every loyal, red-blooded American citizen.

I treasure another Washington incident with patriotic overtones that took place in the old U. S. Supreme Court Room in the Capitol building. I was one of about a dozen who received awards that day from the Freedoms Foundation of Valley Forge. I had received other awards while I was a resident of Cincinnati, but this one had special meaning. In a previous chapter I alluded to the fact that my column, "A Churchman Views the News," in the *Cincinnati Enquirer* had been dropped because I had taken a strong position for separation of Church and State in connection with the presidential candidacy of John F. Kennedy. This bronze medal given me at Washington about a year later was inscribed: "Honoring Dr. James DeForest Murch for his "A Churchman Views the News" series and for outstanding achievement in bringing about a better understanding of the American Way of Life." Kenneth Wells' kind words in presenting the award will aways be remembered with appreciation.

A word about this Freedoms Foundation may well end this chapter on a high patriotic note. The Foundation was established for the purpose of making annual awards, in various categories, to those individuals and institutions which, in the judgment of the judges, have made a real contribution to the American Way of Life in the preceding twelve months. General of the Army Dwight D. Eisenhower was the chairman of the Foundation; Honorable James A. Farley, vice-chairman; Admiral Felix B. Stump, vice-chairman; Don Belding, chairman of the executive committee; and Dr. Kenneth D. Wells, president. At the time of his death Herbert Hoover had been Honorary president for some time. Of the Foundation J. Edgar Hoover said, "Freedoms Foundation stands as a sentinel, as did our revolutionary freedom fighters at Valley Forge."

The Foundation's definition of "The American Way of Life" is graphically portrayed in a chart which has been widely distributed. It features a giant shaft erected on a foundation labeled "Fundamental Belief in God" and "Constitutional Government Designed to Serve the People." It is capped by a block labeled "Political and Economic Rights Which Protect the Dignity and Freedom of the Individual." The inscription on the great shaft details those Rights:

The right to worship God in one's own way.

The right to free speech and press.

The right to peaceably assemble.

The right to petition for the redress of grievances.

The right of privacy in our homes.

The right of Habeus Corpus — no excessive bail.

The right of trial by jury — innocent until proved guilty.

The right to move about freely at home and abroad.

The right to own private property.

The right to free elections and personal secret ballot.

The right to work in callings and localities of one's choice.

The right to bargain with our employers or employees.

The right to go into business, compete, and make a profit.

The right to bargain for goods and services in a free market.

The right to contract about our affairs.

The right to the service of government as a protector and referee.

The right of freedom from arbitrary government regulation and control.

This is truly the American Way of Life!

No wonder my heart beat faster that first Saturday in Washington when the bands went marching by playing "The Star Spangled Banner." There is no land on earth where man is more greatly blessed.

I pledge allegiance to the flag of the United States of America and to the Republic for which it stands — one nation under God, indivisible, with liberty and justice for all.

Episode XXIII

Marooned In Discipledom

It was with mixed emotions that I contemplated the prospect of establishing happy local church relations in Washington. I was aware that great changes had taken place in Christian Churches and Churches of Christ since the days that I had first known our people there, but I was scarcely prepared for what I found.

My first lively contact with the Capital Area brethren came during my editorship of *The Lookout* in the 1920's. When George A. Miller was minister of the Ninth Street Church and later when C. R. Stauffer was pastor, I had invitations to visit that congregation for Bible-school rallies and for conferences with teachers and workers. I really loved George Miller. Maybe the fact that he looked like my father had something to do with it. He not only looked like him, but he talked like him and was committed to the same New Testament doctrine, that he advocated and preached with brilliance and success. In his day the church was the largest of all our congregations in the city and had the largest Bible school. It was on this visit that I became acquainted with Judge Gilbert Nations, who was an elder and taught the largest adult class in the school. He was an ardent Protestant who intelligently recognized the potential dangers of Roman Catholicism to the American Way of Life. As an attorney of distinction he made a thorough study of Canon Law and wrote nearly a dozen books on subjects related to his basic research. I recall reading *The Canon Law and the Papal Throne* and *Papal Sovereignty, or The Government Within a Government.* On the day of my visit there were over a thousand in the Bible school and several additions to the church. The church lived and breathed vital power and success.

This same prosperous condition still existed during C. R. Stauffer's administration, although changing racial and social conditions in the area were intimating new problems that the church must face in the not too distant future. I had gotten acquainted with Stauffer in Cincinnati, where he had built up a remarkable work in the thousand-member Norwood Church. It was strong in its relations with the Disciples Establishment but still preponderantly evangelistic and true to the Book. Stauffer was the most successful pastor I ever knew. It was often said of him "He can't preach for 'cold soup' but he is the reincarnation of the 'good shepherd' in his pastoral ministry." He would go night and day at any hour if he could win a soul to Christ or minister in hours of need. It was this supreme love of mankind that endeared him to everybody and was the secret of his success in Washington. It is my recollection that he invited me to Ninth Street mainly because of my youth ministries, particularly in the field of Christian Endeavor. We had a good time together.

(I have a faint recollection of preaching one Lord's Day morning in the pulpit of Columbia Heights Church then served by A. P. Wilson. This then-prosperous congregation later sold its beautiful building, because of social and racial changes in the community, and is now the North Chevy Chase Church).

Because of my happy associations at Ninth Street I determined to go there on my first Sunday in Washington. It presented a sad contrast to the church I had known in the twenties. There were around three hundred in morning worship which was formal and frigid. The pastor preached as if he had never heard of the New Testament Church or the Restoration Plea. Indeed, I learned later that he had been a United Brethren pastor and had received his preparation for the ministry in Bonebrake Theological Seminary in Dayton, Ohio. Judge Nations had passed to his reward. When I asked about the condition of the church, people just shook their heads and said, "We will likely change our location as soon as we can get a good price for our property." Today its suburban successor is known as the Henson Valley Christian Church and has, even with "open membership", only about 150 members. I crossed Ninth Street off my list. We wanted something better than that.

The next Lord's Day I went to the National City Church on Thomas Circle. I had known this church when it was called the "Garfield Memorial" or the Vermont Avenue Church. In its old location under the long and fruitful ministry of the brilliant Virginian, Frederick D. Power, it had become "a family name" to hundreds of thousands of our people across the nation. Then in Earle Wilfley's day came the propaganda for erecting a magnificent "Disciple Cathedral" that would "truly represent" Discipledom in the Capital City. With a million-dollar gift from lumber tycoon R. A. Long of Kansas City, the dream took root and eventually was realized in the impressive modified Georgian colonial structure on Thomas Circle. During the ministry of Raphael Harwood Miller (Long's long-time pastor in Kansas City) the dream was further realized in pulpit and pew. The stature of Discipledom grew amazingly in the Capital City and, I believe, reached its zenith under his pastorate. Miller was one of our greatest preachers. I had the privilege of knowing him rather intimately over several years, especially when he was editor of the *Christian Evangelist,* and I found him basically true to "our position" and a man of great spiritual depth.

Warren Hastings had become minister of National City before I moved to Washington. He was a Westerner who came from a successful pastorate in Seattle, a good money raiser, evangelistic, and with a breezy, flamboyant style of preaching that appealed to many. He sincerely tried to make the "Cathedral" representative of all elements in the Restoration Movement in America. For instance, he had his sixty-voice choir sing one stanza of a hymn in his morning service without instrumental accompaniment, to represent our A Cappella brethren. With the prodding of the Phillips brothers of Butler, Pennsylvania, who furnished the money, he zealously distributed thousands of copies of L. N. D. Wells' famous doctrinal pamphlet on the Restoration plea, which pleased the brethren of the Center. And, finally, he approved an "associate membership" plan for the unimmersed, which went as far as he dared to please the liberals. He had the habit of coming down from the pulpit, during the singing of the invitation hymn, and moving down the center aisle urging people to accept Christ, which added to the evangelistic appeal of his pulpit messages.

On the particular Sunday I visited the church, he recognized me in the audience and at the conclusion of the service asked me to stand and identified me as "our good friend from the Standard Publishing Company in Cincinnati" which showed how closely he kept in touch with total Brotherhood movements. I appreciated his well-meant cordiality and had many friendly contacts with him before his sudden death which occurred while I was in the city. I was one of the honorary pallbearers at his funeral.

It seemed that everywhere I "went to church" before my family joined me in the city, I was left with something yet to be desired in the way of a church home. In fact, I felt strangely alone in a chilly atmosphere of formal courtesies, a foreigner in a foreign land. Things had changed since I first knew Washington. Later I was to find out why:

Until about 1940 the churches of the Capital Area (District of Columbia, Maryland, Delaware, and contiguous parts of Virginia, West Virginia, and Pennsylvania) were, by and large, true to the Restoration plea and preached, and taught and practiced the Christian Gospel as revealed in the New Testament. Maybe Peter Ainslie's Christian Temple in Baltimore and his few satellite churches would be exceptions to that rule, but even they still had a remnant in their midst who stood boldly for "the faith once delivered." All the churches were rather loosely bound together in the Capital Area Christian Missionary Society, a type of organization similar to those existing in all areas across the nation. They met for fellowship and cooperation in evangelistic undertakings. They had no thought of creating a denominational machine with a hierarchy that would in any way threaten the autonomy of the local church. But in 1944 there was created what was known as "The Christian Church Council of Metropolitan Washington." Few of the *hoi polloi* knew how or why it came into being but, looking back on the historic events which followed, it seems evident that this was to be "in the fulness of time" the nucleus of an area-wide drive to take over the extra-congregational cooperative life of all the churches in "Greater Washington." In 1956 the CACMS was swallowed up by "The Capital Area Council of (Christian) Churches," later named "The Christian Church (Disciples of Christ) Capital Area." Its leadership was predominantly liberal, hierarchally minded with definite orientation toward

"Indianapolis headquarters." J. J. von Burskirk (an unreconstructed Chicago Disciples Divinity House liberal) was installed as full-time "Regional Minister" with all the powers and privileges of a bishop. It was to his "diocese" that I had come. I was being introduced to what "Restructure" would soon accomplish wherever the brethren were docile enough to acquiesce. More of this anon.

Fortunately, the Lord had a church home for us. I think He had something to do with it because we had made no plans to do what we finally did. We bought this lovely house in Chevy Chase and discovered that we were within walking distance of Bethesda Christian Church located at Hunt and Wisconsin, across the street from the Chevy Chase Country Club golf course.

Franklin Gosser was acting as interim minister at the time. Franklin was a U. S. Army chaplaincy colonel stationed in the Washington area — a graduate of Northwest Christian College — and an uninhibited advocate of the Restoration Plea. He was giving the Bethesda brethren sound Gospel sermons and even distributing copies of Hoven's chart on the New Testament church and Reece's Church History chart. He had stimulated a spirit of evangelism which resulted in more than eighty additions to the church before the new minister arrived. Franklin greeted us like "long lost friends."

I learned that my friend Robert W. Shaw (recently removed to First Church, Miami, Florida) had been responsible for the development of the Bethesda Church from a small, struggling, poorly-located congregation, established by a retired minister, William G. Oram in 1937, to the active, growing, strategically located and well-housed assembly on Wisconsin Avenue. I'm sorry we missed being one of Bob's parishioners. I am sure we could have had a most rewarding fellowship in doing the Lord's work.

In "no time at all" Franklin Gosser came to see us at 4711 Trent Court, bringing two elders with him and urging that we place our membership with Bethesda the next Lord's Day. I knew it was an Indianapolis-oriented church and we wanted to get things straight. We first wanted to know whether it was an open membership church or even contemplated being one. The two elders (Dr. O. E. Reed and Robert Alexander) assured us that the church was opposed to the practice and had written a clause into its constitution that would prevent its introduction. I frankly told them that while we would financially support the general program of the local church, we must reserve the right to make our missionary, benevolent, and educational gifts to agencies of our own choice. This was acceptable. With these understandings we became members at Bethesda. Thanks to Franklin's urgings and his perhaps too generous recommendations, the brethren made me an elder a few short weeks later in which office I continued to serve during our entire stay in the city.

I want at this point to speak a good word for the two elders above mentioned. Dr. Reed was a thorough-going disciple of Christ. He knew church history and was well versed in Brotherhood affairs. He was a native Missourian and a graduate and post graduate of the University of Missouri. For several years he had served with distinction on the faculty of the Agricultural College of Kansas State University at Manhattan and had been an elder in the church there. Then the United States Government brought him to Washington to occupy an important post in the Department of Agriculture. Many times he was sent abroad on special missions. His last mission was to India. It was a privilege to visit with the Reeds in their beautiful home and to entertain them in ours. He was active in church affairs in the Capital City and served for many years on the Board of the National City Christian Church Corporation. Robert Alexander was a Tennessean, coming to Washington from Paris, where he was an elder in the First Church. He was a brilliant attorney and a lifetime friend of Cordell Hull, Secretary of State under Franklin D. Roosevelt . . . was chosen by Hull to be his first executive assistant and discharged his duties with such efficiency that he continued in State Department service until his retirement. He, too, knew the history and principles of the Restoration Movement and was constantly alert to any deviations from the New Testament path. A confirmed bachelor, he was frequently in our home for meals. He always did the entertaining and many were the thrilling tales he told of his experiences in top-level circles of government, especially in World War II days. Both have passed to their reward. May they rest in peace.

Bethesda's pulpit committee eventually recommended that W. Kenneth Hoover become our full-time minister. He was strongly recommended by Bob Shaw. In fact, he was his Timothy. Ken, a brilliant and highly-placed member of the political bureaucracy in official Washington, was an agnostic until Bob lovingly, patiently, and effectively convinced him that he should give his life to Christ. When he made that decision he was so enthusiastic about the Way that he decided to give up his position and become a minister of the Gospel. In the days remaining before his leaving for Lexington, Kentucky, to prepare for the ministry, he often taught the united adult classes at Bethesda and won the hearts of all the people. Bob helped him in his reading plans to get background for his life work. Hoover completed his school work at just about the time the pulpit opportunity opened in his "home church."

Ken and Meta were warmly received at Bethesda and they soon proved themselves capable leaders. Ken's sermons were thoughtful and biblical because he leaned more heavily on his Bible than on what he had learned at Lexington. We always worked together in a friendly relationship, although he early learned that there was a difference in our views on many ecclesiastical matters. Part of this knowledge was gained from our association and part from the diocesan establishment. Ken frequently asked me to speak in church-related meetings and once or twice to occupy the pulpit. I was glad to serve in various ways.

274

In the second half of our sojourn at Bethesda a whole stream of high church officials occupied our pulpit, for one reason or another, including — A. Dale Fiers, George Earl Owen, J. J. von Buskirk, Howard Short, W. A. Welsh, and the like. I am sure they warned the brethren that the congregation had been "infiltrated" and that I should be closely watched lest doctrines unapproved by headquarters might be advocated to the detriment of the congregation and the church as a whole. From then on invitations to participate in public meetings and policy-making conferences were few and far between. In one or two instances I was able to ward off efforts to get congregational participation in "diocesan" programs that were unscriptural and out of line with traditional Restoration practice. I was always treated with fine Christian consideration and we still treasure the Bethesda experience as a very happy one. Shortly after our leaving Ken moved to Wilmington, Delaware, to become minister of a mission church. Today the Bethesda church is "open membership" and with no evangelistic urgency. It is much smaller in numbers than in our day and will probably eventually become the victim of ecumenical community mergers — "a disappearing brotherhood."

Shortly after my arrival in Washington I received an invitation from M. B. Brinson, then president of the ministerial fellowship of the area, and pastor at Mount Ranier, to speak at its monthly luncheon in the National City Church. He asked that I tell the story of *Christianity Today* and answer questions. I was warmly welcomed by about thirty ministers and we had a good time together. They asked me to become a member of the fellowship and I gladly accepted, continuing in that relationship during my entire stay in the city. Later on, after my new book *Christians Only* came from the press, I was asked to review the volume and answer questions. This was a mountaintop experience in which great interest was manifested, especially in my view that the Restoration Movement now had three well-defined sectors — Right, Left and Center — and was entering upon its greatest era of growth and influence. I was on my feet for more than an hour answering questions and receiving comment, all in good spirit.

I was often invited to participate in meetings of various sorts at the National City Church, especially after the coming of George R. Davis to its pastorate. I recall bringing a paper on church polity to a laymen's discussion group, supplying as teacher for General Renfro's Bible class, speaking at the annual District of Columbia banquet of "Christian Endeavor Alumni", and "such like." At first I had great hopes for the Davis ministry. I had known him as a participant in early gatherings of the North American Christian Convention. When he arrived we invited him and his wife to be our guests at dinner one evening. They came and we had a perfectly delightful evening. George remembered his NACC days but said that company got too restrictive for his irenic nature. Mrs. Davis said she had studied my textbook on Christian Education in Phillips University. George asked me whether I might be available to supply the pulpit at National City when it was necessary for him to be out of the city. I told him I would. This camaraderie existed for some time but finally cooled, for reasons I could readily understand. National City was virtually owned by the Disciples hierarchy and he could not afford to offend the "powers that be." We still have friendly personal relations.

I would not want to give the impression that Davis was not, generally speaking, a man of strong convictions and independent action. He gave many indications of his courage in given situations. I remember that, shortly after he came to National City, Kring Allen of Los Angeles and a group of extremist allies on the leftist "social gospel" front demanded that the UCMS move in on National City, sponsor a survey of the community which was rapidly turning black, and forcibly integrate its membership and all its organizational structures on a 50-50 basis. George took up the gauntlet and went to the International Convention which was preparing to pass a resolution in favor of Allen's general plan. I heard George on the floor during the discussion in which he presented a masterful plea for the autonomy of the local church in harmony with the Biblical and traditional position of the Disciples. He then said that as long as he was minister at National City he would oppose any effort of extra-congregational authority being imposed on his people. He insisted that there was no racial prejudice at National City and that in due time and in their own way his people would work out their community problem to the satisfaction of the Brotherhood and in the spirit of Christ. He won his case by an overwhelming defeat of the "Allen resolution."

One of the most thrilling things that happened to National City Church during Dr. Davis' ministry was the advent of a Disciples of Christ President of the United States — Lyndon Baines Johnson. President James A. Garfield had been a member of the little church at M and Ninth Streets (later to be moved to Vermont Avenue) but there is a vast difference between the two men and the significance of their churchly influence upon the city. That difference I shall not discuss here.

When President Johnson was catapulted into the President's chair by the assassination of President Kennedy he boldly admitted that he was a member of the Christian Church (Disciples of Christ), although he had never been very active in his church relationship. It seems that, although as a boy his immediate family were Baptists, he had formed a strong attachment to an uncle who was a "Campbellite" and a prominent member of the little congregation at Johnson City, Texas. During a "protracted meeting" in that church little Lyndon "came forward to please his uncle" and was baptized in the Pedernales River near his home. He had "kept his membership" in this church through the years and that was where he kept it when he went to live in Washington. In Washington he seldom if ever went to church. As he rose to political power in the Congress, he and his wife (who is an Episcopalian) occasionally appeared in her church. His children went to public and Roman Catholic

276

schools and later graduated from the posh Episcopal Cathedral School for Girls on Mt. Albans. Dr. O. E. Reed, my elder friend at Bethesda, lived next door to the Johnsons for many years. He often invited them to attend National City where he was then a member. He offered to give the children transportation to Sunday school, but they never accepted.

It is passing strange then that immediately after Mr. Johnson's promotion to the presidency he announced that he would attend services at the National City Church on a given Sunday. It was unusual for a president to tell where he was going to worship on Sunday, for personal precautionary reasons of safety if for no other. But the press and television newsmen played it up. The Murches decided to go and see the show. We got to Thomas Circle two hours in advance. The church yard, the steps, and the whole Circle were crowded with people. Streets in every direction were blocked with traffic. The roofs of all the contiguous buildings were covered with armed policemen. Intelligence men infiltrated the crowds watching for queers and potential assassins. The doors of the church were not to be opened until fifteen minutes before the organ prelude. The presidential party was supposed to enter the sanctuary first. In breathless awe the crowd awaited — the gracious presence of the Spirit of God? No! The President of the United States! Finally here came the presidential party in gorgeous limousines conducted by mounted police, pushing through the crowds. The Johnsons were ushered to choice seats as the organ prelude filled the sanctuary with — what was it? "Pomp and Circumstance"? What did the choir sing? Something appropriate to the very special occasion. What did the preacher preach about? I don't remember. Was the Communion observed? I am not quite certain, but — oh, of course it was! It was a never-to-be-forgotten day.

Discipledom had at long last scored a victory over the Presbyterians, the Methodists, and the Episcopalians. Building the "Cathedral" had been worthwhile! It would have been a shame to have made the President worship in the old slab-sided meeting house on M and Ninth Street! The denomination had been "made"! National City had been "made"! Dr. Davis had been "made"! From that day on as long as LBJ occupied the White House the Church was filled every Sunday morning — with reverent worshipers, of course — but mainly with gawking tourists in the hope that they might catch a glimpse of the President "in the flesh!" The offerings zoomed to such an extent that all current bills and past indebtedness were paid with ease. Out of the surplus, needed repairs were made, the parking lots extended and there was talk of air-conditioning the sanctuary. In heartfelt appreciation LBJ was made an "honorary elder," (whatever that is).

Which leads me to this story: It is said that Billy Graham was occupying the pulpit one Sunday morning at the suggestion of the honorary elder. It was summer and the preachers and congregation were sweltering in the extreme heat and humidity for which Washington is so justly famous. Billy prefaced his sermon by saying the church should be air-conditioned. That brought "amens." Then said Billy, "I suggest that you start a subscription paper for that purpose right away. I know that President Johnson will head it with a generous contribution." The church did, he did and the long-desired project was financed without difficulty. Well, that is one way to make a church prosper!

The longer I stayed in Washington the more I was convinced that the people known as the Christian Church (Disciples of Christ) were for the most part ignorant of their heritage and their reason for being. They were no longer moved by the noble aims of their founding fathers and were degenerating into another denomination. This conviction led me to undertake a project I had long desired — the writing of a history of the Restoration Movement. For nearly twenty years I had been keeping files of notes and data which would be of inestimable value if I ever found the time to write such a book. My library was well stocked with data I needed for background and reference. So, with the Lord's help, I undertook the task in my spare time. I wrote on weekends, by night, and on holidays. I remember writing two chapters in Ohio Governor M. Y. Cooper's mansion in Coral Gables, Florida, while we were supposed to be on vacation. At long last the manuscript was completed and I received the welcome news that Standard would publish it. I am rather certain that if I had not been "marooned in Discipledom," I would never have done it.

There were other histories by such capable men as W. T. Moore, M. M. Davis, Earl West, and there was the so-called "official" history, *The Disciples of Christ,* by W. E. Garrison and A. T. DeGrott. Each in its own way met a felt need but I believed that changing times called for something different. The Restoration Movement was facing an Ecumenical Age. I felt that we had the "message of the hour" for that new era. I wanted to show that the Movement was more than an American movement, that it was indigenous to the life of the universal Christian Church throughout its history. After that, I told the romantic story of the launching of the American phase in 1809 and its amazing, God-guided growth until in its totality it numbered around 5,000,000 adherents. I tried to show that as long as it remained true to Christ and the Holy Scriptures, it grew and prospered, but when it departed from the faith and compromised its mission it failed. I endeavored to show that just as the Movement was born in a situation of universal revival, so it now faced the threat of universal apostasy on the one hand and a universal desire for Christian unity on the other. I delineated the three sectors into which the Movement had splintered (Right, Left and Center), outlined as understandingly as I could, the positions held by each, and described the status of each at the time I wrote. Then I pictured the amazing strength of the total movement around the world. I closed with chapters burdened with the idea that the time had come for unity in the great principles which had brought us into being, and for a challenge to all of God's people that we

278

might together restore the Church of the New Testament in an Ecumenical Age.

When the book appeared it was quite a sensation in our ranks. Hundreds have told me that it is the best thing I have ever done in the book field. It was well received in all three sectors of the Movement. This was so unusual that I want to tell a few interesting stories involved:

When I prepared to write the chapter on the Rightists I called upon B. C. Goodpasture, editor of the *Gospel Advocate,* in his Nashville office and told him about my project. Then I said, "Brother Goodpasture, I want to so fairly and honestly relate the story of the "a cappella" brethren that you and any others you might designate could approve it and recommend it." He leaned back in his chair and laughingly said, "Well, Brother Murch, if you would do that it would be the first time the Disciples ever gave us a square deal." I convinced him that I meant every word I said and he graciously consented to provide information, to review the manuscript, and suggest any changes in it that might be appropriate. When that portion of the manuscript was finished I dispatched it to him. He made xerox copies of it and sent it to such leading educators as Athens Clay Pullias, M. Norvel Young, George S. Benson and Don H. Morris. They read it critically and all sent suggestions which proved immensely helpful in completing that chapter of the volume.

When the book came from the press we sent Dr. Goodpasture one of the first copies. It happened that he was at that time in a Nashville hospital recovering from a major operation. Shortly afterward he wrote me a two-page letter telling how he had read the book through three times in his hospital room and that he considered it the best thing of its kind that had ever been written. He said he would stock it and recommend it to his readers. Furthermore, said he, I expect to keep it on my desk as one of my choice reference works on the Restoration Movement. His endorsement and that of every major editor and bookman of the Churches of Christ made it possible to sell thousands of books among these good people around the world.

I recall with pleasure a long distance call I received while I was on a convention trip in the East. It was from Stewart Hudson (son of John Allen Hudson) in Rosemead, California. Hudson was then directing the Old Paths Book Club. He was very enthusiastic about *Christians Only* and said he would buy 1,000 copies of the book if he could get a discount on it. I told him that such a request would have to go to the publishers in Cincinnati, but that he could tell them that I would forego my royalties on the lot if that would be of any help in disseminating these books. The deal went through and more than this number of books were sold through this club. Hudson's *Old Paths Guide* carried a three-page review of the book headed: *"Christians Only:* A brilliant, enthusiastic, and absorbing comprehensive history of the Restoration Movement, primarily objective and conservative in outlook, idealistic (perhaps some may say occasionally idealistic and unrealistic) but always tremendously stimulating and enlightening. All in all, a Superb Book and a Landmark in Restoration Literature."

I followed the same method in preparing each of the three chapters (Right, Left and Center) and received the same generous cooperation. When the book came to the Disciples, the first cordial review was by Forrest F. Reed, chairman of the Board of the Disciples of Christ Historical Society, in *Discipliana*. Said Brother Reed, "This book, written with serene dignity, represents a serious challenge to the leadership of the Disciples of Christ, Christian Churches and Churches of Christ but not only to them, but to all thinking Protestants."

Then came a lengthy review from Dr. Howard Short, editor of *The Christian,* ending with this comment: "No one can claim to know the thinking of our total movement, without reading *Christians Only,* now that it is here. Nobody who disagrees with the author will think his categories are correct. They don't need to be. We all need to know what a man of Dr. Murch's experience, ability, and devotion thinks about the brotherhood, and he tells us quite clearly in *Christians Only."*

One response stands above all others and I will continue to treasure the memory of it to my dying day. Probably the wealthiest man among the Disciples, one who had given millions during his lifetime to the colleges and universities of the Brotherhood, was sent a special autographed copy of the book. He was a long time acknowledging the gift, but one day I received a long distance call from him. He said, "I have read your book. Parts of it several times. I would like to ask you a lot of questions. Would you come to Pittsburgh for a conference at the William Penn Hotel? I shall be glad to pay all your expenses." Of course, I consented. The day of our meeting was an inspiring experience. This well-known industrialist was thoroughly committed to the Restoration Movement. He believed his Bible and had an intelligent knowledge of its teachings. But he had begun to doubt the wisdom of Disciples' leadership. He had reached the place where he was ready to repudiate it and seek out new missionary, benevolent, and educational objects for his philanthropy. He said to me that day, "Your book has given me a clear picture of the situation. I have no doubts now about what I shall do." Since that interview he and members of his family have given many millions of dollars to Centrist institutions and objectives.

The brethren of the Center responded to *Christians Only* with great enthusiasm. Practically every one of their schools and colleges made it "must" reading or accepted it as their preferred textbook in Restoration history. Thousands of churches and ministers continue to stock it and use it.

In the last few years I lived in Washington I became acquainted with the ministers of our so-called "independent" churches in the area. They were "few and far between." The one church in the District was located at Wheaton. The minister was Kenneth A. Meade. This consecrated young man worked for the government and sacrificially served a struggling congregation housed in an inadequate building which soon had to be abandoned because it stood in the path of a newly-projected freeway. It was too far away from 4711 Trent for us to drive (with my invalid mother) every Lord's Day, but I occasionally visited and helped in various ways. With remarkable wisdom and vision Kenneth led his people to secure a site in the Rockville area known as English Manor Woods where they erected the very attractive first unit of a new building. This church is thriving today and has fine prospects for the future.

In addition to Wheaton there were small churches of like faith at Fork, Glen Burnie, Capitol Heights and Fruitland, in nearby Maryland. Some of these I visited on special occasions. At Bel Air there was a struggling effort to establish Eastern Christian College to serve these and other churches and be the means of evangelizing the area. I went out to lecture there on two occasions.

Some of the brethren were critical of me because I did not give more of my time to strengthening and encouraging their churches. They accused me of being something of a "traitor" to the "independent cause" and giving aid and comfort to the "enemy." It is easy to criticize. I have always felt a brotherly relationship to all who were loyal to the faith regardless of the church in which they held their membership. We had not yet reached the place in our brotherhood life where I could not serve my Master well in many churches of the Right, Left or Center. There were some, of course, in which I could not conscientiously hold membership or serve in any capacity. I had done what I felt was proper in my given situation and I had no regrets. Our decision to go to Bethesda followed very definite prayer and I am sure it was accomplished in the will of the Lord. I made no compromises of the things I most surely believed and all who knew me well were fully aware of that fact.

But toward the close of our stay in Washington I realized that the time had come to take some bold steps toward expanding and strengthening the small nucleus of faithful brethren in the Mid-Atlantic region. There were two main reasons for this. First, due to a continuing population explosion an Eastern megalopolis was rapidly developing extending from Richmond, Virginia, up through Washington, Philadelphia, New York, and on to Boston. Transportation and population experts were saying that eventually this would become the largest metropolitan area in the world. The Capital Area Disciples were not interested in evangelizing this whitening harvest field. Indeed, they had abandoned the Gospel plea and repudiated the Restoration principle. Second, we already had organized groups of loyal brethren evangelizing and planting churches in Virginia, New York, and New England, but the Mid-Atlantic Area was neglected. Something needed to be done and there was real urgency that it be done immediately. We possessed tragically little in prestige, wealth and culture but we had faith in the promises of God.

Several conferences ensued with men like John Mills, J. Thomas Seagroves, Wm. P. Walker, Robert L. Kroh, Rolland A. Steever, Robert Van Lew, Wilbert A. Cunningham and Kenneth Meade. It was their feeling that a fellowship for purposes of evangelism should be created at once. I fully agreed. Accordingly "Mid-Atlantic Christian Church Evangelism, Inc." came into being. I was a member of the first board. John Mills was at the helm. John was minister at the Essex Boulevard Church in Baltimore and doing an exceptional job in building a representative congregation in a rapidly growing suburban area of a great city. (He is now with First Church, Chicago.) A fine group of business and professional men joined in the project. MACCE is today serving a great purpose. It has been the means already of establishing new churches in Creswell, Frederick, Joppatowne, Severna Park and, as I write, it has plans for entering other new fields. The Mountain Church in suburban Baltimore has been a tower of strength to this new venture. This is one of the oldest congregations in the area. It boasts having entertained Alexander Campbell and other heroes of the faith in the early days of the Movement. Under the superb leadership of Dr. Walker it has grown to a congregation of more than 700 members. He led his people in erecting one of the finest and most beautiful Gothic native stone edifices in all that area. The last time I visited them they were planning to add a large education building to be used not only for Bible school purposes but for a Christian Day School serving the whole community. Eastern Christian College under J. Thomas Seagroves has grown in size, strength, and quality of service. New buildings have been erected and the hopes of its founders are beginning to be realized. There is a new day dawning in the Mid-Atlantic area and eventually we may see adequate representation of the Restoration Movement in the Nation's Capital itself.

Probably one of the greatest services I have been able to render the Brotherhood was made possible during my later days in Washington. As I look back on it, I see again the leading of the Lord and the closing and opening of doors. A final determined drive was about to be made by liberal Disciples' leadership to "Restructure the Brotherhood." My "decks had been cleared for action" and I was ready to plunge into the conflict with thousands of faithful brethren across the nation to help "save the day" and an important sector of the Restoration Movement. That story will follow.

I thought I was "marooned in Discipledom" but as it turned out, I had been placed in a strategic position nationally to serve the Lord and the Brotherhood in a time of great need. I sang with new understanding —

Lead on, O King Eternal
The day of march has come;
Henceforth in fields of conquest
Thy tents shall be our home,

Through days of preparation
Thy grace has made us strong
And now, O King Eternal
We lift our battle song.

Lead on, O King Eternal
We follow, not with fears;
For gladness breaks like morning
Where ere Thy face appears;
Thy cross is lifted o'er us;
We journey in its light;
The crown awaits the conquest;
Lead on, O God of might!

Episode XXIV

Restructure

I love the Brotherhood.

When I say that, I mean all those Right, Left, and Center who are committed to the Restoration ideal and are sincerely seeking to serve Christ and to do His will as revealed in the Holy Scriptures.

That is why through all the years I have maintained fellowship with a great company of brethren across extra-congregational lines — a fellowship which has not in the least caused me to compromise my convictions grounded in the Word of God. I shall continue to do this because I think Christ would have me do it and regardless of whether others like it or not.

I have always worked for Christian unity (see Episode X) — the sort of unity which is implicit in Christ's prayer in John 17. My conviction and my spirit in this respect are well expressed in my "Prayer for Unity" which I first published in *Christians Only* and which I repeat here —

Gracious God, our Heavenly Father, we thank Thee for the Church of Jesus Christ. We thank Thee that Thou didst so love us as to send Thine only begotten Son into the world to give His life a ransom for all men who believe upon His Name.

We thank Thee, our God, that we have been purchased by His precious atoning blood, born again and made a part of His glorious body the Church. We thank Thee for the blessed fellowship we know in Thee through Thy dear Son — one flock, one fold and one Shepherd. We find in Jesus Christ our life, our hope, our all.

We thank Thee for Thy Holy Word and the Holy Spirit whereby we are grounded, upheld and guided and preserved in Holy Communion with Thee.

As we look upon the outward divisions of the Church in the world our hearts are pained. God, forgive our humanisms, our perversities and our feverish ways which promote divisions, which keep us from fellowship one with another and which hinder the evangelization of the world. We long for the visible realization of the unity for which Christ prayed. We would surrender our will completely to Thee that Thy will may be done in us to the unity of Thy people and to Thy everlasting glory.

We pray Thy divine blessing upon all those movements and agencies which seek in sincerity the true and ultimate unity of Thy people in the earth. Guide them in Thy Truth to do Thy will. Bless especially, we beseech Thee, those earnest souls who have dedicated their lives to the achievement of this holy purpose. Keep them in Thy will and way. Deliver them from presumptuous thoughts, precipitous acts and shameful compromises.

Hinder and destroy, we beseech Thee, every device of men or of Satan which would mar the pattern of the Church which Jesus built and which His chosen Apostles have revealed to us in Thy Holy Word.

Forbid, O God, that unity which would compromise Thy eternal Truth, condone evil, dampen our zeal for lost souls, consent to barren profession, bear no spiritual fruit, take pride in outward show, seek political power and number in its company a people who praise Thee with their lips but whose hearts are far from Thee. Fulfill the heartening promise of Our Lord that the gates of Hell shall not prevail against Thy Church.

Help us to know the mind of Christ and His will for us in all things pertaining to His Church, that in His greatness we may rise above our littleness, in His strength we shall lose our weakness, in His peace we may bury all discord that in His truth and righteousness we may march — the united Church militant accomplishing the work Thou hast set for us in our day and time.

At last, we pray, enfold us in the one Church triumphant, the family of God, to dwell with Thee forever. And unto Thee we will ascribe all honor and glory through Jesus Christ, our Lord. Amen.

So when I first heard of the "Decade of Decision" I instinctively knew that the Disciples Establishment had come to the point of no return in their long-range planning program which had as its goal the absorption of all the churches of the Left and Center into a huge centralized hierarchy. They had finally decided to build a "Berlin wall" across the Restoration Movement with no one allowed on their side of it but those who would "bow down to the image" in denominational headquarters.

The Establishment did not at first tell the people what they had in mind. The "Decade of Decision" was announced with high-toned spiritual and ecclesiastical objectives with not a word about "Restructure." The local churches welcomed the comprehensive programs suggested. They could now follow directions from headquarters and its experts in "Church Life," in all the functional activities of the local congregation. They were privileged to "goose step" with all other "cooperative churches" in the achievement of "effective ministry, evangelism, stewardship, budget relationships, curriculum, church growth and development, service to racial groups, social welfare, world outreach, missionary policy, ecumenical strategy, and the best in local church life." The churches that accepted the "Decade" program were said to be "cooperative," "united," "responsible," and "approved." They did not know that they were being psychologically conditioned to accept the eventual loss of congregational autonomy and freedom of action which were hallmarks of the Restoration. They did not know that they were being prepared by necessary educational, promotional, organizational, and judicial steps for the achievement of the ultimate "Decade" objective. That objective was the completion of a corporate ecclesiastical metamorphosis that was to deliver the Brotherhood into full-fledged denominational status.

When a "Committee on Brotherhood Restructure" (formed at Denver in 1959) reported at the Louisville assembly of the International Convention of Christian Churches (Disciples of Christ), few were shocked at its findings and proposals for the future. They were not in any way prepared to assess it and realize its implications for the future.

The Louisville Report contained an exhaustive treatment of "The Rationale of Restructure," "The Breadth and Depth of Restructure," "Ways and Means of Restructure," and "Financial Support." The Report said that all previous efforts toward reorganization were inadequate, involving only the agencies which report to the Convention. It insisted that "outmoded procedures" be abandoned and that "a new and imaginative church structure" be devised. It conceded the fact that originally the Disciples had been committed to a Free Church polity, but this was due to "poor means of communication on the frontier and to a lack of intelligent leadership." Early extra-congregational organizations, said the Report, were created for purely pragmatic reasons and were given no official character. Lacking any theology of the Church beyond the local congregation, and refusing to accept denominational status, the churches considered themselves part of a vague Christian unity movement. They felt that a denominationally structured communion would hinder their broad goals. However, the unity movement failed, said the Report, and the Disciples became a separate but irresponsible denomination. It concluded that "no matter what we started out to be," the Disciples are now in deed and in fact a denomination and should act in a "responsible fashion." The Brotherhood should become more than "the sum total of local congregations" and assume the status of a *Church*.

The Louisville Report then turned to future action, proposing that the Disciples develop a new theology of the nature and mission of the Church and proceed to restructure for bigger and broader "involvement" in keeping with an "overall master plan which will relate each part to the whole." The new structure should extend beyond our own borders, including our "historic concern for Christian unity." The time has come, the Report said, to "quit tinkering with the machinery" and seek a new design "rooted in a new Christian conviction concerning the Church." It boldly stated that *every level* in the Brotherhood should be involved in a new denominational structure including "its church members, its ministry, its function, its authority, city unions, district and state conventions and organizations, its International Convention and all agencies reporting to it, colleges, seminaries, benevolent homes, national planning bodies and involvement in all ecumenical bodies." The words "autonomy" and "self-government" should be scrapped, said the Committee, and replaced by "inter-dependence" and "responsibility." The freedom of the local church should be impregnated with a new sense of obligation to proper official authority. At Louisville it was evident that the Establishment had embarked upon a ruthless policy, determined to achieve Restructure with all due speed regardless of the costs involved. Dr. Loren E. Lair, who was president of the International Convention that year, made the statement that "we must have an organization that can move together if we are to have an effective witness. This needs to be achieved, even if it means a breaking away of the anti-organization wing of the Christian Churches, a possible loss of 2,700 churches and 650,000 members." Similar expressions were heard in night sessions of the Campbell Institute, where many leaders of the Restructure spoke. The Louisville Assembly approved the Report of the Committee and authorized the appointment of a Commission on Brotherhood Restructure and actual Restructure of the Brotherhood in depth and breadth.

The brethren assembled at Louisville seemed unaware of the fact that Restructure was already being realized in many ways under supervision of the Establishment. A Panel of Scholars had been at work "behind the scenes" since 1956 drafting the tentative blueprint. Their findings were now published in three volumes under the general title, *The Renewal of Church:* (1) *The Reformation of Tradition*, (2) *Reconstruction of Theology*, and (3) *Revival of the Churches*. Many other volumes designed to prepare church leaders for the abandonment of the Restoration tradition, including the Free Church idea, had long been in circulation and were now promoted with new enthusiasm. Actual restructuring of state and regional "missionary societies" and "associations" was already proceeding step by step as rapidly as the opposition would permit. National agencies were being persuaded to change their constitutions and bylaws so that all legal barriers to complete involvement with the new centralized ecclesiastical structure would be removed. In fact, more was being accomplished in Restructure behind the scenes by pressures from the Establishment than in the much-publicized "open," "democratic actions" of the Convention.

I prayed many times about this situation and asked for guidance as to a course of action. I was supposed to be approaching "retirement." I had very limited resources. I had no Brotherhood connections that would assure me a hearing if I spoke my convictions. But, as always, the Lord provided.

I was in a series of meetings in First Church, Canton, Ohio. (Shades of P. H. Welshimer! What would he do about Restructure if he were alive?) Almost every evening after the services a group of area preachers would go out with me for a snack and a talk-fest. I kept bringing up the Restructure threat to the preservation and perpetuation of the Restoration plea and to that measure of unity that continued to exist in the Brotherhood. I kept saying, "Something must be done." It was the consensus of those meetings that I should write an "open letter to the churches" and that the churches in the Canton area be asked to underwrite the cost of sending it to all the churches and ministers in the Disciples' *Year Book*.

When I went back to Washington I began to draft the Open Letter under the title "Freedom or Restructure?" Then I was called to Elm Court to confer with Mr. and Mrs. B. D. Phillips about other matters. I had a rough draft of the manuscript with me. In the course of our conversations we began to discuss Restructure. I told them about the Canton incident and that I had written the Open Letter. "Do you have a copy with you?" asked B. D. Providentially, I had. He wanted to see it. He took it into his private office and after more than an hour, he emerged waving the manuscript and saying, "This must be sent out to the whole Brotherhood right away. I shall be glad to underwrite the cost. When can we get things moving?"

Almost immediately a meeting of the Canton brethren and others whom Mr. Phillips invited was held in First Church, Canton, at which a "Committee for the Preservation of the Brotherhood" was organized and plans were laid for printing and distributing *Freedom or Restructure?* anonymously.

The brochure was mailed to every church in the Brotherhood, four copies to each congregation. Immediately there was an overwhelming response from the Establishment. Meetings were called by state and area secretaries all over the nation, to which ministers, elders and deacons were invited.

I was in a meeting of the Washington ministerial fellowship the Monday following the general distribution. The Open Letter was the chief topic of conversation. At the luncheon "Bishop" Von Buskirk rose in a highly-agitated manner, called for the floor and asked how many had received the document. Almost everyone had. Said he, "This is the most serious threat to the future of the Church that I have seen in my lifetime. It calls for swift action. I am therefore calling a meeting in Christian Temple, Baltimore, for next Sunday afternoon. I will expect all of our ministers in the area to be present and to bring one or two of their leading elders with them. At that time we will thoroughly review the misrepresentations in the letter and brief those present on the course of action that must be taken in all our churches to counteract the propaganda against Restructure which is bound to result. This is serious. I will expect everyone at Baltimore next Sunday." No one realized that the author of the Letter was present. This incident is probably a fair sample of the way the Establishment received the Letter all over the country. The brochure was vehemently condemned, and plans were laid to discredit the "Committee." There was little attempt made to answer the arguments made against Restructure. The strategy was to disparage the whole Letter because it had been issued anonymously.

The Committee* issued the following apologetic for its method of approach to the Brotherhood:

We wished to have the facts, principles, and issues concerning restructure considered strictly on their own merits. It has been our observation that, in similar situations in the past, principles were forgotten in a welter of personal diatribe and organizational bias. We will not be parties to a repetition of such debacles. After careful and prayerful consideration, we came to the conclusion that the issues would receive far wider attention if the authors and sponsors were not disclosed. Our position has been amply justified. Not in fifty years has there been a response comparable to that received by this pamphlet. The reaction of state and national leaders, in itself, demonstrated the wisdom of our decision. Orders for extra copies have forced us to reprint the pamphlet three times and new orders continue to arrive every day.

Anonymity, alone, without further knowledge should not be condemned. One of the greatest and most influential books ever written on the Restoration Plea was *The Church of Christ,* "By a Layman." It received a far wider reading and had a much greater acceptance because there was no prejudice or preconceived disposition in favor of or against the author. Our Lord, at times, desired anonymity. He charged certain persons, whom He healed, to "tell no man of this." After the Good Confession by Peter, He charged His disciples "that they should tell no man that He was Jesus the Christ." Even following His resurrection, on the road to Emmaus, He saw fit, temporarily, to withhold His identity. The book of Hebrews in the New Testament is credited to no author.

We may say, however, the Committee is a voluntary group, composed of brethren whose ancestors, in some cases, were champions of the Restoration Plea before the beginning of the present century. The project has been financed from sources which have long contributed generously to so-called "official" and "responsible" agencies and institutions of the brotherhood.

Interest in the booklet did not lag. It went through several editions. Then new developments in Restructure called for another "Open Letter." The committee asked me to write it. It was entitled, *The Truth About Restructure.* It called forth from the leaders of Restructure for the first time public recognition of the opposition. Dr. Stephen J. England, president of the International Convention, wrote an "Open Letter" answering the brochures. An issue of *World Call,* the official journal of

---

*The personnel of the "Committee for the Preservation of the Brotherhood," when created, was as follows: B. D. Phillips, Butler, Pa., Chairman; James DeForest Murch, Washington, D. C., Vice-Chairman; Sherriell E. Storey, Canton, Ohio, Secretary-Treasurer; Mrs. Phillips; Dean E. Walker, Milligan College, Tenn.; Murhl H. Rogers, Indianapolis, Ind.; Rolland E. Ehrman, Hershey, Pa.; and Harold E. Davis, Canton, Ohio. At that time, as individuals, half were members of "cooperative" churches and half of "independent" churches.

the Establishment, gave four full pages to *The Truth About Restructure,* including an editorial, "Has the Break Really Come?" All state and area papers joined in publishing condemnatory articles. Following this the CPB issued a four-page *Restructure Report* from time to time keeping the Brotherhood informed concerning developments.

To summarize its position, our Committee opposed Restructure because:

1. It would change the Brotherhood from a voluntary fellowship of individual Christians and local churches, accepting the supreme authority of Christ and seeking to serve Him according to the teaching of the New Testament, into an official, connectional, centralized denomination acknowledging the authority of a liberal Super-Church hierarchy.

2. It would require as a test of Christian fellowship, not only the acceptance of Jesus Christ as Lord and Saviour, but also support of specific official denominational agencies and conventions.

3. It would no longer accept the Bible as sole and ultimate authority in matters of faith and practice.

4. It would permit open membership and condone sprinkling, pouring, and infant baptism.

5. It would reject the free-church polity of the New Testament and replace it with a "modified presbyterian" or "controlled congregational" system in a denominational Super-Church.

6. It would exercise money-raising and money-spending powers over local churches and endanger their right to hold property without regard for any extra-congregational authority.

7. It would require ministers to get extra-congregational authority for ordination, installation, choice, and release.

8. It would create a whole new category of general ministers — national, state and area (similar to bishops) outranking local ministers and exercising a species of unscriptural authority — over local churches.

9. It would limit the local churches in their support of extra-congregational agencies and conventions. Approved agencies and conventions would have to be recognized as parts of "the whole church."

10. Colleges and seminaries would have to be denominationally related. Boards of trustees and administrative policies would be required to have Super-Church approval.

11. Christian unity would be sought, not through the Restoration of the New Testament Church in doctrine, ordinances, and life, but through ecumenical discussion, negotiation, compromise, denominational mergers, and eventual extinction of the Restoration Movement in an Ecumenical World Church similar to the Roman Catholic Church.

12. Local churches could be compelled by extra-congregational authority to enter mergers, close their doors, or change their policies and practices in the interest of ecumenical progress.

290

It soon became evident that the crucial issue in Restructure was church polity and the freedom of the local church. Apart from the work of the Committee, Mr. Phillips commissioned me to write a "scholarly and definitive" treatise on *The Free Church* for the enlightenment of ministers and lay leaders.

Thereby hangs a tale: About this time the Murches were invited to be the guests of the Phillipses in San Juan, Puerto Rico, during the World Convention of Churches of Christ. One day in the San Jeronimo Hilton I met Darrell K. Wolfe, director of the Bethany Press. We fell to discussing Brotherhood affairs, and I casually expressed concern that while the Bethany Press had published many volumes in favor of Restructure, they had issued nothing against it. Mr. Wolfe assured me that this was not due to any bias, but simply because they had received no manuscripts of real quality presenting the opposing view. When I intimated to him that I was contemplating writing *The Free Church,* he immediately expressed an interest in it and asked that I prepare a rather detailed synopsis of the work for consideration of the Book Committee. I told Mr. Phillips about this incident and he immediately saw the value of such an arrangement. So strongly did he favor it that he told Mr. Wolfe that, if money were a problem, the Phillipses would pay the cost of production. Upon my return to Washington, I sent the synopsis, but Bethany Press advised me that, because of previous commitments and a tight publication schedule, it was unable to promise publication. In his cordial letter notifying me of the situation Mr. Wolfe said, "I believe that your manuscript ought to be published without delay." The Christian Board of Publication, because of tight controls by the Establishment, never published anything against Restructure. Not only was I turned down but such a distinguished liberal as Dr. Alfred T. DeGroot, who opposed certain provisions of Restructure, was twice refused publication for two very excellent manuscripts expressing that opposition, which I had the privilege of reading. When *The Free Church* came from the press, Mr. Phillips sent out one thousand copies of the book to key churches free of charge. Two editions of the 140-page book were printed and it still has a wide circulation. It had a tremendous impact on churches willing to thoughtfully and objectively examine the basic issues involved in Restructure.

Others were encouraged by Mr. Phillips to disseminate information about the dangers of Restructure: Dr. R. M. Bell, president of Johnson Bible College, through the college paper, *The Blue and White,* published effective critiques of Restructure. Dr. Dean E. Walker and Dr. W. F. Lown, other college presidents, prepared thoughtful and effective treatises which were widely circulated. Judge B. D. Sartain, noted layman in Central Church, Dallas, Texas, wrote, "Restructure is Unwise, Undemocratic and Unscriptural." Attorney Rolland L. Ehrman, business associate of Mr. Phillips, answered President England's above-mentioned "Open Letter" in a brilliant and comprehensive defense of the Restoration Plea. Dr. Robert W. Burns, pastor of the great Peachtree Christian

Church, Atlanta, Georgia, inspired a thoughtful document, *The Atlanta Declaration,* and led in setting up an "Atlanta Declaration Committee", opposing Restructure.

During the years of the "Decade of Decision" I was in a strategic position to mold thought through reports of the International Conventions in *Christianity Today* and the *Christian Standard.* After I retired from my position with *CT* I was able to be of assistance to Frank Farrell who was assigned to report the conventions. He was an independent Baptist and wholly sympathetic to the Restructure opposition. The *CT* reports reached thousands of Disciples ministers who did not take the *Standard.*

As a result, I was in constant demand as a speaker and a panelist dealing with the Restructure issue. I covered the nation during those years appearing in many churches and conventions of both the Left and Center. I recall especially Atlanta, Ga., (Peachtree); Cleveland, Ohio (Highland); Canton, Ohio (First); Indianapolis, Ind. (Southport); Boise, Idaho (Central); Long Beach, Calif. (First); Los Angeles, Calif. (Bell); and the Pennsylvania and Florida state Conventions. I attended all the International Conventions during the ten-year period to and including St. Louis both as delegate and press representative. I could tell interesting stories about each of the above visits but I shall elaborate on only two, which were in "enemy" territory.

My invitation to speak at Peachtree Church, Atlanta, was most unexpected, although I had known its minister, Robert W. Burns, for some years. This is the largest church of the Disciples in the South with many wealthy and distinguished members. The elders had arranged for two meetings dealing with Restructure — one to be addressed by Howard E. Dentler favoring and the other opposing, which I was to address. The congregation was divided on the issue with the majority taking the Establishment position. Every kindness and courtesy was shown me. I was entertained in the Burns manse and never did a guest have more gracious hosts. I learned that Bob was unalterably opposed to Restructure. He had stood his ground against "open membership" and won his battle, but he was destined to lose on "Restructure." As previously mentioned, he had assembled a group of well-known Establishment ministers and organized them into a group which produced the historic "Atlanta Declaration" in opposition to Restructure. They were to courageously confront the Establishment on the floor of two International Conventions but without success. I told Bob in our conversations that it was impossible to defeat any issue backed by the Establishment in any convention because they had tight and impenetrable control of all authoritative committees, commissions, and the convention machinery itself. That was why our Committee for the Preservation of the Brotherhood took the position that the only way to successfully combat Restructure was for local congregations to withdraw their names from the *Year Book* and assume independent congregational status. He was working from "within." We were working from "without." But we had a wonderful time at Peachtree. Our audience was open and receptive. In the forum that followed my address there were many questions. Discussions were cordial in spirit. At dinner that evening I sat next to H. T. Money, a Lexington product, who had just been called to be Burns' associate. Money favored Restructure and I gathered from comment during the evening that he was slated to succeed Bob when he reached retirement age. He proved to be the Establishment's man to save Peachtree for the new denomination.

Parenthetically, I recall a very interesting conversation with Bob when he came to Washington to address the annual meeting of the Washington District of the Capital Area. He came out for a visit at 4711 which we thoroughly enjoyed. During the course of our conversation we were discussing the Miami Beach International of which he was President. Suddenly he turned to me and said, "Jim, why do you suppose I was elected president? I have always been more or less independent in my views and I was unalterably opposed to 'open membership.' " I said, "Do you want me to be very frank?" "Go ahead, shoot!" he replied. "Well," said I, "I think it was a bit of very carefully calculated strategy to win the conservative vote for Restructure. All the conservatives like you. Indianapolis felt you were 'safe' and that you would have served your purpose and be out of office by the time the crucial decisions had to be made."

Another Disciples church I visited with my Restructure message was Highland, Cleveland, Ohio. This congregation was near Cleveland Christian Children's Home and many of its personnel attended worship there. It happened that at this particular time Stanley A. Ott was the minister. He was opposed to Restructure. The elders had agreed to present both sides of the issue to the congregation. Howard Dentler was to speak in favor and I was to oppose. I had a whole Sunday evening service and Dentler was to appear the following Sunday. Greater Cleveland is a hot-bed of Discipledom and the headquarters of the Ohio "diocese." My appearance was something of an "event" under these circumstances. The building was crowded to the doors with chairs down the aisles. All the "top brass" of Ohio Discipledom was there. It was understood that I was to have the pulpit unmolested with Ott presiding for the forum. As soon as the address was finished there were questions from all over the house. During the course of my comments I made the assertion that "Restructure is not an end in itself but a means to an end; and that end was the merger of the Disciples in the COCU. Restructure is necessary only to divest local congregations of their freedom and concentrate sufficient authority in the hands of a hierarchy which could deliver the churches into the merger." Hardly had the words been uttered before Albert W. Pennybacker, minister of the elite Shaker Heights Church, and nationally prominent Disciple leader, charged down the aisle, took the platform and shouted, "That is a lie!" He then proceeded to say, "If there is any man in the house who knows the truth about Restructure and the COCU I am that man. I am a member of both the Committee on Restructure and the Consultation on Church Union. Restructure has nothing to do with COCU and it is definitely an end in itself for the good of the brotherhood and every local congregation in it." Fortunately I kept my "cool," reached for my portfolio and extracted two documents — one by Granville Walker, chairman of the Restructure committee, and the other by Ronald Osborn, its scribe and interpreter — which said very clearly that the next step beyond Restructure was participation in COCU. Pennybacker hurt himself by having broken the "rules of the game" and by his hot-headed assertion that his own associates denied. Afterward I was overwhelmed by people who expressed their appreciation of my presentation. However, later Brother Ott resigned and Highland Church remains a divided congregation.

What is the state of mind of men like Pennybacker who deliberately mislead the people in their pronouncements? They cannot help knowing the facts they suppress, yet they treat them as non-existent. I relate another incident in this connection. This was in a mass meeting of around 600 ministers during the Dallas International. George Beazley was on the platform and one of the questions he was asked was, "Will the freedom of ministers be in any way limited by either Restructure or COCU?" To which he replied in the Pennybacker manner: "If there is anyone in this room who should know the answer to that question, it is I. I am closely connected with both committees and I can say without equivocation that ministerial freedom is not only protected but will be preserved and perpetuated in both Restructure and COCU." Do you suppose that a man in his vaunted position was unacquainted with the provisions of Articles VI and XI in the "Provisional Design" and with Chapter VII of COCU's "A Plan of Union"? Or was he for certain ulterior purposes "blind in one eye and unable to see out of the other"?

As I have indicated, the two crucial International conventions which were to determine the success of the Establishment's program were Dallas in 1966 and St. Louis in 1967. Everything had been carefully planned with utmost sagacity and precision beginning with the introduction of the Restructure idea in Denver in 1959. At that time a "goose-stepping" temporary committee was announced to explore the possibilities of Restructure. It reported favorably, of course, at Louisville in 1960 and a Commitee on Brotherhood Restructure was appointed consisting of 120 men and women, the overwhelming majority of whom were Establishmentarian in their views. The years 1961-1963 were devoted to study, conference, and necessary political jockeying with the agencies. In 1964 at Detroit the theological and philosophical basis of Restructure was announced and approved. In 1965 there was a big show of carrying the idea to "the people" in regional conventions. Those who came were psychologically conditioned for what was to follow. That brings us to Dallas in 1966 and St. Louis in 1967 about which more will be said. Beyond those conventions came Kansas City in 1968 with the actual but provisional institution of the new denomination on an operative basis.

At Seattle in 1969 the constitution and bylaws were supposed to be adopted. (It will be noticed that the time-table for the gigantic take-over coincides exactly with the dates of the "Decade of Decision.") But in 1969 there were unexpected repercussions and developments that delayed the legalization of the new denomination. Back to Dallas and St. Louis.

B. D. Phillips, deeply interested in the Dallas convention and its outcome, asked his son-in-law and business associate, Rolland Ehrman, and me to be present, report, and interpret the proceedings. More than 10,000 church members registered, making this crucial gathering one of the largest in history. It was evident that the Establishment feared the outcome. They imposed rigid rules in qualifying voting delegates. It was a "packed" convention. They policed the entrances and the seating of voting delegates. It was evident that they had endured a year of rather grueling criticism with a veritable flood of opposition letters, pamphlets, and leaflets. One of these was Dallas Judge Sartain's "Restructure Is Unwise, Undemocratic, and Unscriptural." All distribution of pamphlets was forbidden in or near the auditorium. So strict was the enforcement of this decree that the Judge himself was ordered by police to leave the lobby of the auditorium because he was caught handing one of his booklets to a friend. The whole atmosphere of the place was severely restrictive.

I will spend little time writing of the window-dressing provided by the general program. Suffice to say that all conservatives were banned from it. Liberal establishmentarians were everywhere evident. Special prominence was given to men like Martin Luther King, Roman Catholic Bishop John J. Wright of Pittsburgh and Dean Robert Storey of Southern Methodist University. My chief concern will be with the business sessions.

The convention was headed by Stephen England of Phillips University. He was a Stephen England at Dallas that I never knew before. He had been one of my favorite Disciples leaders. Although loyal to the Establishment he had been generally conservative and biblical in his position. In his *We Disciples* and other writings he had shown a remarkable grasp of the Restoration plea and had in many ways made a fine contribution to the ongoing of the movement. He had shown a fair-minded, sane, and reasonably biblical approach to the ecumenism of the times, serving with distinction on the Faith and Order Commission of the World Council of Churches. But at Dallas he became by all odds the most autocratic, dictatorial, and ruthless presiding officer I have ever seen in the history of parliamentary procedure. He had certainly done his homework on Robert's Rules of Order, and, with the help of an even more ruthless official parliamentarian, hewed to the line in a fashion which could have outdone the legalism of the Scribes and Pharisees in Jesus' day. The Establishment, with his expert guidance, rolled like a Juggernaut over all opposition.

The personnel of the opposition to Restructure at Dallas was largely unknown to Rolland and me. Those who held our views had, as I have previously indicated, long ago come to the conclusion that there was no hope for successful opposition to Restructure within the framework of the Convention. We did not even know who directed the opposition at Dallas with the possible exception of Dr. Burns and his Atlanta Declaration Committee.

The debate on Restructure was spirited. Both sides had their innings. The Burns contingent was courteous in its stance and presented sound biblical and logical reasons why the proposal should be rejected. They pled for "harmony and understanding with all in our Brotherhood." But the general tenor of the unorganized opposition was less than convincing. They inveighed against the "powers that be" and said a "monolithic monstrosity" and a "political machine" was being forced upon the Brotherhood. They said, "You are trying to divide our people." They cried, "This American church which was born in the spirit of the Revolution" would lose all its members who had joined the church "for its patriotic appeal." They summoned to their support the ancestral shade of Alexander Campbell and the Restoration fathers. They claimed that they were "being robbed" of their freedoms. Maybe they "had something," but in their presentation they only succeeded in alienating the thoughtful and open-minded and in making the Liberals hopping mad.

When the determining votes finally came it was not necessary to "divide the house." By tremendous and overwhelming voice votes every Establishment measure was carried. I would estimate that there was at least a four to one majority, for Restructure. The jubilation of the Liberals was complete.

This action constituted the first step in the adoption of the "Provisional Design for Restructure." The document was approved and referred to the churches for suggestions, which might or might not be incorporated in a revised edition, to be submitted at St. Louis for final adoption. The Convention thus turned decisively from the polity that its churches had followed for four generations and faced in a new direction. It did this by repudiating the voluntary mass convention type of extra-congregational international organization by declaring henceforth that its convention business would be conducted by officially elected and approved delegates from the churches. Even more significantly it decided to become a denomination it dubbed "The Christian Church (Disciples of Christ)."

We returned with our report to Mr. Phillips and the "Committee for the Preservation of the Brotherhood." They authorized a redoubled effort to educate the Brotherhood concerning the true meaning of Restructure and to convince local churches that they should take legal action to preserve their congregational freedoms.

Then came St. Louis. I remember having a difficult time getting hotel reservations. Everywhere I turned for a room within a reasonable distance from the convention auditorium, I was told that the Disciples of

Christ had full claim on all their available rooms. I wrote to "headquarters" but was told that all their rooms had been reserved. Finally, in desperation, I telephoned my Lutheran friend, Dr. E. R. Bertermann, who had befriended me on so many occasions. He said, "Don't worry, you will have a place to stay." He was a member of the exclusive Missouri Athletic Club in St. Louis. Within an hour I had my reservation there and lived in luxury during the convention. But I was, from the first, unable to shake a sense of impending doom.

The convention met the first day in a pall of smog, fog, and rain. An atmosphere of gloom pervaded within and without the convention hall. This was the Disciples' first delegate "Assembly" on a national scale. The official count of registration was 9,575. It is interesting to note how successful the advocates of the new system of church government were in achieving official representation of all the churches. A simple exercise in arithmetic reveals: The 1966 *Year Book* of Christian Churches (Disciples of Christ) listed a total of 8,147 churches (both "participating" and "non-participating") in the United States and Canada, with a membership of 1,903,395. Churches numbering 2,100 were said to be represented in St. Louis by 4,805 delegates. (There were 4,770 observers). This means that more than 6,000 churches refused or neglected to have any official voting relationship to the Assembly. Nevertheless, the relatively small group of men and women who controlled and directed the convention assumed to act for the whole Brotherhood at St. Louis. Indeed they told the press in their official releases that they represented and spoke for "a brotherhood of more than 8,000 congregations with almost two million members."

The Assembly was superbly staged. Everything moved according to plan. The main sessions were efficiently expedited under the leadership of President Forrest L. Richeson and his assistants. There were breakfasts, luncheons, and dinners galore. Top speakers, largely imported from denominations involved in the Consultation on Church Union (COCU), set an ecumenical pattern. Liturgy, music, and stage effects were highly appropriate. There was an atmosphere of expectancy as the Assembly faced revolutionary changes.

Restructure of the "Brotherhood" was, of course, the chief concern. On the opening night President Richeson in his keynote address said, "The Disciples of Christ have suffered from an exaggerated emphasis upon the autonomy of the local congregation . . . In this Convention our brotherhood is entering upon a new day. Through the adoption of a voting delegate Assembly at the national level, we have already left behind that which was . . . Our times are forcing us to redefine the roles and the relationships of our congregations, their regional, national, and agency life, hence the need for Restructure."

In the morning session next day the executive secretary of the Convention, A. Dale Fiers, in his "State of the Church" address, pled for the adoption of the *Provisional Design for the Restructure of the Brother-*

hood. Somewhat facetiously he compared the Assembly to a jet plane flight, saying, "We will, however, have to fly at 40,000 feet in order to remain above the squalls and thundershowers taking place at the lower levels. While we may encounter some turbulence along the way we expect to land safely and on time."

Chairman of the Commission Granville T. Walker, advised the delegates that some 9,000 ideas for improvements were received since Dallas. He said revisions were made (largely semantic) and that the document was now ready for adoption.

The *Provisional Design* was presented first to the Recommendations Committee. Kenneth L. Teegarden, administrative secretary of the Commission on Restructure, spoke in favor of acceptance. Then Kenneth Johnson, of Portland, Oregon, spoke in opposition on behalf of the Atlanta Declaration Committee. He asserted that more than one thousand churches were opposed to Restructure because it would turn the Disciples into a tight little denomination, set up a new order of ministry, destroy congregational freedom, and substitute a system of connectional authority over the churches. The Atlanta position was rebutted by Herald B. Monroe, general secretary of the Ohio Society of Christian Churches. Then the Recommendations Committee made short shrift of the issue by approving the *Design* without a single dissenting vote.

When the *Design* came to the Assembly Saturday morning, the position of the Atlanta Committee was heard in the person of Thomas O. Parish, Sr., of Wichita, Kansas. He expressed concern that the *Design* would, in effect, disregard the noble heritage of the Restoration movement and return the brotherhood to the sectarianism against which our fathers had rebelled; it would lead to merger with other denominations; it would set up a professional order of the ministry, giving regional and national ministers unprecedented and unacceptable authority over their brethren; it would set up a connectional authoritative power structure which would destroy the freedom of the local church; and it would result in a serious loss of fellowship with many ministers and churches. Dr. Parish warned that *recommendation* of the *Design* (which was being asked for) would be tantamount to *adoption* and urged the delegates to vote against it. He was given a respectful hearing and generous applause, but he made few converts. The voting delegates knew what they had come to do and they intended to do it as soon as they got their cue from the officers of the Convention.

Defense of the official view came from Ohio's Herald Monroe. He charged that virtually all opposition to Restructure had been addressed to interpretations of the *Design* and said that the text itself provides no support for the charges leveled against it.

In contrast to the steamroller tactics employed at Dallas, President Richeson allowed considerable freedom for discussion both pro and con relating to all the issues. Floor debate, however, was inconclusive except to clear the decks for action on the Provisional Design on Monday.

Parenthetically, it should be observed that, according to the rules of the Assembly, no new business could be voted on. The proposal of the Recommendations Committee to *recommend* the *Design* could only be voted "up" or "down," or "referred" to the Committee for further consideration. Under this *modus operandi* six resolutions embodying delaying tactics, some of which were inspired by Dr. Burns and his Atlanta Committee, were disposed of in order, and the Assembly moved to make its historic decision.

When the vote was called for Monday morning it was overwhelmingly in favor of Restructure. So loud were the "ayes" that no one had any question about the completeness of the Establishment's victory. The "nays" were weak and scattered and I would generously estimate them as scarcely more than a hundred. Delegates from two thousand churches had made tragic division inevitable for a great Movement.

I had anticipated such a result but I was unprepared for the shock when I realized that from henceforth I had no connection with this body of believers. That shock was so strong that it affected me physically. There may have been other contributing factors, but I was suddenly stricken with blood hemorrhages so persistent that I had to take a taxi to my room. There I could get no relief. I knew no doctors in St. Louis, but suddenly I realized that we had Christian Hospital in St. Louis — at that time our only "independent" hospital in the nation. I called Mrs. Selina Hulan, president of the Christian Women's Benevolent Association who was in charge. I told her of my condition and she immediately put me in touch with her own personal physician who ordered me to the Emergency Ward of Christian Hospital immediately. His preliminary examination caused him to order me to X-ray at once and to make arrangements for me to be admitted to a private room for treatment. When the x-ray pictures came through he shook his head and said, "Dr. Murch, you are a very sick man. There are evidences of malignancy. You are to stay here for treatments for two or three days and then I think you will be able to go home, contact your physician, and arrange for surgery." Through the kindness of my friend, Leonard Wymore, who was attending the Convention, he saw me through arrangements for the plane trip to Cincinnati and transportation to my home.

There is no need to describe in detail the happenings of the next few weeks. This was undoubtedly the most serious illness I have ever experienced. I had one of Cincinnati's finest surgeons for the operation which was definitely for cancer. I put my whole trust in the Lord. I told Him I was ready to go to my eternal home if that were His will. If He spared me, I said, I would consider it an evidence of the fact that He still had work for me to do and that I would gladly serve Him as He might direct. Though we made no announcement of my illness somehow the word got around and we received hundreds of letters of sympathy. Word came of thousands who were praying for my recovery, some in specially called church meetings. That was four years ago. I am alive and as I write, am reasonably well for a man of my age. Some of the things I have been able to do since then will be yet recorded in this volume.

St. Louis was my last Disciples' International convention. My first, as I have previously noted, was the Pittsburgh "Centennial Convention" in 1909. When I attained maturity I found some way to attend almost all of them and sought in many ways to promote all the *good things* they stood for. I reserved the right to be critical of the bad. But the St. Louis assembly marked the end of a beautiful fellowship. Many of the faithful disciples I knew who went out with the new denomination remain my personal friends, but the "Berlin wall" that was built at St. Louis I consider an abomination unto the Lord. I can have no part nor lot in it.

Episode XXV

A Continuing Brotherhood

When the International Convention of Christian Churches (Disciples of Christ), meeting in Kansas City, Missouri, September 27 to October 2, 1968, legally changed its form from that of a loose federation of congregations to that of a Church, it automatically divorced itself from the Restoration Movement, and built a wall of separation from approximately 4,600 autonomous congregations with a membership of 1,020,000 in the United States and Canada. These brethren elected to continue in the faith and practice that had characterized the Restoration Movement from its beginnings. I was of that number.

One could have read the newspapers, magazines and periodicals of the time and never have known that there was a continuing brotherhood which refused to enter the new denomination. The 4,600 churches were not affected in any way. They continued to hold their services and carry on their work patterns as always. But they had to do a great deal of explaining to the secular and religious world at large, as to their national status — who they were and by what right they existed as a separate people. At wit's end they began to say to one another, "Why doesn't somebody do something about it?"

In 1927 brethren of the same mind and heart had organized the North American Christian Convention (to which I have previously alluded) but the leaders of the Convention said it had no right to speak or act for the Brotherhood. The fact is, no organization or individual has that right.

Finally, after being approached many times and urged to "do something" about "telling the world," I was foolish enough to send a news story to the Religious News Service. I had served RNS as a reporter for many years and they readily accepted my copy. Here is the history-making document:

Million Members Not in
Disciples Restructure Plan

CINCINNATI, Ohio.—When the International Convention of the Christian Church (Disciples of Christ) voted to become a full-fledged denomination at Kansas City, Missouri, last October, at least 4,600 autonomous congregations did not recognize its authority. These churches with over one million members and 4,300 ministers, are continuing in an "undenominational fellowship."

This fellowship of Christian Churches and Churches of Christ traces its roots to an American movement "to restore the New Testament church in doctrine, ordinances and life" initiated by Thomas and Alexander Campbell, Walter Scott, Barton W. Stone, and others in the early part of the Nineteenth Century. Many of its churches, always strictly congregational in polity, were formerly reported in the *Year Book* of the "Disciples of Christ." Many others refused or neglected such listing, but are now listed in a *Directory of the Ministry* published at Springfield, Illinois.

While this continuing fellowship of churches recognizes no exclusive extra-congregational structure and its thousands of congregations remain free, independent, and completely autonomous units, they voluntarily cooperate in many ways to further their common purposes. . . .

The news story continued, to speak of the North American Christian Convention, the missionary, educational, benevolent and journalistic accomplishments of the fellowship. It contained facts that were an "eye-opener" to thousands who read it.

One of the problems which our ministers faced was their inability to get endorsements from the Chaplaincy Commission of the Disciples, essential if they were to be accepted by the U.S. government as chaplains in the Armed Forces and government institutions. This situation had existed long before Kansas City and I had warned our brethren that something must be done in fairness to our own qualified men. We held a series of informal *ad hoc* meetings to discuss the problem. Finally (1) I called an exploratory conference at Louisville in 1967 attended by C. R. Gresham, W. F. Lown, Edwin Hayden, J. T. Segroves and Jack Bliffen. After much discussion we decided to poll our Bible colleges and a representative number of churches to determine whether they would favor the launching of a Chaplaincy Endorsement Commission. (2) This was accomplished and an open meeting was called in Cincinnati, in the Continental Room of the Netherland Hilton Hotel, July 10, 1968, to take some definite action. Around fifty or sixty brethren assembled, heard the presentation of the proposal, discussed it at length and finally created the "Chaplaincy Commission of the Churches of Christ/Christian Churches." They chose the following twelve men to serve as members of the first Commission: James DeForest Murch, Chairman; Ralph M. Small, Vice Chairman; C. R. Gresham, Secretary and Sherriell Storey, Treasurer; Paul Benjamin, Jack Bliffen, Russell Blowers, Harold Ford, Lewis Foster, W. F. Lown, Russell Martin, and J. T. Segroves. The first meeting of the new commission was set for September 16 at which time a report would be made on the steps necessary to secure governmental acceptance, and to adopt a constitution and by-laws.

When the brethren assembled in the TWA Conference Rooms at the Greater Cincinnati Airport, it was proposed that (1) application should be made to the U.S. Armed Forces Chaplains Board, based on the constituency of churches listed in the *Directory of the Ministry,* (2) that the

Commission on Chaplains and Service for Military Personnel of the National Association of Evangelicals be asked to facilitate all Washington contacts, (3) that a proposed Constitution and By-Laws be adopted; and that, upon proper clearance, (4) applications for endorsement be received and processed. There was prolonged discussion but finally all proposals were adopted. Then came months of negotiations, correspondence, telephone calls until early in April, 1969, I received the following letter:

Department of Defense
Armed Forces Chaplains Board
Washington, D.C.

James DeForest Murch, Chairman
Chaplaincy Endorsement Commission
Christian Churches and Churches of Christ

Dear Mr. Murch:

The Armed Forces Chaplains Board is pleased to recognize the Christian Churches and Churches of Christ as an official ecclesiastical endorsing agency and Mr. Floyd Robertson as authorized endorsing agent.

The application was considered on 1 April and acceptance was unanimous. We look forward to a most cordial and mutually beneficial relationship. Please call on us for assistance whenever needed. . .

Sincerely,
Hans E. Sandrock
Chaplain, Colonel USAF
Executive Director

The commission was also assured that its endorsement would be respected in connection with chaplains already serving if they should desire to transfer from one endorsing agency to another. We were in business. Since that day many men have received endorsement for Armed Forces chaplaincies, institutional chaplaincies (both state and national) and Civil Air Patrol chaplaincies.

In August 1969 I went to Washington to attend the annual conference of the "Ecclesiastical Indorsing Agency Representatives", as representative of our Commission. Here at the War College and at Patton Hall in Fort Myer we met for two days. I was introduced to all the "top brass" and publicly recognized as the representative of the newest agency admitted to their distinguished company. It was quite a thrill, especially when it was freely prophesied in some quarters that we could never qualify. We were given "off the record" briefings on important developments in the Far East and Middle East political and military situations. There was extended discussion of mutual problems. Chaplain (Major General) Francis L. Sampson was the presiding officer.

After this I asked to be relieved of any administrative connection with the Commission although I remained a much concerned member. Ralph M. Small succeeded me and carried on with distinction. Special mention should be made of the yeoman service rendered by Charles E. Gresham, who bore much of the detailed responsibility for a functioning operation, in connection with his duties as a member of the faculty of Emmanuel School of Religion. We had won a great victory and had set a precedent which was of tremendous help in the solution of other problems that were to arise.

During the time when we were seeking government approval for our Chaplaincy Commission, we were faced with the fact that the Christian Churches and Churches of Christ were not listed in the *Yearbook of American Churches.* We were told time and again that if we had that listing the problem could be solved sooner.

It seems that the United States Census Bureau once had a division known as the United States Religious Census, but now has no such service. The USRC was always in a hassle with denominational leaders about figures which the churchmen rejected as inaccurate. Finally the government threw up its hands and abandoned the field. Inasmuch, however, as the government has many occasions and faces many situations in which accurate figures concerning the churches are essential, it has an unwritten rule to accept as standard the figures of the *Yearbook of American Churches,* published by the National Council of Churches.

This complicated the problem which faced us in securing listing. Our churches were one hundred percent opposed to the Council and some of our people, including myself, were rather aggressive in the opposition to the Council. However, the editors of the volume claim to produce an unbiased, objective and all-inclusive statement of figures furnished by the churches themselves and to reflect the current state of affairs in the total American church picture.

Acting on the assumption that the AYBC would welcome information about our churches, the men present at the Cincinnati meeting of the Chaplaincy Commission authorized me to approach the editors of the *Yearbook,* explaining our situation and asking for listing. A statement for publication was approved by the Commission on motion by Sherreill Storey and seconded by Lewis Foster. It read as follows:

CHRISTIAN CHURCHES AND CHURCHES OF CHRIST

This "undenominational fellowship" had its origin in the movement "to restore the New Testament church in doctrine, ordinances and life" initiated by Thomas and Alexander Campbell, Walter Scott, and Barton W. Stone in 1809. Its churches, always strictly congregational, were formerly reported with the Disciples of Christ. When the International Convention of Christian Churches (Disciples of Christ) adopted a connectional system of church government at Kansas City, Missouri in 1968, thousands of congregations elected to continue as free, independent and completely autonomous local churches.

No General Organization

Churches: 4,673. Inclusive Membership: 1,001,969
Ordained clergy having charges: 4,447
Voluntary agencies serving the churches:

Conventions

North American Christian Convention (founded 1927), 3533 Epley
Road, Cincinnati, Ohio 45239.

National Missionary Convention (founded 1947), 509 West Jefferson
Street, Joliet, Illinois 60434.

Periodicals

Christian Standard (w), 8121 Hamilton Avenue, Cincinnati, Ohio
45231. Edwin V. Hayden, Ed.

Restoration Herald (m), 5664 Cheviot Road, Cincinnati, Ohio 45239.
Harvey C. Bream, Jr., Ed.

Directory of the Ministry (a), 1525 Cherry Road, Springfield, Illinois
62704. Ralph D. McLean, Ed.

Then began a long and sometimes frustrating correspondence with
Rev. Lauris B. Whitman, at that time editor of the *Yearbook*. It was
quite evident that there was resistance against the listing, which undoubtedly came from the Disciples. Our statement sent in November,
1968, was said to be controversial, our figures inaccurate and lacking
confirmation, our committee *ad hoc* and lacking in the ecclesiastical
authority usually required. We were told, also, that our copy had been
received too late for publication in the 1969 book. We were then sent
forms to fill out with information for the 1970 book. This was sent
promptly. Then there was a change of editors in New York and Dr.
Glen W. Trimble took up our application. We had to go over all the
ground covered with Mr. Whitman. There were still grave doubts in the
minds of the NCC "top brass" as to just what ought to be done with us.
We were in the dark as to what decisions had been made by them until
we saw the 1970 Yearbook. We were not listed. Then another change
in editorship ensued. The new man, Mr. Constant H. Jacquet, seemed
to be quite fair-minded but he had to be briefed from the beginning.
Finally, it seemed that the crucial issue was whether or not our figures
were accurate. We reminded the New York office that we had on several occasions sent copies of the *Directory of the Ministry* containing
detailed accurate information. Mr. Jacquet professed not to have seen
any such book. So I sent him a copy air mail, special delivery, and
"insured" so as to require his signature upon delivery. At long last we
were informed that a statement and listing would appear in the 1971
volume. It did, but with many changes in the statement, limited recognition, and without any figures concerning total membership. The
symbol NR, in the latter connection, indicated that we had made no
report of membership. It became evident that there had been a challenge of our figures — by whom, we were not informed. However, it was

quite evident that the Disciples had again resisted our efforts to gain recognition. Then ensued further correspondence, with Mr. Jacquet's final acceptance of our figures as "reasonably accurate." Also, at our request he promised to list the names of our publications, our accredited colleges and to give us unlimited recognition in the 1972 book. If this had not been done we were prepared to take such action, legal or otherwise, as might be necessary to secure the recognition that was rightfully ours. Now we are thankfully able to say that the *Yearbook of American Churches* is "reasonably accurate" in its claim to be unbiased, objective, and all-inclusive in its compilation of religious information.

This experience served to underline the fact that our *Directory of the Ministry,* published by Ralph and Zella McLean at Springfield, Illinois, is of tremendous importance to the welfare of our "continuing Brotherhood." Its ancestor was a book published by Vernon M. Newland in 1955. Successive volumes appeared in 1957, 1958 and 1960 under his supervision. Facing financial and other problems he turned the publication over to the McLean's in 1963 and it has been published annually ever since. The voluntary task performed so well by this consecrated couple has been a sacrificial one and, I regret to say, unappreciated by large numbers of our people. At Ralph's request I did some "spade work" in setting up an Advisory Board which is now assisting them in their work. Ralph also asked me to prepare an "apologetic" for the book which he had disseminated widely and which I include here for the information of those who may be interested:

WHY "A DIRECTORY OF THE MINISTRY"?

A Directory of the Ministry of the Undenominational Fellowship of Christian Churches and Churches of Christ, published annually at Springfield, Illinois, contains a voluntary listing of approximately 5,000 churches, 6,000 ministers, 1,000 missionaries, 40 institutions of higher education, and 50 benevolent agencies (hospitals, children's homes, and homes for the aged) not listed elsewhere.

The term "Christian Churches" does not refer to congregations legally and officially related to the Christian Church (Disciples of Christ) with headquarters at Indianapolis, Indiana. The term "Churches of Christ" does not refer to congregations of the same name which make the use of missionary societies and instrumental music in worship tests of fellowship. The churches listed are identified as parts of the Restoration Movement which had its American origins in the early part of the Nineteenth Century.

The publication of such an encyclopedia of information was made necessary because of legal requirements of various agencies of government at national, state, and local levels. The U. S. Internal Revenue Service in many cases refused to grant tax exemptions to local churches, to schools and colleges, and to benevolent institutions until they could prove they were related to a valid and authentic fellowship of churches.

Missionaries unrelated to such a fellowship were often denied visas and U.S. State Department protection in foreign lands. Many donors to churches, missionaries, and institutions have been refused tax exemption for their gifts. These governmental requirements were developed as the result of a plethora of irresponsible, independent religious racketeers seeking tax exemption and other government favors illegally. Many U.S. Military Draft Boards refused to grant exemption to ministers and students in Bible colleges and seminaries unless they could prove a valid and authentic relationship to a recognized fellowship of churches. Applicants for U.S. military and institutional chaplaincies were for similar reasons unable to qualify for service. In many other situations, free and autonomous congregations, ministers, missionaries, and educators serving them were embarrassed by being unable to prove their status and enjoy the rights and privileges which were theirs in a free land. "A Directory of the Ministry of the Undenominational Fellowship of Christian Churches and Churches of Christ" solves these and many other problems. It is now accepted and recognized by the United States government and its various agencies in lieu of an official national religious census. It is also accepted and recognized by the *Yearbook of American Churches.*

In this same connection, courts of law recognize the rights and privileges of local congregations, listed in the Directory, to hold their property in fee simple and in perpetuity, without regard to claims of any outside organization or denomination, such as The Christian Church (Disciples of Christ). Churches so listed are considered valid beneficiaries of the free congregational polity which continues to be maintained through the long history of the Restoration Movement in America.

There are many practical benefits provided by the *Directory.* It acquaints brethren with the facts concerning the rapidly growing fellowship of Christian Churches and Churches of Christ in America and around the world. It lists widely utilized publications, voluntary agencies, conventions, conferences, Christian Service camps, campus ministries, schools, colleges, seminaries, radio and television broadcasts, giving addresses and other information. It contains a directory of home and foreign missionaries, mission stations, and mission fields which are widely supported. Ministers seeking churches and churches seeking ministers find a fund of valuable information in its pages. Brethren moving from city to city and community to community often find agreeable new church homes by reference to the book.

The volume constitutes an impressive testimony to the amazing growth and influence of the Restoration Movement at home and abroad. It serves to promote wider fraternal relations with like-minded brethren and intelligent participation in worthy cooperative ministries. It contributes to a deeper loyalty and inner strength for the Movement as a whole and guards against an incipient isolationism which sometimes plagues free churches. It cannot be studied without giving a new dimension to and a new appreciation of brotherhood life.

Listings in the *Directory of the Ministry* offer no official ecclesiastical sanction or status. Applications for listing are purely voluntary. Withdrawals are possible upon request. Listings do not delineate barriers to wider fellowship. Churches and agencies are free to determine the limitations and the latitude of their fellowship without regard to Directory listings of any nature whatsoever.

The *Directory* is chartered under the laws of the State of Illinois as a corporation not for profit. It operates with the assistance of a self-perpetuating advisory board of well-known and trustworthy brethren who are members of Christian Churches and Churches of Christ. The present board (1971) consists of Burris Butler, John Carter, James W. Greenwood, Henry Gruenberg, Earl C. Hargrove, W. E. McGilvrey, James DeForest Murch, Floyd M. Strater, and Leonard G. Wymore. The publication is capably edited and managed by Ralph and Zella McLean.

Lately I have been deeply concerned that all those churches qualified to be listed in this *Directory* of the continuing Brotherhood should be invited to enroll. I am convinced that there are at least 2,000 congregations that have no conscious national or international relationship to their brethren in Christ. This conviction came to me by way of an incident which occurred in 1970. I was examining a copy of the current Disciples' *Yearbook* to see how many of the Ohio churches I knew were still listed. During my lifetime I had visited hundreds of churches in my native state and I pretty well knew all of them, in some connection or other. I was amazed at the number I once knew which are now missing. I then looked in the *Directory* and found many but searched in vain for others. I had a copy of the 1960 Disciples *Yearbook* which I then compared with their 1970 volume and was again amazed at the large number of churches that had been dropped by the editors. Having some time on my hands I made an accurate listing of the missing Ohio churches and — believe it or not! — there were 294 whose names were in the 1960 Disciples' book but were *not listed anywhere* in 1970. I added to these the number of churches (42) in the 1970 Disciples' book which were listed as "non-participating" and I had a grand total of 336 churches in the Buckeye State that were in the category of "forgotten brethren." I said to myself, if this is true of Ohio, what must be the total picture in the nation? So I set myself to the task of finding out. I learned that there were 3,078 churches that had been dropped by the Disciples in ten years' time and not listed elsewhere. If I added to these the "non-participating" churches in their 1970 book (761) I had a total of 3,839 that would seem to be of the "continuing Brotherhood." By this time, I, too, was saying "Why doesn't somebody do something about it?"

Accordingly, I got in touch with Ralph McLean. He was greatly interested but he did not have the office help necessary to properly process the names. We agreed that more than mere mailings would be necessary. Personal contacts should be made. We then shared the information we had obtained with Leonard Wymore and Ralph Small. They both had facilities essential to a comprehensive and thorough survey. As I write, all three of these men are directing different phases of the task and we are persuaded that when the work is accomplishd we will have at least 2,000 additional churches listed in the *Directory of the Ministry*. I am assisting as I am able.

Most of the churches involved are small town and rural congregations. Some of them do not have regular preaching, but they are faithful in gathering about the Lord's Table on the Lord's Day and carrying on an educational work in small Bible schools. They have a limited vision which hardly extends beyond their own community. They have little money to give for general missions, education, and benevolence. Under these circumstances their near neighbors ought to feel a brotherly desire to help and encourage them in the Lord's work, so that they may grow in grace, in the knowledge of God's Word, and in a more acceptable service for Christ and His Kingdom.

One such church was brought to my attention recently by George C. Fisher, who is directing the work of the Virginia Evangelizing Fellowship. Located in a small village, this congregation suffered the loss of their building by fire. Two elders turned to Disciples' headquarters at Richmond for help. They were met by only a lukewarm interest in their problem, but the state minister promised to send a committee to their village to look over the situation and offer advice. The men came and this was their advice: "We feel that in the interest of ecumenicity you should merge with one of the denominational churches in the community. Furthermore, scientific surveys indicate that there is no future for rural or small town churches in view of the universal exodus to the large cities. We would not be interested in getting you a loan to erect a new building." The elders were shocked, as were all the leaders of the congregation. Someone had heard of the Virginia Evangelizing Fellowship and the elders paid Fisher a visit. He immediately helped them finance a new building project locally, and, with a great deal of contributed labor, the church soon had a better building than before the fire. Fisher put them in touch with a fine man from one of our Bible colleges who became their minister. It was not long until the Bible school was averaging around two hundred a Sunday, as compared with a former average of around fifty. Many souls were won to Christ and a strong, vigorous testimony was given the Restoration plea in this community. This could be the story in many of the 2,000 forgotten churches that are constantly on my mind, as I write.

With success on several fronts in our effort to effect status for the Christian Churches and Churches of Christ in key positions, it occurred to some of us that we had no representation in the *Encyclopedia Britannica* and similar works. Again, the Lord provided a channel. It happened that I had been admitted to the ranks of the official contributors to the *Encyclopedia Britannica* while I was in Washington and I had been responsible for writing the articles on the National Association of Evangelicals and other evangelical organizations. With the agreement of several of our brethren, I opened a correspondence with the editors of the *Encyclopedia Britannica* to effect proper representation. I encountered the same hesitancy as we had met from the editors of the *American Yearbook of Churches,* but I am confident we shall achieve eventual recognition. A million and a quarter commited people cannot be ignored!

As I think of our continuing brotherhood, I am reminded of the over two million brethren in those Churches of Christ who will not use instrumental music in their worship. There ought to be no "Berlin wall" between us. As far as I am personally concerned there is none. We are one in the Lord. Previously in these Memoirs I have written about the efforts toward unity that Brother Claud F. Witty and I made many years ago. I am just as much interested in that cause now as I was then. During my years of so-called "retirement" I have had the privilege of making several very rewarding contacts with these brethren, which I would like to share with my readers.

One day shortly after I had written *The Free Church* and while I was still living in Washington, I had a long-distance telephone call from Abilene, Texas. The voice in Texas said, "I am John Allen Chalk, the speaker for the Church of Christ nationwide radio broadcast "Herald of Truth." I have just finished reading your book, with which I fully agree. How many people among the Disciples believe this?" I answered, "About a million and a half." "Why," he said, "this is astonishing! This is our belief! Why haven't we realized long before this that we are united on the matter of church polity?" Then he went on to ask specifically for the use of certain quotes from *The Free Church* in radio addresses that he was preparing. I was glad to give him permission without any royalty charge.

About a month later I had another long-distance call from Chalk advising me that he and his radio committee were coming to New York City for a conference with radio network executives. Then he went on to say that it was the unanimous wish of this committee that I be invited to meet them in Hotel Barclay for a day's conference. He said my expenses would be paid and that they would stay over in New York an extra day for this occasion. Of course, I went gladly and had a most enriching experience. Most of our time was given to their questions and my answers. We covered every phase of our church life — polity, doctrine, and practice in worship, missions, education, benevolence, and service. There was a remarkable meeting of minds. They were not trying to convert me. I was not trying to convert them. We were learning of the possibilities of better understanding and closer unity. After three sessions, as the hands of the clock were nearing twelve midnight, it was suggested that we get down on our knees in our hotel room and pray for the unity of God's people. Only God knows how wide were the beneficial repercussions of that event which, as far as I know, has never before been publicly mentioned.

Another resulting rapprochement between our two groups came through this same book. I blush to make the quote, but this is exactly what Editor Reuel Lemmons said about it in *Firm Foundation:* "One of the clearest and most concise treatments of the theme of congregational independence we have ever seen comes from the pen of the great writer among conservative Christian churches, James DeForest Murch. Fired up by the "restructure" struggle which threatens the complete apostasy of the liberal wing of the Christian church, Brother Murch has done one of the greatest works of his life in this book. The case for congregational autonomy has been clearly set forth and every member in our own Churches of Christ can read it with profit." Beginning with this, Brother Lemmons and I had a most rewarding correspondence over many months. Eventually we worked out a mutual plan to bring together six of their ministers and educators and six of ours in Memphis, Tennessee, June 12-14, 1969, for conference and prayer. Growing out of that meeting came another in St. Louis, Missouri, September 18-20, 1969, between twelve of their men and twelve of ours in which papers were read and discussions were held dealing with each of the critical issues that had led to separation many years before. Never have I been in unity meetings where the spirit was finer and where there were more personal professions of brotherly kindness and love than at Memphis and St. Louis.

Possibly a special word needs to be written about the Saint Louis meeting. It was one of the most representative I have ever attended. Those who accepted invitations and were present were:

Churches of Christ: Jimmy Allen, noted evangelist and Harding College faculty member, Searcy, Arkansas; Robert Bell, elder and executive of Wyatt's Cafeterias, Dallas, Texas; E. A. Cayce, elder and executive of Ralston-Purina Company, St. Louis, Missouri; Harold Hazelip, Harding Graduate School of Religion, Memphis, Tennessee; William Humble, Dean, Abilene Christian College, Abilene, Texas; Hulen Jackson, Trinity Heights Church of Christ, Dallas, Texas; Raymond Kelsey, vice-president, Oklahoma Christian College, Oklahoma City, Oklahoma; Hardeman Nichols, Walnut Hill Church of Christ, Dallas, Texas; Tom Ulbricht, professor in Abilene Christian College, Abilene, Texas; Frank Pack, head of the Department of Religion and dean of Graduate Studies, Pepperdine College, Los Angeles, California; J. W. Roberts, professor of New Testament and Greek, Abilene Christian College; Jay Smith, business manager of *Twentieth Century Christian,* Nashville, Tennessee; Earl West, historian and lecturer, Indianapolis, Indiana; Norvel Young, president of Pepperdine College; and Reuel Lemmons, editor of *Firm Foundation.*

Christian Churches/Churches of Christ: Russell Boatman, Dean, St.

Louis Christian College, St. Louis, Missouri; William Boice, minister, First Church, Phoenix, Arizona and president, North American Christian Convention; A. Dale Crain, campus minister, Terre Haute, Indiana; C. C. Crawford, professor of New Testament, Dallas Christian College, Dallas, Texas; Dwain Dunning, professor, Platte Valley Bible College, Scottsbluff, Nebraska; Robert O. Fife, professor of history, Milligan College, Johnson City, Tennessee; Lewis Foster, dean of the Graduate School, Cincinnati Bible Seminary, Cincinnati, Ohio; John Greenlee, minister, Westside Church, Wichita, Kansas; R. J. Kidwell, professor in Graduate School, Cincinnati Bible Seminary; W. F. Lown, president, Manhattan Bible College, Manhattan, Kansas; Max Randall, professor in missions department, Lincoln Christian College, Lincoln, Illinois; Ben Schiller, professor in missions department, Ozark Bible College, Joplin, Missouri; John Wade, executive, Standard Publishing, Cincinnati, Ohio; L. Palmer Young, minister, South Louisville Church, Louisville, Kentucky; and J. D. Murch.

Following treatises on "Authority" given at Memphis by J. D. Murch and J. D. Thomas, an agenda of significant studies was presented at St. Louis: "History — Retrospect and Prospect" by W. F. Lown and Wm. Humble; "Faith and Opinion" by Lewis Foster and Reuel Lemmons; "Worship" by R. J. Kidwell and J. W. Roberts; "Evangelism" by C. C. Crawford and Raymond Kelsey; and "Fellowship" by Robert Fife and Frank Pack.

Since the open break came between these two sectors of the Restoration Movement in 1907-1909 there has been little disposition to do more than debate the issues of disagreement. While the brethren who came together at Memphis and St. Louis faced these issues frankly, they did so in good spirit and with constructive purposes in view. There was complete mutual acceptance of one another as "brethren in Christ" and a determination to break down the "middle wall of partition" which has separated them in the past. They were aware of the fact that none of the participants could speak for anyone but himself. No resolutions could be passed nor votes taken that would bring unity. But there was an amazing evidence of individual commitment to the task of promoting and practicing unity in every way possible in the days to come. Among the approaches to unity discussed were:

Prayer. Definite private and congregational prayer for unity, seeking the will of Christ. Survey. Seeking to determine how much the two groups have in common in faith and practice. Fellowship. Establishing individual friendly ministerial relations by exchange of fraternal courtesies and union meetings. Cooperation. In enterprises and projects which will not involve compromise of convictions. The fields of evangelism, foreign missions and higher education were particularly considered as ready for immediate developments. Study and Discussion. Open-minded study and humble discussion of the things which at present divided, in order to discover the way to complete and permanent unity.

312

I am persuaded that the Lord is using our gathering together in ways that we know not, to His glory and the eventual unity of His people. For me, as I have said before, there is no longer any "middle wall of partition."

As Paul put it in Ephesians 2: "But now in Christ Jesus, ye who sometime were afar off are made nigh by the blood of Christ. For he is our peace, who hath made both one, and hath broken down the middle wall of partition between us: Having abolished in his flesh the enmity, even the law of commandments contained in ordinances; for to make in himself of twain one new man, so making peace; and that he might reconcile both unto God, in one body by the cross, having slain the enmity thereby: and came and preached peace to you which were afar off, and to them that were nigh. For through him we both have access by one Spirit unto the Father. Now, therefore, ye are no more strangers and foreigners, but fellow citizens with the saints, and of the household of God; and are built upon the foundation of the apostles and prophets, Jesus Christ himself being the chief corner stone; in whom all the building fitly framed together groweth unto an Holy temple in the Lord: in whom ye also are builded together for an habitation of God through the Spirit." AMEN!

That is the New Testament pattern for a continuing and everlasting brotherhood!

Episode XXVI

Retirement

That delightful old curmudgeon Dr. Johnson, author of the *Dictionary,* faced with retirement, gave this advice: "Exert your talents and distinguish yourself, and don't think of retiring from the world until the world will be sorry that you retire. I hate a fellow whom from pride or cowardice or laziness drives himself into a corner, and then does nothing but sit and growl. Let him come out, as I do, and bark!"

When I reached seventy, five years after the modern deadline for retirement, and left my office in *Christianity Today,* I began to think about what I might do with the rest of my life. What happened was that when the word got about, I was simply deluged with invitations and offers. This was evidence to me that the Lord still had a work for me to do, whether some men felt so or not. Writing ten years later and looking back on those years I am amazed at the record, some of which I shall attempt to recount.

One of my most important undertakings was the supervision of the indexing of the *Christian Standard.* B. D. Phillips, son of one of its founders, had long realized the importance of such a project to historians, scholars, and interpreters in the field of church history. He talked to me about his dream many times and finally decided to underwrite the tremendous cost and retain the expert services of Claude E. Spencer, former curator of the Disciples of Christ Historical Society, to do the job. Mr. Phillips' decision to go ahead was somewhat contingent on my willingness to oversee the undertaking and bring it to a successful conclusion. Associated with us in this task was attorney Rolland L. Ehrman, son-in-law and business associate of Mr. Phillips. As I write, we are within a few weeks of the issuance of the six-volume *Index* containing more than 600,000 entries covering one hundred years of weekly publication together with a complete microfilm service covering all issues of the journal from its beginnings. I might dwell on the importance of this accomplishment but I have written about it in some detail both in the *Christian Standard* and *Discipliana,* official organ of the DCHS. Today, with the centripetal and centrifugal forces at work in the life of the Restoration movement, this *Index* will release to scholars, researchers, and students sources of information that will better enable them to evaluate these forces and better understand the issues at stake. With Mr. Phillips, we can all devoutly hope that the *Index* will contribute to the realization of a greater unity in and a deeper understanding of the high ideals that have made the Restoration movement such a vital force in Christendom.

During this ten-year period I undertook for the Standard Publishing Company the comprehensive survey of all their periodical publications for the Sunday School to which I have previously alluded. I was charged with the task of reporting at length and in detail upon each one, and with the additional assignment of making suggestions for their improvement. It was understood that I would take my textbook, *Christian Education and the Local Church,* as the criterion in my judgments. The project also involved the detailed examination of the competitive materials issued by all the major American denominational and independent publishers in this field. Fortunately I had a large "rec" room in my home which I took over completely as my workshop. My wife generously agreed to "look the other way" as to the condition of this room in comparison with her perfectly-kept house. I plunged into the monumental and seemingly-interminable task with zest and enthusiasm. After all, this had been one of my major interests for many years and was still a matter of deep concern in changing times. When my report was finished it embraced more than five hundred pages. I still have somewhere in my effects a complete copy which I shall include in the papers I will turn over to Milligan College one of these days. I have been assured by my Standard brethren that the report was of considerable value in their planning for the future. I enjoyed every minute of this huge undertaking.

Growing out of the weeks and months involved in the Standard project, came some very deep convictions about changes that must take place in the traditional program of Christian education in the local church if it was to meet the needs of the hour in the era we were facing. I felt a very deep sense of the guidance of the Holy Spirit in the preparation of a work that would state these convictions succinctly and challengingly to the religious world. Thus began the preparation of my manuscript for *Teach or Perish.* When I had finished it I sent it to my old friend, William B. Eerdmans, of Grand Rapids for publication. I was hardly prepared for what happened. Only a week or so later I had a long-distance midnight telephone call in Washington. It was from Mr. Eerdmans. He said, "I have just finished reading your tremendously challenging manuscript on Christian education. I like it so much that I decided to call you and tell you that Eerdmans Publishing Company will gladly publish it and enthusiastically promote it." We discussed some of the features of the book for several minutes over the phone and I could tell by the relevancy of his questions and comments that Mr. Eerdmans held much the same views I had expressed. When the volume came from the press I had a wonderful response from reviewers. My friend Dan Poling liked it so well that he asked the privilege of carrying two chapters as feature articles in the Sunday School section of *Christian Herald.*

One of the finest reactions came when the national organization of evangelical denominational directors of Christian education invited me to their annual meeting in Nashville, Tennessee, to present the essence of my proposd program in two lectures, followed, in each case, by an hour of questions and discussion. We met in the conference rooms of the national headquarters of the National Association of Free Will Baptists under the most cordial circumstances. It was the consensus of the gathering that this book could well have a strong influence upon the future planning of the forty or fifty denominations represented. Its proposals are still live issues as is indicated by the fact that I still get sizable author's royalty checks from Eerdmans.

I have previously (Episode XVI) mentioned my experience in producing the book, *Protestant Revolt*. It reached the height of its influence in my retirement years. Because of the efforts of J. Howard Pew, Roger Hull, and other leading laymen of the United Presbyterian Church in the USA, to encourage the distribution of this book, I had many invitations to speak in Presbyterian churches across the land. *The Presbyterian Layman*, the national publication of the Presbyterian Lay Committee, carried two generous excerpts from *Protestant Revolt*. This, too, had considerable influence in my behalf. I was unable because of the press of other obligations to accept many of these invitations but I have happy recollections of meetings in Fourth Church, Chevy Chase Church, and the National Church in Washington; Covenant-First, College Hill and Seventh churches in Cincinnati. The book also paved the way for an invitation from J. W. Fifield and his Free Church Association to speak before the Freedom Club in the great First Congregational Church in Los Angeles.

Speaking of invitations to speak in the churches during my retirement years — naturally most of them have come from our own people. I have never kept a record of them, but in those years I recall having spoken outside the Capital area in Central Church of Christ, Portsmouth, Ohio; First Church, Hillsboro, Ohio; Indianola Church, Columbus, Ohio; First Church, Canton, Ohio; Broadway Church, Lexington, Kentucky; Memorial Church, Detroit, Michigan; First Church, Johnson City, Tennessee; North Highlands and Parkview Churches, Fort Wayne, Indiana; Englewood Church, Indianapolis, Indiana; First Church, Washington, Indiana; First Church, Phoenix, Arizona; First Church, Angola, Indiana; First Church, Lincoln, Illinois; and Central Church, Pittsburgh, Pennsylvania; and there were the scores of churches in California and other points west. But of those a later reference. It has been thrilling to meet thousands of pople I had never seen before who greeted me like "a long-lost brother" because we had become acquainted through the years by the medium of books, articles, editorials, and correspondence. I think there is no ministry for Christ that has rewards equal to those which come to Christian writers. You can't retire from this!

While my mind is reminiscing about traveling and speaking I am confronted with a long list of engagements with schools and colleges during these ten years, in answer to invitations to lecture, give commencement addresses, and the like. Here they are as they come to mind,

316

running down the alphabet: Atlanta Christian College, Atlanta, Georgia; Bethany College, Bethany, West Virginia; Bethany College, Newton, Kansas; Biola College, La Mirada, California; Berkshire Christian College, Lenox, Masachusetts; Cincinnati Bible Seminary, Cincinnati, Ohio; Dana College, Blair, Nebraska; Dallas Christian College, Dallas, Texas; Emmanuel School of Religion, Milligan College, Tennessee; Evangelical Congregational School of Theology, Myerstown, Pennsylvania; Eastern Christian College, Bel Air, Maryland; Fort Wayne Bible Institute, Fort Wayne, Indiana; Fuller Theological Seminary, Pasadena, California; Great Lakes Bible College, Lansing, Michigan; Johnson Bible College, Knoxville, Tennessee; Lincoln Christian College, Lincoln, Illinois; Louisville Bible College, Louisville, Kentucky; Moody Bible Institute, Chicago, Illinois; Milligan College, Milligan College, Tennessee; Manhattan Christian College, Manhattan, Kansas; Midwest Christian College, Oklahoma City, Oklahoma; Minnesota Bible College, Minneapolis, Minnesota; Messiah College, Grantham, Pennsylvania; Malone College, Canton, Ohio; Maritime Christian College, Charlottestown, Prince Edward Island, Canada; Nebraska Christian College, Norfolk, Nebraska; Puget Sound College of the Bible, Seattle, Washington; Pacific Christian College, Long Beach, California; Pepperdine College, Los Angeles, California; St. Louis Christian College, Florissant, Missouri; San Jose Bible College, San Jose, California; Tabor College, Hillsboro, Kansas; Talbot Theological Seminary, La Mirada, California; Upland College, Upland, California; Washington Bible College, Washington, D. C. Did I miss any? If so, my regrets for having a faulty memory. If all the addresses and lectures I gave in these institutions could be put together, they would make a book or two. Why didn't I do it?

I could tell some interesting stories about each of these college visits and pay tributes to the capable, self-sacrificing men and women who headed them and compose their faculties, but, of course, this is not feasible in a book that has already exceeded the number of pages I had originally planned. There are some things, however, I would like to say about a few of these schools:

Take historic Bethany: (Strangely enough, I spoke at another Bethany College, in Kansas, a General Conference Mennonite institution, where a number of delightful contacts were made.) I mean, of course, the institution Alexander Campbell founded, in the beautiful hills of West Virginia. I have visited our Bethany many times, but this last visit was extremely rewarding. President Perry Gresham did me the high honor of inviting me to speak in chapel on Founders' Day and also at the service commemorating the hundredth anniversary of the death of Campbell.

Olive and I arrived the day before and had opportunity to tour the area, including the site of the old Brush Run Church, the pool where the Campbells were baptized, the Alexander Campbell mansion, the old Bethany church, and all the rest of the hallowed spots that make Bethany the shrine of many precious memories to advocates of the Restoration plea. I had been there many times before but this time it seemed to have a special appeal. Above all, we admired again the Gothic beauty of the buildings constructed by Alexander Campbell, the founder and first president of the college. These are reminiscent of the main buildings of Glasgow University where he sat under the tutelage of Scotland's most distinguished scholars. Sequestered in the beautiful hills of West Virginia the Bethany campus is always a startling inspiration.

That evening we were taken to Pendleton Heights, the traditional home of Bethany's presidents, for dinner and what proved to be a long-remembered visit. Olive and Aleece found many things in common and enjoyed each other's company. Perry and I almost immediately began to talk about the "state of the Brotherhood" and kept up our conversation to well past midnight. I learned what I never knew before, that Perry was inspired to enter the ministry by Dr. James E. Davis, then minister of Central Church, Denver, Colorado, and president of one of our first independent schools, Colorado Bible College (now defunct), which was housed in this church building. Of course, he completed his education in Texas Christian University and the University of Chicago. While not a strict conservative, he always had an understanding and an appreciation for that point of view. He was always fairminded and considerate in dealing with this sector of our Brotherhood life. We got to talking about "Restructure" and I found him to be very critical of its strictures of our traditional freedoms and of many of the men who were foremost in its advocacy. Then he said, "I have read your book, *The Free Church,* and find myself in agreement with much that you have written. Now, Jim, we are going to have a testimonial luncheon for you after the Founders' Day exercises, and I want you to speak afterward to the students who are members of the Christian Church. I am going to tell them about your book and advise them to get it. I want you to feel free to talk with them about any of the issues you have raised." This was totally unexpected, and the incident served to show this broad concept of the "academic freedom" that should prevail on our college campuses.

The services of Founders' Day were dignified and inspiring. From the opening strains of the organ in the old chapel and the academic procession there was a mood worthy of the Bethany tradition. Perry liked my address (which was published later in the *Christian Standard*) and I noted recently a quote from it in *The Gresham Years,* his biography by James W. Carty. B. D. and Mildred Phillips drove down from Butler, Pennsylvania, to be in both services and to lay a beautiful wreath on the last resting place of Campbell. B. D. had my address xeroxed and sent to many of his friends. That was before "Restructure." Bethany and Perry grudgingly went along with it. What else could they do? They were caught unalterably in the web of Disciples' institutionalism and establishmentarianism. And wasn't the "President of the Church" on the board?

My speaking engagement at Fuller Theological Seminary brought me

318

face to face with the tremendous progress that had been made since the Charles E. Fullers made their millions-of-dollars grant for its establishment. Well housed and set for expansion in the heart of Pasadena, its faculty was the equal of that in any AATS theological seminary in the United States. Graciously introduced by President David A. Hubbard I gave the large audience, almost exclusively of men, a "leaf or two" out of my book, *Teach or Perish,* stressing the value of a strong church school emphasis in a succesful Gospel ministry. I was particularly interested to meet afterward quite a group of Christian church and Church of Christ students, most of them drawn to Fuller by the outstanding work being done by our own Dr. Donald McGavran who headed the School of World Mission. I want to pay tribute to this good man:

I first knew Dr. McGavran when he was a missionary for the United Christian Missionary Society in India. Despite the trends in that organization he remained aggressively evangelistic and committed to the idea that the pagan world must be brought to personal commitment to Jesus Christ as Saviour and Lord. I was not surprised later when I learned that he had launched an independent Institute of Church Growth at Eugene, Oregon, with the encouragement of Northwest Christian College. Here he directed a program of research scholarships and church growth lectureships and published *The Dynamics of Church Growth* and *Church Growth and Christian Mission.*

Dr. McGavran broke with the socio-political and humanistic concepts of the liberals and much of the traditional methodology of denominational missions. He early incurred the opposition of mission board members and supporters who felt that Church Growth threatened their vested interests — faithful missionaries whose long service in resistant fields has reacted against McGavran's "harvest theology," missionaries who have no growth because of paternalism and bad missionary methods, ethnocentric missionaries whose methods were Western and individualistic and had a predisposition against group decision-making, and those who refused to accept his frame of reference in the use of the Holy Scriptures. But the work at Eugene went on. The only problem was funds to underwrite the extensive plans of the director.

Then came the move to Fuller Theological Seminary at Pasadena, California, where the Institute of Church Growth is now located. On the occasion of my visit, I saw it in operation. It was at the time of their special intensive studies and surveys on the Mexican mission field. I was truly amazed at the thoroughness and efficiency of the work and the professional capabilities of those in charge. Every question I raised was answered with thoroughness, efficiency, precision, and satisfaction.

Dr. McGavran and his associates were seeking to restudy every mission field in the world in the light of new dimensions of economics, social structure, culture change, and primitive religions, majoring on mission theology, mission theory, and mission practice. They were committed to the idea of individual conversion and the establishment of churches as vital to the whole missionary enterprise. They were not afraid to think big and to participate in community and mass evangelism. They were for a more radical return to the New Testament and fuller cultural, sociological, and psychological adaptations of the Gospel to meet the needs of the hour.

Dr. McGavran and his staff have produced comprehensive studies of mission fields in Africa, the Philippines, Mexico, Brazil, Nigeria, Korea, Liberia, and Japan. They are not of equal quality, but as a total collection they present an amazing assembly of up-to-date data and each adds to the general weight of church growth methods and theory. They have drawn from many missionary sources which would not otherwise have been tapped. For instance, in my examination of the Mexican data I was glad to see full information about our "independent" missions and those conducted by our "a cappella" Church of Christ brethren. Here, too, were facts, figures, and data of various kinds about the missionary work of Pentecostals, "faith missions," and other agencies which the traditional surveys of the major Protestant denominations utterly ignored. Here was "the whole story" of "things as they are."

At Fuller McGavran had the financial support he needed, the academic standing and specific degree program for those who desire to organize their studies and research projects. Here he had access to more anthropological credentials than in any missionary school in the country. These already produced cover more areas of Church Growth than any other collection extant. His annual School of World Mission offered a service to evangelical Christian missionaries unexcelled. It is indeed a privilege to have known a man whose impact for good on world missions will be felt for decades to come.

My trip to Emmanuel School of Religion was to deliver the address for the second annual Commencement and the first graduating class to receive degrees for graduate work done exclusively in ESR. This greatly needed institution, set up on strictly AATS standards, had been struggling for recognition since its beginnings in the dreams of Dr. Dean E. Walker and Dr. Joseph Dampier of Milligan College. I found both faculty and student body enthusiastic about their accomplishments and the news that the Phillips family would soon provide them with a thoroughly adequate $2,000,000 home on a separate campus across the highway from the campus of Milligan. Dr. Fred Thompson was scheduled to become president — a man whom I had admired and honored for many years not only for his theological fitness and awareness but also for his administrative abilities. It had been my privilege to visit him several times while he was pastor of First Church, Chicago, where he laid strong foundations for the perpetuation of the Restoration plea in one of the nation's greatest cities. The Lord is continuing to bless Emmanuel in its loyalty to the faith and its preparation of well-qualified men for the Gospel ministry. It is going to have a great future.

When I received an invitation to preach on Easter Sunday in Central

Church, Charlottetown, the capital of Prince Edward Island, Canada, and give a week of lectures in Maritime Christian College, I accepted gladly. I had long wanted to visit this area which had produced so many outstanding American preachers and leaders through the years and which had stood so long four-square for "the faith once delivered." The churches of Christ in the Maritimes were comparatively small and few in number, but they have served the Lord courageously and well. To the Maritimes we owe a great debt for the life and ministry of A. McLean, who gave our American churches their foreign mission conscience. And here was born J. A. Lord, who served for many years as editor of the *Christian Standard.* Many of our great preachers, such as John H. McNeill, came from the Maritimes.

We had a great Easter service at Charlottetown with the church edifice overflowing. This church is now our largest in all of Canada. It has recently organized two new congregations in the capital city — they are evangelistic, a feat seldom encountered in Canada these days. It is this church that has mothered and encouraged Maritime Christian College which occupies adjacent buildings. Besides the college personnel, visitors from some twenty-five or thirty churches in the Maritime provinces were present for my lectures on the Restoration Movement and the modern Ecumenical Movement. We had a good time together. I never had audiences more eager to learn. The open forum periods were replete with intelligent questions and many keen expressions of loyalty to the Restoration plea.

The history of higher educational ventures in Canada has recorded many failures, largely due to the fact that supporting constituencies have been small and financial undergirding inadequate. MCC is fortunate in the leadership of its president, Kenneth T. Norris, who has built wisely and well. The success of the school will have much to do with the success of the cause in the Maritimes in years to come. I was glad to make a small contribution to its ongoing.

I was intrigued with the history of our people. One day Kenneth took me out to the historic Cross Roads meeting house, where our oldest church in the Maritimes was organized. In the adjoining cemetery I stood by the grave of John Knox, its founder. He had been born in Scotland, schooled in Edinburgh University, and awarded a medical degree in London. He came to the Maritimes as a physician and a missionary of the Church of England, but he soon came under the influence of the Scotch Baptists and began preaching in their churches with great acceptance. Then he began to read the *Millennial Harbinger* and the works of Alexander Campbell with the result that Cross Roads became a congregation after the New Testament pattern (1842). Knox also founded the churches at Three Rivers (Montague), South Lake and East Point. How the heart of this hero of the faith would rejoice if he could see the progress being made today by those who followed in his steps.

My invitations to visit institutions of higher education outside our own fellowship usually came because of my leadership in the National Association of Evangelicals and its associated agencies. I will take my visit to Tabor College as an example. Tabor was an accredited liberal arts college owned and operated by the Mennonite Brethren in Christ. This small denomination had its headquarters in Hillsboro, Kansas, in the center of its Mid-western numerical strength and here it had planted its major educational institution. Stretching out in every direction were the rich and prosperous farming lands of these good people — truly a heart-warming sight to behold. I had learned from my first contacts with the MBC that they were a Restoration Movement related to the earliest efforts in German-speaking European lands to restore the New Testament Church in doctrine, ordinances and life. All its leaders were men of deep consecration and spiritual power. When I have visited them in their homes I have been impressed with the fact that the Bible is at the center of their very existence and the guide and guardian of their lives. Prayerfully, at meals, in the morning and at night, they turn to its sacred pages as a family for inspiration for the daily tasks. Modern psychologists and social scientists tell us that this simply cannot be done in modern times, but the Mennonite Brethren do it and are greatly blessed thereby. So it was a pleasure to renew old contacts at Tabor, to look into the faces of several hundred young people and be privileged to say some word that might encourage them and endow them with strength to meet the problems they must some day face in a pagan world. Tabor? Whence the name? They tell this story:

When John Hus was burned at the stake long ago in Hungary because of his decision to take the Bible and the Bible alone as his rule of faith and practice, they say his last words were: "God give me a fearless heart, a right faith, a firm hope, a perfect love that for Thy sake I can lay down my life with patience and joy." Among those who saw him die that day was Jan Zizka, of the little town of Tabor. Back home he led the remnant of the faithful in the every Lord's Day observance of the Lord's Supper despite priestly bans, taking both the bread and wine. This practice became so well known that the cup became the symbol of the "Taborites." And at the foot of Tabor Hill was a pool called Jordan, where great numbers were immersed upon profession of their faith in the Lord Jesus Christ.

These people I met in Hillsboro, Kansas, that day were the spiritual (and possibly some of them the genealogical) descendants of John Hus and/or Jan Zizka set down in America. What a privilege to be their friend and brother in Christ as they carry on for God.

And then there was Pepperdine College. Pepperdine is the largest and most favorably-known institution of Christian higher education on the Pacific coast, supported by those Churches of Christ that do not use instrumental music in worship. Dr. M. Norvel Young was president and Dr. William S. Banowsky, chancellor, when I received their invitation to speak at a tribute dinner there in honor of B. D. Phillips. This was to be an invitational affair with one hundred Christian Church and one hundred Church of Christ ministers and their wives in attendance. This was one of the most courageous and irenic ventures in Christian unity ever attempted in this area. Mr. Phillips had but recently passed away. He was well known for his philanthropic interest in institutions of both sectors of the Restoration Movement. What more salutary occasion for cementing common ties in the Lord's work?

I was glad to accept and at their suggestion flew to Los Angeles a day in advance of the affair. I was met at the airport and whisked away on a tightly scheduled series of events. We had lunch at Knott's Berry Farm as the guests of Mr. Knott. Afterward he took us on a personal tour of his "empire," including the perfect replica of the original Independence Hall where the Declaration of Independence was signed. Then we visited the offices of Kenneth Hahn, Supervisor of the County of Los Angeles, where I was inducted with due ceremonies as an "honorary citizen." Dinner at one of the swank clubs of the city topped a very busy day. The next morning we were transported to the campus of the College for a tour and then to the site for the new Malibu campus of Pepperdine University overlooking the Pacific Ocean. I could not fail to be impressed with the capable and wide-visioned leadership of these brethren as they faced the future in a very competitive field.

When the hour came for the tribute dinner every available space was taken in the Friendship Hall and many had to be turned away. An exquisitely catered full-course dinner was served. There was music by the Pepperdine A Cappella Choirs. In the presence of Mrs. B. D. Phillips and a number of representatives of the Phillips Family who were guests of honor, a striking bas relief plaque was unveiled bearing an appropriate tribute to Mr. Phillips. My address on this occasion was entitled, "Benjamin Dwight Phillips — Indomitable Advocate of the Restoration of New Testament Christianity." I tried to express his views, which I knew very well after years of association with him; enumerated some of his outstanding philanthropies; and closed with an appeal for the unity of God's people in their common task of winning the world to Christ and restoring the Church of the New Testament in doctrine, ordinances, and life. When I finished I was startled and shaken by the spontaneous response of the whole audience in deafening long-lasting applause. Then all of us stood together and sang "Blest Be the Tie That Binds Our Hearts in Christian Love." It was a never-to-be-forgotten experience. Until past midnight many of us spent hours talking and praying about the possibilities of a united testimony in the days ahead.

Next day was Commencement Day for the college, but in the morning at the suggestion of Dr. Banowsky I went with a group of brethren to their Up-town Church of Christ meeting house in Long Beach for worship. Bill preached that morning on "Christian Unity." It was the finest sermon of the kind I have ever heard. Afterward I urged him to put it into print, but to my knowledge he never has done so. If he would do this I am sure it would evoke the greatest movement toward real unity we have witnessed since the days of the Campbells. I was warmly received as I was introduced and as they sang together my hymn "I'll Put Jesus First in My Life" from *Great Songs of the Church*. I would estimate that there were some eight hundred people in the audience. They were all my brethren and I was perfectly at home among them.

In the afternoon came the Commencement exercises in a packed auditorium when Mrs. Phillips delivered the address in true Welshimer style. Her father would have been proud of her. I marched in the Academic Procession and had part in the program. I hope and pray that the small mustard seeds of Christian unity sown in those days together may grow into a tree the branches of which may some day cover the world.

A major experience of my retirement years was the call to become Visiting Professor of Christian Education and Contemporary Christianity on the faculty of Pacific Christian College, at Long Beach, California. This was largely the doing of President Kenneth Stewart and G. B. Gordon, vice-president and director of development, although I was told that it was the unanimous decision of the entire faculty.

Though almost everyone in the current generation had forgotten, I was one of the founders of the institution. I think I have previously mentioned the fact that upon the call of a number of deeply concerned brethren I went to Los Angeles in 1928 and assisted them in the organization of the "Pacific Bible Seminary," patterned after our then young Cincinnati Bible Seminary. Under the presidency of Dr. George P. Rutledge the school opened in the quarters of the then Alvarado Church of Christ (now the Golden West Christian Church). Much water had flowed over the dam since those days, with struggles and sacrifices untold. Finally, under the new name Pacific Christian College it had become a most significant factor in the life and growth of the Restoration cause in southern California. It is apparent that I had a more than passing interest in making some contribution to the ongoing of this institution.

Under Kenneth's leadership and the capable help of Dean Harold W. Ford and many others, PCC had been accredited by the Association of Bible Colleges and was on the verge of acceptance by the Western Association of Schools and Colleges Accrediting Association (accomplished by the end of my second year on the faculty). New buildings adequate for the effective operation of the school had been erected and there was encouraging growth in enrollment and financial support.

Another touch with Southern California had come while I was chairman of the Trustees of The Clarke Estate, also previously mentioned. Working with men like C. C. Root, Reuben Anderson, and Ralph Dornette we had financial fellowship in the establishment of about twelve new churches in this rapidly developing area. I think I can still name them: Culver City, Elsinore, La Habra, Oxnard, Montebello, Pomona, San Fernando, National City, Torrance, Van Nuys, Victorville, and Anaheim (Knott Avenue). A few of these had "fallen by the wayside" but most

324

of them were still serving their communities well. I was eager to see these churches that we had aided through the years.

So in 1967 I arrived in beautiful California and began my services in the classroom as instructor in Christian Education, Church Polity, and Church History. I also conducted seminars in the Ecumenical Movement and Christianity Today. I was working with many dedicated and capable teachers such as Harold W. Ford, T. R. Applebury, Wm. Harvey Beard, Franklin O. Bixler, Kenneth C. Hanson, John W. Koekkoek, Harrold W. McFarland, Paul R. McReynolds, Park H. Netting, Roger Koerner, Richard Derby, John Rowe, and Ralph Swearingen. It was a wonderful fellowship. They took me into their homes and hearts. We were like one great Christian Family working together for the glory of God and the building of His Kingdom in the midst of a host of young men and women with the same intents and purposes. There are many advantages in the small college and we had all of them.

My extra-curricular activities were almost as strenuous as my teaching responsibilities. G. B. Gordon directed these with the thought in mind of developing friendly relations with the churches, colleges, religious and social agencies in the area and the community as a whole. I cannot begin to list all of the engagements he arranged for me, but I shall try to enumerate a few and then elaborate upon some that might be of special interest to my readers. I will make no effort to allocate them by specific dates.

I began with a series of lectures in McCall Chapel on the Restoration Movement which drew interested auditors from many surrounding churches, including quite a number from the A Cappella Churches of Christ, and created a new interest in "Christians Only." The last lecture had to do with Restructure and its bearing on the future of the Movement, which aroused an interest that increased throughout my tenure.

Then followed engagements at Anaheim, Bell, Fullerton, Garden Grove, Hollywood, Huntington Beach, Inglewood, Lawndale, Long Beach, Compton, Glendale, Los Angeles proper, Montebello, Riverside, Santa Ana, Tujunga, Burbank, Westwood Hills, Ceres, San Jose, and points as far away as Caldwell and Boise, Idaho.

I remember two great Sunday school conventions: GLASS and BRASS. I had known the Los Angeles area was probably the best organized of all the metropolitan groups aligned with the National Sunday School Association. They had an annual convention which enrolled four or five thousand delegates. Then they had district conventions with names like GLASS (Greater Los Angeles) and BRASS (Bernardino-Riverside). Cyrus Nelson and Henrietta Mears were the "power houses" back of these successful operations. I addressed GLASS with some 2,000 present and BRASS wth over 1,000. In each instance I gave my address, "Christian Education the Hope of the World," and conducted a conference based on my book, *Teach or Perish*. It was thrilling to meet scores and scores of people who had read and studied my books and other writings in this field and had been helped by them. I was no stranger to them. At Riverside I was pleased that our own Paul Neal, pastor of the University Church, introduced me. He told me that there were many of "our people" in the audience and that they were enthusiastic in their cooperation in BRASS.

In this connection I might mention my week-end visit to Ceres which was in the nature of a Sunday School conference. It involved lectures, open forums, and preaching on the Lord's Day. Many of our churches in the area were represented and a large number of students from San Jose Bible College registered. Also an evening Sunday school rally in University Church, Los Angeles, with many of our LA schools represented. In my evening classes in Christian Education at the college we had many Sunday school workers enrolled from churches in the area. In a once-a-week, two-hour session, I devoted one hour to answering questions concerning their problems and tried to make the period as practical as possible.

I met many ministers' groups. I recall one of ours, exceptionally well attended, at Crenshaw Boulevard in Inglewood where Restructure was my subject. There was keen interest, especially on the part of men who were serving congregations that were distinctly Disciples oriented. Some of them thought I was extreme in my criticisms and prophecies concerning the future. (I wonder what they think now?) Twice I had the privilege of speaking to the interdenominational Evangelical Ministerial Fellowship of Long Beach. Both times they asked me to talk on the National and World Councils of Churches and trends in the modern Ecumenical Movement. The NAE is quite strong in Southern California and maintains an office at Fullerton with a full-time secretary to serve a growing number of churches.

I was deeply interested in the glowing evangelistic spirit which characterized our free churches in the area. I enjoyed attending more than one of the dinner meetings of the Southern California Evangelistic Association. During my first year Ragon Flannery was executive director; during my second year, Ralph Dornette. These meetings were capacity affairs and there was keen interest as reports were heard from the new mission churches. All told of progress and enlargement. I was time after time impressed with the "population explosion" in Los Angeles and Orange counties with the new suburban housing developments "all over the place." There is nothing like it anywhere in the United States. If careful surveys are made, choice locations obtained, and good leadership obtained, the success of a new church is almost assured from the start. They grow naturally with population increase. One of the finest services offered by the SCEA is "The Churches of Christ Building and Loan Fund." It provides loans for the construction of new church buildings, on a unit plan, and guarantees a favorable impression of permanence to all our new churches which avail themselves of its services. There is now over $2,000,000 in the Fund, which is operated under charter from the state as a building and loan association. I am sure the ink will not be dry on this book before that sum will have been enlarged many times. Ralph Dornette is one of my special friends among the oncoming generation of ministers. He is a Timothy of our Westwood-Cheviot congregation in Cincinnati and has remarkably fine abilities for his task.

When Joseph Merle Appelgate resigned a most successful ministry with the Crenshaw Boulevard Church to become associate minister with Jesse R. Kellems at Westwood Hills, he brought me into the picture. (Merle, by the way, had been an Army Air Force chaplain and was an airplane pilot of distinction, and took me on several thrilling trips in his little Cessna over Los Angeles and adjoining territory, just to add a little spice to my stay.) Westwood Hills has one of the finest church edifices in the Los Angeles area. It is located opposite the main entrance to the campus of the University of California Los Angeles (UCLA) and, indeed, is about surrounded by magnificent buildings of the school. It is a striking Gothic structure with a worshipful sanctuary and has adequate quarters for its church school. Its choir is quite noted in the city. Its organ is one of the finest. On my visits there I was impressed with the growing youth groups, which indicated to me that the church was not only serving the exclusive residential area of Westwood Hills but also the student body of the University, one of the largest in the world.

There would be no Westwood Hills Church without the life and ministry of Jesse Kellems. Since few people today know of him I believe it would be most appropriate for me to tell a bit of the Kellems story. He was born the son of David Clinton Kellems, a distinguished professor in what is now Northwest Christian College. Early in life Jesse began to preach. He seemed born to the pulpit and preaching evangelism. After graduating from college he entered the evangelistic field, holding tremendously successful meetings in the greatest Christian Churches in the country. He lectured in our schools and colleges and had soon produced a number of best-selling books: *The Deity of Jesus, New Testament Evangelism, The Resurrection Gospel* and *Studies in the Forgiveness of Sins.* Feeling the need of further education he enrolled in Edinburgh University and received his Ph.D. about the time that he was called to evangelize South Africa under the Thomas Mission. The Kellems-Richards evangelistic team was responsible for organizing many churches in that area which still exist today and form the nucleus of the Restoration community in that distant land.

Then, due to unfortunate domestic problems, he was practically ostracized by our people. Marrying the beautiful daughter of an aristocratic Venezuelan family he became immensely wealthy and spent much of his time in world travel and further studies in noted European universities on the Continent. During this time he converted and baptized his wife and her mother, former Roman Catholics. He never departed from his early faith and finally the old urge to preach stirred him to locate permanently in Westwood Hills and establish the church here.

He was not at all welcome to many of our people, but he persevered in his determination to serve the Lord, as a free lance if necessary. As a memorial to their only child who had died at an early age, the Kellems erected the beautiful building I have previously described, worth in its wonderful location over $2,000,000. Here and now many victories have been won for Christ through the years and now in happy fellowship with many in the free and independent undenominational communion of Christian Churches and Churches of Christ, Westwood Hills has a prospective future of ever enlarging proportions.

One of Jesse Kellems' dreams was the establishment of a graduate school of religion on the Pacific Coast where ministers could be trained for effective service. While I was in Los Angeles I met with committees he appointed to explore the possibilities of such an educational venture. Other men like Dean E. Walker, then president of Milligan College, were called in for advice and counsel. The hindrances to such a move, however, were at that time so monumental that nothing definite was accomplished. The Kellems are still living as I write and it may be that this dream may yet come true. I was entertained in their beautiful home several times. I was especially impressed with the intelligent understanding and appreciation of Mrs. Kellems for the Restoration Movement. On one occasion I gave them a copy of my book, *The Free Church,* which they appreciated so much that they bought a number of copies and sent them to their friends. They rejoice in the way the Lord has blessed the North American Christian Convention and the whole loyal Brotherhood which is growing by leaps and bounds wherever the Word is faithfully preached. Myron Taylor, one of our greatest preachers, now occupies the pulpit at Westwood Hills and is doing an important work in this strategic location.

While I was teaching at Pacific Christian I received word from B. D. Phillips that he and Mrs. Phillips, and possibly some other members of the Phillips family would be touring the Pacific Coast. A combination of incentives inspired them to make this decision. B. D. had not been on the Coast since he had made the tour as a small boy in company with his parents. He was interested in visiting the scenes of some of his childhood experiences and in seeing first-hand evidences of the remarkable economic progress California had made since that time. The Sprankles and the Ehrmans had become interested in a new process for the production of oil from a certain type of shale in California. They wanted to investigate. Both B. D. and Mildred were interested in the progress of the Restoration cause in this rapidly developing area. Time for a vacation was coming up, so why not tour California, Oregon, and Washington?

President Stewart and his assistants at the College made immediate preparations to welcome them to Southern California. When they arrived they were greeted with a testimonial banquet at which the B. D. Phillipses were presented with a plaque honoring their philanthropic interest in Christian higher education. Mildred was invited to speak to the women of the LA-LB churches under the auspices of the women's auxiliary of PCC. An overflow audience in McCall Chapel greeted her enthusiastically. The party had opportunity to visit the leading churches of the area and see the phenomenal evangelistic progress being made. B. D. noted the splendid location of the College opposite the Municipal Golf Course and within walking distance of the Long Beach campus of the University of California. With characteristic generosity he expressed his interest in the ongoing of the school and its loyalty to the Restoration plea by making a contribution to the purchase of additional property for future expansion.

We had opportunity to enjoy visits with the party to the area's finest gourmet restaurants, Knott's Berry Farm, Disneyland, and view the gorgeous scenery and special points of interest on the seacoast and in the mountains. The visit of the Phillipses was indeed a bright spot in my tour of duty at PCC.

A red-letter occasion was my visit to Boise, Idaho, upon invitation of the brethren in the Northwest Regional Christian Unity Conference. They asked me to give four addresses involving Christ's prayer for unity, the "Declaration and Address," the modern Restoration Movement, and the challenges of the modern Ecumenical Movement. The meetings were held in the Central Christian Church, across the street from the state capital building. The church was crowded for all sessions which drew visitors from four or five states. There were representatives from all three sectors of the Movement — Right, Left, and Center. I was particularly pleased with the large number of Church of Christ (non-instrumental) brethren present. A whole bus load of students and faculty members from their Magic Valley Christian College, at Albion, Idaho, was present throughout. The area minister for Disciples churches, Burton R. Brown, was there with a splendid representation of their churches. Practically every "independent" church of the area was represented together with members of faculty and student body of Boise Bible College. The spirit of the whole conference was ideal and I think I had greater liberty in speaking than in any other meeting of its kind in which I ever participated. My pleas for unity as well as those of all who took part on the program were warmly received and I am sure that the benign influence of that gathering continues to be felt in all that Northwest area.

At the insistent solicitation of a large number of brethren I arranged toward the end of the Conference to speak and hold an open forum on "Restructure" in a non-scheduled separate meeting. This, too, I felt, would be in the best interests of Christian unity. The fellowship hall was jammed beyond capacity with many people standing, indicating the deep concern over the new proposal of the Disciples' leadership. The issue had been previously raised in the Idaho-Utah area in the shape of re-organization proposals. So strong had been the opposition that most of the larger churches in the area had withdrawn from the new organization and several congregations had divided. I refused to get involved in regional problems and confined myself to an analysis and interpretation of the "Provisional Design" for Restructure. My presentation was well received although a few criticized me for "introducing a divisive issue."

On the Lord's Day I enjoyed worshipping with First Church, Caldwell, Idaho, and its minister, my good friend of long standing, Dr. Ernest H. Chamberlain. He asked me to preach and I gladly consented. This is one of the largest churches of our fellowship in the area. It has a beautiful and adequate building in the heart of the city and numbers in its membership many of its prominent business and professional people. "Ernie," a former minister at West Seattle and past president of the North American Christian Convention, is one of our outstanding national leaders whose guidance and wisdom have meant much to the Cause through the years. What a fellowship!

At the close of my second term as Visiting Professor, I felt that I could not continue another year, because of my wife's health problems and other demands upon my time. Under normal conditions I would have enjoyed another term, or maybe more, if my services would have been of value. When I made my decision known the faculty voted unanimously (with generous words of appreciation) to grant me the honorary degree of L. H. D. at the forthcoming commencement. The citation was read by Dean Ford, and the diploma and hood presented by President Stewart. The Commencement address was delivered by Dr. M. Norvel Young, president of Pepperdine, and one might have thought he was conferring the degree, with all the kind things he had to say about my ministry in the Restoration movement. My concern for Pacific Christian College continues and I welcome every advance it makes in the field of Christian higher education. As I write, the highly capable Dr. Medford Jones is serving as President, succeeding Kenneth whose health necessitated his resignation in 1964.

There is much more that could be recorded, but I cannot hope to encompass completely all the services I have been privileged to render. As I look back upon my years of work and travel as a minister, leader of youth groups, as magazine editor, as author, as founder and leader of many organizations, as teacher, as lecturer and consultant, I am repeatedly struck with the mystery of how I got into all this. I have been happy in my work and would not have chosen to change anything. Yet even today I do not feel that the control of events has been entirely in my hands. In mysterious and wonderful ways, I have been directed. I devoutly believe that there has been God's purpose in the scheme of things. If I have made some worthwhile contributions to His Cause and Kingdom I am content. To Him be the glory!

Episode XXVII

"Tribute to Whom Tribute"

But for the prayers, the encouragement, the cooperation, the aid in multitudinous ways of hundreds of people, I would have been able to accomplish very little in the service I tried to render to Christ and His Cause. It has been said that a man has all the friends he deserves, but I feel that I have had more than I could ever deserve. I wish I could recall all of these wonderful people and here record their individual contributions to my life and my work, but it is manifestly impossible to include them all. Some of them I have mentioned in previous chapters. Maybe, in the providence of God, in "the land beyond the river" I may be able to say a personal "thank you" to every one.

In this chapter, however, I want to pay tribute to those who have been most closely and intimately involved in my life story.

I shall begin with my father. I have already described in my early chapters at some length his influence in guidance, instruction, discipline, and helpfulness. I will not repeat, but take up the thread of his life story and pursue it to the end. His crowning ministry, measured by human standards, was with First Church, Athens, Ohio, at the seat of Ohio University, the oldest state institution of higher education west of the Alleghenies. Eschewing the temptation to compromise the Word of God and appeal to the popular "forward looking" socio-scientific elements in the university community, he preached sermons "true to the Bible" and lifted up Christ, the divine Son of God, in a way that marked him the leading exponent of evangelical Christianity in the area. Here, again, he had a second pastorate. In his first he built the church from 500 members housed in an inadequate frame building to one of 1,100 and led in the purchase of a new centrally located building site and the drawing of the plans for the present edifice. His second ministry was made necessary by a division in the church that threatened to destroy its future influence. The elders said, "Only Brother Murch can put the pieces together again." He returned and he did. In one of his longest ministries he saw the Bible school reach a 600 average attendance, the new sanctuary filled for morning and evening services, additions almost every Lord's Day, and a remarkable evangelical Christian testimony to the communities of both "town and gown."

It was a similar situation of local-church schism that persuaded him to move from Athens to East Palestine (near Youngstown). A new building had been erected here, but through a series of unfortunate ministries, the church had actually divided into two congregations, one meeting in the new building and the other in the old one. The Ohio Christian

Missionary Society added Father to its staff and underwrote his salary as minister at East Palestine in the hope that unity could be achieved. It was not long until he had the two groups together again and not long after that until the church became self supporting. He continued as pastor for eleven years, until his death. The whole community, recognizing his part in the remarkable rebirth of First Church, conferred many honors upon him and recognized him as one of its leading citizens. It was my privilege to visit him many times in those years and on two occasions to act as evangelist in revival meetings which the Lord blessed with many souls won to Christ. In the eleven years great changes took place in our Brotherhood life, many of which I have already treated at some length. Father's heart and soul were torn between loyalty to many Establishment leaders whom he had known and loved for a lifetime, and loyalty to what he very clearly and definitely knew to be the teaching of the Word of God and the essentials of the Restoration plea, to which he had given his life. Gradually he came to take his stand unequivocally with those who refused to compromise our historic position. The East Palestine church is today one of the pillars of strength to the Cause in the Western Reserve.

The day of Father's passing was remarkable in many ways. He had been advised by his personal physician that he had a heart condition which would make it unwise for him to continue in an active pastoral relationship. We had worked out a retirement plan for him and purchased property in Blanchester, Ohio (near an area of southern Ohio with which he had long been familiar) where he could live in peace and contentment. On September 13, 1936, he preached his "farewell sermon" at East Palestine with the sanctuary crowded to its doors. He was at his best and lifted up Christ in a marvelous way. Tears and tributes were showered upon him as he stood at the main entrance and shook hands with his parishioners for the last time. Afterward he went with Mother to the parsonage nearby. Here he said, "I am overly tired and I think I will lie down for a rest before lunch." Those were his last words. Fifteen minutes later he had passed to his reward.

It happened that on this September 13 I was to preach at Blanchester in the morning worship hour and in the afternoon to address the quarterly meeting of the Clinton County churches at the Sabina Camp Grounds. As I pronounced the benediction at Blanchester, I was approached by a local undertaker who said I was wanted to answer a long-distance telephone call from East Palestine. The word was that Father had suffered a heart attack, that he was not likely to survive, and that I should come at once. I immediately canceled the afternoon engagement and drove swiftly to East Palestine, too late to see Father alive, but able to take charge of funeral arrangements.

What a blow! This was the first death in our immediate Murch family. Anyone who has faced that experience will appreciate how I felt and how I had to orient myself in a personal way to those great passages of

Christian hope I had used so many times as I had officiated at funeral services. The passage that stood out for me at this time was 2 Corinthians 4:16-18: "For which cause we faint not; but though our outward man perish, yet the inward man is renewed day by day. For our light affliction which is but for a moment, worketh for us a far more exceeding and eternal weight of glory; while we look not at the things which are seen, but at the things which are not seen: for the things which are seen are temporal; but the things which are not seen are eternal." Christ had traveled this way himself and proved the validity of that wonderful doctrine. I was content!

There were many ways in which I inherited the high regard in which Father was held wherever he went. The East Palestine Church, in the years following his death, often invited me to assist in special services. I recall especially being the guest speaker for their "Golden Anniversary," when N. B. Martin was their minister. That and the other days I spent with them were always rich with blessings.

There were, likewise, many happy occasions spent with the Athens church, where Olive had grown up and where I, in my student days at the university, had once served as superintendent of the Bible school. After Father's second pastorate there, he was succeeded by several liberal ministers. Their terms of service were marked by loss of attendance and financial difficulty. One day in Cincinnati I got a long-distance call from the Chairman of the Board. He said, "DeForest, we are having troubles getting a new minister. We wish we could get another like your father. Would you come over and fill our pulpit next Sunday and meet with our elders to discuss the situation?" I consented and we had a regular "homecoming" at the morning worship service. They asked first if I would be interested in accepting the pulpit. I said, "No, I have a great ministry which I cannot abandon." They readily agreed and then asked if I could recommend a good man "like your father" for the vacancy. Within weeks, during which I supplied the pulpit, I learned of the availability of Joe Maffet, who had just resigned the church at North Tonawanda, New York. He was a sound Gospel preacher, had been active in Erieside Christian Service Camp and in the North American Christian Convention. At my suggestion P. H. Welshimer and W. R. Walker, who knew him well, sent fine letters of recommendation to the Athens Board. Joe was called to the pastorate and served for nearly twenty years. However, about half way through his ministry the Athens church literally froze in its relationship with me. I knew something was wrong. What happened was that the Pedigo, Fierce, Vermillion and other families, strongly committed to the Establishment, had persuaded the Ohio Christian Missionary Society to bring pressures to bear on Joe to change church policy. Mrs. S. E. G. Pedigo was elected head of the women's work in the state. The OCMS underwrote the salary of a student pastor to work with the Disciples in the University. A veritable flood of special day speakers from Headquarters appeared. There was even an effort made to get the church to adopt the practice of open membership. Joe was able to forestall any such action. He continued to preach the Gospel. But he was forced to compromise on church policy. Today the Athens church is a mere shadow of its former self during Father's last ministry. It is firmly in control of the "powers that be" in Cleveland and Indianapolis and practices open membership. My name is anathema except among a faithful few whose feeble testimony for the "faith once delivered" is all but smothered. I tell this story parenthetically as typical of many situations where the blight of liberalism and ecclesiastical tyranny has all but destroyed great churches with a long history of loyalty to the Faith.

There is no higher tribute I can pay my father in the flesh and my father in the ministry than through the medium of Paul the Apostle's words, "He fought a good fight, he finished his course, he kept the faith; henceforth there is laid up for him a crown of righteousness, which the Lord, the righteous judge, shall give him at that day: and not to him only but to all them also that love Christ's appearing."

After Father's passing, Grandmother (Mrs. Frances Savage) and Mother went to live with my brother-in-law and sister, Dr. and Mrs. Edwin E. Higgins, at Gallipolis, Ohio, where Edwin was at that time Superintendent of Schools. As the years passed this arrangement was a happy one until death took Grandmother in her one hundredth year (May 28, 1941). Later, Mother came to live with us in Chevy Chase, Maryland. This, too, was a happy relationship until she was called in her ninety-seventh year to her heavenly home, March 5, 1963. It was at Mother's knee I learned to lisp my first prayer. Throughout her life she was an ever available help. Whatever my situation, sometimes criticized and abased even in the circle of our friends, Mother fiercely defended me. In good repute or bad I was her son and she was certain I could do no wrong. One of her absorbing interests in her Maryland home was the making of gift-books from pictures she cut out of old Christmas cards supplied by the scores by our friends. She had a remarkable ability to arrange these pictures artistically and meaningfully. Local hospitals were glad to get them for use among convalescent children, who thoroughly enjoyed them. Other hundreds of these booklets went to children in the foreign mission stations of our Christian Churches and Churches of Christ. Once when Mother read in the Washington papers that little Caroline Kennedy, the daughter of our President, was ill and confined to her bed, she insisted on sending Caroline one of her booklets. Mother received a personal acknowledgment from the White House — a letter which she treasured until her dying day. The Washington papers recalled the incident when they carried the news of her passing. Who can measure the joy she brought to thousands of children during the closing years of her life?

According to many physicians, who know my biological history, I owe to Mother and Grandmother the blessing of longevity that I still enjoy in my eightieth year. The Lord uses many ways and means of accomplishing His purposes. I can never be thankful enough for the home life in which I was born and nurtured to do God's will.

My sister, Frances, was ten years younger than I. The "generation gap" hindered the development of a close family relationship, but, of course, I loved her dearly. Upon her graduation from Ohio University she married a classmate, Edwin E. Higgins, member of a respected Athens County family. He early became principal of the East Palestine High School. This was a happy arrangement as far as Frances was concerned because Father was then minister of First Christian Church there. Edwin's tour of duty in East Palestine was followed by post-graduate study in Columbia University where he was awarded his Master's degree. His reputation as a successful schoolman soon earned him the superintendency of the public schools of Gallipolis, county-seat of Gallia County, where he spent all the remaining years of a very successful career. He was recognized by many educational associations. He became highly influential in the business, social, and religious circles of the city. Frances joined him in all these relationships. Upon his retirement he was awarded an honorary doctorate by nearby Rio Grand College. Later he became a member of the faculty of the college and served in that capacity for several years. We have many happy relationships which help to make our declining years most rewarding.

Jeremy Taylor once said, "A good wife is heaven's last, best gift to man." I agree, and that is the blessing I have had in Olive Cameron Murch. I have previously mentioned my marriage. Despite the changing marital mores of the time, we have lived together for nearly sixty years. Olive has all the qualifications necessary to have built a career of her own but she chose to build one that has been of immense help to me in my life and ministry. She has been loyal to Christ and His Church from the beginning. When we came to Cincinnati and became members of the historic Richmond Street Church she became active in the Bible school and Christian Endeavor Society, teaching and directing the activities of children and youth. In later years there she became teacher of the Loyal Women's Bible Class, the largest in the school. When the church moved to Price Hill, adopting the new name, Western Hills Church of Christ, she continued in that capacity. Then, when we transferred our membership to the Westwood-Cheviot Church she almost immediately assumed a similar position, teaching for more than thirty years the Loyal Women's Class there, which again was the largest in the Bible school. Olive was and is a "woman's woman." When women meet her they recognize that quality in her and almost instinctively accept her leadership and her ability to counsel, teach, and lead them. In many ways she has been a helpmate in all the work I have undertaken.

When I was editor of *The Lookout* she wrote a column of helps for the social life of youth groups which was of such high quality that Standard Publishing asked her to put the cream of her work in book form, *Let's*

Have a Good Time, by Olive Cameron. Later she prepared helps for Christian Endeavor prayer meetings for the same magazine. As opportunity afforded she attended our church conventions, accompanying me on several occasions to foreign lands. When I assumed leadership in the Cincinnati Bible Institute and the Cincinnati Bible Seminary, she gave gladly of her time to counsel the young women students and help build up the woman's auxiliary, composed of members from the churches of Greater Cincinnati.

But the thing in which she achieved highest distinction was leadership in the secular social milieu of women's clubs. Her college sorority, Alpha Delta Pi, the oldest in America, early made her a province president. Wherever she went in her official visitations she was able to counsel and guide in such an effective way that she was promoted to the position of vice-president of the national organization and made a member of the Grand Council, a position which she occupied with distinction for many years. She had been instrumental as a student in Ohio University in organizing a chapter of ADPi there. In Cincinnati she helped found the chapter in the University of Cincinnati. Later she was appointed by Grand Council to reorganize and revive the chapter at the University of Maryland (near our Chevy Chase home). She was awarded the highest distinctions her sorority had to offer. She still remains an honored member.

In Greater Cincinnati Olive became well known for her club activities. She began as president of the Westwood Woman's Club, then moved up to become the president of the Western Hills Federation of Women's Clubs, and later secretary of the Ohio Federation of Women's Clubs. She could have gone on to take positions of even higher responsibility in this area of club work, but she declined because she felt such obligations would require neglect of her domestic responsibilities.

Then came a most unexpected honor. She had been accepted as a member of the exclusive Cincinnati Woman's Club with accompanying recognition by the Blue Book of Queen City society. She was offered the presidency of the Club and served with distinction for two terms. She was the only woman ever chosen for this position from the western area of the city; the only minister's wife ever so recognized. The Club occupied one of the most beautiful club houses of its kind in the nation, and its programs, involving all phases of the social graces, arts, and letters, were of an exceedingly high order. Through the years she had contacts with many of the great and near-great who visited Cincinnati. I basked in her reflected glory and reaped many social rewards for which I was, I am afraid, ill fitted. This was a dimension of my life which, I am sure, would never have been developed had it not been for her remarkable abilities in this area.

When we went to the Nation's Capital, her reputation had gone before her. She almost immediately was invited to become a member of the exclusive Washington Woman's Club housed in the famous "Cissy"

Patterson mansion on DuPont Circle (once the temporary residence of the President of the United States, Calvin Coolidge). She was given successive promotions in administrative positions and I believe would have been eventually elected president had we chosen to remain in the Washington area, rather than moving back to Cincinnati for final retirement. Here in Washington I was also able through her social connections to meet many distinguished persons from at home and abroad — an experience which helped to broaden my personal contacts and open doors of wider influence.

Olive has more than fulfilled her marriage vows in her loyalty "in prosperity and in adversity." When misfortune beset me she rose by mental force to be "the comforter and supporter of her husband, abiding with unshrinking firmness the bitterest blasts of adversity." Her business capabilities made it possible for me to have great freedom in travel in the discharge of my nationwide responsibilities through the years. Altogether I could not have had a more rewarding marital relationship.

Our son, James DeForest II, has always been a comfort and joy. From the day when I baptized him into Christ not far from the rural stream where I met my Lord, he has never given us a moment's concern. After his graduation from Ohio University he was immediately inducted into the armed forces of the second World War. First as a "grease monkey" he accepted his responsibilities without a murmur. After training at famous Vultee in Nashville, Tennessee, he moved up quickly in the Air Force arm to a position of importance at the great Patterson Field and Wright Field center at Dayton, Ohio. This was considered the service focus, backbone, and axis of the total air operation of the United States throughout the world. "Dee," as we like to call him, became a warrant officer. In his position he was sent to air-force centers all over the world to ascertain their supply needs and provide them. His conduct throughout the war was highly exemplary. I remember: A prominent Cincinnati businessman told me he had met Dee on a transcontinental train in a bar with men who were his superiors. When drinks were ordered, Dee asked for milk and nobody "kidded" him for his choice. "You can be proud of him, Jim," said my friend. He had the respect of all and was "in the cards" for promotion when the war ended. He chose not to continue in the service and became associated with the advertising department of the Rike-Kumler department store in Dayton. He served this noted mercantile establishment for many years, retiring recently from an executive position of considerable importance. May 1, 1943 he married Gene Atwood, of Lakewood, Cleveland, whom he met in Ohio University. She has been a highly regarded teacher in the Dayton public schools for many years. Their daughter, Ann, also a graduate of OU, is now a stewardess for the American Airlines. All of the family were active church workers in Dayton. Dee is now a trustee of his church and well respected for his moral stamina and good business judgment.

I gladly pay tribute to the succession of capable secretaries with whom I have been blessed through the years. Proverbially, at least half of an executive's success is due to the aid of a dedicated, efficient office assistant who can handle the details of the day's work, take dictation and transcribe it accurately, write error-proof letters, arrange interviews, and meet callers. My first secretary was Miss Clara Luskey, when I was assistant editor of the *Christian Standard*. She later became the first Mrs. Edwin R. Errett. Then came Virginia Young, who served during my early years as editor of *The Lookout* and later became a missionary to India. She was succeeded by Miss Mildred Covington, who was so well fitted for her job that she was soon rewarded by appointment to an assistant editorship. Then in my CRA days I remember Miss Agnes Howie, who stood out above many CBS helpers. I recommended her so highly that Edwin Errett, editor of *Christian Standard,* "stole" her for his secretary. Later she became Mrs. Orval M. Morgan. Back at Standard in the early 1930's I was fortunate to secure the services of Mrs. Catherine Logan, who had been secretary to Russell Errett, "Mr. Standard Publishing." She was a perfectionist in everything she undertook. Later she became the second Mrs. C. J. Sharp. I had no idea that I could find a new secretary with the abilities of Mrs. Logan, but like "manna from heaven" came Miss Verda Bloomhuff. Verda was a successful teacher in the Cincinnati public schools, but sought an opportunity to serve in the field of religious publishing and thus came to Standard. Guy Leavitt offered her a position in *The Lookout* office, which she accepted, but she hardly had arrived until I "stole" her to fill the vacancy left by Mrs. Logan's marriage. Miss Bloomhuff held two degrees from the University of Cincinnati. She had distinguished herself in school as a linguist and a semanticist and could turn out a letter or a manuscript as nearly error proof as is humanly possible. With a bit of guidance she developed into a very capable editor. During her stay at Standard she prepared a number of program books and played a large part in mounting my development program which produced an entirely new Standard line of Bible school quarterlies and helps for teachers and workers.

When I was fired from my position as Managing Editor, Verda was offered a promotion if she would remain with the Company and break off all relationships with me. Because her high principles were outraged by my summary and unfair dismissal, she indignantly refused the offer — and within days had secured a new position in the office of the Vice-president of the University of Cincinnati. When I opened my new offices at 111 East Fourth Street, I offered her a renewal of our previous contract and she returned to my employ. As a true friend and associate in the Lord's work she embraced my objects as her own and became another mind bent on the same end — enjoying it, ensuring it, reflecting it, and delighting in her devotion to it. Her name went on the masthead of *United Evangelical Action* magazine and with distinction remained there even after I had gone to Washington as Managing Editor of

Christianity Today. During these fourteen years she received many honors. She was elected secretary of the Evangelical Press Association and served in a similar capacity in a number of evangelical organizations. She was honored with a listing in *Who's Who of American Women.* She held offices in the Worldwide Baraca-Philathea Bible Class Movement and also in the Cincinnati Business and Professional Women's Club.

When Verda decided that she would like a change in her work she asked me to assist her in locating a position worthy of her talents. It happened that I was having dinner with Dr. Cyrus Nelson, president of Gospel Light Publications, one evening during the Denver Convention of the National Sunday School Association. He asked me if I knew of someone who could take an editorial position with his concern. When he described the duties of the editor, I immediately replied, "I know exactly the person who would fill that spot with distinction. She is Miss Verda Bloomhuff." To make a long story short, she accepted GLP's offer and went to Glendale, California, where she remained until her retirement. Today in Cincinnati she finds opportunity to serve as an editorial assistant on the staff of *The Lookout,* the same office where she began her editorial career.

I pay the highest possible tribute to this "modern Phoebe" whose helpfulness over some twenty years of my ministry cannot be too greatly praised.

I hesitate to single out any from among our host of friends who have made wonderful contributions to our life and work, for special mention in this chapter; but I feel obligated, beyond ability to repay, to two couples — Mr. and Mrs. B. D. Phillips and Mr. and Mrs. Walter Eckert.

I had known both B. D. and Mildred Phillips for many years and had come to esteem them highly, both personally and for their work's sake. I first met Mildred because of a common interest in the Christian Endeavor movement. Later, through my associations with Standard, I became one of the circle of friends of the P. H. Welshimers in Canton. Mildred always impressed me as being "the living image" of her distinguished father. She was so deeply committed to Christ and the Church and to the Restoration Movement that she "talked his language" everywhere she went. With her remarkable talents she served as teacher, writer, editor, lecturer, and leader in every good work. I knew her and worked with her in Christian Endeavor rallies, Sunday school conventions, Christian Service camps, and many gatherings for the advancement of the Restoration Plea. We were pleasantly associated on the editorial staff of Standard. When she went to Milligan College as teacher and as Dean of Women I followed her ministries with interest. When I learned of her marriage to B. D. Phillips, I remarked, "Surely, this is a marriage that was made in heaven."

As far as B. D. was concerned, I always stood in awe of him because of his great wealth, his distinction in the world of business, and his well-known philanthropies to the Lord's work. I honored him for his clear

grasp of the essentials of the Christian faith and the Restoration plea —
a true son of a great father, Thomas W. Phillips, author of *The Church
of Christ, by a Layman*. When he read my book, *Christians Only*,
there began to develop between us a close and vital friendship based on
a common belief and a common purpose in the Lord's work. (When he
passed to his reward, I was asked to write his biography. If the reader
cares to learn in depth my high regard for this man he should read my
B. D. Phillips: Life and Letters.) After B. D.'s marriage to Mildred it
was only natural, in the providence of God, that the Murches were invited to spend a weekend at Elm Court, the palatial Phillips mansion.
We flew over from Washington to Pittsburgh and they met us for the
short drive to Butler. Olive and Mildred reviewed and renewed old
friendships. B. D. and I talked mainly about the Brotherhood and some
of the trends which were so disturbing. We saw eye to eye, and were
of one mind as to some of the steps that should be taken to preserve and
perpetuate the Restoration movement. When we were ready to return
home we were told that the room we occupied was to be considered our
"very own" any time we chose to visit Elm Court.

Then came "Restructure," the story of which is told in Episode XXIV.
I truly believe that, had it not been for the concern and cooperation of
the Phillipses, we would have been able to salvage only a small portion
of the great host that finally stood unswervingly for the "faith once for
all delivered." It was a joy to work with them. During those crucial
years we were often at Elm Court. We were also the guests of the
Phillipses at a number of state, national and world conventions. In a
time of supposed "retirement" I enjoyed an activity in the Lord's work
unsurpassed by that of any other period of my life.

Today Mrs. Phillips stands out as "The Queen Esther of the Brotherhood." I believe she has "come to the Kingdom for such a time as this."
As the administratrix of the large philanthropies of her late husband she
is instrumental, under God, in advancing the cause of higher Christian
education in many ways that would gladden the hearts of both B. D.
Phillips and her father, P. H. Welshimer. Thus the cause they both
loved will be better enabled to triumph over the vicissitudes of the past
and enter into a new day of accomplishment to the glory of Christ. It
has been a high privilege to be numbered among the friends of Benjamin
Dwight Phillips and Mildred Welshimer Phillips.

Walter and Marie Eckert were neighbors of ours for many years, but
we never knew them well until I became ad interim minister of the
Westwood-Cheviot Church. During this time Walter took a renewed
interest in the cause of Christ and the Restoration plea. I have already
related how he was later instrumental in advising and helping the congregation in its financial problems. When I left Cincinnati for Washington he said to me, "Now J. D., if I can ever be of service to you in any
way feel free to call upon me. And I mean *in any way!*" Marie echoed
his sentiments. When I realized I was soon to retire I faced the "facts

of life" and proceeded to "put my house in order." Unfortunately, I had never been connected with any concern that had a pension plan for its employees. All of those I served now have such a plan, but I just missed being a beneficiary of any of them. One day as I was passing through Cincinnati, I dropped off my plane at the airport and called the offices of the Cheviot Building and Loan Company and asked for Mr. Eckert. I reminded him of his generous promise to be of service in a time of need. I briefly explained my desire to "put my house in order" and asked whether he would advise me. He gladly assured me he would and we set up a date for a conference. My wife and I had been frugal and careful in our financial affairs. We had a small inheritance and had been fortunate in several real estate transactions. This constituted a nucleus for an investment the income from which might care for our retirement needs. With great wisdom Walter outlined what he would do under the circumstances and offered the help of his Company in implementing and realizing the plan. Truly, the psalmist spoke well when he said, "Trust in the Lord and do good; so shalt thou dwell in the land, and verily thou shalt be fed . . . When the steps of a man are ordered by the Lord, he delighteth in his way. Though he fall, he shall not utterly be cast down; for the Lord upholdeth him with his hand. I have been young but now I am old; yet have I not seen the righteous forsaken nor his seed begging bread." Today we have modest holdings which, the Lord willing, will care for us as long as this life shall last. We feel a real warmth of friendship for Walter and his good wife because of their faith and encouragement and we find great satisfaction in continuing to work with them in advancing Christ's cause.

Above all things earthly, I would give thanks and pay tribute to God for His guidance and goodness and blessing. I rejoice that I have known Christ and walked and talked with Him all the days of my Christian life. To Him I owe my life and breath. To Him I owe my salvation and the privilege of service in His name. To Him I owe the blessings of answered prayer. To Him I owe the joys of conscious forgiveness when I have strayed from His will and His way. To him I owe the achievements and the victories I have experienced. What I have done is worthy of nothing. Only what God has done for me and through me is worthy of everlasting and thankful praise.

Episode XXVIII

Looking Forward

In my later years I have been thrust into something approximating the role of a patriarch by my brethren in the Christian Churches and Churches of Christ. Frequently in the closing moments of gatherings someone is likely to say, "And now, Brother Murch, what word of admonition do you have for us?" or "Brother Murch, what of the future of the cause we all love?" It might, therefore, be appropriate to end these memoirs with such a word.

It occurs to me that nothing of this sort could be more apropos than the thoughts expressed in a Commencement address I delivered before the graduating classes of Emmanuel School of Religion, at Milligan College, Tennessee, and of the Puget Sound College of the Bible, at Seattle, Washington (circa 1970). Here it is:

OUR MISSION IN A CHANGING WORLD

We are living in a revolutionary age. Revolutions are as necessary to society as storms and waves on a lake, that it may not become a stagnant marsh. Revolutions are like a fire that tests men and institutions. If they are built on sound foundations they will endure. If they are not, they will perish.

We must be prepared in a revolutionary age to witness the passing of outmoded scientific and religious dogmas and philosophies. We must expect institutions and bureaucracies that have outlived their usefulness to be destroyed. We shall see pharisaism, sophistry, charlatanism, hypocrisy and deception challenged and exposed. But we shall also see truth and right exalted. Many will come to see the validity of the Apostle Paul's word to the Church at Corinth, "Other foundation can no man lay than that is laid, which is Jesus Christ" (I Corinthians 3:11).

Such a day is a good day for the movement to restore the New Testament Church in message and mission, in doctrine, ordinances and life. The demolition squads are preparing the way for us. The high places are being brought low and the low places are being lifted up for the coming of a new and better day.

All humanity is becoming vaguely conscious of a need for something different, something better in every phase of life.

Education, long dominated by Greek modes of thought and crass humanistic pseudo-scientisms, has come to the end of its tether. Like lost souls wandering in a wilderness of futility without chart or compass, liberal educators and student leaders have turned to riot and burning. Wildly berating the status quo and without any constructive proposals for

342

change or future action they have taken over thousands of college campuses in total disregard for the welfare of the majority of young men and women who desire to seriously pursue their studies and prepare for useful careers. For the lack of courageous administrators and boards of trustees capitulation is now called negotiation; absence of all principle, reason; irrational whim, youthful idealism; and hairy savages, men of noble commitment. What has happened really is that the godless philosophies and programs adopted at the beginning of the Twentieth Century are now bearing fruit. Sane and responsible people who have been the chief supporters of these institutions are calling for something different.

In religion, there is unprecedented chaos and confusion. The powerful Roman Catholic Church, long the bulwark of ecclesiastical conformity and tyranny, is in serious trouble with its theology, its moral teaching, its social action, and its repressive policies. Over 10,000 priests have left the church. Scores of them are asking to be released from their vows of celibacy so they can marry. No less an authority than Hans Kung of Tubingen says that the Church is ripe for reform in every area of its life.

Protestantism is in a ferment of trouble with its new theology and its new morality. All ethics are seen as situational and relativistic, governed only by the attribute of a questionable "love."

The United Presbyterian Church has surrendered its traditional commitment to the Westminster Confession of Faith. Its New Confession of 1967 substitutes seven Confessions of Faith as testimonies to the faith of the church but not as tests of the faith of any minister or church leader. No church member is required to hold any distinctive doctrine concerning the fundamentals of the Christian faith. Each member can believe what he wishes and discover in his own way the path to God and salvation. Every major Protestant denomination is similarly afflicted. Modern ecclesiastical emphasis is not upon the Gospel of Christ for the salvation of souls, but upon the secularization and urbanization movements of the day. Man's religious response is measured in terms of his concern with the conflicts of race, class, politics and nations. There is an obsession about mergers and unions which are bringing in their wake new divisions and thousands of closed churches. The *United States News and World Report* recently declared that there were 70,000 closed Protestant churches in America.

Many are seeking solutions for this tragic situation in theology. In these latter days of the Twentieth Century new schools of theology are born with dizzying frequency, have their short day, and die. Reigning Protestant religious theory yesterday was classic Modernism, the theology of divine immanence. Then came Neo-orthodoxy with its theory of divine transcendence. The latest major thought form, now in its dying days, is Existentialism, the theology of subjectivity. The survival span of modern alternatives to the simple truth of the New Testament becomes shorter and shorter with the passing years. In the parade are Bultmann, Kaseman, Thielicke, Stauffer, Pannenberg, Tillich, Hordern, Altizer and

343

Moltmann. To these notables can be added a vast number of lesser lights whose tentative religious writings reject traditional formulations and reflect the tides of the modern spirit. They cover theories of sociological salvation, theories of cosmological salvation, attempted syntheses of the sacred and the secular, and even ventures into the occult. A vast emptiness now pervades the field of modern theology and independent thinkers are coming to the conclusion that man, basing his theories on purely humanistic premises, can have no cognitive knowledge of God. Many are plunged into a metaphysical agnosticism. Fortunately, an increasing company are being driven to the simplicity, the depth and the satisfactions of the truth of God to be found alone in the Holy Scriptures. Eventually we may see the creation and inscripturation of the revealed Word of God.

Other solutions are being sought in modern ecumenicity. In America the Ecumenical Movement is synonymous with the National Council of Churches with a claimed constituency of 30 million and COCU — the Consultation on Church Union. Nine major Protestant denominations in COCU are moving rapidly toward merger into what will probably be known as the "United Church of Christ."

At the global level the World Council of Churches, with a claimed constituency of 450 million, is creating a melange of national united churches which will eventually acknowledge the supremacy of either Geneva or Rome. Actual negotiations are being directed in some 40 areas involving over 100 denominations through the World Council's Faith and Order Commission with the United Church of South India as a pattern.

Beyond the Councils of Churches, which have lost their distinctly Protestant character, there are liaison agencies already functioning to bring about union with the Roman Catholic Church. The Roman Catholic Secretariat for Christian Unity is doing a remarkably successful work in this regard. Archbishop Ramsey of the Church of England said the other day that he would not be averse to accepting the Pope of Rome as the primate of a united world church. Dr. W. B. Blakemore, dean of the Disciples Divinity House at the University of Chicago, upon his installation as president of the Chicago Church Federation, boldly declared that as far as he was concerned he was ready now to accept the Pope as Head of the Church.

The unity which is being promised Christendom in the modern Ecumenical Movement is not the unity for which Christ prayed in John 17. The only result of its studies, conferences, consultations, conventions, resolutions, covenants and legislative and judicial actions will be the creation of a monolithic Ecclesiastical Monopoly, exactly the same thing that eventuated following the Great Apostasy in the Third Century. Monopolism — whether in business, government or religion — easily becomes the instrument of tyranny. The totalitarian church is as much to be feared as the totalitarian state — possibly more so because the monopolistic church can wield control over the hearts and consciences of men as well as over their social and political structures. What is being proposed is a neo-Catholicism which can become, as did the old Catholicism, the symbol of oppression, exercising dominion over every phase of life and destroying human freedom around the world.

The true unity of the Church derives, not from some centralized ecclesiastical structure, but from real spiritual substance. It is not something that can be achieved by voting it or desiring it. It is more than a sentimental "togetherness"; more than a sanctified camaraderie; more than fellowship in a coffee house; more than worship in a common liturgy; more than association under a common name; more than participation in a common socio-political program issued from a central headquarters or an encyclical pronouncement by an infallible primate; more than the outflowing of some sentimental and intangible spirit of good will. This institutional structural concept of a united Church-anity is bound eventually to interpose itself between men and God to such a degree that the life in Christ described in the Holy Scriptures cannot be fully realized. As a result people will be disillusioned about the Church, becoming either formal or lukewarm in their profession, or abandoning it altogether. The proposed merger of many denominations into an institutional behemoth can only mislead Christians and the world at large into identifying the true Church with an institution, and the living Christ with an ecclesiastical hierarchy. Where this united Church is achieved it will definitely not be the Church that Jesus built.

But there is an effective solution to the world's ills in a return to the Christ of the New Testament, to His teaching and to the Church which He founded. I say this because I have faith in the soul of man. In the time of crisis it will refuse to surrender its liberty to the tyranny of government, of industry, of science, of society or of a monopolistic ecumenical church. It will not allow its finer aspirations to be destroyed by systems or institutions. It will, in its extremity, turn to God and that finest exemplification of Himself, His will and His way which can alone be found in Jesus Christ, His Son and our Saviour, in His Holy Word and in His Holy Church.

This soul of man is about ready to welcome a rebirth — a restoration — of the Church in terms of its pristine message and mission, its doctrine, its ordinances and its life. The soul of man is yearning for the rebirth of a Christianity which excludes malignity, subdues selfishness, regulates the passions, subordinates animal appetites, quickens the intellect and exalts the highest affections. A Christianity which promotes industry, honesty, truth, purity and kindness; humbles the proud; exalts the lowly; upholds law and order; favors liberty and would unite men in one great brotherhood. If we are ever to see such a new day, we must reject all humanly-devised creeds and churches which call themselves "Christian," we must deny all humanistically-based theologies, the shibboleths of pragmatic skepticism, the optimistic religions of a self-sufficient humanity, the pseudo-scientific theories regarding human conduct and go to the Bible and the Bible alone for directives and guidance in the great task before us.

This rebirth — this restoration — can come through the Restoration Movement if we are willing to pay the price for that leadership. What will it cost?

We dare not in this crucial hour in world history assume a negative and reactionary attitude, spending our time in criticizing the shortcomings of others, and failing to undertake what God is clearly calling us to do. We must read the signs of the times and move to bring in a new day under the guidance of God's Spirit and in harmony with God's Word.

To begin with, we have much for which we must repent. We need to ask God to forgive our divisions, our humanisms, our perversions, our feverish ways, which promote misunderstanding, keep us from vital fellowship with one another, and hinder the evangelization of the world. We need to know more fully the mind of Christ and His will for us in all things pertaining to His church, that in His greatness we may rise above our littleness, that in His strength we may lose our weakness. We need to learn His peace that we may bury all discord and in His truth and righteousness we may march as the united church to accomplish the work He has set for us in this day and time.

We are challenged anew to lift up the Christ of the Scriptures. In the modern Ecumenical Movement there is much said of Christ. He is said to be the author of all its doings. But who is their Christ? Is he the Christ of Church tradition? Is he the Christ of the "inner consciousness"? Is he the Christ of "divine-human encounter"? Such a Christ is not the Christ revealed in the words of the Bible. He is a man-created counterfeit. The world is perishing for want of the Christ of the Scriptures. As the Apostle Paul put it in his letter to the Colossians: All they that are alienated and enemies of God in their minds and wicked works must be reconciled in the body of his flesh through death if they are to be holy and unblamable and unreprovable in the sight of God. Only the Christ of the Scriptures can do that. In the words of Karl Barth, "The quest for the unity of the church must be identical with the quest for Christ as the Head and Lord of the Church. The blessing of unity cannot be separated from Him who blesses, for in Him (the Christ of the Scriptures) it has its source and reality, through His Word and His Spirit it is revealed to us, and only in faith in Him can it become a reality among us."

We are challenged to a restudy of the Word of God. Fresh touch with the living, written Word of God apart from our preconceived ideas can, under the guidance of the Holy Spirit, give New Testament Christians a new birth of freedom of thought and launch us out into a united movement of such broad proportions that it can sweep the world. The modern Ecumenical Movement has virtually scrapped the Bible as its guidebook, leaving the way open to us to be the true missioners for the world's good, for its salvation, its guidance, and its spiritual nourishment.

We are challenged to present to Christendom the true nature of the Church. We must make clear that a mere union of denominations or a federation of churches is not true Christian unity. Such a union would be merely something which the Church would have in common with human societies and undertakings in general. The true Church consists, first of all, of a vertical relationship between God and man. When our Lord prayed to the Heavenly Father for the unity of His Church, as recorded in the seventeenth chapter of John, He asked that His followers might be one "as thou Father art in me and I in thee that they may be one in us." Without this vital spiritual relationship there can be no true Christian unity. But there is also a horizontal relationship between Christians. In the work and worship of the visible, organized churches this spiritual unity must be reflected. It is in this area that true ecumenicity needs to be demonstrated more effectively. We must build a united church that is both spiritually creative and spiritually conventional.

We are challenged to give new emphasis to the true mission of the Church. The modern Ecumenical Movement rejects the idea that man is lost in sin and can be saved only by the acceptance of and obedience to the Christian Gospel. It sees at the core of all creeds and religions a nucleus of religious intuition which is as valid in the sight of God as the Christian faith. It accepts the establishment of a redeemed society as the mission of the church. This is a far cry from the first great ecumenical gathering at Edinburgh, Scotland, in 1910 called by that great missionary statesman John R. Mott and which had as its slogan the salvation of the world in "this generation." We must emphasize anew the fact that man is lost in sin, corrupt, guilty, threatened with eternal punishment and called to repentance, obedience and forgiveness of sin; and the fact that the Church is a redemptive fellowship, separate from the world and the spirit of evil, but willing to identify itself with lost mankind for its salvation. In this conviction we need to pray for revival. God is willing to move among us. Only our lack of true Christian unity prevents.

To this end we must preach the Gospel. I can hear the Apostle Paul speaking again to the young Timothies of our day, and to all of us who love the Lord: "I charge thee, therefore before God, and the Lord Jesus Christ, who shall judge the quick and the dead at his appearing and his kingdom; Preach the Word! be instant in season, out of season; reprove, rebuke with all long suffering and doctrine. For the time will come, (and now is!) when they will not endure sound doctrine; but after their own lusts shall they heap to themselves teachers having itching ears; and they shall turn from the truth, and shall be turned unto fables. But watch thou in all things, endure afflictions, do the work of an evangelist, make full proof of thy ministry" (II Timothy 4:1-5).

Finally, New Testament Christians are challenged to demonstrate in a more effective manner the social implications of the Gospel. New

Testament Christians have a social conscience but we revolt at the idea of using the temporal power of the church to force world revolution according to any humanly devised plan. We must formulate a dynamic philosophy of social action built on biblical theology and once again make the Church a mighty force for righteousness in the nations, ministering to the needs of humanity and promoting social justice.

God has blessed our fellowship in the bold and uncompromising stand we have taken for the "faith once for all delivered" in the midst of doubt and apostasy. We have built great churches, great Bible institutes, colleges and seminaries, missionary and benevolent enterprises that span the world, publishing houses, radio ministries and independent functional agencies that show every mark of the blessing of God. But if we are going to allow these works of our hands to bulk so large in our thinking and our loyalties as to cut us off from fellowship with others of like mind and heart, we are failing Him who made it possible to achieve great things for the Kingdom. We need to see today's problems from the viewpoint of God and be as big and as broad in our concerns as He is. Any barriers that we allow to keep us from having a love for mankind as wide as the love which our Lord Jesus Christ demonstrated on Calvary should be pulled down *now!* Tomorrow may be too late in the schedule of God's plan for the ages.

We need to mobilize all the forces of every existing group committed to the Restoration ideal, our endowments, and personnel in our local churches, in inter-church agencies, in education, in evangelism, in journalism, in radio and television, in missions — in all fields and spheres of Christian service — for a movement of such proportions that God can take it and use it for the accomplishment of His purposes. This calls for the absolutely complete and unwithholding surrender of our intellectual, material, and spiritual resources and a wholehearted determination to match and exceed the highest and best that liberalism, humanism, and paganism have to offer.

The ultimate victory is certain, because above and beyond our resources and our will to serve is the promise the Eternal God made to Zerubbabel over twenty-five hundred years ago as he faced the seemingly insurmountable odds which were keeping him from restoring the Temple in Jerusalem. God said, Victory will come, "not by might, nor by power, but by my Spirit" (Zechariah 4:1-7). O, Lord of Hosts, be with us yet, lest we forget!

FINIS

WORKS OF JAMES DeFOREST MURCH

Books and Brochures

Successful Prayer Meetings 1930

Christian Action Bible Studies 1934

Christian Action Study Manual 1934

Junior Quiz Book 1934

Christian Ministers Manual 1937

Studies in Christian Living 1937

Sunday School Handbook 1939

God Still Lives 1941

Christian Education and the Local Church 1943

Evangelical Sunday School Lesson Commentary 1948-1952

The Growing Super-Church 1952

The Coming Great Church 1955

Cooperation Without Compromise: History of the NAE 1956

Teach Me to Pray 1958

The World Council of Churches: An Analysis and Evaluation 1961

Christians Only: A History of the Restoration Movement 1961

God's Answers to Life's Problems 1963

Teach or Perish 1963

Church-State Relations: The American Way 1963

The National Council of Churches: A Critique 1966

The Free Church 1966

Christian Endeavor Essentials 1966

Protestant Revolt 1968

B. D. Phillips: Life and Letters 1970

Gift Books in Color

Prelude to Prayer 1939

Bible Treasures 1940

Portals to Bible Study 1940

Holy Matrimony 1940

The Call of the Church 1940

Cheer Along the Way 1941

Victorious Christian Living 1942

Precious Promises of God 1943

Chapters Contributed

Editorials

Numerous articles in Christian Standard, The Lookout, Christian Herald, Sunday School Times, Christian Endeavor World, Moody Monthly, Cincinnati Enquirer, etc.

Quarterly commentaries on Bible lessons published by Standard Publishing, Scripture Press, Higley Press, Gospel Light Publications, etc.

Hymns and tunes: "I'll Put Jesus First in My Life," "Trysting Place with Jesus," "Hymn to God Our Father," "Restoration Hymn," "Here Am I, Send Me," etc.

INDEX